MW00777829

Constructing Basic Liberties

Constructing Basic Liberties

A Defense of Substantive
Due Process

JAMES E. FLEMING

The University of Chicago Press
Chicago and London

The University of Chicago Press, Chicago 60637
The University of Chicago Press, Ltd., London
© 2022 by The University of Chicago
All rights reserved. No part of this book may be used or reproduced in any
manner whatsoever without written permission, except in the case of brief
quotations in critical articles and reviews. For more information, contact the
University of Chicago Press, 1427 E. 60th St., Chicago, IL 60637.
Published 2022
Printed in the United States of America

31 30 29 28 27 26 25 24 23 22   1 2 3 4 5

ISBN-13: 978-0-226-82139-9 (cloth)
ISBN-13: 978-0-226-82140-5 (paper)
ISBN-13: 978-0-226-82141-2 (e-book)
DOI: https://doi.org/10.7208/chicago/9780226821412.001.0001

Library of Congress Cataloging-in-Publication Data

Names: Fleming, James E., author.
Title: Constructing basic liberties : a defense of substantive due process /
    James E. Fleming.
Description: Chicago : University of Chicago Press, 2022. |
    Includes bibliographical references and index.
Identifiers: LCCN 2021059029 | ISBN 9780226821399 (cloth) |
    ISBN 9780226821405 (paperback) | ISBN 9780226821412 (ebook)
Subjects: LCSH: United States. Supreme Court. | Due process of law—
    United States. | Civil rights—United States. | Liberty. | Law and ethics.
Classification: LCC KF4765 .F54 2022 | DDC 347.73/05—dc23/eng/20220128
LC record available at https://lccn.loc.gov/2021059029

♾ This paper meets the requirements of ANSI/NISO Z39.48-1992
(Permanence of Paper).

For Linda, Sarah & Katherine

Due process has not been reduced to any formula; its content cannot be determined by reference to any code. The best that can be said is that through the course of this Court's decisions it has represented the balance which our Nation, built upon postulates of respect for the liberty of the individual, has struck between that liberty and the demands of organized society. If the supplying of content to this Constitutional concept has of necessity been a rational process, it certainly has not been one where judges have felt free to roam where unguided speculation might take them. The balance of which I speak is the balance struck by this country, having regard to what history teaches are the traditions from which it developed as well as the traditions from which it broke. That tradition is a living thing. A decision of this Court which radically departs from it could not long survive, while a decision which builds on what has survived is likely to be sound. No formula could serve as a substitute, in this area, for judgment and restraint.

JUSTICE JOHN MARSHALL HARLAN II, *Poe v. Ullman* (1961) (dissenting)

The identification and protection of fundamental rights is an enduring part of the judicial duty to interpret the Constitution. That responsibility, however, "has not been reduced to any formula." *Poe v. Ullman* (1961) (Harlan, J., dissenting). Rather, it requires courts to exercise reasoned judgment in identifying interests of the person so fundamental that the State must accord them its respect. That process is guided by many of the same considerations relevant to analysis of other constitutional provisions that set forth broad principles rather than specific requirements. History and tradition guide and discipline this inquiry but do not set its outer boundaries. See *Lawrence v. Texas* (2003). That method respects our history and learns from it without allowing the past alone to rule the present.

The nature of injustice is that we may not always see it in our own times. The generations that wrote and ratified the Bill of Rights and the Fourteenth Amendment did not presume to know the extent of freedom in all of its dimensions, and so they entrusted to future generations a charter protecting the right of all persons to enjoy liberty as we learn its meaning.

JUSTICE ANTHONY KENNEDY, *Obergefell v. Hodges* (2015)

CONTENTS

ONE

A Second Death of Substantive Due Process?

The liberal constitutional wit John Hart Ely quipped that "substantive due process"—the protection of substantive liberties such as privacy and autonomy under the Due Process Clauses of the US Constitution—is "a contradiction in terms."[1] Justice Antonin Scalia, the most prominent conservative critic of the doctrine, similarly characterized it as an "oxymoron."[2] Worse still, Justice Clarence Thomas has blasted substantive due process as a "dangerous fiction" that imperils both religious liberty and our democracy itself.[3] Many progressive critics, on the other hand, have argued that leading substantive due process cases are rightly decided, but that the Supreme Court should "rewrite" them to ground the rights in the Equal Protection Clause.[4] The rights of privacy and autonomy, as they are described in these withering attacks from all sides, seem so nonsensical, dangerous, or misconceived that one might wonder whether they can be defended as coherent and integral to our constitutional democracy.

These issues were at the heart of *Obergefell v. Hodges* (2015), in which a bitterly divided Supreme Court held 5-4 that the fundamental right to marry extends to same-sex couples. Justice Anthony Kennedy's opinion of the Court proclaimed that "the right to personal choice regarding marriage is inherent in the concept of individual autonomy." Kennedy declared that denying gays and lesbians the right to marry denies them equal dignity and respect and fails to afford them and their children the status and benefits of equal citizenship.[5] In dissent, Chief Justice John Roberts contended that Kennedy's majority opinion had "no basis in the Constitution or this Court's precedent" and that it revived the "grave errors" of *Lochner v. New York* (1905), an infamous substantive due process decision.[6]

In the *Lochner* era, the Court gave heightened judicial protection to substantive economic liberties under the Due Process Clauses of the Fifth and

Fourteenth Amendments.[7] In 1937, during the constitutional revolution wrought by the New Deal, *West Coast Hotel v. Parrish* repudiated the *Lochner* era, marking the first death of substantive due process.[8] Nevertheless, the ghost of *Lochner* has haunted constitutional law ever since, manifesting itself in charges that judges are "Lochnering" by imposing their own "philosophical predilections and moral intuitions" in the guise of interpreting the Constitution.[9] The cries of Lochnering have been most dogged with respect to *Roe v. Wade* (1973), which held that the Due Process Clause protects a realm of substantive personal liberty or privacy "broad enough to encompass a woman's decision whether or not to terminate her pregnancy."[10] More generally, *Roe* embodied the practice of protecting rights "implicit in the concept of ordered liberty."[11] Despite these cries, *Planned Parenthood v. Casey* (1992) reaffirmed the central holding of *Roe* instead of marking the second death of substantive due process by overruling it.[12] *Obergefell* further solidified the Court's commitment to substantive due process by resting its holding primarily on the Due Process Clause, but as intertwined with the Equal Protection Clause.[13] To Scalia's outraged charge that such cases stem from "a new mode of constitutional adjudication," *Casey* and *Obergefell* retorted that the Supreme Court in protecting these basic liberties is "exercis[ing] that same capacity which by tradition courts always have exercised: reasoned judgment."[14]

After *Casey* and *Obergefell*, one might have expected that the long-anticipated second death of substantive due process would be unlikely to come anytime soon. But in both 2016 and 2020, Donald Trump campaigned on a promise to appoint to the Court justices in the same vein as Justice Scalia who would overrule *Roe/Casey* and *Obergefell* (though Trump stated that he personally was "fine" with *Obergefell* and accepted it as "settled").[15] As president, Trump made significant progress toward fulfilling that promise. His appointment of Justice Neil Gorsuch (a self-styled originalist in the mold of Scalia) to succeed Scalia is likely to be a wash with respect to substantive due process.[16] The succession of Justice Kennedy (a notable proponent of substantive due process in the joint opinion in *Casey* and the majority opinion in *Obergefell*) by Justice Brett Kavanaugh (an evident critic of the doctrine), however, may augur change.[17] After the death of Justice Ruth Bader Ginsburg (a vigorous defender of reproductive rights as well as gay and lesbian rights), the confirmation of Justice Amy Coney Barrett (an avowed originalist and protégé of Scalia) will very likely move the Court in a staunchly conservative direction and away from protecting such rights.[18] Given this renewed possibility of a second death of substantive due process, I offer this book as a timely and vigorous defense of it.[19] I aim to fend off the ghost of *Lochner* by showing that the practice of constructing basic liberties that are essential for personal self-government in building out our commitment to ordered liberty is not illegitimate. Rather, it is integral to our constitutional democracy.[20]

Our practice of substantive due process over the last half century—in particular, through vindication of the rights of gays and lesbians—implicates classical controversies over law and morality. Conservatives like Justice Scalia have warned for decades that protecting a right of same-sex couples to intimate association would put us on a slippery slope not only to same-sex marriage but indeed to "the end of all morals legislation."[21] This warning presupposes that our governments may enforce traditional morality. Yet many conservatives object that when government prohibits discrimination against gays and lesbians, it improperly legislates morality and thereby denies liberty. Liberals and progressives often flip these two complaints about governmental moralizing, condemning traditional morals legislation and advocating governmental measures to secure a different moral objective: the status and benefits of equal citizenship for all. It seems, to paraphrase Mark Twain, that nothing so needs reforming as other people's morals.[22] The gay and lesbian rights debate is thus the latest round of an old problem in liberal societies: the proper relationship between law and morality. I will show how this debate points to the appropriate scope of the legal enforcement and promotion of morals and public values.

Furthermore, substantive due process cases pose a long-standing interpretive issue that turns on the relationship between law and morality: does constitutional interpretation involve determining the original meaning of the Constitution, conceived as historical facts (originalism), or does it involve making normative judgments concerning the best understanding of our constitutional commitments (moral reading)? By "moral reading," I refer to conceptions of the Constitution as embodying abstract moral and political principles—not codifying concrete historical rules or practices—and of interpretation of those principles as requiring normative judgments about how they are best understood—not merely historical research to discover relatively specific original meanings.[23] *Obergefell* plays out this clash, with Justice Kennedy's majority opinion exemplifying a moral reading and the dissents more or less reflecting originalism. What is more, Chief Justice Roberts in his dissent articulates a general view that the Constitution does not "enact" a particular moral theory but is "made for people of fundamentally differing views" (invoking Justice Oliver Wendell Holmes Jr.'s dissent in *Lochner*).[24] He maintains that, where there is deep moral disagreement concerning a right and recognizing a right would depart from historical practices, the courts should leave the matter to the democratic processes. I criticize Roberts's assertions that Kennedy's moral reading has no basis in the Constitution or judicial precedents and is undemocratic. I show that Roberts's democratic objections are overstated and misplaced, given the best understandings of constitutional interpretation (moral reading) and of the form of democracy embodied in our constitutional practice (a constitutional democracy, in which basic liberties limit majority rule).[25] I argue that our practice of substantive due process reflects an attractive moral reading of the Constitution and is justifiable on the basis of constitutional imperatives: protecting the basic liberties significant for personal self-government and securing the status and benefits of equal citizenship for all. This reading and these imperatives aspire to realize the promise of liberty together with equality and to fulfill the best understanding of the relationship between law and morality in our circumstances of moral pluralism.[26]

I begin with an overview sketching the arguments of each chapter.

Part I: Our Practice of Substantive Due Process

In part I (chapters 2–3), I develop an account of our practice of protecting basic liberties under the Due Process Clause. I argue that the line of cases culminating in *Obergefell*—far from being a nonsensical "oxymoron" or "dangerous fiction"—makes sense as a coherent and structured practice of deciding what basic liberties are significant preconditions for personal self-government in our scheme of constitutional self-government. I show that common criticisms have exaggerated the stringency of protection of basic liberties under the Due Process Clause and thus the dangers of protecting such liberties.

The Coherence and Structure of Substantive Due Process

Our practice of substantive due process after 1937 has protected the following basic liberties: liberty of conscience and freedom of thought; freedom of association, including both expressive association and intimate association, whatever one's sexual orientation; the right to live with one's family, whether nuclear or extended; the right to travel or relocate; the right to marry, whatever the gender of one's partner; the right to decide whether to bear or beget children, including the rights to procreate, to use contraceptives, and to terminate a pregnancy; the right to direct the education and rearing of children, including the right to make decisions concerning their care, custody, and control; and the right to exercise dominion over one's body, including the right to bodily integrity and ultimately the right to die (at least to the extent of the right to refuse unwanted medical treatment).[27]

There are two radically different views concerning this list of basic liberties. The first is Justice Scalia's view that it is a subjective, lawless product of judicial fiat and that the enterprise of protecting such liberties is indefensibly indeterminate and irredeemably undemocratic.[28] The second is that the list represents what Justice John Marshall Harlan II in dissent in *Poe v. Ullman* (1961), the joint opinion of Justices O'Connor, Kennedy, and Souter in *Casey*, and the majority opinion of Justice Kennedy in *Obergefell* called a "rational continuum" of ordered liberty stemming from "reasoned judgment"[29] concerning "the individual's right to make certain unusually important decisions that will affect his own, or his family's, destiny."[30] It has been constructed through common law constitutional interpretation: reasoning by analogy from one case to the next and making judgments about what basic liberties are significant for such personal self-government.[31] In chapter 2, I defend the latter view, articulating the coherence and structure of this practice against arguments that it is unbounded and anomalous in our constitutional scheme.

The practice of substantive due process over the past half century has been a battleground between these two competing views, encapsulated respectively in *Washington v. Glucksberg* (1997) and *Casey*. On the *Glucksberg* view, the liberty protected by the Due Process Clause is a deposit of "careful[ly] descri[bed]" concrete historical practices (originalism);[32] on the *Casey* view, it is a "covenant" of abstract aspirational ideals to be realized over time through judgments about the best understanding of our constitutional commitments (moral reading).[33] The battle between these views came to a head in *Obergefell*, with the majority adopting the *Casey* framework[34] and the dissenters that of *Glucksberg*.[35] I argue that the *Casey* framework better fits and justifies the line of cases protecting basic personal liberties culminating in *Obergefell* and that, going forward, we should build out that line with coherence and integrity to secure those liberties significant for personal self-government. My account shows that the practice of substantive due process has steered a middle course between Scylla (Scalia)—the rock of liberty as concrete historical practices—and Charybdis—the whirlpool of liberty as unbounded license.[36]

The Rational Continuum of Ordered Liberty

Dissenting in *Lawrence v. Texas* (2003), Justice Scalia stated that, under the Due Process Clause, if an asserted liberty is a "fundamental right," it triggers "strict scrutiny" that almost automatically invalidates any statute restricting that liberty. Otherwise, he wrote, it is merely a "liberty interest," which triggers rational basis scrutiny that is so deferential that the Court all but automatically upholds the statute in question.[37] In attempting to limit the protection of substantive liberties under the Due Process Clause, Scalia argued for a narrow approach to what constitutes a "fundamental right" and a broad approach to what constitutes a mere "liberty interest."

Lawrence deviated from Scalia's regime. The Court did not hold that gays' and lesbians' right to sexual privacy or autonomy was a fundamental right requiring strict scrutiny. Nor did it hold that their right was merely a liberty interest calling for highly deferential rational basis scrutiny. Instead, the Court applied an intermediate standard—what many have called rational basis scrutiny with "bite"[38]—and struck down the statute forbidding same-sex sexual conduct.[39] Scalia chastised the Court for not following a rigid two-tier framework that all but automatically decides rights questions one way or the other.[40]

In chapter 3, I expose the myth of two rigidly policed tiers under the Due Process Clause.[41] Contrary to what it sounds like, this myth aims not at stringently protecting fundamental rights, but at raising the bar for protecting them and delegitimizing our more complex actual practice of substantive due process. I show that the only substantive due process case officially to recognize a fundamental right implicating strict scrutiny—requiring that the statute further a compelling governmental interest and be necessary to doing so—was *Roe*.[42] And those aspects of *Roe* were overruled in *Casey*, which pointedly avoided calling the right to decide whether to terminate a pregnancy a "fundamental right" and substituted an "undue burden" standard for strict scrutiny.[43] Moreover, the leading due process cases *protecting* liberty and autonomy—from *Meyer v. Nebraska* (1923) through *Casey*, *Lawrence*, and *Obergefell*—have not applied Scalia's rigid two-tier framework. Instead, actual practice in these cases reflects what *Casey*, *Obergefell*, and Justice Harlan in *Poe* called "reasoned judgment" and maps onto a "rational continuum" of ordered liberty, with several intermediate levels of review. The only cases that have applied Scalia's framework have been those *refusing to recognize* asserted rights: *Bowers v. Hardwick* (1986), *Michael H. v. Gerald D.* (1989), and *Glucksberg*.[44]

Part II: Substantive Due Process Does Not "Effectively Decree the End of All Morals Legislation"

In part II (chapters 4 and 5), I defend our practice of substantive due process against familiar objections relating to the legal enforcement of morals. I rebut the argument that protecting the rights of same-sex couples to inti-mate association and to marry puts us on a slippery slope to "the end of all morals legislation." I refute the related contention that if moral disapproval alone is not an adequate reason to justify traditional morals legislation, then all such legislation is unconstitutional.

Is Substantive Due Process on a Slippery Slope to "the End of All Morals Legislation"?

In *Lawrence*, which recognized a right of gays and lesbians to intimate as-sociation, Justice Scalia protested in dissent that the case "effectively de-crees the end of all morals legislation." Is Scalia right that there is really no distinction between same-sex intimate association and, to quote his list, "bigamy, same-sex marriage, adult incest, prostitution, masturbation, adul-tery, fornication, bestiality, and obscenity"?[45] Similarly, in *Obergefell*, which recognized the right of same-sex couples to marry, Chief Justice Roberts sug-gested in dissent that the decision puts us on a slippery slope to protecting a right to plural marriage.[46]

In chapter 4, I criticize Scalia's slippery slope argument, insisting that we can draw significant distinctions between same-sex intimate association and marriage on the one hand, and most of the types of conduct on his list on the other. I also refute Chief Justice Roberts's slippery slope argument, show-ing that it would be a much bigger leap to recognize plural marriage than it was to protect the right of same-sex couples to marry. I demonstrate that we have many tools available in our constitutional practice to get traction on such slippery slopes. These are forms of constitutional argument that we make in drawing lines as we build out our constitutional commitments through common law constitutional interpretation. Whether *Lawrence* and *Obergefell* "effectively decree[] the end of all morals legislation" depends upon our answers to the following types of questions:

· *How we conceive the right being protected.* Does *Lawrence* presuppose that I have a liberty to choose to do whatever traditionally immoral things I wish to do? Or does it presuppose simply that the rights of spatial privacy and intimate association already recognized for straights extend to gays and lesbians?

· *How we justify protecting the right.* Do *Lawrence* and *Obergefell* justify protect-ing the rights of gays and lesbians to intimate association and to marry on the ground that individuals have a right (1) to choose whom or what to have sex with, (2) to decide whom or what to marry, and (3) to choose to

do whatever they damn well please with their bodies—a right to choose
without regard for the moral good of what is chosen? Or do these cases to
the contrary justify protecting the right to intimate association and to marry
on the ground that doing so promotes moral goods (the same moral goods
for same-sex couples as for opposite-sex couples): for example, intimacy,
commitment, and loyalty within a worthy relationship.[47]

· *How we understand the processes of constitutional change that have brought us
to recognize the right.* Do we conceive the processes of constitutional change
(as Scalia did) in terms of Supreme Court justices arbitrarily imposing their
"philosophical predilections" or "moral intuitions" upon the rest of us?
Or do we conceive those processes in terms of common law constitutional
interpretation: reasoning by analogy from one case to the next, building out
lines of doctrine interpreting our constitutional commitments on the basis
of experience, new insights, moral progress, and evolving consensus, all
of which contribute to moral judgments about the best understandings of
those commitments?

The moral of the story is that the tools or forms of argument I elaborate
help us answer these questions and avert any slide down Scalia's slippery
slope. I argue that, far from being "the end of all morals legislation," *Lawrence* and *Obergefell* are the beginning of legitimate morals legislation: legislation that does not demean or humiliate the ways of life of people who are
entitled to the status and benefits of equal citizenship.

Is Moral Disapproval Enough to Justify Traditional Morals Legislation?

Some defenders of Justice Scalia argue, contrary to chapter 4, that he was
not really making a classic slippery slope argument. They argue that he was
instead contending that if moral disapproval alone is not an adequate reason to justify traditional morals legislation—if the Supreme Court is going
to put any "bite" into its rational basis scrutiny of such legislation, as it did
in *Lawrence*—then, as Scalia put it, "[e]very single one of these laws is called
into question."[48] In other words, any requirement of a good reason to justify
these traditional moral prohibitions "effectively decrees the end of all morals legislation."

In chapter 5, I assess this alternative interpretation by doing a "take two"
on Scalia's warning in *Lawrence*. I distinguish several versions of the claim
that moral disapproval alone is not an adequate justification for traditional
morals legislation. And I develop several types of (nontraditional) arguments beyond moral disapproval that—contrary to Scalia's warning—do

provide good reasons to justify prohibitions of most of the types of conduct on his list. These include arguments about (1) preventing harm to others; (2) prohibiting conduct where we have good reason to fear lack of meaningful consent; (3) protecting institutions worth protecting because of their important civic and social functions; and (4) securing the status and benefits of equal citizenship for all. I argue that Kennedy's majority opinion in *Lawrence*, even on this alternative interpretation of Scalia's warning, does not entail that all of the traditional morals prohibitions on his list are unconstitutional. Nor does Kennedy's majority opinion in *Obergefell*. Indeed, to continue the argument of chapter 4, instead of decreeing "the end of all morals legislation," *Lawrence* and *Obergefell* require decidedly moral inquiries like those involved in making or assessing the foregoing forms of arguments. Those cases emphatically do not reject moral arguments as such as a basis for justifying laws.

Part III: Substantive Due Process Does Not Enact a Utopian Economic or Moral Theory

In part III (chapters 6–7), I defend our practice of substantive due process since 1937 against criticisms that it illegitimately reads a controversial utopian economic or moral theory into the Constitution in the guise of interpreting it. I reject Justice Scalia's and Chief Justice Roberts's claims that substantive due process cases including *Obergefell* repeat the "grave errors" of *Lochner*. I refute Roberts's charge that cases such as *Obergefell* read the Constitution as enacting John Stuart Mill's *On Liberty*.

The Ghost of Lochner v. New York

A recurring issue surrounding judicial protection of substantive liberties is the so-called double standard between economic liberties and personal liberties. The question is whether the Supreme Court can justify aggressively protecting personal liberties like the right to marry while deferring to legislative regulation of economic liberties. Put more concretely, can the Court simultaneously justify its repudiation of *Lochner*'s aggressive judicial protection for economic liberties and its embrace of *Roe*'s and *Obergefell*'s heightened judicial protection for personal liberties? To get at this issue, we must ask, why is *Lochner* infamous? What is the ghost of *Lochner* that haunts modern constitutional law? Although critics of substantive due process sometimes speak as if there is an agreed-upon account, in chapter 6 I show that every theory of constitutional interpretation and judicial review has different implications for what, if anything, was wrong with *Lochner* (as well as for the relationship between *Lochner* on the one hand, and *Roe* and *Obergefell* on the other).

I argue that economic liberties and property rights, like personal liberties, are fundamental liberties secured by the Constitution. In fact, economic liberties are so fundamental in our constitutional scheme, and so sacred in our constitutional culture, that there is neither need nor good argument for aggressive judicial protection of them. Rather, such liberties are properly "judicially underenforced," for their fuller enforcement and protection is secure with legislatures and executives in "the Constitution outside the courts."[49] That is hardly the case with personal liberties such as reproductive freedom and freedom to marry, which are vulnerable in the political processes. On this view, the Court was wrong to protect economic liberties aggressively in *Lochner*, but right to protect personal liberties stringently in *Roe* and *Obergefell*. Thus, contrary to Scalia's and Roberts's charge, *Obergefell* does not revive the "grave errors" of *Lochner*.

Does Substantive Due Process Enact Mill's On Liberty?

In *On Liberty* (1859), John Stuart Mill argued that the only justification for government to restrict individual liberty is to prevent harm to others.[50] This famous "harm principle" figures prominently in arguments against the legal enforcement of traditional morals. Dissenting in *Obergefell*, Chief Justice Roberts charges that Justice Kennedy's majority opinion reads Mill's harm principle into the Constitution. In doing so, Roberts echoes Justice Holmes's dissent in *Lochner* by asserting: "[T]he Fourteenth Amendment does not enact John Stuart Mill's *On Liberty* any more than it enacts Herbert Spencer's *Social Statics*."[51] This makes *Obergefell* and the practice of substantive due process sound undemocratic and illegitimate: importing foreign normative authority and imposing it on the rest of us! In reality, I argue in chapter 7, Kennedy makes a moral argument from constitutional principles of liberty, equality, and fairness, reflecting a moral reading of the Constitution. Roberts misconceives this argument and accuses Kennedy of applying extra-constitutional authority, the moral theory of Mill. The lesson here is that the Constitution embodies a morality of its own and that explicating and applying that morality is the function of constitutional interpretation.

I begin by examining the leading substantive due process precedents, showing that they have not been animated by Mill's *On Liberty*. I point out basic differences between the generic right to privacy or autonomy those cases protect and Mill's harm principle and comprehensive moral conception cultivating individuality as a perfectionist ideal of the good life. More generally, I demonstrate that our practice of substantive due process has not involved liberals reading their ideal normative moral theories into the Constitution. For example, Justice Blackmun's majority opinion in *Roe* reflects conservative concerns for family stability and family planning, rather than liberal concerns for autonomy or the sexual revolution of the 1960s and 1970s.[52] And the joint opinion of Justices O'Connor, Kennedy, and Souter in *Casey* as well as Justice Kennedy's majority opinion in *Obergefell* stem from a preservative conservative constitutional jurisprudence prefigured by Justice Harlan (as contrasted with the counterrevolutionary or movement conservativism epitomized by Justice Scalia).

Part IV: Conflicts between Liberty and Equality

In part IV (chapters 8–9), I take up the relationship between liberty and equality, exploring conflicts between these two commitments. I assess arguments by some liberals and progressives that certain basic liberties protected under the Due Process Clause would be on firmer ground if they instead were based on the Equal Protection Clause. I ask whether (as some conservatives have argued) securing basic liberties and the status and benefits of equal citizenship for gays and lesbians, including the right to marry and the right not to be discriminated against, has imperiled the religious liberty of opponents of such rights.

The Grounds for Protecting Basic Liberties: Liberty Together with Equality

Some argue that cases like *Roe* and *Obergefell* reached the right result but that we need to "rewrite" the opinions to provide better justifications. Such critics explore topics such as "What *Roe* Should Have Said" and "What *Obergefell* Should Have Said."[53] The answer commonly provided is that the Court should have grounded the right—to decide whether to terminate a pregnancy or to marry—in the Equal Protection Clause instead of the Due Process Clause. In chapter 8, I assess these arguments, examining the relationship between these two clauses. I argue that rather than being in opposition, liberty and equality overlap and are intertwined: both provide sound grounds for protecting basic liberties essential to securing ordered liberty and the status and benefits of equal citizenship for all. I also argue that *Casey* and *Obergefell*, while officially grounded primarily in due process, are also rooted in equal protection; indeed, the opinions intimate the very concerns for the status of equal citizenship that the rewriters articulate. Thus, we need not rewrite *Casey* or *Obergefell*—those opinions already contain and intertwine the best liberty arguments and threads of the best equality arguments needed to justify them adequately.

Although I argue for liberty together with equality as grounds for basic liberties essential to equal citizenship, I develop criteria for deciding which—liberty or equality—might seem to the Court to provide a sounder ground for certain rights in certain circumstances. I then apply these criteria to the circumstances of *Roe, Casey,* and *Obergefell.* I also bring out what might have seemed to the Court to be advantages of grounding certain rights in liberty instead of equality. For example, in *Obergefell,* the conservative Justice Kennedy might have thought that rooting the right of same-sex couples to marry in liberty rather than equality would enable him to avoid drawing analogies between discrimination on the basis of sexual orientation and that on the basis of race, and thus to sidestep the dissenters' arguments that he was equating opposition to same-sex marriage with racial prejudice and bigotry. He also might have thought that by taking the liberty route instead of the equality route he could avoid deciding (or implying an answer to) the question liberals and progressives might have wanted him to decide: whether all forms of discrimination on the basis of sexual orientation are unconstitutional.

Accommodating Gay and Lesbian Rights and Religious Liberty

In chapter 9 I focus on another type of conflict between equality and liberty: conflicts between gay and lesbian rights (protected through antidiscrimination statutes together with substantive due process decisions like *Obergefell* safeguarding the right of same-sex couples to marry) and religious liberty. Recent developments have dramatically posed the question whether laws recognizing same-sex marriage and protecting against discrimination on the basis of sexual orientation or gender identity (including in the marketplace) should grant exemptions to businesspeople who disapprove of such rights on religious grounds. The changed composition of the Supreme Court likely will make it more receptive to the religious liberty claims in such conflicts.

The four justices who dissented in *Obergefell* have warned that protecting the right of same-sex couples to marry threatens the religious liberty of those who oppose that right.[54] Yet Chief Justice Roberts, in dissent, acknowledged that every state that had recognized same-sex marriage had created religious exemptions.[55] I argue that nothing in *Obergefell* implies that the state statutes already granting such exemptions were unconstitutional, nor would it prohibit legislatures prospectively from creating exemptions as long as they do not impose a substantial burden on the rights of others. *Obergefell* leaves room for the democratic processes to continue to operate as before in creating religious exemptions. To be sure, exemptions will not satisfy those who oppose same-sex marriage altogether. Nor will they satisfy many supporters of equal rights. Yet, in circumstances of rapid cultural and constitutional change, limited exemptions might seem to some to be a reasonable prudential approach to ameliorating clashes between gay and lesbian rights and religious liberty and minimizing backlash against such rights. Still, we might hope that the need for such exemptions will wither away along with religious objections to such marriage.

What is more, I suggest that the Supreme Court, in attempting to resolve conflicts between rights in "culture war" controversies—in particular, between gay and lesbian rights and religious liberty—might be a civic educative institution, teaching lessons to citizens concerning how to accommodate such conflicts. Judicial opinions might model how to secure the central range of application of each conflicting right rather than vindicating one right absolutely to the exclusion of the other, with one side winning it all. They also might teach how to speak with respect concerning both gay and lesbian rights and religious liberty. I focus on the US Supreme Court's decision in *Masterpiece Cakeshop, Ltd. v. Colorado Civil Rights Commission* (2018)[56] but also discuss the New Mexico Supreme Court's decision in *Elane Photography, LLC v. Willock* (2013).[57] Such cases teach (1) that antidiscrimination laws properly exact a commitment to nondiscrimination in the marketplace as "the price of citizenship" (to invoke a phrase from *Elane Photography*) and (2) that it is an obligation of government to afford equal respect both to gays and lesbians and to religious opponents of gay and lesbian rights. Moreover, I caution that religious exemptions for businesses from antidiscrimination laws undercut the significant moderating influences of trade in large commercial republics such as the US. They undermine the salutary civic function of trade in facilitating contact, moderating difference, promoting tolerance and respect, and securing the status and benefits of equal citizenship for all.

Part V: The Future

The Future of Substantive Due Process

In concluding, chapter 10 reflects upon what is likely to change in constitutional law with the succession of Justice Kennedy by Justice Kavanaugh and of Justice Ginsburg by Justice Barrett. Is substantive due process likely to become a relic of the past? Instead of a liberal forecast of gloom and doom concerning the future of the Supreme Court, I offer some more constructive thoughts: (1) a pep talk for dismayed liberals and progressives—or proposals for what to do next—and (2) some words of caution for jubilant conservatives—be careful what you wish for. The long-awaited conservative counterrevolution—with its restoration of the Constitution that has been in exile since the New Deal liberal revolution in 1937—may come back to haunt conservatives and doom the Court to an infamy even worse than that of the *Lochner* Court. In fulfilling such conservative wishes, rather than protecting basic personal liberties in substantive due process cases culminating in *Obergefell*, the Court would truly repeat the "grave errors" of *Lochner*.

The upshot of my analysis is that—though it always has been and will continue to be controversial, and though it requires complex judgments—constructing basic liberties significant for personal self-government through reasoned judgment has proven to be a durable feature of US constitutional practice, one that should survive changes in the composition of the Court. Substantive due process is a worthy practice that we should continue to build out with coherence and integrity on the basis of moral judgments about the best understanding of our constitutional commitments to protecting ordered liberty and securing the status and benefits of equal citizenship for all.

A Note on Terminology

This book analyzes Supreme Court cases from the last half century protecting reproductive freedom (e.g., *Roe* and *Casey*) and the rights of gays and lesbians or same-sex couples to intimate association and to marry (e.g., *Lawrence* and *Obergefell*). *Roe* and *Casey* speak of protecting the right of a "pregnant woman" to decide whether to terminate her pregnancy (and *Casey* includes intimations of a feminist gender equality justification for that right). Today, there has been an important, necessary shift toward the more inclusive language of "pregnant person" to acknowledge that some people who become pregnant do not identify as women or are gender nonbinary. *Lawrence* speaks of "homosexuals" or "homosexual persons" or "gays and lesbians," and *Obergefell* uses the terms "gays and lesbians" or "same-sex couples." Today, I, like many, would use more inclusive formulations like LGBTQ+. In both contexts, many of us now hold more fluid conceptions of gender identity and sexual orientation.

In some instances, we can update the language in the cases to non-offensive terms without extending the holdings of those cases (e.g., from "homosexuals" to "gays and lesbians" or "same-sex couples"). But in other instances, updating the language used in the opinions to more inclusive terms (like LGBTQ+) may imply protection of rights for groups (transgender and gender nonbinary people) not explicitly guaranteed by or contemplated within those opinions. Indeed, the farthest the Supreme Court has ever gotten in a constitutional law case is to LGB in *Romer v. Evans* (1996)—where the invalidated state constitutional amendment had explicitly referred to "Homosexual, Lesbian, or Bisexual Orientation"[58]—though it recently interpreted Title VII's statutory prohibition of discrimination on the basis of sex to include discrimination on the basis of sexual orientation or gender identity in *Bostock v. Clayton County* (2020).[59] The same may be true with updating "pregnant woman" to "pregnant person."

To acknowledge these issues, I have attempted to remain true to the language of the opinions themselves, while updating language where I can do so without changing the meaning or reach of the opinions. I would argue that the rationales in those opinions extend more broadly. Given that the current Supreme Court is markedly more conservative than it was at the time of *Roe*, *Casey*, *Lawrence*, and *Obergefell*, however, we must acknowledge that it might limit the precedents narrowly to their specific circumstances (if not overrule them) rather than extending them on the ground that their rationales apply more broadly. At any rate, we cannot take it for granted that the Court will recognize rights that liberals or progressives would argue are clearly implicit in the opinions.

PART ONE

Our Practice of Substantive Due Process

TWO

The Coherence and Structure of Substantive Due Process

The Fourteenth Amendment includes three clauses that might serve as textual bases for protecting fundamental rights or basic liberties: (1) the Privileges or Immunities Clause, (2) the Due Process Clause, and (3) the Equal Protection Clause, respectively:

> No State shall make or enforce any law which shall abridge the privileges or immunities of citizens of the United States; nor shall any State deprive any person of life, liberty, or property, without due process of law; nor deny to any person within its jurisdiction the equal protection of the laws.

The Privileges or Immunities Clause might seem to be the most promising textual basis for protecting basic liberties. After all, it speaks of "privileges or immunities" of citizenship, which might appear to include such freedoms. The Due Process Clause speaks of "due process of law," which might seem to be limited to guaranteeing that the government must follow processes established under existing law, whatever the law is. That is, it might permit the government to deprive anyone of any liberty, provided that it follows prescribed processes for doing so. Finally, the Equal Protection Clause speaks of "equal protection of the laws," which might appear to be limited to assuring equal protection under existing laws, whatever they are. That is, it might permit the government to treat everyone equally badly.

Yet in *The Slaughter-House Cases* (1873), the first judicial interpretation of the Fourteenth Amendment, given five years after its ratification, the Supreme Court gutted the Privileges or Immunities Clause. Although the dissenters interpreted the Fourteenth Amendment as a whole as "a new Magna Charta" and the Privileges or Immunities Clause in particular as protecting "natural and inalienable rights," "those which of right belong to the citizens of all free governments,"[1] the majority limited the Clause to protecting only those rights "which owe their existence to the Federal Government, its National character, its Constitution, or its laws."[2] According to Justice Field in dissent, this interpretation reduced the Fourteenth Amendment to a "vain and idle enactment, which accomplished nothing, and most unnecessarily excited Congress and the people on its passage."[3]

Thus, to interpret the Fourteenth Amendment to secure basic liberties, the Court had to (1) overrule much of *Slaughter-House* (and resurrect the Privileges or Immunities Clause), (2) find another clause to bear the burden, or (3) look beyond the constitutional document for justification (for example, to read it to incorporate natural and inalienable rights). Despite recurring protests, the justices have opted to use the other clauses—the Due Process Clause doctrine of substantive due process and the fundamental rights or interests strand of Equal Protection Clause doctrine—to protect basic liberties. Protecting substantive basic liberties through the Due Process Clause results from this choice to give meaning to the Fourteenth Amendment after *Slaughter-House* and is not a nonsensical "oxymoron" or "dangerous fiction," notwithstanding the assertions of Justices Scalia and Thomas.[4]

An Overview of Our Practice of Substantive Due Process

In this book, I defend the protection of "unenumerated" substantive fundamental rights or basic liberties. I focus on substantive due process, but briefly mention the fundamental rights or interests strand of Equal Protection doctrine. I put "unenumerated" in quotation marks because I agree with Ronald Dworkin and Charles Black that many of our constitutional commitments—for example, to liberty, equal protection, and freedom of speech—are abstract and do not "enumerate" their specific contents. On this view, it is "spurious" to object to protecting a basic liberty on the ground that it is not "enumerated" in the word "liberty," just as it would be "bogus" to object to protecting the right to burn flags on the ground that it is not "enumerated" in the words "freedom of speech."[5]

As noted above, the text of the Due Process Clause might make it seem problematic as a basis for protecting substantive fundamental rights or basic liberties. Accordingly, the joint opinion of Justices O'Connor, Kennedy, and Souter in *Planned Parenthood v. Casey* (1992) begins: "Although a literal reading of the [Due Process] Clause might suggest that it governs only the procedures by which a State may deprive persons of liberty. . . ." On that reading, the controlling word in the Clause is "process." But, *Casey* continued: "at least . . . since *Mugler v. Kansas* (1887), the Clause has been understood to contain a substantive component as well." On that understanding, as *Casey* put it, "[t]he controlling word in the cases before us is 'liberty.'"[6] The doctrine of substantive due process interprets the word "liberty" to secure basic liberties.

Many critics of substantive due process, including Justice Scalia, have tried to tar it with the brush of an infamous earlier case, *Dred Scott v. Sandford* (1857).[7] Because I, like the joint opinion in *Casey*, conceive substantive due process as the practice of interpreting the word "liberty" in the Due Process Clauses to protect basic liberties that are not "enumerated" specifically in the text of the Constitution, I do not view *Dred Scott* as a substantive due process case. In *Dred Scott*, Chief Justice Taney stated: "And an act of Congress which deprives a citizen of the United States of his liberty or property, merely because he came himself or brought his property into a particular Territory of the United States, and who had committed no offence against the laws, could hardly be dignified with the name of due process of law." Taney immediately added: "[T]he right of property in a slave is distinctly and expressly affirmed in the Constitution." He mentioned Article V's express entrenchment of slavery in the Constitution for at least twenty years: "The right to traffic in it, like an ordinary article of merchandise and property, was guarantied to the citizens of the United States, in every State that might desire it, for twenty years." He also referred to the Fugitive Slave Clause of Article IV, Section 2, Clause 3: "And the Government in express terms is pledged to protect it in all future time, if the slave escapes from his owner. This is done in plain words—too plain to be misunderstood."[8] In short, Taney claimed that what the government had unconstitutionally denied was Sanford's "right of property in a slave"—a right he insisted was recognized in the "express terms" and "plain words" of the Constitution. Clearly, Taney did not claim to be protecting any "unenumerated" liberty of Sanford.

By contrast, modern critics of substantive due process object to the practice of protecting "unenumerated" fundamental rights or basic liberties through the Due Process Clauses. For example, Justice Scalia objected to protecting the right to decide whether to terminate a pregnancy because "the Constitution says absolutely nothing about" abortion.[9] Similarly, he objected to protecting a right to die because "the Constitution has nothing to say about the subject."[10] Protecting rights to property "enumerated" in the "plain words" and "express terms" of the Constitution is not what we today conceive as substantive due process, and thus *Dred Scott* is not part of that practice.

I shall distinguish three phases in judicial protection of fundamental rights or basic liberties: (1) from 1887 to 1937, (2) from 1937 to 1973, and (3) from 1973 to the present.

1887 to 1937: The Lochner Era

During the first phase, the era of *Lochner v. New York* (1905), the Court aggressively protected economic liberties—such as liberty of contract—along with personal liberties—such as the liberty of parents to direct the upbringing and education of their children—without distinguishing between the two. Both were seen as essential liberties to be protected under the Due Process Clauses. *Meyer v. Nebraska* (1923) gave a classic formulation concerning liberty during the *Lochner* era:

> While this court has not attempted to define with exactness the liberty thus guaranteed, the term has received much consideration and some of the included things have been definitely stated. Without doubt, it denotes not merely freedom from bodily restraint but also the right of the individual to contract, to engage in any of the common occupations of life, to acquire useful knowledge, to marry, establish a home and bring up children, to worship God according to the dictates of his own conscience, and generally to enjoy those privileges long recognized at common law as essential to the orderly pursuit of happiness by free men. *Slaughter-House Cases* [1873]; *Yick Wo v. Hopkins* [1886]; *Minnesota v. Barber* [1890]; *Allgeyer v. Louisiana* [1897]; *Lochner v. New York* [1905]; *Twining v. New Jersey* [1908]; *Truax v. Raich* [1915]; *Adams v. Tanner* [1917]; *Truax v. Corrigan* [1921]; *Adkins v. Children's Hospital* [1923].[11]

Note that most of these liberties that have been "definitely stated" in the precedents are not enumerated in the Constitution. Those that are—freedom of speech and freedom of religion—are enumerated only as against the federal government. They have been incorporated through the Due Process Clause of the Fourteenth Amendment and made applicable to the state governments.[12]

Meyer conceived liberty more abstractly as including not only the things enumerated in the Constitution or "definitely stated" in the precedents, but also "those privileges long recognized at common law as essential to the orderly pursuit of happiness by free men."[13] Here the Court prefigured later formulations of the Due Process inquiry such as those in *Palko v. Connecticut* (1937) ("implicit in the concept of ordered liberty") and *Loving v. Virginia*

(1967) ("essential to the orderly pursuit of happiness by free men").[14] Still more abstractly, *Meyer* intimated a fundamental theory of liberty—of "the relation between individual and state"—as prohibiting the state from "submerg[ing] the individual and develop[ing] ideal citizens."[15] Two years later, *Pierce v. Society of Sisters* (1925) articulated this theory of liberty as forbidding the state to "standardize" children by treating them as "the mere creature[s] of the state" to be crafted into its vision of ideal citizens.[16] *Meyer* and *Pierce* upheld the right of parents to direct the upbringing and education of their children by striking down, respectively, a state statute prohibiting the teaching of any modern language other than English in any public or private grammar school and a state statute requiring parents to send their children between the ages of eight and sixteen to public schools rather than private schools.

In both cases, the Court anticipated what has come to be known as the "level of generality problem" in the formulation of rights recognized in precedents or traditions: how abstractly or specifically to frame rights. The Court clearly conceived liberty as an abstract principle, not a concrete historical practice or a specific original meaning. That is, the Court did not frame the rights specifically or limit them to their concrete factual contexts—in proto-Scalian or *Glucksbergian* style, to be explained below—as being about the right of parents to contract with teachers to teach their children the German language or the right of parents to send their children to Catholic schools or military academies.

The most famous (or infamous) decision of this era was its namesake, *Lochner*. The case involved a challenge to a New York law providing that "no employee shall be required or permitted to work" more than sixty hours in one week. The law was ostensibly an exercise of the state's police power: the power to protect the health, safety, morals, or welfare of the people. Stringently protecting liberty of contract against governmental regulation, the Court invalidated the law. The Court viewed the state's professed police power concern—to protect the health of bakers or the welfare of the public—as a mere "pretext" for "other motives"—"simply to regulate the hours of labor between the master and his employees." The Court seemed to fear that upholding such legislation under the police power would put us on a slippery slope leading to the end of all constitutional limitations upon government: "the supreme sovereignty of the state to be exercised free from constitutional restraint."[17]

During the *Lochner* era, the Court struck down a number of state and federal economic regulations on the ground that they denied liberty of contract. During that period and since, *Lochner* has been a symbol of illegitimate

judicial review. Yet just what was so wrong about *Lochner* is a matter of per-
ennial controversy, as I show in chapter 6.

In *West Coast Hotel v. Parrish* (1937)—at the height of the confrontation
between President Franklin Roosevelt and the Supreme Court concerning
the constitutionality of the New Deal—the Court repudiated the *Lochner*
era and therewith aggressive judicial protection of economic liberties under the Due Process Clauses. The Court instead began to apply what has
come to be known as "deferential rational basis scrutiny" in deciding the
constitutionality of economic regulations: "regulation which is reasonable
in relation to its subject and is adopted in the interests of the community
is due process."[18] Applying this deferential standard, the Court upheld a
state minimum-wage law against the challenge that it violated liberty of
contract. In justifying this shift, the Court took judicial notice of "recent economic experience" during the Great Depression. It stated that "the liberty
safeguarded [by the Constitution] is liberty in a social organization which
requires the protection of law against the evils which menace the health,
safety, morals and welfare of the people" and concluded that "[e]ven if the
wisdom of [legislative] policy be regarded as debatable and its effects uncer-
tain, still the Legislature is entitled to its judgment."[19]

Although it may not have been clear in 1937, it turned out that the Court
left undisturbed the cases from the *Lochner* era protecting personal liberties
(such as the right to direct the upbringing and education of children in
Meyer and *Pierce*), but it repudiated those vindicating economic liberties
(such as liberty of contract in *Lochner*). Ultimately the Court built upon the
former cases from 1965 to the present in protecting substantive personal
liberties.

1937 to 1973: Eschewal of the Due Process Clause
for the Equal Protection Clause

During the second phase, from 1937 to 1973, the Court eschewed protecting fundamental rights or basic liberties on the basis of the Due Process
Clauses alone. In *Skinner v. Oklahoma* (1942), the Court considered the constitutionality of an Oklahoma statute requiring sterilization of "habitual
criminals"—persons convicted two or more times for some felonies involving "moral turpitude." The statute excepted certain "white collar" crimes:
"offenses arising out of the violation of the prohibitory laws, revenue acts,
embezzlement, or political offenses."[20] Jack Skinner, who had been convicted of stealing chickens and of robbery with firearms, challenged the pro-
ceedings to order his sterilization.

The Court opened the opinion by waxing eloquent about "important . . . human rights," speaking of "the right to have offspring" or to procreate as a "fundamental" or "basic civil right."[21] But it did not hold that the state may not sterilize anyone on the ground that there is a fundamental right to procreate rooted in the Due Process Clause. The recent repudiation of substantive due process in *West Coast Hotel* foreclosed that straightforward option. Instead, the Court protected the right to procreate by establishing what came to be known as the "fundamental rights or interests" strand of Equal Protection doctrine (as distinguished from the "suspect classifications" strand). The Court held the Oklahoma statute unconstitutional on the ground that equal protection requires that the state must either (1) sterilize embezzlers along with larceners or (2) sterilize neither class of "habitual criminals." All or none. Retrospectively, though, the Court has sometimes cited *Skinner* as if it were a substantive due process case involving the fundamental right to procreate—which the state may not deny to anyone—rather than an equal protection case merely holding that the state must treat everyone equally.[22]

Over the next three decades, the Court developed the fundamental rights or interests strand of Equal Protection doctrine—sometimes called "substantive equal protection"—and avoided protecting substantive liberties under the Due Process Clause alone.[23] Two prominent cases that might seem to be counterexamples, but which in fact confirm the point, are *Griswold v. Connecticut* (1965) (protecting the right of privacy through invalidating a law prohibiting the use of contraceptives by married couples), and *Loving* (1967) (protecting the right to marry by invalidating a law prohibiting interracial marriage).

Writing for the Court in *Griswold*, Justice Douglas, a veteran of the New Deal critique of *Lochner*, officially avoided reviving substantive due process as the basis for protecting the right of privacy. Rather than deriving that right from the word "liberty," he grounded it in the language and "penumbras" or "emanations" of "specific guarantees in the Bill of Rights," namely, the First ("privacy in one's associations"), Third (privacy of the home), Fourth (privacy of the person and the home from unreasonable searches and seizures), and Fifth Amendments (freedom from compulsory self-incrimination).[24] Douglas invoked the command of the Ninth Amendment—"The enumeration in the Constitution, of certain rights, shall not be construed to deny or disparage others retained by the people"—to justify going beyond the bare enumeration of the foregoing rights so as not to exclude the protection of the penumbras or emanations that were not explicitly enumerated.[25] Finally, connecting the dots of the letters and penumbras, Douglas stated that this case "concerns a relationship lying within the zone of privacy created by several fundamental constitutional guarantees."[26] In concluding, Douglas indicated that the Court was protecting the right of marital privacy—or freedom of intimate association—to protect the "intimate relation of husband and wife," a "sacred" association that promotes "noble" purposes.[27] Justice Harlan in concurrence would have none of Douglas's letters and penumbras approach, arguing instead for grounding the right of marital privacy squarely on substantive due process. Harlan thundered: "The Due Process Clause stands on its own bottom."[28]

Two years later, *Loving* held that Virginia's miscegenation statute prohibiting and punishing interracial marriage violated both the Equal Protection and the Due Process Clauses. First, Chief Justice Warren's opinion of the Court held that the law reflected invidious racial discrimination that denied equal protection.[29] Second, it added that the law denied the fundamental right to marry in violation of the Due Process Clause. Warren began by stating that "[t]he freedom to marry has long been recognized as one of the vital personal rights essential to the orderly pursuit of happiness by free men." He continued:

> To deny this fundamental freedom on so unsupportable a basis as the racial classifications embodied in these statutes, classifications so directly subversive of the principle of equality at the heart of the Fourteenth Amendment, is surely to deprive all the State's citizens of liberty without due process of law. The Fourteenth Amendment requires that the freedom of choice to marry not be restricted by invidious racial discriminations.[30]

This passage demonstrates the thoroughgoing overlap between the Court's due process holding concerning the fundamental right to marry and its equal protection holding concerning invidious racial discrimination. The Court does not rest the decision on substantive due process alone.

Bruce Ackerman reports that Warren's first draft of the opinion in *Loving* cited *Meyer*, the substantive due process precedent from the era of *Lochner*, but that Justice Black, an adamant opponent of substantive due process, objected.[31] Warren deleted the specific citation to *Meyer*, and instead intertwined the due process holding with the equal protection holding concerning invidious racial discrimination. But he still managed to insert into *Loving* a formulation characterizing the right to marry as "essential to the orderly pursuit of happiness by free men"[32] that closely tracks the famous line from *Meyer* quoted above—the Due Process Clause protects "those privileges long recognized at common law as essential to the orderly pursuit of happiness by free men." That is, *Loving* did not signal a full-blown revival of substantive due process "stand[ing] on its own bottom" any more than *Griswold* did. Still, it did represent a step in that direction.

In *San Antonio v. Rodriguez* (1973), the Supreme Court shut down expansion of the fundamental rights or interests strand of Equal Protection doctrine, holding that there was no judicially enforceable right to an equal education. Specifically, the Court upheld a state system of financing public education based in part on property taxes, which resulted in the amount of school expenditures varying widely from district to district.[33] The Court took a "thus far and no further" approach, declining to recognize "new" fundamental rights or interests such as education (or "new" suspect classifications such as wealth). It did not overrule the fundamental rights or interests equal protection cases that had come before. It simply stopped further developing that line of doctrine, proclaiming that "[i]t is not the province of this Court to create substantive constitutional rights in the name of guaranteeing equal protection of the laws."[34]

Just two months earlier, though, in *Roe v. Wade* (1973), the Supreme Court officially revived substantive due process: protecting a substantive liberty—the right of a woman to decide whether to terminate her pregnancy—under the Due Process Clause alone.[35] Rarely is history so tidy: the Court shut down use of the Equal Protection Clause to protect fundamental rights at the very moment that it revived use of the Due Process Clause to do so. A common understanding is that the early Burger Court was wary of and wanted to curb what it saw as the Warren Court's egalitarian revolution, but was comfortable with protecting basic liberties developed in a line of decisions through common law constitutional interpretation.

1973 to the Present: The Flight from Abstract Aspirational Principles to Concrete Historical Practices and Back

According to the Supreme Court in *Roe*, the criterion for deciding what substantive liberties are protected under the Due Process Clauses against encroachment by either the federal government or the state governments is whether the asserted liberty is "implicit in the concept of ordered liberty."[36] In some cases since *Roe*, the Court has applied an alternative formulation: whether the asserted liberty is "deeply rooted in this Nation's history and tradition."[37] In some earlier cases, the Court had offered this formulation: whether the asserted liberty comes within a "principle of justice so rooted in the traditions and conscience of our people as to be ranked as fundamental."[38] Yet another well-known formulation was: "fundamental principles of liberty and justice which lie at the base of all our civil and political institutions."[39] These formulations raise the question of what constitutes a tradition and therefore the baseline for what liberties are protected by the Due Process Clauses.

Tracing the Due Process inquiry from *Roe* (1973) to *Obergefell v. Hodges* (2015) reveals how the Court and individual justices have waged a contentious battle among three available conceptions of tradition and liberty:[40]

- *abstract aspirational principles*—liberty is an abstract principle to which we as a people aspire, and for which we as a people stand, whether or not we have always realized it in our historical practices, statute books, or common law (for example, Justice Cardozo's opinion of the Court in *Palko*, and Justice Brennan's dissenting opinion in *Michael H. v. Gerald D.* [1989]);[41]
- *concrete historical practices*—liberty includes whatever liberties were protected specifically in the statute books or recognized concretely in the common law when the Fourteenth Amendment was adopted in 1868 (for example, Justice Scalia's plurality opinion in *Michael H.* and Chief Justice Rehnquist's opinion of the Court in *Washington v. Glucksberg* [1997]);[42] and
- a *"rational continuum"* that is a *"living thing"* or evolving consensus—liberty is a "rational continuum," a "balance struck by this country, having regard to what history teaches are the traditions from which it developed as well as the traditions from which it broke. That tradition is a living thing" (for example, Justice Harlan's dissenting opinion in *Poe v. Ullman* [1961] and the joint opinion in *Casey*).[43]

The third conception is for all practical purposes similar to the first, although the first seems to contemplate a more philosophical inquiry in elaborating an abstract principle of liberty, the third a more historical inquiry in articulating an evolving consensus concerning liberty.

Between *Roe* and *Bowers v. Hardwick* (1986), an important change occurred in the Supreme Court's conception of the Due Process inquiry. The Court moved from (1) considering whether an asserted fundamental right or basic liberty is "of the very essence of a scheme of ordered liberty," or is required by a "principle of justice so rooted in the traditions and conscience of our people as to be ranked as fundamental," to (2) considering only whether it historically has been protected against governmental interference. The former formulations call for an inquiry into traditions conceived as *abstract aspirational principles*, while the latter makes an inquiry into traditions understood as *concrete historical practices*.

Roe conceived due process as encompassing the basic liberties implicit in a scheme of ordered liberty embodied in our Constitution—or again, the fundamental principles of justice to which we as a people aspire and for which we as a people stand—whether or not we have actually realized them in our historical practices, common law, and statute books. On this view, our aspirational principles may be critical of our historical practices, and our basic liberties and traditions are not merely the Burkean deposit of those practices. Cases such as *Roe*, as well as *Bolling v. Sharpe* (1954) and *Loving*, broke from historical practices in pursuit of aspirational principles.[44]

In *Bolling*, Chief Justice Warren wrote that "[c]lassifications based solely upon race must be scrutinized with particular care, since they are contrary to our traditions and hence constitutionally suspect."[45] Warren's argument necessarily presupposes a conception of traditions as aspirational principles—for example, the Declaration of Independence's proclamation that all persons are created equal—given our shameful history of slavery and historical practices of enacting laws that drew classifications based solely on race, even after the ratification of the Civil War Amendments and Reconstruction. Similarly, Warren's statement in *Loving* that "[t]he freedom to marry has long been recognized as one of the vital personal rights essential to the orderly pursuit of happiness by free men"[46] necessarily reflects a similar conception of aspirational principles, given our shameful historical practices of enacting statutes forbidding interracial marriage.

In *Bowers* (1986), by contrast, the Court per Justice White narrowly conceived the Due Process inquiry as a backward-looking question concerning historical practices, stripped of virtually any aspirational force or critical bite with respect to the status quo. White simply recounted our nation's historical practices disapproving of "homosexual sodomy" and dismissed the claim that the Due Process Clause protects "a fundamental right [of] homosexuals to engage in acts of consensual sodomy" as "at best, facetious."[47]

Justice Scalia's plurality opinion in *Michael H.* (1989) was an attempt to narrow the *Bowers* Due Process inquiry even further, limiting substantive due process to include only those rights that have actually been protected through historical practices, common law, and statutes. Scalia argued against conceiving protected rights abstractly, insisting on framing them at "the most specific level [of generality] at which a relevant tradition protecting, or denying protection to, the asserted right can be identified."[48] For example, in *Michael H.*, in rejecting an unwed biological father's assertion of parental visitation rights, Scalia framed the right at issue not in abstract terms of rights of parenthood (as Justice Brennan did in dissent), but in highly specific terms as the right to have a state "award substantive parental rights to the natural father of a child conceived within, and born into, an extant marital union that wishes to embrace the child."[49] That same year, concurring in *Cruzan v. Director, Missouri Dept. of Health* (1990), and arguing against recognizing a right to die, Scalia warned that if the Court used the Due Process Clause to try to protect the citizenry from "irrationality and oppression" through recognizing substantive liberties, "it will destroy itself."[50] For the ghost of *Lochner* lurks. We should note, however, that in *Cruzan* the majority took a broader view of liberty than did Scalia, "assum[ing]" that the Due Process Clause protected the right to refuse unwanted medical treatment.[51]

To avoid the destruction that he feared would follow in the wake of engaging in reasoned judgment concerning aspirational principles—veering into the whirlpool of liberty as unbounded license—Scalia steered into the rock of liberty as "hidebound" historical practices and narrowly conceived original meaning. As Justice Brennan aptly put it in his dissent in *Michael H.*, "[t]he document that the plurality [opinion of Justice Scalia] construes today is unfamiliar to me. It is not the living charter that I have taken to be our Constitution; it is instead a stagnant, archaic, hidebound document steeped in the prejudices and superstitions of a time long past."[52] Brennan had taken our Constitution to be one of aspirational principles.

In *Casey* (1992), reaffirming the central holding of *Roe*, the joint opinion rejected Scalia's *Michael H.* jurisprudence as "inconsistent with our law," namely, the line of decisions protecting substantive liberties under the Due Process Clause.[53] *Casey* instead accepted the third approach identified above: that of Justice Harlan in dissent in *Poe*. I shall distill several characteristics of Harlan's substantive due process jurisprudence and then elaborate them in the next section. First, Harlan conceived the liberty guaranteed by the Due Process Clause as a "rational continuum" of ordered liberty, not a "series of isolated points pricked out" in the constitutional document. It is an abstract principle (as *Casey* put it, "ideas and aspirations"), not a list of concrete, enumerated rights. Second, he conceived interpretation of abstract commitments like liberty as a "rational process" of "reasoned judgment," not a quest for a formula, code, or bright-line framework to avoid exercising such judgment. Third, interpreting liberty requires judgment about the balance between liberty and order ("ordered liberty") and involves common law constitutional interpretation, reasoning by analogy from one case to the next. Finally, while Harlan like Scalia believed that judgments about liberties must be grounded in history and tradition, he conceived tradition as a "living thing" or evolving consensus, not historical practices as of the time the Due Process Clause was ratified (in 1868).[54]

The joint opinion in *Casey* followed Harlan's lead and conceived the Due Process inquiry as requiring "reasoned judgment" in interpreting the

Constitution, understood as a "covenant" or "coherent succession" whose "written terms embody ideas and aspirations that must survive more ages than one" and guarantee "the promise of liberty." It concluded: "We accept our responsibility not to retreat from interpreting the full meaning of the covenant in light of all of our precedents."[55] *Casey* clearly conceived liberty as an abstract aspirational principle to be built out over time through common law constitutional interpretation, not a concrete historical practice whose meaning was settled in the past.

In *Glucksberg* (1997), in which the Court declined to extend the right to refuse unwanted medical treatment to include the right to "physician-assisted suicide" or aid in dying, Chief Justice Rehnquist sought to rein in the *Poe-Casey* formulation of the Due Process inquiry. Rehnquist wrote that the Court's "established method of substantive due process analysis has two primary features." (Whenever the Court says something like "our established method is" or "it is well settled that," it is likely about to put forward a new method and to utter something controversial. This is certainly borne out here.) The supposed two primary features were: "First, we have regularly observed that the Due Process Clause specially protects those fundamental rights and liberties which are, objectively, 'deeply rooted in this Nation's history and tradition,' . . . and 'implicit in the concept of ordered liberty.' . . . Second, we have required . . . a 'careful description' of the asserted fundamental liberty interest."[56] In calling for a "careful description" of the asserted right and an "objective[]" inquiry into "[o]ur Nation's history, legal traditions, and practices," Rehnquist called to mind Scalia's formulation of the Due Process inquiry in his plurality opinion in *Michael H.*—framing rights specifically rather than abstractly, and narrowly limiting liberty to concrete historical practices.

In *Lawrence v. Texas* (2003), however, Justice Kennedy's opinion of the Court repudiated the framework of *Glucksberg* in favor of an understanding like that in *Casey*. *Lawrence* overruled *Bowers*, holding that the Due Process Clause protects gays' and lesbians' right to privacy or autonomy regarding consensual sexual conduct or intimate association.[57] It signaled a return to a conception of liberty as a rational continuum or evolving consensus of aspirational principles. In fact, one reason Scalia was so indignant in dissent in *Lawrence* was his belief that *Glucksberg* had "'eroded'" *Casey*'s conception of the Due Process inquiry.[58] Kennedy wrote in *Lawrence*:

> Had those who drew and ratified the Due Process Clauses of the Fifth Amendment or the Fourteenth Amendment known the components of liberty in its manifold possibilities, they might have been more specific. They did not

presume to have this insight. They knew times can blind us to certain truths and later generations can see that laws once thought necessary and proper in fact serve only to oppress. As the Constitution endures, persons in every generation can invoke its principles in their own search for greater freedom.[59]

This passage underscores that the Court conceived the Constitution as an abstract scheme of principles such as liberty to be elaborated over time—in a "search for greater freedom"—not as a specific code of historical practices and enumerated rights (or an expression of the framers' and ratifiers' original meanings and expectations to be discovered and preserved).

If Kennedy did not claim to ground the right to privacy or autonomy in original meaning or concrete historical practices, where did he ground it? The answer is in the line of privacy or autonomy cases beginning with *Griswold* and running through *Roe* and *Casey* and in an understanding of tradition as an evolving consensus embodying aspirational principles.[60] Kennedy conceived tradition not as a positivist, historicist, or traditionalist deposit of "millennia of moral teaching" (to quote Chief Justice Burger's concurrence in *Bowers*),[61] but as an evolving consensus about how best to realize liberty (and by implication equality) as an aspirational principle.

Since *Lawrence*, the practice of substantive due process has continued to be a battleground between the two competing views encapsulated in *Glucksberg* and *Casey*. This battle came to a head in *Obergefell*, with the majority adopting the *Casey* framework—in extending the fundamental right to marry to same-sex couples—and the dissenters that of *Glucksberg*—in objecting to that extension. In dissent, Chief Justice Roberts argued that Justice Kennedy's majority opinion has "no basis in the Constitution or this Court's precedent."[62] Whether it does depends, of course, upon our conceptions of (1) the Constitution and (2) precedent. Thus, the clash between Kennedy and the dissenters is between two competing understandings of *the Constitution*: Is it a basic charter of abstract aspirational principles like liberty and equality? Or a code of specific, enumerated rights whose meaning is determined by the deposit of concrete historical practices extant at the time of the adoption of the Fourteenth Amendment in 1868? The clash is also between two competing understandings of how abstractly or concretely we conceive *precedents* and *traditions*: Do we limit precedents to specific holdings and limit traditions to concrete historical practices? Or do we build upon them in extending our line of cases through making recourse to the basic reasons underlying precedents and the aspirational principles embodied in traditions?

To continue: Roberts in his dissent argues that "[the majority's] aggressive application of substantive due process breaks sharply with decades of precedent."[63] Really? What about all the precedents since 1973 involving the fundamental rights to intimate association and to marry, together with all the precedents affording equal liberty and dignity to gays and lesbians? Consider *Romer v. Evans* (1996), *Lawrence*, and *United States v. Windsor* (2013).[64] *Romer* invalidated a state constitutional amendment prohibiting the protection of gays and lesbians from discrimination, *Lawrence* struck down a state law denying them the right to intimate association, and *Windsor* invalidated the federal Defense of Marriage Act (defining marriage for purposes of federal law as the union of one man and one woman). To be sure, Roberts may think all of these precedents themselves are baseless and wrongly decided, but they are precedents which still stand. In light of them, *Obergefell* was not a "sharp break," but rather the next step in a line of cases that has unfolded through common law constitutional interpretation, reasoning by analogy from one case to the next.

Thus, Roberts's dissent in *Obergefell* seems curiously dated and out of touch with our practice of substantive due process and protection of gay and lesbian rights. The Chief Justice, to paraphrase the musician Prince, "parties like it's 1973."[65] His dissent reads like one he could have written for *Roe*, the 1973 case that revived substantive due process after *West Coast Hotel* repudiated *Lochner* in 1937. He writes as if nothing has changed in constitutional law since 1973, as if there have been no cases protecting substantive liberties under the Due Process Clause and protecting the rights of gays and lesbians to the common benefits of equal citizenship under the Equal Protection Clause. He also writes as if the Court has learned nothing from its grave errors in denying gays and lesbians the right to intimate association in the infamous 1986 decision of *Bowers*, overturned in the 2003 decision of *Lawrence*. In short, Roberts's dissent ignores the many developments in constitutional law since 1973 that provide a firm foundation for Kennedy's majority opinion. The fact is that, although always controversial, protecting substantive liberties under the Due Process Clause has proven to be an enduring feature of our constitutional practice (and more solidly so over the years between 1973 and 2015, when the Court decided *Obergefell*).

Yet there is no reason to expect that *Obergefell* will be the last word concerning the Due Process inquiry. The pendulum likely will continue to swing back and forth between the competing understandings of what liberties are embodied in our traditions. Indeed, there is good reason to believe that—with the retirement of Justice Kennedy and the death of Justice Ginsburg, and their subsequent successions by Justices Kavanaugh and Barrett—the *Glucksberg* framework will emerge as the dominant approach for the next generation. In the next section, I argue that the *Casey* framework better fits and justifies the line of cases protecting basic personal liberties over the past century than does the *Glucksberg* framework.

The Battle between the *Casey* and *Glucksberg* Frameworks

An Imaginary Archaeological Excavation

Imagine that you are a constitutional archaeologist who digs up the following bones and shards of a constitutional culture:

· liberty of conscience and freedom of thought;
· freedom of association, including both expressive association and intimate association, whatever one's sexual orientation;
· the right to live with one's family, whether nuclear or extended;
· the right to travel or relocate;
· the right to marry, whatever the gender of one's partner;
· the right to decide whether to bear or beget children, including the rights to procreate, to use contraceptives, and to terminate a pregnancy;
· the right to direct the education and rearing of children, including the right to make decisions concerning their care, custody, and control; and
· the right to exercise dominion over one's body, including the right to bodily integrity and ultimately the right to die (at least to the extent of the right to refuse unwanted medical treatment).[66]

This list distills familiar basic liberties which the Supreme Court has recognized through our practice of substantive due process.[67] The challenge that you face is to decide whether these bones and shards fit together into, and are justifiable within, a coherent structure.[68]

Let us consider how originalist and moral reader archaeologists—proponents of the *Glucksberg* and *Casey* frameworks, respectively—might view these materials. If you were an originalist archaeologist, you might conclude that, because these bones and shards were not specifically enumerated in the constitutional document or deposited in the concrete historical practices, you had unearthed the junk pile of the constitutional culture. From that viewpoint, the only thing these relics have in common is that they are anomalies that have nothing to do with the language and design of the Constitution. Or you might decide that what they have in common is that they evince the hubris and futility of judges episodically succumbing to the temptation of imposing their "philosophical predilections" or "moral intuitions" on the polity in the guise of interpreting the Constitution. Indeed, you might speculate that you had exhumed a ghost town, and that these shards were lying here together because judicial protection of them culminated in the destruction of the Supreme Court and the Constitution.[69]

But if you were a moral reader archaeologist, you would accept these bones as stipulated features (or fixed points) of a skeleton that you had a responsibility to construct. You would be obligated to strive to construct the unity of these bones in a structure of basic liberties that is an integral part of the body of the Constitution. From that standpoint, you would comprehend that all of these bones constitute basic liberties that reserve to persons the right to deliberate about and decide how to live their own lives, with respect to certain matters unusually important for personal self-governance, over the course of a complete life (from cradle to grave). Put another way, the bones represent basic liberties that are significant preconditions for persons' capacity to make certain fundamental decisions affecting their destiny, identity, or way of life, and spanning a complete lifetime. Hence, moral readers would fit these bones together and justify them within a coherent structure of rights significant for personal self-government and, as such, essential to the concept of ordered liberty. I defend the latter view.[70]

What Unifies the Basic Liberties Protected through Substantive Due Process?

Returning from this imaginary archaeological excavation to our constitutional practice, we can find many familiar understandings of what unifies, and what is at stake in protecting, the basic liberties listed above. For example, in dissent in *Bowers*, Justice Stevens famously wrote that the Court's privacy or autonomy decisions had actually been animated by fundamental concerns for "the individual's right to make certain unusually important decisions that will affect his own, or his family's, destiny" and "the abiding interest in individual liberty that makes certain state intrusions on the citizen's right to decide how he will live his own life intolerable."[71] In dissent in *Bowers*, Justice Blackmun characterized this liberty in terms of "freedom of intimate association" and the "decisional and the spatial aspects of the right to privacy."[72] His discussion built on Justice Brennan's analysis of the right to intimate association in *Roberts v. United States Jaycees* (1984): "The Court has long recognized that, because the Bill of Rights is designed to secure individual liberty, it must afford the formation and preservation of certain kinds of highly personal relationships a substantial measure of sanctuary from unjustified interference by the State."[73] This protection, Brennan stated, "safeguards the ability independently to define one's identity that is central to any concept of liberty."[74]

Similar conceptions appear in *Casey*, not only in the concurring opinions of Justices Stevens and Blackmun, but also in the joint opinion of Justices O'Connor, Kennedy, and Souter. As Stevens put it, "Decisional autonomy must limit the State's power to inject into a woman's most personal deliberations its own views of what is best," because a woman's decision to terminate her pregnancy "is nothing less than a matter of conscience."[75] He emphasized liberty of conscience and decisional autonomy (as well as equal dignity and respect for women).[76] Likewise, Blackmun's opinion in *Casey* emphasized that cases protecting the right to privacy embody "the principle that personal decisions that profoundly affect bodily integrity, identity, and destiny should be largely beyond the reach of government."[77] He too stressed personal self-government or self-determination (along with gender equality).[78]

The joint opinion in *Casey* spoke of a woman's liberty at stake in the decision whether to have an abortion as

> involving the most intimate and personal choices a person may make in a lifetime, choices central to personal dignity and autonomy. . . . At the heart of liberty is the right to define one's own concept of existence, of meaning, of the universe, and of the mystery of human life. Beliefs about these matters could not define the attributes of personhood were they formed under compulsion of the State.[79]

The joint opinion's explication of this personal liberty is rooted in personal autonomy and bodily integrity. (Like the opinions of Stevens and Blackmun, the joint opinion intertwines concerns for personal liberty and gender equality.)[80]

Landmark cases such as *Meyer*,[81] *Pierce*,[82] *Griswold*,[83] *Loving*,[84] *Eisenstadt v. Baird* (1972),[85] *Moore*,[86] *Roe*,[87] *Carey v. Population Services International* (1977),[88] *Lawrence*,[89] and *Obergefell*[90] illustrate similar conceptions of personal autonomy and exemplify *Casey*'s conception of the Due Process inquiry. Furthermore, *Lawrence* and *Obergefell* intertwined concern for liberty as autonomy with concern for the status of equal citizenship for gays and lesbians. We see this most clearly in Kennedy's arguments in both cases that it "demeans the lives" of gays and lesbians not to afford them the rights to intimate association and to marry already recognized for straights.[91]

These eloquent formulations, expressed in the contexts of abortion, intimate association, and marriage, also apply to the other types of personal decisions encompassed by the rights on the foregoing list (recall our archaeological excavation). They succinctly capture what is at stake in these unusually important decisions and why such decisions lie in "a realm of personal liberty which the government may not enter."[92]

In previous work, I have argued that the basic liberties on the foregoing list cohere in and are integral to a theory of *securing constitutional democracy*, a guiding framework with two fundamental themes: first, securing the basic liberties that are preconditions for *deliberative democracy*, to enable people to apply their capacity for a conception of justice to deliberating about and judging the justice of basic institutions and social policies; and second, securing the basic liberties that are preconditions for *deliberative autonomy*, to enable people to apply their capacity for a conception of the good to deliberating about and deciding how to live their own lives. Together, these themes afford everyone the status of equal citizenship in our morally pluralistic constitutional democracy. They reflect two bedrock structures of our constitutional scheme: democratic and personal self-government. The second theme bounds the right to autonomy by limiting it to protecting basic liberties that are significant preconditions for persons' development and exercise of deliberative autonomy in making certain fundamental decisions affecting their destiny, identity, or way of life. As against charges that rights of autonomy like those protected through substantive due process are anomalous or rootless, I have shown that deliberative autonomy is rooted, along with deliberative democracy, in the language and overall design of the Constitution. In response to objections that protecting such basic liberties is undemocratic, I concede that doing so limits majority will—but I argue that it is integral to our constitutional democracy, in which basic liberties constrain majority preferences. Our scheme of constitutional self-government protects basic liberties essential to both democratic and personal self-government (or deliberative democracy and deliberative autonomy).[93] Unless those basic liberties are secure, the majority has no legitimate title to rule.[94]

The Casey *Framework Better Fits and Justifies Our Substantive Due Process Cases than Does the* Glucksberg *Framework*

We should ask which of the competing frameworks for the Due Process inquiry, that of *Glucksberg* or that of *Casey*, is more consistent with our law in the area of substantive due process. That is, which account better fits and justifies the cases protecting the rights on the foregoing list? The *Casey* methodology wins hands down over the *Glucksberg* methodology. The former can account for all of these cases—as the joint opinion in *Casey* did through the framework of "reasoned judgment"—while the latter can account for none of them. None of these cases protected a right as a matter of vindicating long-standing, concrete historical practices as the *Glucksberg* framework conceives them—practices embodied in and specifically protected by statutes and common law. But all of them are justifiable on the basis of realizing aspirational principles as the *Casey* framework conceives them—principles that may be critical of such practices for failing to live up to our commitment to liberty.

This should come as no surprise, for it is very likely that, as an original matter, both Chief Justice Rehnquist (the author of *Glucksberg*) and Justice Scalia would have dissented in all of these cases protecting basic liberties; in fact, Rehnquist and Scalia did dissent in some of them. It is also very likely that, if they had had the votes to do so, they would have overruled these cases. (Whether the new 6-3 conservative majority now has the votes to overrule them remains to be seen.) Through the *Glucksberg* framework, Rehnquist, like Scalia, was engaged in damage control: his concerns were not merely to decline to extend this line of cases, but also to gut the cases of any vitality or generative force for future cases. By contrast, those applying the *Casey* framework accept these cases as rightly decided and accordingly accept the responsibility to extend the line of cases further through common law constitutional interpretation.

As noted above, the battle between these two conceptions continued in *Obergefell*, with the five justices in the majority adopting the *Casey* framework and the four dissenters that of *Glucksberg*. In dissent, Chief Justice Roberts protested that *Obergefell* "effectively overrules" *Glucksberg*, which he called the "leading modern case" on substantive due process.[95] Indeed, *Obergefell* is inconsistent with *Glucksberg*. So are *Lawrence* and *Casey*. In fact, every decision in the past century that has protected a basic personal liberty under the Due Process Clause is inconsistent with *Glucksberg*. None would have come out as they did had the Court been applying *Glucksberg*'s framework. *Glucksberg* is the leading modern substantive due process case only for those who wish to shut down that doctrine. The *Casey* framework better fits and justifies the line of cases protecting basic liberties from *Meyer* through *Obergefell* and, going forward, we should build out that line with coherence and integrity.

Ironically, in *Obergefell* Justice Kennedy did to *Glucksberg* what it advocated doing to all of our substantive due process precedents protecting basic liberties: he limited it to its facts, as a one-off decision, draining it of any generative vitality for future cases. "While [the *Glucksberg*] approach may have been appropriate for the asserted right there involved (physician-assisted suicide), it is inconsistent with the approach this Court has used in discussing other fundamental rights, including marriage and intimacy."[96]

Notwithstanding well-known claims by Justice Scalia and Chief Justice Roberts that substantive due process cases represent liberal justices reading their own "philosophical predilections" or John Stuart Mill's *On Liberty* into the Constitution, I argue that Justice Kennedy's majority opinion in *Obergefell* is best understood as a conservative opinion in the mold of Justice Harlan, the most conservative member of the Warren Court. Kennedy's opinion in *Obergefell*—like the joint opinion of Justices O'Connor, Kennedy, and Souter in *Casey*—invokes and evokes Harlan's conservative constitutional jurisprudence as manifested famously in his dissenting opinion in *Poe* and his concurring opinion in *Griswold*.[97] The dissenters in *Obergefell*—like those in *Casey*—are a new breed of culture war or movement conservatives who have rejected Harlan's conservative jurisprudence. The battle in *Obergefell*—like that in *Casey*—is between these two types of conservatives, whom I elsewhere have called preservative conservatives versus counterrevolutionary conservatives. Preservative conservatives (like Justices Harlan, Powell, O'Connor, and Kennedy) mostly attempt to preserve precedents and principles—rather than immediately overruling decisions that they, as an original matter, might have decided differently—perhaps conservatively developing those precedents and principles in subsequent cases rather than liberally extending them. Counterrevolutionary conservatives (like Justices Scalia and Thomas) seek to purge constitutional law of precedents and principles manifesting liberal error at the earliest available opportunity or—if they do not have the votes to do so—to reinterpret decisions so as to extirpate any generative force from them for future cases.[98]

What are the central characteristics of Harlan's and Kennedy's substantive due process jurisprudence? There are five defining characteristics of their jurisprudence that set it apart from that of the four dissenters in *Obergefell*. First, Harlan and Kennedy conceive the Constitution as a "basic charter" of abstract principles promising liberty, not a code of specific, enumerated rights or a deposit of concrete historical practices.[99] They are decidedly anti-originalist: on their view, the framers and ratifiers did not presume to specify liberty in all its particulars. Instead, they committed us to a basic charter of abstract aspirational principles to be built out over time.

Second, Harlan and Kennedy conceive constitutional interpretation of abstract commitments like liberty as a "rational process" of "reasoned judgment," not a quest for a "formula," code, or bright-line framework that would allow justices to avoid exercising such judgment.[100] In interpretation, we have to make reasoned judgments about the best understanding of our constitutional commitments. The framers and ratifiers were not authoritarian fathers who decided our questions for us and ordered us to follow their specific understandings and expectations. They established a framework of constitutional self-government to be built out over time on the basis of experience, new insights, and moral progress.

Third, applying these conceptions of liberty and interpretation proceeds through common law constitutional interpretation. In making reasoned judgments about the best understanding of our constitutional commitments, we build on precedents that have gone before, reasoning by analogy from one case to the next. And in deciding how to develop and extend those precedents, we make judgments stemming from the basic reasons for protecting the rights recognized in those precedents—we should not confine precedents narrowly to their factual circumstances, nor should we reduce abstract constitutional commitments to liberty to the specific understandings and expectations of the framers and ratifiers of the Fourteenth Amendment in 1868.

Fourth, while Harlan and Kennedy agree with the four dissenters in *Obergefell* that judgments about the meaning of our commitment to liberty must be grounded in history and tradition, they conceive traditions as abstract aspirational principles, not concrete historical practices as of the time the Due Process Clause was ratified.[101] They conceive traditions as the principles to which we as a people aspire, and for which we as a people stand, whether or not we have always realized them in our historical practices. Again, the Declaration of Independence's proclamation—that all persons are created equal—is part of our tradition, even though our historical practices of slavery, racial discrimination, and gender discrimination have failed to honor it. As stated above, Harlan conceived tradition as a "living thing," saying that constitutional interpreters must have "regard to what history teaches are the traditions from which it developed as well as the traditions from which it broke." Harlan contemplated the possibility that we might break from historical practices in pursuit of our traditions as aspirational principles.[102] As Kennedy similarly put it in *Obergefell*, "history is the beginning" but not the end of the analysis. For our historical practices regarding the fundamental right to marry—for example, limiting it to the union of one man and one woman—have proven to fall short of our aspirational principles to liberty and equality.[103]

Finally, in elaborating the basic reasons underlying our constitutional commitments and the legal precedents that interpret them, Harlan and Kennedy make recourse to the moral goods promoted by protecting our freedoms. Harlan's conservative jurisprudence recognizes considerable latitude for the state to promote the moral soundness of its people, to inculcate civic virtues, and to encourage responsible exercise of rights.[104] Let's draw a stylized distinction here between two kinds of arguments justifying the protection of constitutional rights like that to autonomy, including the right to marry. One kind, which I'll call *liberal*, stresses the right of the individual to make choices, without regard for the moral good of what is chosen. This idea is reflected in the familiar liberal formulation of an individual "right to choose." The other kind of argument, which I'll call *conservative*, emphasizes the moral goods promoted by protecting the right to autonomy.[105]

Applied to marriage, the liberal argument stresses my right as an individual to choose whom to have sex with, to decide whom to marry, and to do whatever I damn well please with my body—a right to choose without regard for the moral good of what is chosen. By contrast, the conservative argument emphasizes the moral goods promoted by protecting that right and the institution of marriage. In *Obergefell*, Kennedy quotes the stirring language from *Griswold* (recognizing a right of marital privacy) about the noble purposes of marriage: promoting intimacy, harmony, and loyalty within a worthy relationship.[106] He also quotes the Massachusetts Supreme Judicial Court's formulation concerning moral goods in *Goodridge v. Department of Public Health* (2003) (recognizing a right of same-sex couples to marry): because marriage "fulfils yearnings for security, safe haven, and connection that express our common humanity, civil marriage is an esteemed institution." That court also mentions the moral goods of "commitment" along with "mutuality, companionship, intimacy, fidelity, and family."[107] On Harlan's and Kennedy's conservative view, we protect the fundamental right to marry because marriage is an intimate association and a valuable institution for furthering noble purposes and promoting moral goods. Kennedy justifies extending the fundamental right to marry to same-sex couples on the ground that doing so not only respects their basic liberty, but also promotes these moral goods, just as opposite-sex marriage does. I return to this point in chapter 4 when I rebut Scalia's misguided claim that substantive due process cases have put us on a slippery slope to "the end of all morals legislation." Indeed, as we see in chapter 3, it is notable that many of the leading substantive due process decisions, far from emanating from liberal "philosophical predilections" and "moral intuitions," were written by conservative justices who embraced Harlan's jurisprudence: Justices Powell, O'Connor, and Kennedy.

In sum, the *Casey* framework, as prefigured by Justice Harlan and as carried forward by Justice Kennedy in *Obergefell*, better fits and justifies our substantive due process cases protecting basic liberties than does the *Glucks-berg* framework.

The Scope of Substantive Due Process: Limited to Significant Preconditions for Personal Self-Government

Why do only the foregoing rights appear on the list of basic liberties? Our practice of substantive due process since 1937 has limited the scope of autonomy to protecting basic personal liberties that are "essential to the concept of ordered liberty":[108] those which are *significant* preconditions for personal self-government.[109] All of the liberties listed earlier satisfy this criterion. They do not stem from more abstract libertarian or liberal principles of liberty, autonomy, or individuality which are broader and encompass liberties that are not essential or significant in this sense.

I should make clear that the question framed by the criterion of what liberties are essential to or significant for personal self-government is not subjective, as in: "What liberties does a particular person need to enable them to pursue their particular conception of the good?" It is instead: "What liberties in principle are significant for everyone, regardless of their particular conceptions of the good and irrespective of whether particular persons happen to value those liberties?" In recognizing the significance of the basic liberties on the foregoing list—and the rights of persons to make decisions of the sort encompassed by them—we need not embrace any particular view of the ultimate meaning or importance of such decisions within any specific comprehensive conception of the good life (though we might well find considerable overlap among a variety of such conceptions, all of which would affirm that the right is significant).

Admittedly, basic liberties such as those listed earlier are controversial. They are controversial precisely because they are significant for personal self-government. The criterion of significance is double-edged, for a government may have obligations with respect to certain matters because of their importance for ordered liberty, or for the ordered reproduction of society over time—for example, marriage and family—but may nonetheless be prohibited from standardizing people with respect to such matters precisely because they are so important.

In the contemporary US, persons may try to dress up relatively insignificant liberty claims in the garb of fundamental rights to privacy or autonomy. But our practice of substantive due process has not recognized such liberties. All of the basic liberties protected through that practice are "essential to the concept of ordered liberty." By accepting this limitation,

I do not mean to imply that the basic liberties on the foregoing list make up a complete, closed list. But limiting the right to autonomy to protecting basic liberties that are significant for personal self-government renders it less vulnerable to arguments (like Scalia's) that it is hopelessly indeterminate or irredeemably undemocratic. To be sure, these rights—like all rights—limit majority will, but that does not mean that protecting them is problematically undemocratic. Once again, the form of democracy our Constitution embodies is not a majoritarian democracy but a constitutional democracy, properly understood as securing basic liberties essential to not only democratic self-government but also personal self-government. As Justice Kennedy put it in *Obergefell*, quoting famous lines from *West Virginia v. Barnette* (1943): "The idea of the Constitution 'was to withdraw certain subjects from the vicissitudes of political controversy, to place them beyond the reach of majorities and officials and to establish them as legal principles to be applied by the courts.'" He continued: "This is why 'fundamental rights may not be submitted to a vote; they depend on the outcome of no elections.'"[110]

Between Scalia and Charybdis

Our practice of reasoned judgment concerning what rights are essential to ordered liberty has charted a middle course between Scylla (Scalia)—the rock of liberty as concrete historical practices—and Charybdis—the whirlpool of liberty as unbounded license. Haunted by the ghost of *Lochner*, Scalia wrote ominously about the dangers that judicial protection of basic liberties through the Due Process Clause, which he found perilously unbounded, posed for destruction.[111] But veering into either the rock or the whirlpool brings destruction. Tethering the Due Process inquiry to the structure of basic liberties significant for personal self-government might help stem the Court's characteristic temptation to flee from aspirational principles (and the *Casey* framework) to concrete historical practices (and the *Glucksberg* framework) in this area, as well as steady its return to aspirational principles (as in *Lawrence* and *Obergefell*).

In constructing basic liberties, we do not write on a blank slate concerning significance for personal self-government. Nor do we operate in a philosophy seminar, elaborating an abstract or utopian conception of autonomy wherever unguided speculation might take us. Instead, we work within our ongoing constitutional democracy, which has a long-standing practice and tradition of protecting fundamental rights or basic liberties that are essential to our "scheme of ordered liberty"[112] or to the "orderly pursuit of happiness."[113] In the first instance, my argument here is retrospective, contending that a criterion such as significance for personal self-government accounts for why the categories of personal decisions encompassed by the foregoing list of basic liberties are indeed essential and should be on the list. Put simply, it fits and justifies the cases. That established, my proposal is prospective, arguing for using such a criterion in further specifying the basic liberties presupposed by our constitutional democracy through common law constitutional interpretation. Needless to say, offering a criterion of significance will not resolve all questions concerning the scope and content of the basic liberties protected under the Due Process Clause. It will, however, help frame and guide our reflections and judgments regarding those questions, which can be resolved only as they arise.

And so, continuing our practice of substantive due process, exercising reasoned judgment in building out our rational continuum of ordered liberty, we should interpret the Constitution to secure the basic liberties that are significant preconditions for personal self-government. By interpreting the Constitution in this manner, to recall the joint opinion in *Casey*, we would face up to the responsibility to give full meaning to our constitution of principle, a covenant of aspirations and ideals that guarantee the promise of liberty and that must survive more ages than one.[114] And, to recall Justice Kennedy's opinion in *Lawrence*, we would not "presume"—any more than the framers and ratifiers of the Constitution did—exhaustively to specify "the components of liberty in its manifold possibilities."[115] As Kennedy similarly put it in *Obergefell*: "The generations that wrote and ratified the Bill of Rights and the Fourteenth Amendment did not presume to know the extent of freedom in all of its dimensions, and so they entrusted to future generations a charter protecting the right of all persons to enjoy liberty as we learn its meaning."[116] Through our practice of substantive due process, we have built out our commitments to liberty over time on the basis of experience, new insights, and moral learning. Through a process of common law constitutional interpretation, we make reasoned judgments about the best understanding of those commitments, building on precedents that have gone before, reasoning by analogy from one case to the next. In deciding how to develop and extend those precedents, we make judgments stemming from the basic reasons for protecting the rights recognized in the precedents. Therein lies the coherence and structure of our practice of substantive due process.

THREE

The Rational Continuum of Ordered Liberty

In chapter 2, I observed that opponents of substantive due process, most notably Justice Scalia, Chief Justice Rehnquist, and Chief Justice Roberts, have deployed the *Glucksberg* framework as a method of damage control: not overruling the precedents protecting basic liberties, but narrowing them to their specific facts and draining them of any generative vitality for reasoning by analogy in future cases. In this chapter, I take up their tandem attempt to truncate the development of this line of cases through what I call the myth of two rigidly maintained tiers—either strict scrutiny for fundamental rights or deferential rational basis scrutiny for every other claim—under the Due Process Clause.[1] Contrary to what it sounds like, this myth aims not at stringently protecting fundamental rights, but at raising the bar for protecting them and delegitimizing our more complex actual practice of substantive due process. In reality, our practice of protecting basic liberties has mapped onto what I call our rational continuum of ordered liberty, with several intermediate levels of review. In analyzing the cases to support this claim, I also confirm in fuller detail my contention in chapter 2 that the *Casey* framework fits and justifies all of the cases protecting rights under the Due Process Clause and the *Glucksberg* framework fits and justifies none of them.

Dissenting in *Lawrence v. Texas* (2003), Justice Scalia stated that, under the Due Process Clause, if an asserted liberty is a "fundamental right," it triggers "strict scrutiny" that almost automatically invalidates any statute restricting it. For strict scrutiny requires that the challenged statute, to be upheld, must (1) further a "compelling governmental interest" and (2) be "necessary" or "narrowly tailored" to doing so. Scalia also wrote that if an asserted liberty is not a fundamental right, it is merely a "liberty interest," which triggers rational basis scrutiny that is so deferential that the Court all but automatically upholds the statute in question. For deferential rational basis scrutiny requires merely that the challenged statute, to be valid, might be thought to (1) further a "legitimate governmental interest" and (2) be "rationally related" to doing so.[2] In attempting to limit the protection of substantive liberties under the Due Process Clauses, Scalia argued for a narrow approach to what constitutes a "fundamental right" and a broad approach to what constitutes a mere "liberty interest."

Lawrence deviated from Scalia's regime. The Court did not hold that the right of gays and lesbians to sexual privacy or autonomy was a fundamental right requiring strict scrutiny. Nor did it hold that their right was merely a liberty interest calling for highly deferential rational basis scrutiny. Instead, the Court applied an intermediate standard—what many have called rational basis scrutiny with "bite"[3]—and struck down the statute forbidding same-sex sexual conduct. Instead of deferring to the state's proffered "legitimate governmental interest" in preserving traditional sexual morality, the Court (explicitly in *Romer v. Evans* [1996] and implicitly in *Lawrence*) put some teeth into its analysis.[4]

Consequently, Scalia chastised the Court for not following a rigid two-tier framework that all but automatically decides rights questions one way or the other.[5] Many scholars and judges have questioned whether the Court's actual practice has followed or should follow this framework.[6] I expose the myth of two rigidly policed tiers under the Due Process Clause. Scalia's formulation of the framework sounds familiar and uncontroversial. Yet I show that the only substantive due process case officially to recognize a fundamental right implicating strict scrutiny—requiring that the statute further a compelling governmental interest and be necessary to doing so—was *Roe v. Wade* (1973).[7] And those aspects of *Roe* were overruled in *Planned Parenthood v. Casey* (1992), which pointedly avoided calling the right to decide whether to terminate a pregnancy a "fundamental right" and substituted an "undue burden" standard for strict scrutiny.[8] Moreover, the leading due process cases *protecting* liberty and autonomy—from *Meyer v. Nebraska* (1923) through *Casey* (1992), *Lawrence* (2003), and *Obergefell v. Hodges* (2015)—have not applied Scalia's rigid two-tier framework. Instead, these cases reflect what *Casey*, *Obergefell*, and Justice Harlan in *Poe v. Ullman* (1961) called "reasoned judgment" and map onto a "rational continuum" of "ordered liberty,"[9] with several intermediate levels of review.

Nevertheless, opponents of substantive due process have advanced this myth of two rigid tiers in opinions *refusing to recognize* asserted rights. Examples include: Justice White's majority opinion in *Bowers v. Hardwick* (1986), rejecting a right of gays and lesbians to sexual privacy[10] (*Bowers* was overruled in *Lawrence*, hence provoking Scalia's rage in dissent); Scalia's plurality opinion in *Michael H. v. Gerald D.* (1989), rejecting a right of unwed fathers to visit their biological children;[11] Rehnquist's majority opinion in *Washington v. Glucksberg* (1997), rejecting a right to die including "physician-assisted suicide" or aid in dying;[12] and, most pointedly, Scalia's dissent in *Lawrence*.

These opponents of substantive due process perpetuate this myth in order to narrow the interpretation of the Due Process Clause and make it harder to justify protecting rights under it. I grant that many strong defenders of substantive due process have argued for strict scrutiny for fundamental rights because they want stringent protection for rights of privacy or autonomy. Indeed, typically in constitutional law, what drives jurists and scholars to apply or argue for strict scrutiny is a desire stringently to protect the right in question, as is the case with the First Amendment and the Equal Protection Clause, two main areas of strict scrutiny. We do not, for example, trust government when it restricts freedom of speech on the basis of the content of ideas, and we are suspicious of government when it passes laws reflecting racial prejudice.

I acknowledge that in some substantive due process cases protecting basic liberties, while the Court does not explicitly recognize a right as fundamental and as warranting strict scrutiny, it still—for all practical purposes—treats the right as fundamental and as deserving relatively stringent scrutiny. *Lawrence* itself is a case in point. Laurence H. Tribe famously argued, in an essay titled "The 'Fundamental Right' that Dare Not Speak Its Name," that "the strictness of the Court's standard in *Lawrence*, however articulated, could hardly have been more obvious."[13] To be sure, rational basis scrutiny with "bite" was stringent enough that the Court readily invalidated the statute in that case. My point is that Justice Kennedy was never going to speak of a fundamental right triggering strict scrutiny because he is a conservative rather than a liberal like Tribe. The conservative justices who have written most of the majority or plurality opinions in substantive due process cases protecting rights after *Roe*—including *Moore, Casey, Troxel, Lawrence,* and *Obergefell,* to be discussed below—did not accept the liberal project of protecting fundamental rights to privacy or autonomy through applying strict scrutiny. These conservative justices may have been wary of this project because they accepted greater latitude for the government to regulate, for example, reproduction or the family.[14]

In any case, Justice Kennedy's majority opinion in *Lawrence* provoked Justice Scalia, a culture war conservative, to dissent vigorously and attempt to recast the tools liberals originally forged for stringently protecting fundamental rights into a framework for limiting the recognition and protection of such rights by raising the bar for doing so. Indeed, the twofold result of

Scalia's and Rehnquist's myth is (1) to make it harder to recognize rights under the Due Process Clause and (2) to make all cases recognizing rights but not tracking this doctrinal template of strict scrutiny—which is to say, all cases protecting rights under substantive due process (besides *Roe*, itself repudiated in this respect in *Casey*)—seem problematic and unrigorous. Because of their myth, every time the Court does not use the formulations "fundamental right," "strict scrutiny," "compelling," and "necessary," some people claim that something illegitimate is going on.

If not a two-tier framework of strict scrutiny and deferential rational basis scrutiny, what framework or standards has the Court actually applied? Put another way, what framework best fits and justifies the line of cases actually protecting substantive liberties under the Due Process Clause? I have already given away the answer: Harlan's conception of the Due Process inquiry, advanced in his dissent in *Poe*. I offer interpretations of his conception that bring out how well it fits and justifies the cases over and against Scalia's and Rehnquist's conception.

Reasoned Judgment Concerning the Rational Continuum of Ordered Liberty

The joint opinion of Justices O'Connor, Kennedy, and Souter in *Casey* embraced Justice Harlan's conception of the Due Process inquiry as put forward in dissent in *Poe*. It quoted the following two passages from Harlan:

[T]he full scope of the liberty guaranteed by the Due Process Clause cannot be found in or limited by the precise terms of the specific guarantees elsewhere provided in the Constitution. This "liberty" is not a series of isolated points pricked out in terms of the taking of property; the freedom of speech, press, and religion; the right to keep and bear arms; the freedom from unreasonable searches and seizures; and so on. It is a rational continuum which, broadly speaking, includes a freedom from all substantial arbitrary impositions and purposeless restraints . . . and which also recognizes, what a reasonable and sensitive judgment must, that certain interests require particularly careful scrutiny of the state needs asserted to justify their abridgment.

Due process has not been reduced to any formula; its content cannot be determined by reference to any code. The best that can be said is that . . . it has represented the balance which our Nation, built upon postulates of respect for the liberty of the individual, has struck between that liberty and the demands of organized society. If the supplying of content to this Constitutional concept has of necessity been a rational process, it certainly has not been one where judges have felt free to roam where unguided speculation might take them. The balance . . . is the balance struck by this country, having regard to what history teaches are the traditions from which it developed as well as the traditions from which it broke. That tradition is a living thing. A decision of this Court which radically departs from it could not long survive, while a decision which builds on what has survived is likely to be sound. No formula could serve as a substitute, in this area, for judgment and restraint.[15]

Interpreting these passages, the joint opinion in *Casey* added:

The inescapable fact is that adjudication of substantive due process claims may call upon the Court in interpreting the Constitution to exercise that same capacity which by tradition courts always have exercised: reasoned judgment. Its boundaries are not susceptible of expression as a simple rule. That does not mean we are free to invalidate state policy choices with which we disagree; yet neither does it permit us to shrink from the duties of our office.[16]

Clearly, the joint opinion is implying that originalists like Justice Scalia would have judges "shrink from the dut[y]" to decide cases responsibly, exercising reasoned judgment.

In chapter 2, I elaborated five defining characteristics of Harlan's conception of the Due Process inquiry (manifested in the *Casey* framework and in Justice Kennedy's majority opinion in *Obergefell*) that set it apart from that of the four dissenters in *Obergefell* (which reflected the *Glucksberg* framework). If the Supreme Court were to have applied Harlan's conception, what would our substantive due process jurisprudence look like? Instead of having two tiers—strict scrutiny and deferential rational basis scrutiny—we would have a spectrum of standards or continuum of judgmental responses.[17] That is, this jurisprudence would look basically the very way our Due Process jurisprudence looks today! To preview my findings, figure 3.1 shows the spectrum of standards or continuum of judgmental responses we will see in the substantive due process cases. I have ordered them from the most stringent review to the most lenient or deferential review.

In analyzing each case, I ask what type of framework (or standards) the Court applies as well as how abstractly or concretely the Court formulates the right(s) at issue. I conclude that Harlan's framework (rational continuum of ordered liberty) can fit and justify all of the cases protecting rights under the Due Process Clause, and that Scalia's and Rehnquist's (rigid two-tier framework of strict scrutiny and deferential rational basis scrutiny) can fit and justify none of them. Furthermore, going through the cases in detail,

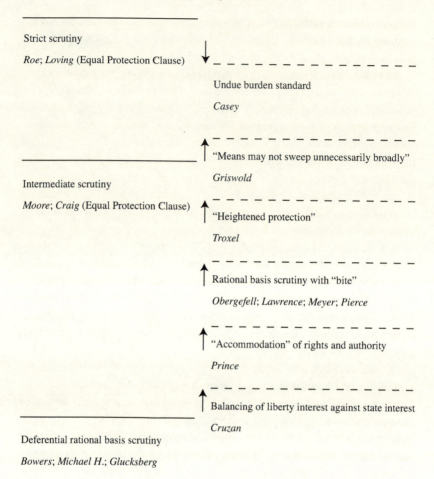

Strict scrutiny

Roe; *Loving* (Equal Protection Clause)

Undue burden standard

Casey

"Means may not sweep unnecessarily broadly"

Griswold

Intermediate scrutiny

Moore; *Craig* (Equal Protection Clause)

"Heightened protection"

Troxel

Rational basis scrutiny with "bite"

Obergefell; *Lawrence*; *Meyer*; *Pierce*

"Accommodation" of rights and authority

Prince

Balancing of liberty interest against state interest

Cruzan

Deferential rational basis scrutiny

Bowers; *Michael H.*; *Glucksberg*

3.1. The spectrum of standards in protecting ordered liberty

I find additional support for the argument I advanced in chapter 2 that the *Casey* framework (abstract aspirational principles) can account for all of the cases protecting basic liberties, while the *Glucksberg* framework (concrete historical practices) can account for none of them.

The Substantive Due Process Cases from *Meyer* to the Present

Meyer v. Nebraska *(1923)*

In 1919, Nebraska passed a law prohibiting the teaching of any modern language other than English in any public or private grammar school. Meyer, a parochial school instructor, was convicted of violating this act by teaching German to a ten-year-old boy. The Court invalidated the law as a deprivation of liberty in violation of the Due Process Clause.[18]

The Court proclaims: "That the state may do much, go very far, indeed, in order to improve the quality of its citizens, physically, mentally and morally, is clear; but the individual has certain fundamental rights which must be respected." It gives several formulations of those fundamental rights: the teacher's right "to teach"; the parents' right "to contract" with the teacher to instruct their children; and the parents' right to control the upbringing and education of their children. More abstractly, *Meyer* intimates a fundamental theory of "the relation between individual and state" precluding the state from freely crafting its vision of ideal citizens (by contrast with the theory of Plato's ideal commonwealth in *The Republic*).[19]

The Court frames the inquiry thus: "The established doctrine is that this liberty may not be interfered with, under the guise of protecting the public interest, by legislative action which is arbitrary or without reasonable relation to some purpose within the competency of the state to effect." But it adds: "Determination by the Legislature of what constitutes proper exercise of police power is not final or conclusive but is subject to supervision by the courts."[20] Although the initial formulation resembles our language of deferential rational basis scrutiny, in application the form that this "supervision" takes is more like rational basis scrutiny with teeth.

What is the end that the state legitimately may pursue? The Court states: "The desire of the Legislature to foster a homogeneous people with American ideals prepared readily to understand current discussions of civic matters is easy to appreciate." Does the challenged statute bear a "reasonable relation" to that end? The Court answers: "Perhaps it would be highly advantageous if all had ready understanding of our ordinary speech, but this cannot be coerced by methods which conflict with the Constitution—a desirable end cannot be promoted by prohibited means." While the Court appears quite deferential to the legitimacy of the end of fostering a homogeneous people with American ideals and a common tongue, it puts bite into its scrutiny of whether the law promotes another asserted end, that of "protect[ing] the child's health by limiting his mental activities." The Court writes: "As the statute undertakes to interfere only with teaching which involves a modern language, leaving complete freedom as to other matters, there seems no adequate foundation for the suggestion that the purpose was to protect the child's health by limiting his mental activities."[21]

Justice Holmes in dissent shows us what deferential rational basis scrutiny would look like in this case. He is quite deferential as to end—the law pursues "a lawful and proper [end]." He is also quite deferential as to fit between means and end—the law "might . . . be regarded as a reasonable or even necessary method of reaching the desired result." Because this is "a question upon which men reasonably might differ," Holmes concludes that the Constitution does not "prevent[] the experiment [from] being tried."[22]

Pierce v. Society of Sisters *(1925)*

In 1922, Oregon enacted a statute requiring parents to send their children between the ages of eight and sixteen to public schools rather than private schools. The Society of Sisters of Holy Names, a Catholic religious order that operated several parochial schools in the state, and the Hill Military Academy, a private school, sued in federal district court. The Court struck down the statute under the Due Process Clause.[23]

The Court frames the right in question as "the liberty of parents and guardians to direct the upbringing and education of children under their control," citing *Meyer*. *Pierce* further sketches a "fundamental theory" of the relation between the individual and the state, intimated in *Meyer*, which forbids the state to craft its vision of ideal citizens: "The fundamental theory of liberty upon which all governments in this Union repose excludes any general power of the state to standardize its children by forcing them to accept instruction from public teachers only." The Court proclaims: "The child is not the mere creature of the state; those who nurture him and direct his destiny have the right, coupled with the high duty, to recognize and prepare him for additional obligations."[24]

The Court frames the test as follows: "[R]ights guaranteed by the Constitution may not be abridged by legislation which has no reasonable relation to some purpose within the competency of the state."[25] What is the purpose that the state legitimately may pursue?

> No question is raised concerning the power of the state reasonably to regulate all schools, to inspect, supervise and examine them, their teachers and pupils; to require that all children of proper age attend some school, that teachers shall be of good moral character and patriotic disposition, that certain studies plainly essential to good citizenship must be taught, and that nothing be taught which is manifestly inimical to the public welfare.[26]

The Court does not explicitly inquire whether the statute bears a "reasonable relation" to that purpose. It simply states the two famous propositions quoted above concerning the "fundamental theory of liberty" and that the "child is not the mere creature of the state." It then concludes, holistically, that the statute denies protected liberty. Clearly, the Court is putting some "bite" into its analysis. It is not deferring to the legitimacy of the end and to the rationality of the fit between means and end. As in *Meyer*, so here, though the language looks like our language of deferential rational basis scrutiny, in application the framework seems more like rational basis scrutiny with teeth.

As observed in chapter 2, both *Meyer* and *Pierce* clearly conceive liberty as an abstract principle, not a concrete historical practice. The Court does not frame the rights specifically or limit them to their concrete factual contexts—in proto-Scalian or *Glucksbergian* style—as being about the right of parents to contract with teachers to teach their children the German language or the right of parents to send their children to Catholic schools or military academies.

Prince v. Massachusetts *(1944)*

Prince is the third of the early parental liberty cases often cited as a group to support the venerable roots of substantive due process. Unlike *Meyer* and *Pierce*, however, *Prince upholds* the statute being challenged. Massachusetts's child labor laws prohibited boys under twelve and girls under eighteen from selling, exposing, or offering for sale "any newspapers, magazines, periodicals or any other articles of merchandise of any description . . . in any street or public place." The statute imposed a fine and imprisonment of up to five days on "any parent, guardian or custodian having a minor under his control who compels or permits such minor to work in violation" of the laws. One night, Sarah Prince, the aunt and legal custodian of nine-year-old Betty Simmons, allowed Betty to distribute copies of "Watchtower" and "Consolation," publications of the Jehovah's Witnesses, on the streets of Brockton. Prince was convicted of violating the law. The Court upheld the law against her claims of parental liberty and freedom of religion as well as of the child's religious liberty.[27]

The Court states: "It is cardinal with us that the custody, care and nurture of the child reside first in the parents, whose primary function and freedom include preparation for obligations the state can neither supply nor hinder," citing *Pierce*.[28] As in *Meyer* and *Pierce*, so here, the Court does not put forward any framework or test that can be said to presage "strict scrutiny." Instead, it emphasizes the "clash" between parents' and children's rights on the one hand, and state authority on the other, and the need for making "accommodation" between them. And the Court credits the state's claim that the law is "necessary to accomplish its legitimate objectives," including the healthy development of children.[29] Therefore, the Court upholds the statute. "Parents may be free to become martyrs themselves. But it does not follow that they are free . . . to make martyrs of their children before they have reached the age of full and legal discretion when they can make that choice for themselves."[30] In this often-quoted formulation, the Court stresses governmental authority to protect children's development, even when that authority entails restricting adult exercises of parental and religious liberty that may hinder such development.

The Court proclaims that decisions like *Meyer* and *Pierce* have respected the "private realm of family life which the state cannot enter." This line is often quoted in subsequent cases recognizing a right of privacy or autonomy. "But," the Court insists, "the family itself is not beyond regulation in the public interest, as against a claim of religious liberty. And neither rights of religion nor rights of parenthood are beyond regulation." Here, the Court engages in a "two-step" seen in much of its constitutional family law about the regulation of marriage and parental rights and responsibilities: immediately after step one—a declaration that something is "fundamental" and "private"—is step two—a clarification that it is neither absolute nor beyond regulation. In making the "accommodation" or resolving the "clash," the Court holds that "the state has a wide range of power for limiting parental freedom and authority in things affecting the child's welfare."[31] This lends no support to Scalia's framework of two rigid tiers.

Moreover, the Court formulates the parents' rights and "the private realm of family life which the state cannot enter" quite abstractly (*Casey*-style). It does not formulate these rights or this realm specifically (*Glucksberg*-style) in terms of concrete historical practices forbidding children from distributing newspapers in the street.

Griswold v. Connecticut *(1965)*

A Connecticut statute made it a crime to use or to aid, abet, or counsel use of "any drug, medicinal article or instrument for the purpose of preventing conception." The Executive Director of Planned Parenthood League of Connecticut and a physician who was Medical Director for the League violated the law by publicly advising married persons about the use of contraceptives. They were arrested, tried, convicted, and fined $100. The Court invalidated the law as a violation of the right of privacy.[32]

The Court says: "The present case . . . concerns a relationship lying within the zone of privacy created by several fundamental constitutional guarantees."[33] (In chapter 2 I discussed the Court's analysis of these guarantees, along with their "penumbras" or "emanations," and pointed out that the majority opinion, unlike Justice Harlan's concurrence, avoided grounding the holding on "liberty" and substantive due process "stand[ing] on its own bottom.") It continues: "Such a law cannot stand in light of the familiar principle, so often applied by this Court, that a 'governmental purpose to control or prevent activities constitutionally subject to state regulation may not be achieved by means which sweep unnecessarily broadly and thereby invade the area of protected freedoms.'"[34] Here the Court is drawing an analogy to First Amendment overbreadth analysis. It does not cite any Due Process precedents as having engaged in such analysis. Implying that prohibition of the use of contraceptives by married couples sweeps too broadly, the Court concludes, rhetorically, "Would we allow the police to search the sacred precincts of marital bedrooms for telltale signs of the use of contraceptives? The very idea is repulsive to the notions of privacy surrounding the marriage relationship."[35] However, the Court does not engage in the formulaic, two-pronged analysis of whether the end is compelling and whether the means is necessary to further it. It seems fair to say that *Griswold* applies a form of what we today would call intermediate scrutiny: not as stringent as strict scrutiny, but not as lenient as deferential rational basis scrutiny.

What is more, as suggested in chapter 2, the Court conceives the right of privacy quite abstractly (*Casey*-style), as a right of intimate association concerned with protecting the marriage relationship, not as a specific right of privacy (*Glucksberg*-style) protecting a concrete historical practice concerning the use of contraceptives.

Loving v. Virginia *(1967)*

Loving holds that a miscegenation statute prohibiting and punishing interracial marriage violates both the Equal Protection and Due Process Clauses. The Court begins with its equal protection holding. Here, the Court rejects deferential rational basis scrutiny: "[W]e do not accept the State's contention that these statutes should be upheld if there is any possible basis for concluding that they serve a rational purpose."[36] Instead, because the case involves invidious racial discrimination, the Court writes: "At the very least, the Equal Protection Clause demands that racial classifications, especially suspect in criminal statutes, be subjected to the 'most rigid scrutiny' and, if they are ever to be upheld, they must be shown to be necessary to the accomplishment of some permissible state objective, independent of the racial discrimination which it was the object of the Fourteenth Amendment to eliminate."[37] The Court clearly is well on its way toward articulating the canonical formulation of strict scrutiny under the Equal Protection Clause. It holds that the statute fails that test.

The Court opens its due process analysis by saying: "The freedom to marry has long been recognized as one of the vital personal rights essential to the orderly pursuit of happiness by free men." It continues: "Marriage is one of the 'basic civil rights of man,' fundamental to our very existence and survival."[38] Furthermore, the Court holds,

> To deny this fundamental freedom on so unsupportable a basis as the racial classifications embodied in these statutes, classifications so directly subversive of the principle of equality at the heart of the Fourteenth Amendment, is surely to deprive all the State's citizens of liberty without due process of law. The Fourteenth Amendment requires that the freedom of choice to marry not be restricted by invidious racial discriminations.[39]

Note the intertwining of the Court's due process and equal protection holdings. To begin, when the Court characterizes the right to marry as a "basic civil right of man," it does so by reference to *Skinner v. Oklahoma* (1942), an equal protection case.[40] And when it holds that the statute denies due process, it emphasizes the invidious racial discrimination that subverts the principle of equality. Let me be clear: I am not reducing *Loving*'s due process holding to an equal protection holding (in the way some have, such as casebook editors who edit out the due process holding[41]). To the contrary, as I argue in chapters 2 and 8, the Due Process and Equal Protection Clauses overlap, and so it is no surprise that the Court would hold that this statute denies both due process and equal protection for overlapping reasons. What I am suggesting is that *Loving* may not say much by way of articulating a doctrinal framework of fundamental rights and strict scrutiny under the Due Process Clause in general, or where we don't have a similar intertwining with the Equal Protection Clause and invidious racial discrimination (which implicate that clause's framework of strict scrutiny).

That said, it is undeniable that *Loving* is an important root for a fundamental right to marry. And the case conceives the right to marry as an abstract right (*Casey*-style), not as a right whose meaning is exhausted by the concrete historical practices concerning marriage as of 1868 (Scalia- or *Glucksberg*-style). Those practices certainly did not protect interracial marriage.

Roe v. Wade *(1973)*

Texas made it a crime to "procure an abortion" or to attempt one, except "an abortion procured or attempted by medical advice for the purpose of saving the life of the mother." The Court invalidated the statute on the ground that it violated the right of a woman to decide whether to terminate her pregnancy, a right rooted in personal privacy.[42] As I acknowledged, *Roe* is a substantive due process case that characterizes the right being protected as a "fundamental right." The Court, in explicating the "roots" of the right of privacy in various precedents (in the First Amendment, the Fourth and Fifth Amendments, the penumbras of the Bill of Rights, the Ninth Amendment, or the concept of liberty guaranteed by the Fourteenth Amendment), writes: "[T]hese decisions make it clear that only personal rights that can be deemed 'fundamental' or 'implicit in the concept of ordered liberty,' are included in this guarantee of personal privacy."[43]

As I also acknowledged, *Roe* is the one substantive due process case protecting an asserted liberty that explicitly applies strict scrutiny:

> Where certain "fundamental rights" are involved, the Court has held that regulation limiting these rights may be justified only by a "compelling state interest," *Kramer v. Union Free School District* (1969); *Shapiro v. Thompson* (1969); *Sherbert v. Verner* (1963); and that legislative enactments must be narrowly drawn to express only the legitimate state interests at stake. *Griswold v. Connecticut* (1965); *Aptheker v. Secretary of State* (1964); *Cantwell v. Connecticut* (1940); see *Eisenstadt v. Baird* (1972) (White, J., concurring in result).[44]

It is striking that, in support of the idea that where "fundamental rights" are involved it should apply strict scrutiny, the Court invokes two Equal Protection cases (*Kramer* and *Shapiro*), a First Amendment case (*Sherbert*), and no Due Process cases. It is also striking that, in support of the requirement that laws "must be narrowly drawn to express only the legitimate state interests at stake," the Court cites a concurrence in an Equal Protection precedent (*Eisenstadt*), two First Amendment precedents (*Aptheker* and *Cantwell*), and *Griswold* (and recall that *Griswold* itself drew an analogy to First Amendment overbreadth doctrine but cited no Due Process precedents). That is, *Roe* bases its application of strict scrutiny on analogies to Equal Protection and First Amendment jurisprudence, without purporting to be applying established Due Process jurisprudence. Be that as it may, *Roe* is the closest approximation to what Scalia offers as the Court's authoritative framework of requiring strict scrutiny when protecting fundamental rights under the Due Process Clause. Still, the Court conceives the right of personal privacy quite abstractly (*Casey*-style); it emphatically does not reduce liberty to a deposit of concrete historical practices concerning abortion (*Glucksberg*-style).

Moore v. City of East Cleveland *(1977)*

The next major substantive due process case, *Moore*, is a vindication of Justice Harlan's conception of the Due Process inquiry (rational continuum of ordered liberty) over Scalia's conception (two rigidly policed tiers of strict scrutiny and deferential rational basis scrutiny). It is also a shining example of how the *Casey* framework better fits and justifies our practice of substantive due process than does the *Glucksberg* framework.

At issue in *Moore* was an ordinance of East Cleveland, Ohio limiting occupancy of each dwelling unit to members of a single family, with "family" defined essentially as the nuclear family of parents and their children. (The ordinance, however, permitted grandparents to live with their children and their children's children, provided that all of the grandchildren were siblings rather than cousins.) Inez Moore shared her home with her son and two grandsons who were cousins rather than brothers; thus, her extended family was too extended under the ordinance. She was convicted of violating it. The plurality concluded that this ordinance was unconstitutional under the Due Process Clause.[45]

In the plurality opinion, Powell writes: "This Court has long recognized that freedom of personal choice in matters of marriage and family life is one of the liberties protected by the Due Process Clause of the Fourteenth Amendment."[46] He continues: "A host of cases, tracing their lineage to *Meyer v. Nebraska* (1923) and *Pierce v. Society of Sisters* (1925), have consistently acknowledged a 'private realm of family life which the state cannot enter.'"[47] He also speaks of the Due Process Clause as protecting "choices concerning family living arrangements." The city had made a proto-Scalian/*Glucksbergian* attempt to define the rights recognized in prior cases at a highly specific level, limiting the force of precedents to their factual circumstances involving nuclear families. But Powell does not accept the city's attempt to limit rights in this way. To the contrary, he focuses on the basic reasons we protect those rights—the force and rationale of those precedents—and concludes that they justify protecting extended family living arrangements along with nuclear families. He invokes Harlan's dissent in *Poe* to justify this approach.[48]

Powell quotes Harlan: "The home derives its pre-eminence as the seat of family life. And the integrity of that life is something so fundamental that it has been found to draw to its protection the principles of more than one explicitly granted Constitutional right."[49] Here Harlan is saying that family life is fundamental in the sense that the family is a fundamental institution of our society. This formulation is about the need to protect traditional institutions because of the substantive moral goods they foster, not an argument for protecting individual fundamental rights against those traditional institutions. Supporting this interpretation is Powell's argument that "[o]ur decisions establish that the Constitution protects the sanctity of the family precisely because the institution of the family is deeply rooted in this Nation's history and tradition." The extended family, he states, "has roots equally venerable and equally deserving of constitutional recognition" as the nuclear family. East Cleveland's ordinance, by contrast, would "cut[] off any protection of family rights at the first convenient, if arbitrary boundary—the boundary of the nuclear family."[50] In sum, Powell clearly conceives our traditions as abstract principles, not concrete historical practices. He does not (*Glucksberg*-style) point to specific common law or statutory protection for extended families to substantiate his conclusions, and he rejects the Scalia-style attempt to limit the reach of the precedents to the nuclear family.

Likewise, Powell avoids the language of strict scrutiny. He writes: "Of course, the family is not beyond regulation. See *Prince*." He continues: "But when the government intrudes on choices concerning family living arrangements, this Court must examine carefully the importance of the governmental interests advanced and the extent to which they are served by the challenged regulation. See *Poe* (Harlan, J., dissenting)."[51] Powell's formulation is clearly not Scalia-style strict scrutiny: he articulates no requirement of a compelling governmental interest and necessary relationship to furthering it. In fact, his formulation sounds more like intermediate scrutiny, as developed in interpreting the Equal Protection Clause in *Craig v. Boren* (*Moore* was decided in 1977, and *Craig* in 1976). *Craig* requires an "important governmental objective[]" and that the means be "substantially related" to serving it.[52] Powell assimilates this intermediate level of review into Harlan's conception of the Due Process inquiry in his *Poe* dissent.

Finally, let's examine Powell's application of this intermediate standard of review. He writes: "The city seeks to justify [the ordinance] as a means of preventing overcrowding, minimizing traffic and parking congestion, and avoiding an undue financial burden on East Cleveland's school system." He concludes: "Although these are legitimate goals, the ordinance before us serves them marginally, at best."[53] This language, if anything, sounds like rational basis scrutiny with "bite" concerning the "marginal" fit between the means and the asserted "legitimate" end. In any case, it sounds more like a form of intermediate scrutiny than strict scrutiny.

In conclusion, Powell's opinion in *Moore* is quintessentially Harlanian. Interpreting our commitment to liberty entails a rational process of reasoned judgment: a form of judgment lying on a continuum at an intermediate point between strict scrutiny and deferential rational basis scrutiny.

Cruzan v. Director, Missouri Dept. of Health *(1990)*

Missouri required that evidence of an incompetent person's wishes as to the withdrawal of life-sustaining treatment be proven by clear and convincing evidence. The guardians of Nancy Cruzan, a person in a "persistent vegetative state," challenged this law under the Due Process Clause. The Court upheld the requirement.[54]

Chief Justice Rehnquist for the Court notably avoids speaking of any "fundamental right" to die. Instead, he speaks of a "liberty interest" in refusing "unwanted medical treatment," a much weaker claim. He distinguishes between a "generalized constitutional right of privacy" and a "liberty interest."[55] By not citing to any of the substantive due process cases from *Meyer* through *Roe*, he seems to suggest that the privacy/autonomy cases are not relevant. The only cases relevant on his view are those specifically involving refusing "unwanted medical treatment."

Rehnquist does not apply strict scrutiny, instead writing: "whether respondent's constitutional rights have been violated must be determined by *balancing* his liberty interests against the relevant state interests."[56] The "balancing" he contemplates seems highly general, with no weight on the scales in favor of any "liberty interest." On our continuum of standards, balancing of this sort is clearly less stringent than the forms of intermediate scrutiny seen in *Griswold* and *Moore*. Yet the Court seems to imply that it would give the "liberty interest" in refusing "unwanted medical treatment" more weight than, say, the "liberty interest" of opticians to pursue their livelihood in *Williamson v. Lee Optical* (1955), the canonical case exemplifying deferential rational basis scrutiny.[57]

Thus, *Cruzan* lends no support whatsoever to Rehnquist's and Scalia's formulation of the Due Process inquiry as a rigid two-tier framework (either strict scrutiny or deferential rational basis scrutiny). However, its highly specific formulation of the right in question as a right to refuse "unwanted medical treatment," instead of as a right to die with dignity or right to bodily integrity, does embody their *Glucksberg* methodology rather than that of

Casey. That does not undermine the argument of this chapter, though, for in *Cruzan* the Court did not protect the asserted right.

Planned Parenthood v. Casey *(1992)*

As stated above, the joint opinion in *Casey* embraces Harlan's conception of the Due Process inquiry. *Casey* reaffirms the "central holding" of *Roe* concerning the right of a woman to decide whether to terminate her pregnancy before viability. However, it pointedly avoids calling the right in question a "fundamental right." And it explicitly jettisons *Roe's* framework of strict scrutiny together with the trimester framework.[58] The joint opinion replaces strict scrutiny with an undue burden standard. This standard inquires whether a state regulation "has the purpose or effect of placing a substantial obstacle" to or undue burden upon a woman's exercise of the right to make the "ultimate decision" whether to have an abortion.[59]

On our spectrum of standards, the undue burden standard lies between strict scrutiny and deferential rational basis scrutiny. It is a form of intermediate scrutiny, though it does not follow the analytics of, say, intermediate scrutiny under the Equal Protection Clause (requiring an important governmental interest or means substantially related to furthering that interest). And, it certainly affords more stringent protection than the "balancing" test of *Cruzan*. How does the undue burden standard compare with rational basis scrutiny with "bite"? Its analytics are not the same, that is, it does not put teeth into analysis of ends and fit between means and ends.

In two more recent cases, *Whole Woman's Health v. Hellerstedt* (2016) and *June Medical Services, LLC v. Russo* (2020), the Supreme Court, applying the undue burden standard, struck down ostensible health regulations that had the effect of shutting down virtually every abortion clinic in Texas and Louisiana, respectively.[60] In dissents in both cases, Justice Thomas objected that the majority had toughened up the undue burden standard as compared with its formulation in *Casey*.[61] Even if that were true, the undue burden standard in those cases still would be less stringent than (and would apply different analytics than) strict scrutiny.

Washington v. Glucksberg *(1997)*

This case concerned the constitutionality of a Washington law prohibiting "physician-assisted suicide" or aid in dying.[62] The Court rejected the asserted right to die and, as observed in chapter 2, took the occasion generally to seek to narrow the Due Process inquiry. For one thing, Chief Justice

Rehnquist's opinion of the Court specifically rejected Harlan's conception of the Due Process inquiry, which had been embraced by the joint opinion in *Casey*. For another, Rehnquist took steps toward propounding the myth of two rigid tiers under the Due Process Clause.

Rehnquist wrote that the Court's "established method of substantive due process analysis has two primary features":

> First, we have regularly observed that the Due Process Clause specially protects those fundamental rights and liberties which are, objectively, "deeply rooted in this Nation's history and tradition" . . . and "implicit in the concept of ordered liberty." . . . Second, we have required . . . a "careful description" of the asserted fundamental liberty interest.[63]

Rehnquist's call for a "careful description" of the asserted right and for an inquiry into "[o]ur Nation's history, legal traditions, and practices" sounded like Scalia's formulation of the Due Process inquiry in his plurality opinion in *Michael H.* As discussed in chapter 2, Scalia advocated a specific or narrow, rather than abstract or broad, formulation of asserted rights and a conception of tradition as concrete historical practices instead of abstract aspirational principles.

Nonetheless, in *Glucksberg*, Rehnquist framed the asserted right highly abstractly, as "a right to commit suicide which itself includes a right to assistance in doing so,"[64] even though several more specific formulations were readily available to him. Those formulations arguably have greater support in our traditions, whether they are understood as concrete historical practices or abstract aspirational principles. For example, Rehnquist did not frame the asserted right as the court of appeals did in its en banc decision: the right of terminally ill, competent adults to control the manner and timing of their deaths by using medication prescribed by their physicians.[65] Nor did he frame it as Breyer did in concurrence: "a right to die with dignity," which Breyer characterized as "a different formulation, for which our legal tradition may provide greater support."[66] Nor did Rehnquist heed Stevens's objections in concurrence that, even if "[h]istory and tradition provide ample support for refusing to recognize an open-ended [or 'categorical'] constitutional right to commit suicide," our Constitution protects a "basic concept of freedom" that "embraces not merely a person's right to refuse a particular kind of unwanted treatment, but also her interest in dignity, and in determining the character of the memories that will survive long after her death."[67]

To Justice Souter's argument in concurrence that *Casey* had adopted Justice Harlan's conception of the Due Process inquiry, Chief Justice Rehnquist retorted:

> In Justice Souter's opinion, Justice Harlan's *Poe* dissent supplies the "modern justification" for substantive-due-process review. But although Justice Harlan's opinion has often been cited in due-process cases, we have never abandoned our fundamental-rights-based analytical method. . . . True, the Court relied on Justice Harlan's dissent in *Casey*, but . . . we did not in so doing jettison our established approach.[68]

Rehnquist argued further that only if the Court recognizes a "fundamental right" will it "requir[e] more than a reasonable relation to a legitimate state interest to justify the action." He claimed that it applies a dichotomous two-tier framework: either "more than a reasonable relation" (if a fundamental right is in play) or deferential rational basis scrutiny (if no fundamental right is in play). Once the Court in *Glucksberg* holds that there is no fundamental right at stake, it falls back on deferential rational basis scrutiny and readily upholds the law prohibiting "physician-assisted suicide."

Who provides the better account of the "established method of substantive-due-process analysis," Rehnquist or Souter (who embraces Harlan's conception in *Poe*)? In chapter 2, I raised that question. Now that we have gone through many of the leading cases in greater detail, it is time to return to it. Are *Meyer*, *Pierce*, *Griswold*, *Loving*, *Roe*, *Moore*, and *Casey* more consistent with Rehnquist's account or Souter's? Which method better fits and justifies these cases protecting liberties? Souter clearly can account for all of these cases—as the joint opinion in *Casey* did through the framework of "reasoned judgment." He also could readily account for the subsequent cases of *Troxel*, *Lawrence*, and *Obergefell*, to be discussed below. Rehnquist can account for none of them.[69] These cases do not narrowly or specifically frame the rights they are protecting (*Glucksberg*-style). Nor do they justify protecting the rights on the ground of vindicating long-standing, concrete historical practices as Rehnquist and Scalia conceive them, that is, historical practices embodied in and specifically protected by statutes and common law. But all of these cases are justifiable on the basis of realizing aspirational principles that are critical of such practices.

As observed in chapter 2, Chief Justice Rehnquist is offering this "established method" as a method of damage control—he did not have the votes to overrule the substantive due process cases protecting basic liberties, but he could try to drain them of any generative vitality for future cases. We can also see that he is laying the groundwork for the myth of two rigidly maintained tiers (either fundamental right or mere liberty interest) under the Due Process Clause subsequently to be fully propounded by Scalia in dissent in *Lawrence*. The only cases where the Court has taken pains to insist that, to receive protection, the right must be "fundamental" and the regulation will trigger "strict scrutiny" have been cases like *Bowers*, *Michael H.*, and *Glucksberg*, where the Court rejected the asserted right. And in all of those cases, the opinions were met with criticisms in dissents or concurrences that their ways of formulating the rights were not true to the challengers' claims or to our history and tradition.[70]

Troxel v. Granville *(2000)*

At a time when the Court was narrowing its interpretation of the Due Process Clause in cases like *Glucksberg*, *Troxel* affirmed the vitality of the "big three" early substantive due process cases. Justice O'Connor's plurality opinion in *Troxel* cited *Meyer*, *Pierce*, and *Prince* in support of its statement that "the interest of parents in the care, custody, and control of their children . . . is perhaps the oldest of the fundamental liberty interests recognized by this court."[71]

Under a Washington statute, grandparents were permitted to petition a court for visitation of grandchildren, and the court was permitted to order visitation rights if they served the best interest of the children, over and against a mother's judgments concerning the care, custody, and control of her children. The Court struck down the statute under the Due Process Clause.

The plurality opinion of Justice O'Connor states: "The Fourteenth Amendment . . . includes a substantive component that 'provides heightened protection against government interference with certain fundamental rights and liberty interests.'"[72] The opinion simultaneously reiterated the rhetoric of "fundamental" parental liberty, while declining to apply strict scrutiny.[73] That is why Justice Thomas objects, in concurrence: "I would apply strict scrutiny to infringements of fundamental rights."[74]

If not "strict scrutiny," what standard of "heightened protection" does the plurality apply? Without specifying a framework, the plurality concludes that the statute is "breathtakingly broad" in allowing "any third party seeking visitation to subject any decision by a parent concerning visitation of the parent's children to state-court review." The constitutional flaw the plurality identifies is the failure, in the statute and in its application by the state court, to "give

[any] special weight at all" to the "presumption that fit parents act in the best interests of their children." As the plurality puts it: "[S]o long as a parent adequately cares for his or her children (i.e., is fit), there is normally no reason for the State to inject itself into the private realm of the family to further question fit parents' ability to make the best decision" regarding their children "simply because a state judge believes a 'better' decision could be made."[75]

Justice Stevens's dissent brings out that in cases like *Troxel*, the Court has engaged in "balancing" of interests rather than "strict scrutiny" protecting well-nigh absolute fundamental rights. He writes: "A parent's rights with respect to her child have thus never been regarded as absolute . . . [but] must be balanced against the State's long-recognized interests as *parens patriae* . . . and, critically, the child's own complementary interest in preserving relationships that serve her welfare and protection." Stevens argues: "[W]e have never held that the parent's liberty interest in this [parent-child] relationship is so inflexible as to establish a rigid constitutional shield, protecting every arbitrary parental decision from any challenge against a threshold finding of harm."[76]

Troxel, like many cases surrounding the legal regulation of the family (for example, *Prince* and *Moore*), demonstrates the following two-step framework that amounts to a form of intermediate scrutiny:

· Determine that the right in question—for example, the right to marry, the right to decide one's family living arrangements, or the right to parental liberty—is fundamental.
· Conclude that even though the right is fundamental, it does not require strict scrutiny or entail that reasonable regulations are unconstitutional.[77]

Clearly, *Troxel* does not support Scalia's (and Thomas's) claim that cases involving "fundamental rights" apply "strict scrutiny" under the Due Process Clause. Moreover, Justice O'Connor frames the right in question quite abstractly (*Casey*-style)—as a right of parents to direct the care, custody, and control of their children—not as a deposit of concrete historical practices concerning grandparents' visitation rights (*Glucksberg*-style).

Lawrence v. Texas *(2003)*

Lawrence invalidated a Texas law criminalizing certain same-sex sexual conduct under the Due Process Clause.[78] It overrules *Bowers* and rejects its narrow specification of the asserted right as a "fundamental right [of 'homosexuals'] to engage in sodomy."[79] Echoing Blackmun's dissent in *Bowers*, Kennedy says that *Bowers* and *Lawrence* are no more about the right to commit "homosexual sodomy" than *Griswold* is about the right to have sexual intercourse using contraceptives. Instead, both cases are about liberty "in its spatial and more transcendent dimensions," including personal autonomy and intimate association.[80] Thus, *Lawrence* emphatically rejects *Bowers*'s (and by implication *Michael H.*'s and *Glucksberg*'s) conception of the Due Process inquiry.

The Court does not explicitly ask whether the asserted liberty is a "fundamental right." Nor does it explicitly apply strict scrutiny. Yet, it does not for that reason fall back on deferential rational basis scrutiny, unlike *Bowers* and *Glucksberg* but very like the Due Process cases protecting asserted liberties. It does not articulate or apply any particular framework of scrutiny. Instead, *Lawrence* implicitly applied rational basis scrutiny with "bite."

Did the Court in *Lawrence* embrace Harlan's conception of the Due Process inquiry as the joint opinion had in *Casey*? This option certainly would seem to have been on the table. All three authors of the joint opinion in *Casey*—Kennedy, O'Connor, and Souter—were in the majority of six in *Lawrence*. The Court did not explicitly do so. The majority did not make Harlan's concurrence in *Poe* the centerpiece of the opinion. But its approach is true to Harlan's approach in several senses.

First, the Court frames the right asserted quite abstractly—as liberty in its spatial and more transcendent dimensions—not as *Bowers* framed it—a "fundamental right to engage in homosexual sodomy." Second, the Court conceives tradition as a "living thing" or evolving contemporary consensus, not, as *Bowers* assumed, concrete historical practices (what was on the statute books or in the common law as of 1868). Thus, Kennedy's opinion focuses on the "emerging awareness" of the past fifty years,[81] or how we have "broken from" (to recall Harlan's formulation) tradition conceived as concrete historical practices regarding gays and lesbians toward realizing an abstract aspirational principle of liberty (and equality) for all. Indeed, Kennedy's opinion retraces *Bowers*'s steps, saying that the pattern of twenty-six out of fifty states repealing their anti-sodomy laws between 1961 and 1986 should have signaled, even in 1986 (when *Bowers* was decided), that we were witnessing tradition as a living thing, reflecting an evolving contemporary consensus against criminalization of sexual intimacy and in favor of respecting sexual autonomy.[82]

Third, the *Lawrence* opinion embodies common law constitutional interpretation, making recourse to the basic reasons for protecting rights in the precedents: the Court reasons by analogy from rights already protected for straights to protecting analogous rights for gays and lesbians. Indeed, the Court concludes that it would be anomalous to protect intimate association for straights but not the analogous right for gays and lesbians. Finally, *Lawrence* is Harlanian in its ease with carefully scrutinizing a statute without laboring under any compulsion to articulate a rigid formula or framework that will substitute for making reasoned judgments.

Given these affinities, why didn't the Court explicitly embrace Harlan's conception of the Due Process inquiry, as the joint opinion did in *Casey*? I can only speculate, but there is a theory available that is so obvious that it may in fact be sound. In *Poe*, Harlan propounded his conception and applied it to sexual privacy. While he argued for an abstract "right to be let alone" as part of the rational continuum of ordered liberty, he confined that right basically to a right of marital privacy for opposite-sex couples within the home. He specifically exempted any right of gays and lesbians to sexual privacy.[83] To be sure, one can embrace Harlan's conception of the Due Process inquiry in general without accepting his own application of it as of 1961. There is no contradiction in general and certainly not in particular if tradition is indeed a "living thing" that could have evolved between 1961 (*Poe*) and 2003 (*Lawrence*). For example, Charles Fried, famously the law clerk for Harlan at the time of *Poe*, embraced Harlan's method but argued that *Bowers* was wrongly decided.[84] Laurence Tribe and Michael Dorf also took this approach.[85] For whatever reasons, the Court did not go that route. But again, its conception of the Due Process inquiry and its application of it are Harlanian in spirit if not in name.

Obergefell v. Hodges *(2015)*

As I showed in chapter 2, Justice Kennedy's majority opinion in *Obergefell* embodies the Harlan/*Casey* framework over and against the arguments of the dissenters for the *Glucksberg* framework. In *Obergefell*, Kennedy writes:

> The identification and protection of fundamental rights is an enduring part of the judicial duty to interpret the Constitution. That responsibility, however, "has not been reduced to any formula." Poe v. Ullman (1961) (Harlan, J., dissenting). Rather, it requires courts to exercise reasoned judgment in identifying interests of the person so fundamental that the State must accord them its respect. See *ibid*. That process is guided by many of the same considerations relevant to analysis of other constitutional provisions that set forth broad principles rather than specific requirements. History and tradition guide and discipline this inquiry but do not set its outer boundaries. See *Lawrence*. That method respects our history and learns from it without allowing the past alone to rule the present.[86]

Here I shall examine whether the case lends any support to Scalia's argument that the Court rigorously applies a two-tier framework. The Court certainly does characterize the right to marry as a "fundamental right."[87] But it does not for that reason apply "strict scrutiny" to the laws limiting marriage to opposite-sex couples, just as it did not apply such scrutiny to laws prohibiting same-sex sexual intimacy in *Lawrence*. Yet, again like *Lawrence*, *Obergefell* did not for that reason fall back on deferential rational basis scrutiny. In fact, it did not articulate or apply any particular framework of scrutiny. It seems fair to say that, like *Lawrence*, *Obergefell* implicitly applied rational basis scrutiny with "bite."

Debunking the Myth of a
Rigidly Policed Two-Tier Framework

Having analyzed our history of substantive due process, I can now assess Scalia's dissent in *Lawrence*. Again, Scalia says that the Court's established framework for the Due Process Clause has two rigidly policed, dichotomous tiers: if the Court is not prepared to declare an asserted liberty a "fundamental right" triggering strict scrutiny, it must view it as a mere liberty interest and fall back on deferential rational basis scrutiny. Moreover, applying these two tiers, the Court either automatically invalidates the statute or automatically upholds it. For Scalia and Rehnquist, there is nothing in between—notwithstanding all of the cases which I have shown to apply forms of review that lie in between. Through my analysis of the major substantive due process cases protecting basic liberties, I have shown that this framework is not true to the cases.

Scalia and Rehnquist have propounded the myth of two tiers under the Due Process Clause to make it harder to protect liberties. For them (not to mention White in *Bowers*), the ideal state of affairs would be to abolish substantive due process altogether, to overrule all of the precedents protecting substantive liberties under the Due Process Clause and, going forward, to protect no such substantive liberties. But they did not have the votes to accomplish this result. For them, the second-best state of affairs was to formulate a rigid two-tier framework that would (1) make it difficult if not impossible to protect "new" liberties under the Due Process Clause by raising the bar for protecting them and (2) make it easy to uphold laws restricting such liberties. Tellingly, opinions by White, Scalia, and Rehnquist (in *Bowers*, *Michael H.*, and *Glucksberg*) proclaim that this is the established framework and cite one another (cases denying protection of liberties) in support of this claim, but they do not cite cases actually *protecting* rights as supporting this framework. For none of those cases employs this framework.

Notwithstanding Justice Scalia's myth of two rigidly maintained tiers of strict scrutiny or deferential rational basis scrutiny, the cases protecting basic liberties under the Due Process Clause reflect what *Casey* and Justice Harlan called "reasoned judgment" concerning our "rational continuum" of "ordered liberty." What is more, contrary to Scalia's assertions, the justices who have championed and epitomized this continuum have not been liberal justices imposing their subjective, unbounded conceptions of autonomy upon the people. Instead, they have been what I have called preservative conservatives—from Harlan to Powell to O'Connor, Kennedy, and Souter—building out this line of cases through common law constitutional interpretation, reasoning by analogy one case at a time. The counterrevolutionary culture war conservatives—Rehnquist, Scalia, Thomas, and Alito initially and now probably Gorsuch if not also Kavanaugh and Barrett—have tried to shut down this line through the tandem of the *Glucksberg* framework and the myth of two dichotomous tiers.

This concludes my initial account of our practice of substantive due process, showing its coherence and structure as well as examining the stringency of its protection of basic liberties, debunking Scalia's myth of two rigidly policed tiers. In the next two chapters, I turn to the legal enforcement of morals, defending our practice against another myth propounded by Scalia, that substantive due process cases "effectively decree[] the end of all morals legislation."

PART TWO

Substantive Due Process
Does Not "Effectively Decree
the End of All Morals Legislation"

FOUR

Is Substantive Due Process on a Slippery Slope to "the End of All Morals Legislation"?

In US politics and constitutional law, many have argued that recognizing constitutional rights of gays and lesbians under the Due Process Clause puts us on a slippery slope to protecting . . . (they then fill in the blank with their chosen horrible outcome). For example, in *Lawrence v. Texas* (2003), which recognized a right of gays and lesbians to intimate association, Justice Antonin Scalia protested in dissent that the case "effectively decrees the end of all morals legislation." Is Scalia right that there is really no distinction between same-sex intimate association and, to quote his list, "bigamy, same-sex marriage, adult incest, prostitution, masturbation, adultery, fornication, bestiality, and obscenity"?[1] Similarly, in *Obergefell v. Hodges* (2015), which recognized the right of same-sex couples to marry, Chief Justice John Roberts suggested in dissent that the decision puts us on a slippery slope to protecting a right to plural marriage or polygamy.[2]

Let us distinguish two quite different responses to Scalia's slippery slope argument. The first, taken by some libertarians, is to embrace it, greasing the slide down the steep slope to the end of all morals legislation! The second response, which I shall take, is to rebut Scalia's slippery slope argument, insisting that we can draw significant distinctions between same-sex intimate association and marriage on the one hand, and most of the types of conduct on his list on the other.

I should also distinguish between a slope that is slight or gradual and one that is slippery or precipitous. To illustrate the former, imagine a culture in which, five hundred years ago, parents arranged all marriages for their children (without taking the children's wishes or choices into account). Imagine that, over the centuries, children gradually pressed for and were afforded more choice concerning whom to marry and that there finally came a point at which children generally exercised autonomy in deciding whom to marry. Imagine further that there came a point, five hundred years after this process began, when the culture recognized a right of same-sex couples to marry. We emphatically would not say that beginning to allow children some choice five centuries ago had put us on a slippery slope to recognizing same-sex marriage, although we might acknowledge that doing so might have infinitesimally increased the likelihood that over a period of five hundred years of evolution the culture eventually would recognize such marriage. Scalia's alarmist warning in *Lawrence* surely does not contemplate such a slight slope, but rather, a precipitous one.

I begin by making some general observations about the circumstances in which slippery slope arguments are prevalent: circumstances in which Justice Scalia's and Chief Justice Roberts's arguments in *Lawrence* and *Obergefell* would be persuasive to many. Next, I rebut Scalia's argument about the slippery slope from same-sex intimate association and marriage to "the end of all morals legislation," sketching five tools or forms of argument that are available in our constitutional practice for getting traction on such slopes. Finally, I criticize Chief Justice Roberts's argument about the slippery slope from same-sex marriage to plural marriage, applying three of those tools. I should make clear at the outset that I do not argue against a right to plural marriage. Rather, I argue that Roberts was wrong to suggest that it would have been a smaller step to plural marriage than to same-sex marriage and to imply that *Obergefell* itself makes the case for protecting plural marriage.

The Circumstances for Slippery Slope Arguments

Slippery slope arguments are so common in US politics and constitutional law that many simply take them for granted as a tool in the political and legal analyst's toolkit.[3] But they are featured as an illustration of a "logical fallacy" and a form of "bad argument" in the clever book, *An Illustrated Book of Bad Arguments*.[4] And some, like the British conservative Edmund Burke, have suggested that slippery slope arguments are a peculiarly American phenomenon:

> In other countries [than the American colonies], the people . . . judge of an ill principle in government only by an actual grievance; here they anticipate the evil, and judge of the pressure of the grievance by the badness of the principle. They augur misgovernment at a distance and snuff the approach of tyranny in every tainted breeze.[5]

Slippery slope arguments certainly are not peculiar to the US. But there is no doubt that they are more prevalent and more extreme in the US than elsewhere. In other countries, people might think you were paranoid if you made the kind of slippery slope arguments that are common in the US political and constitutional cultures—especially those made with respect to the First Amendment's protection of freedom of speech, the Second Amendment's protection of the right to bear arms, and the Fourteenth Amendment's protection of substantive liberties like the right to privacy or autonomy. But in the US, people often are persuaded by such slippery slope arguments.

This leads me to ask, what is it about the US political and constitutional cultures that fosters slippery slope arguments? Or, what are the circumstances in which slippery slope arguments are prevalent? Understanding these circumstances may help us better understand what might contribute to slippery slope arguments like Scalia's and Roberts's.

1. *Circumstances of distrust of government in general.* For example, slippery slope arguments are likely to flourish in a culture in which many view government as, at best, a "necessary evil" (to use the term from Garry Wills's well-known book)[6] rather than a force for positive good. In such circumstances, where many distrust government, slippery slope arguments are the coin of the realm, not only among libertarians who hate government but also, for example, among ACLU liberals who fear government. And these arguments gain more general currency in such political and constitutional cultures.

2. *Circumstances of diversity, moral pluralism, and deep disagreement on fundamental moral, political, and constitutional questions.* In such circumstances, people may not trust those with whom they deeply disagree to wield political or judicial power reasonably or with appropriate respect for the principled development of constitutional commitments. We might expect slippery slope arguments to be less common or less extreme in societies that are more homogeneous morally or where people's trust of one another and of their government is greater.

3. *Circumstances of distrust of common law constitutional interpretation.* In such circumstances, judges and the people themselves may not have confidence in the very possibility of reasoning by analogy from one case to the next, and of the possibility of making reasoned judgments in drawing lines and maintaining cogent distinctions in building out constitutional doctrines. Consider, for example, Scalia's book, *A Matter of Interpretation* (1997), which is a jeremiad against common law constitutional interpretation and

in favor of originalism (and the view that authoritarian founders already made our judgments for us).[7] See also his dissents in *Planned Parenthood v. Casey* (1992), *Lawrence,* and *Obergefell,* which are all-out attacks on the very possibility of "reasoned judgment" in interpreting abstract constitutional commitments to liberty and equality as distinguished from arbitrary imposition of justices' subjective preferences.[8] For Scalia, evidently the only thing that averts the slippery slope is following the relatively specific commands of the founders or the specific practices of the past.

4. *Circumstances of moral flux and change together with fear of further change.* Many conservatives are wary of moral flux and change. As part of what Albert Hirschman famously called the "rhetoric of reaction," they stir up opposition to change by conjuring up slippery slopes or parades of horribles concerning where that change might take us.[9] And some conservatives, most famously Lord Patrick Devlin, seem to believe that traditional morality is a seamless web, and that any change in it leads to the "disintegration" of the moral fabric of a society.[10] In expressing a similar view, Scalia has characterized change in terms of "destruction" and "rot."[11] Therefore, to forestall such disintegration, destruction, or rot, conservatives warn against taking the next step in a line of development, lest it hurl us down a slippery slope to "the end of all morals legislation." Seen in this light, slippery slope arguments like Scalia's, far from being evidence of his cogent reasoning or rigorous thinking, are part of his conservative strategy for resisting change and what liberals and progressives would see as moral progress and the extension of basic liberties to all.

Do these circumstances for slippery slope arguments sound familiar? Don't they sound like the very circumstances of the US political and constitutional cultures at the present time? Elsewhere, I have argued that the prevalence of extreme slippery slope arguments in the US—in particular, with respect to the right to bear arms—is a symptom of political and constitutional dysfunction or pathology.[12] The same may be true in the context of substantive due process.

Scalia's Slippery Slope from *Lawrence* to "the End of All Morals Legislation"

Let us turn to assessing Justice Scalia's slippery slope argument in *Lawrence.* Does recognizing a right of gays and lesbians to intimate association really spell "the end of all morals legislation"? Is there really no distinction between same-sex intimate association and, to recall Scalia's list, "bigamy, same-sex marriage, adult incest, prostitution, masturbation, adultery, fornication, bestiality, and obscenity"? Constitutional law is not for the squeamish, and I shall be discussing some of these horribles on Scalia's list, even though we do not ordinarily talk or write about such things in polite society!

At the end of the majority opinion in *Lawrence*, Justice Anthony Kennedy articulated some limits on the scope of the liberty being recognized there, presumably in response to Scalia's warnings in dissent about the slippery slope. Kennedy stressed the following. (1) "The present case does not involve minors." Instead, it involves adults. (2) "It does not involve persons who might be injured or coerced or who are situated in relationships where consent might not easily be refused." In other words, the sexual intimacy does not inflict injury upon others. And it involves consenting adults. Furthermore, it does not involve, for example, incest or sex trafficking. (3) "It does not involve public conduct or prostitution." Instead, it involves sex between consenting adults, without pay, in private. (4) "It does not involve whether the government must give formal recognition to any relationship that homosexual persons seek to enter." That is, they are not seeking the right to marry. Aha! you may interject, because you know that, twelve years later, same-sex couples did seek and win the right to marry in *Obergefell*. But below I shall distinguish between extending the principles in precedents through the ordinary processes of common law constitutional interpretation (as in the development from *Lawrence* to *Obergefell*) and sliding down a slippery slope. Earlier in the opinion, Kennedy had emphasized that protecting the right of gays and lesbians to sexual intimacy (5) does not involve "injury to a person or abuse of an institution the law protects." Again, he is saying that there is no injury to others. And there is no abuse of the institution of marriage, an institution worth protecting (for example, the case did not involve incest, adultery, or bigamy).[13] These limits, Kennedy suggests, distinguish the sexual intimacy protected in *Lawrence* from the types of conduct on Scalia's list.

According to Justice Kennedy, same-sex intimate association is analogous to opposite-sex intimate association, not to what Scalia views as the horribles on his list. Kennedy judged gays' and lesbians' sexual intimacy and way of life to be as morally worthy and entitled to respect as that of straights. Therefore, he wrote that petitioners are entitled to "respect for their private lives." He concluded that the state may not "demean their existence or control their destiny by making their private sexual conduct a crime."[14] Accordingly, his majority opinion held that the right of intimate association already recognized for straights in previous constitutional cases extended to gays and lesbians. That holding represents the principled extension of a right through the ordinary processes of common law constitutional interpretation, reasoning by analogy from one case to the next, building out a line of cases interpreting our constitutional commitments to liberty and equality on the basis of experience, new insights, moral progress, and evolving contemporary consensus. Those ordinary processes of constitutional interpretation do not put us on a slide down a slippery slope to the end of all morals legislation. Indeed, they embody moral judgments about the best understanding of our constitutional commitments. And they reflect moral judgments about what ways of life are entitled to respect.

Tools for Getting Traction on Scalia's Slippery Slope

Next, I move from explicating Justice Kennedy's particular limits to examining more generally the tools or forms of argument available in our constitutional practice for rebutting Justice Scalia's slippery slope argument in his dissent in *Lawrence*. I sketch five tools and illustrate how they operate in that case.

How We Conceive the Right Being Protected

How we conceive the right being protected has important implications for whether recognizing the right puts us on a slippery slope or simply reflects the principled extension of rights already recognized. I shall give two examples to illustrate this first tool.

Example one: (1) Does *Lawrence* presuppose that I have a liberty to choose to do whatever traditionally immoral things I wish to do? If so, it indeed does hurl us down the slippery slope to "the end of all morals legislation." And there is no distinction between the conduct protected in *Lawrence* and the types of conduct on Scalia's list. For I have a right to do all of these traditionally immoral things. (2) Or does *Lawrence* presuppose simply that the rights of spatial privacy and intimate association already recognized for straights in constitutional law precedents extend to gays and lesbians? If so, it does not put us on the slippery slope. For we can readily draw lines after that extension since there are significant distinctions between the conduct protected in those precedents and most of the sorts of conduct on Scalia's list. And *Lawrence* grows out of the extension of principles in precedents through the ordinary processes of common law constitutional interpretation. It simply entails that gays and lesbians have the rights of spatial privacy and intimate association that straights have.

Example two: (1) Does *Lawrence* launch a libertarian revolution by holding or presupposing that moral disapproval as such is not a legitimate basis for laws?[15] If so, it shoves us down Scalia's slippery slope. And none of the laws on his list, to the extent they are based on moral disapproval alone, is constitutional. (2) Or does *Lawrence* instead seek to secure the status of equal citizenship for gays and lesbians by striking down laws that "demean their existence": an existence that we judge to be a morally worthy way of life entitled to respect? If so, it holds merely that moral disapproval that demeans the existence of a group whose members are worthy of the status of equal citizenship and respect is not a legitimate basis for laws. Thus understood, *Lawrence* does not push us down Scalia's slippery slope. For there is a distinction between the conduct and way of life protected there and, for example, bestiality: if the person wanting to have sex with or to marry their horse complains that the law prohibiting bestiality demeans their existence and reduces them to the status of second-class citizenship, we are not going to be moved. We are not going to accept the proposed analogy. (Not to mention harm to animals and lack of consent as grounds for continuing to prohibit bestiality.)

Justice Kennedy's opinion in *Lawrence* (like that in *Obergefell*) intertwines concern for protecting liberty and the aspiration to securing equality in a way that makes clear that the Court was protecting the liberty of gays and lesbians to intimate association and to marry in order to secure the status and benefits of equal citizenship for them. Bringing out the aspiration to secure such equality for a morally worthy group of persons shows that we don't have to worry about sliding down a slope to the morally unworthy horribles on Scalia's list.

How We Justify Protecting the Right

A second, related tool concerns how we justify protecting the right recognized in the cases. Do *Lawrence* and *Obergefell* justify protecting the right of gays and lesbians to intimate association and to marry on the ground that individuals have a right (1) to choose whom or what to have sex with, (2) to decide whom or what to marry, and (3) to choose to do whatever they please with their bodies—a right to choose without regard for the moral good of what is chosen? If so, those precedents put us on Scalia's slippery slope to bigamy, adult incest, prostitution, adultery, and bestiality.

Or do *Lawrence* and *Obergefell* to the contrary justify protecting the right of same-sex couples to intimate association and to marry on the ground that doing so promotes moral goods? In *Obergefell*, as discussed in chapter 2,

Kennedy quotes the stirring language from *Griswold v. Connecticut* (1965) about the noble purposes of marriage: promoting intimacy, harmony, and loyalty within a worthy relationship.[16] He also quotes the Massachusetts Supreme Judicial Court's formulation concerning moral goods in *Goodridge v. Department of Public Health* (2003): because marriage "fulfils yearnings for security, safe haven, and connection that express our common humanity, civil marriage is an esteemed institution, and the decision whether and whom to marry is among life's momentous acts of self-definition." That court also mentions the moral goods of "commitment" along with "mutuality, companionship, intimacy, fidelity, and family."[17]

If we protect the right to marry for same-sex couples because marriage is an "esteemed institution" for furthering such noble purposes and promoting such moral goods, doing so does not hurl us down Scalia's slippery slope. To work down his list, if someone says, for example, that they need the right to engage in adultery or prostitution to enable them to pursue the moral goods of intimacy, commitment, and loyalty, we will not be persuaded to protect any such rights. We are not going to accept those rights as justified by those moral goods or as analogous to intimate association and marriage for straights as well as for gays and lesbians.

How We Understand the Processes of Constitutional Change

The third tool or form of argument concerns how we understand the processes of constitutional change that have brought us to recognize the right. Do we conceive extant processes of constitutional change (as Scalia does) as involving idiosyncratic judges arbitrarily imposing their subjective preferences on the rest of us? Or do we conceive those processes in terms of common law constitutional interpretation: reasoning by analogy from one case to the next, building out lines of doctrine interpreting our constitutional commitments on the basis of experience, new insights, moral progress, and evolving contemporary consensus, all of which contribute to making moral judgments about the best understandings of those commitments? I have defended the latter view in my book, *Fidelity to Our Imperfect Constitution: For Moral Readings and Against Originalisms*.[18]

If we hold the former view of the processes of constitutional change, we will worry about Scalia's slippery slope, because who knows where the "philosophical predilections" or "moral intuitions" of five subjective, willful justices on the Supreme Court might lead us? But if we hold the latter view, we will not be worried about such a slippery slope. We will understand that in making judgments about the best understanding of our constitutional

commitments, justices do not go it alone. For example, in making judgments about evolving contemporary consensus, justices might look for evidence of desuetude, under-enforcement of old laws on the books, and democratic repeal of such laws. In fact, Cass Sunstein argues that desuetude is a
good ground for the decision in *Lawrence*: "Without a strong justification,
the state cannot bring the criminal law to bear on consensual sexual behavior if enforcement of the relevant law can no longer claim to have significant
moral support in the enforcing state or the nation as a whole."[19]

On this second view of the processes of constitutional change, we will
understand that courts generally do not lead but instead follow, consolidating democratic change that is already occurring, invalidating outlier statutes,
and embodying evolving contemporary consensus. Furthermore, we will
understand that as these processes of constitutional change unfold, social
movements are hard at work drawing analogies between rights already recognized in previous cases and the rights they are seeking to vindicate (as we
have seen with the gay and lesbian rights movement). For example, in *Bowers v. Hardwick* (1986), Justice Byron White's 5-4 majority opinion asserted
that none of the precedents protecting a right of privacy or intimate association "bears any resemblance" to the right gays and lesbians sought. By the
time of *Lawrence*, seventeen years later, the gay and lesbian rights movement
was much farther along, and the majority recognized the close resemblance
between these rights—indeed, that gays and lesbians were seeking the same
rights of privacy or intimate association that straights already had.[20]

If one thinks that courts are in the vanguard of constitutional change, and
impose change before social movements and the democratic processes do
their work in securing the preconditions for it, one might fear the slippery
slope. But if one thinks courts come along and consolidate change in understanding of constitutional commitments that is already underway through
social movements and the democratic processes, one should not fear the
slippery slope. For those preconditions for constitutional change—such as
social movements, desuetude, under-enforcement, and democratic repeal—
simply are not in place for most of the types of conduct on Scalia's list.

How We Limit the Extension of Liberty: Harm Arguments

Tool four involves how we limit the extension of liberty through making
harm arguments. Recall that Justice Kennedy's majority opinion in *Lawrence*
mentions, as one limit on the reach of the liberty protected through its
holding, that recognizing the right of gays and lesbians to intimate association does not involve "injury to a person or abuse of an institution the law

protects."[21] This formulation may seem to evoke John Stuart Mill's harm principle as a limit on governmental regulation. In *On Liberty* (1859), Mill famously argued that the only justification for government to restrict individual liberty is to prevent harm to others.[22]

But Kennedy is not using a comprehensive harm principle as a *sword* to strike down all traditional morals legislation that does not prevent harm to others. Instead, he is mentioning that same-sex intimate association does not harm others as a *shield* to limit further extension of liberty: he is implicitly acknowledging that some practices really do inflict harm on others or on institutions that are worth protecting—and that those practices might be outlawed for that reason.

Let me sharpen this distinction between sword and shield in light of how plaintiffs make arguments and how courts write opinions in US constitutional law. Plaintiffs do not successfully make arguments, as a matter of first principle, that they have a right to do X because doing X is a purely self-regarding act that imposes no harm on others or on institutions. That would be making harm arguments as a sword. Instead, plaintiffs make arguments for extending rights through the ordinary processes of common law constitutional interpretation and, when pressed for limits on the extension of those rights or when confronted with dire warnings about the harmful consequences of extending the rights, they reply that protecting the right will not impose the feared harmful consequences upon others or institutions. That is making harm arguments as a shield.

Put another way, justices on the Supreme Court do not write opinions making arguments that an asserted right causes "no harm to others" affirmatively as a sword to carve out a boundary between the proper jurisdiction of governmental regulation and that of individual liberty. Instead, they advance other grounds for recognizing the right and then mention "no harm to others" defensively as a shield to deflect warnings that the recognized liberty is boundless, unruly, or poses substantial risks of harmful consequences to others or to institutions. And litigants and judges typically use harm arguments to justify not extending precedents to recognize asserted liberties—as we will see when we turn to rebutting Roberts's arguments about the alleged slippery slope from same-sex marriage to polygamy.

How We Test Slippery Slope Arguments: Comparative Constitutional Inquiry

The fifth tool concerns comparative constitutional inquiry. In *Lawrence*, Justice Scalia objected to Justice Kennedy's reference to a "wider civilization" beyond the US in justifying protecting the right of gays and lesbians to inti-mate association.[23] Quoting Justice Clarence Thomas, Scalia protested that "this Court . . . should not impose foreign moods, fads, or fashions on Americans." He insisted that the only thing that matters is *this Nation's* his-tory and tradition" (emphasizing "this Nation's").[24]

Yet Scalia's objection to the majority's engaging in comparative consti-tutional inquiry to *support* protecting the right did not stop Scalia himself from engaging in such inquiry to *oppose* protecting it. As discussed below, he warned that, just as Canada moved from protecting intimate association for same-sex couples to protecting marriage for them, so too, were we likely in the US to slide down that slope in the aftermath of *Lawrence*.[25] In *Oberge-fell*, Chief Justice Roberts likewise engaged in comparative constitutional inquiry to oppose protecting same-sex marriage, as we will see in rebutting his arguments about the supposed slippery slope to polygamy.[26]

Despite the resistance in US constitutional law to comparative consti-tutional inquiries in judicial decisions, these inquiries would seem useful to test slippery slope arguments. In response to the warning that protect-ing right X leads ineluctably down the slippery slope to protecting right Y (and that that's a bad thing), we might test that warning by asking, have the countries that have protected right X ended up (or are they moving to-ward) protecting right Y? Or have they been able to draw lines and main-tain significant distinctions and thus to avert the slide? Or, in response to the worry that *not* protecting right X leads inexorably to evil Y, we should inquire whether evil Y has come to pass in other countries that have not protected right X.

For example, in his opinion for the Court of Appeals for the Seventh Circuit in *American Booksellers Ass'n v. Hudnut* (1985), Judge Frank Easter-brook made a well-known slippery slope argument in the context of the First Amendment's protection of freedom of expression. He objected that upholding the Indianapolis antipornography ordinance (affirming the sta-tus of equal citizenship for women in regulating pornography) against a First Amendment challenge would amount to subjecting people to a regime of "thought control" through favoring the viewpoint that women are equal to men over the viewpoint that women are subordinate to men. He pro-claimed that doing so would put us on a slippery slope leading to "totalitar-ian government."[27]

Comparative inquiry suggests how parochial, unfounded, and over-blown such slippery slope arguments can be. For Canada, our reasonable and freedom-loving neighbor to the north, came to the opposite conclusion regarding a similar antipornography law. In *Butler v. The Queen* (1992), the

Supreme Court of Canada, while acknowledging that the country's criminal obscenity law restricted freedom of expression, upheld the law on the ground that it was justifiable to ban pornography that harms women.[28] It's been thirty-seven years since *Hudnut* and thirty years since *Butler*. The last time I checked, Canada had not fallen down the slippery slope into totalitarian government.

Such comparative constitutional inquiries might help deflate overblown slippery slope arguments, whether made by conservative judges like Easterbrook and Scalia or liberal organizations like the ACLU. Engaging in such analysis is a far cry from following "foreign moods, fads, or fashions." It is not even arguing affirmatively for protecting a right. Rather, doing so is putting a check on slippery slope arguments.

Thus, the fifth tool, comparative constitutional inquiry, through providing empirical test cases, may suggest that fears of slippery slopes are overstated. We'll use this tool below to test the supposed slippery slope from same-sex marriage to polygamy.

To conclude: If we use these five tools or forms of argument, we will be able to get some traction on Justice Scalia's purported slippery slope from *Lawrence*'s recognition of the right of gays and lesbians to intimate association to "the end of all morals legislation." We will be able to see that, far from being "the end of all morals legislation," *Lawrence* is the beginning of legitimate morals legislation: legislation that does not demean or humiliate the morally worthy ways of life of people who are entitled to the status and benefits of equal citizenship and to equal dignity and respect. *Lawrence* entails and undertakes a decidedly moral inquiry: determining whether a way of life is morally worthy of not being demeaned or humiliated, and whether laws denying basic liberties and the status of equal citizenship to persons leading that way of life are demeaning or humiliating to them. It does not stem from a rejection of morals as such as a basis for justifying laws. (I will develop these points further in chapter 5.)

Roberts's Slippery Slope from *Obergefell* to Plural Marriage

Now let us take up Chief Justice Roberts's slippery slope from *Obergefell*'s protection of the right of same-sex couples to marry to recognition of the right to plural marriage. First, we should observe that Roberts's slippery slope argument is not as precipitous, sweeping, and overwrought as Scalia's. Unlike Scalia, Roberts is not saying that once you recognize a right to X, there is no limiting principle and we are in a free fall! Instead, Roberts is suggesting that if you accept the principles Kennedy articulates in his majority opinion in *Obergefell* to justify recognizing the right to marry for same-sex couples, the logical next step in applying those principles is to recognize a right to polygamy. More precisely, he is saying that it would have been a smaller leap from those principles to polygamy than to same-sex marriage.[29]

Second, as suggested above, we should distinguish between (1) sliding down a slippery slope and (2) the principled extension of a line of cases through extending their holdings and rationales in a new case. Just because one case (e.g., *Lawrence*) proves to be a building block for another (e.g., *Obergefell*) does not mean that the first case put us on a slippery slope to the second. In light of this distinction, we might argue that the movement from *Lawrence* to *Obergefell* was not down a slippery slope toward the end of all morals legislation; instead, the principled development of the line of cases that led to protecting the right to intimate association in *Lawrence* in turn led to protecting the right to marry in *Obergefell*.

Whether we conceive Roberts's argument in dissent as a slippery slope argument or more narrowly as an argument against the way the majority opinion in *Obergefell* extended the principles articulated in the line of cases protecting the right to autonomy—including the right to marry—I focus on two arguments he makes: the first from history and tradition and the second from the majority's reasoning in *Obergefell*.

This Nation's History and Tradition

As discussed in chapter 2, one of the doctrinal tests for deciding whether an asserted liberty is protected by the Due Process Clause is whether it is "deeply rooted in this nation's history and tradition," *Moore v. City of East Cleveland* (1977).[30] Purportedly applying that test, Roberts contends that "from the standpoint of history and tradition, a leap from opposite-sex marriage to same-sex marriage is much greater than one from a two-person union to plural unions, which have deep roots in some cultures around the world. If the majority is willing to take the big leap, it is hard to see how it can say no to the shorter one." He mentions the cultures of "the Kalahari Bushmen and the Han Chinese, the Carthaginians and the Aztecs."[31]

Not so fast. Roberts's argument from history and tradition seems completely disingenuous. After all, as discussed in chapter 2, Roberts himself advocates *Washington v. Glucksberg*'s (1997) approach to the Due Process inquiry instead of Kennedy's approach, which is represented in *Casey*, *Lawrence*, and *Obergefell*. *Glucksberg* had sought to rein in and narrow *Casey*'s approach—"reasoned judgment" about the full meaning of our constitutional commitments to abstract moral principles of liberty—to a positivist inquiry into concrete historical facts concerning "this Nation's history and tradition." *Glucksberg*'s approach does not look to the historical practices of "some cultures around the world" in interpreting the Due Process Clause of the US Constitution; under it, those practices are irrelevant. *Glucksberg* stresses that what matters is "*this nation's* history and tradition" (as noted above, Scalia added the emphasis to "this nation's"). *This nation's* history and tradition does not include any legal recognition whatsoever of plural marriage, whatever may have been the case with Roberts's examples of the Kalahari Bushmen, the Han Chinese, the Carthaginians, the Aztecs, and others. From the standpoint of *this nation's* history and tradition—which includes evolving contemporary consensus toward protecting gay and lesbian rights but not toward protecting plural marriage—it would be a much greater leap to plural marriage than it was to marriage for same-sex couples.

The Majority's Reasoning in Obergefell

Chief Justice Roberts also writes in his dissent in *Obergefell*: "It is striking how much of the majority's reasoning would apply with equal force to the claim of a fundamental right to plural marriage."[32] Maybe so, if constitutional interpretation and change is basically a matter of justices sitting in a constitutional theory colloquium—and applying abstract principles and general phrases from precedents to new cases we might hypothesize—rather than engaging in a dialogue about constitutional interpretation and change with other institutions and social movements in our constitutional culture. But it is not. Constitutional interpretation and change proceed through processes of common law constitutional interpretation, democratic deliberation, and social movements. None of the preconditions for constitutional change that were in place for recognizing a right of same-sex couples to marry in *Obergefell* is in place with respect to recognizing a right to plural marriage.

Before making that argument, I want to observe that Roberts's dissent in *Obergefell* may have given a boost to the arguments for a right to plural marriage. Imagine that you are a lawyer who has been trying to make the case for a right to polygamy. You have just read *Obergefell* and understandably have been emboldened by Roberts's dissent arguing that its principles "would apply with equal force to the claim of a fundamental right to plural marriage." You also have taken heart from his claim that it would be a smaller step to protect plural marriage than to recognize same-sex marriage. Imagine that you copy and paste the key language from *Obergefell* into a complaint challenging the Montana statute prohibiting bigamy. Imagine that you do a "find and replace": find every "gays and lesbians" or "same-sex couples" in the language from *Obergefell* and replace it with "polygamists" or "plural marriage."

Do these things and you will have practically drafted the complaint actually filed in *Collier v. Fox*.[33] In August 2015, not long after Roberts filed his dissent in *Obergefell*, Christine Collier, Victoria Collier, and Nathan Collier filed such a complaint in federal district court in Montana challenging that state's marriage laws for not recognizing plural marriage. This sounds like clever lawyering. Roberts's dissent in *Obergefell*, combined with Scalia's dissents in *Lawrence* and *United States v. Windsor* (2013), practically cried out for advocates of plural marriage to try this! In fact, Scalia's dissent in *Windsor*—objecting that the reasoning of the majority in striking down the federal Defense of Marriage Act entailed a federal constitutional right to marry for same-sex couples—was cited by lower court judges in justifying reaching exactly that conclusion after *Windsor* (2013) and before *Obergefell* (2015).[34] And so, we could have expected to see a similar thing happen with Roberts's dissent in *Obergefell* regarding the right to plural marriage.

When are conservative justices going to learn not to write dissents like these? Instead of engaging in such doom-and-gloom prophesying about the radical implications of the majority's reasoning in cases like *Lawrence*, *Windsor*, and *Obergefell*, one might think that they would learn to be more prudent in trying to control the damage (as they see it) by arguing that the opinions in these cases were narrowly limited to deciding the specific issues before the Court (and had no implications for deciding other worrisome questions that might arise farther down the line). In *Windsor*, Roberts, unlike Scalia, took the more prudent, limiting approach in dissent. He stressed the opinion's federalism grounds for invalidating the federal law defining marriage as limited to opposite-sex couples, which entailed that the Court had stopped short of saying that every state must recognize a right of same-sex couples to marry.[35] In *Obergefell*, however, Roberts wrote a dissent more like Scalia's, warning about the radical implications of the majority's reasoning as well as about the slippery slope.[36] One might ask, who is the audience for these evidently self-fulfilling and self-defeating dissents? Perhaps conservative cause organizations seeking to raise funds and rally troops in the culture war. Perhaps the Republican Party Presidential Platform Committee. Perhaps, as Scalia sometimes said in speeches and interviews, the law students who represent the next generation and who may, in the long term, fight to correct the error. From a progressive standpoint, Justice Ginsburg expressed a similar view in stating that "dissents speak to a future age."[37]

We'll have to wait and see whether Roberts's dissent ends up being invoked by a court to support recognizing a right to polygamy. In *Collier*, the federal magistrate dismissed the case on the ground that plaintiffs lacked standing to challenge Montana's law. The Colliers had filed suit after a county clerk refused to issue a marriage license for Christine to legally marry Nathan, who was already legally married to Victoria. In the letter denying the license, the county clerk had told the applicants that obtaining a second marriage license would be considered polygamy. But in the letter, the government did not explicitly threaten them with prosecution. That is why the magistrate concluded that plaintiffs lacked standing to sue.[38]

Tools for Getting Traction on Roberts's Slippery Slope

Even if a court were to conclude that plaintiffs did have standing to challenge bans on plural marriage, I doubt that such a lawsuit would succeed anytime soon, for all the reasons I gave above for why I do not believe *Lawrence* and *Obergefell* put us on Justice Scalia's slippery slope. That is, we can use the tools or forms of argument I discussed above to criticize Chief Justice Roberts's slippery slope by drawing distinctions between same-sex marriage and plural marriage. Let's apply three of those five tools: (1) understanding of change; (2) comparative constitutional inquiries; and (3) harm arguments.

How We Understand the Processes of Constitutional Change

Chief Justice Roberts excoriates Justice Kennedy's majority opinion in *Obergefell* for putting a stop to the democratic process, through which the people have been deliberating about whether to change the institution of marriage to recognize marriage between same-sex couples. I am going to use Roberts's very arguments here to undercut his suggestion that *Obergefell* puts us on a slippery slope to plural marriage. Roberts's objections to recognizing a right to same-sex marriage are flawed, but they may be good reasons for not expecting a court to protect a right to polygamy—at least not at the present time.

Roberts quotes Justice Ginsburg's famous criticism of the Court in *Roe v. Wade* (1973) for its "heavy-handed judicial intervention" just as the people through the democratic processes were considering whether and how to liberalize abortion laws, and he contends that her criticism applies to *Obergefell* as well.[39] (I should observe that, despite her criticism, Ginsburg believed that *Roe* was rightly decided.[40]) Even if we concede for the sake of argument that Ginsburg's criticism was sound with respect to *Roe*, it is not sound as against *Obergefell*. For we as a people were much farther along in the national and state-by-state debates about same-sex marriage as of June 25,

2015 (the day before *Obergefell*) than we were in the corresponding debates about abortion as of January 21, 1973 (the day before *Roe*). *Roe* had the effect of invalidating the abortion statutes in forty-nine states, whereas by the time of *Obergefell* thirty-seven states already had recognized same-sex marriage (and more if we count states recognizing civil unions providing all or most of the rights, responsibilities, and benefits of marriage to same-sex couples).[41] There had been a tireless social movement working to secure the status and benefits of equal citizenship for gays and lesbians over the course of two generations—from Stonewall (1969) through *Bowers* (1986), *Romer v. Evans* (1996), *Lawrence* (2003), *Goodridge* (2003), and *Windsor* (2013). Moreover, public opinion polls indicated remarkable social change: that a majority of the people nationwide supported marriage for same-sex couples and that there was a decided generational gap in favor of supporting it.[42] These developments led many to believe that strong nationwide acceptance of same-sex marriage was inevitable, merely a matter of time. That was hardly the case with abortion in 1973 or, for that matter, now.

Thus, Roberts's analogy between *Obergefell* and *Roe* putting a stop to the democratic process is overblown. And his objections to the Supreme Court being in the vanguard of social change and of transformation of the basic institution of marriage are wildly exaggerated. The Court is hardly in the vanguard of social change in *Obergefell*. It is following and consolidating social change that has been occurring through democratic and judicial processes—along with conversations over the family dinner table—throughout the nation over a period of nearly fifty years (since Stonewall), and especially in the years since the defeat in *Bowers* in 1986 mobilized the gay and lesbian rights movement. Indeed, Roberts practically concedes as much when he acknowledges that the proponents of same-sex marriage had "the winds of change . . . at their backs."[43]

Nothing like this has happened with respect to polygamy: proponents of plural marriage do not have the winds of change at their backs. The Supreme Court would be taking a much bigger leap if it were to recognize plural marriage than it did when it recognized same-sex marriage in *Obergefell*. Not a single state legislature has repealed its laws prohibiting bigamy so as to recognize plural marriage—compared with thirty-seven states repealing their laws prohibiting sodomy by the time of *Lawrence* and thirty-seven states recognizing same-sex marriage by the time of *Obergefell* (and, again, more if we count states recognizing civil unions affording all the rights, responsibilities, and benefits but not the name of marriage).

Moreover, not a single federal or state court has recognized a right to plural marriage. In *Brown v. Buhman* (2013), the case involving Kody Brown of reality television show *Sister Wives* fame, a federal district court struck down a law prohibiting polygamous "cohabitation." But the court treated *Reynolds v. United States* (1878), which upheld a prohibition on bigamy, as binding with respect to polygamous marriage.[44] In any case, the federal court of appeals reversed on the ground that plaintiffs lacked standing to sue: because local prosecutors had a policy of not prosecuting most polygamy cases, the plaintiffs had no credible fear of being prosecuted. The Supreme Court subsequently declined to hear the appeal from the court of appeals' decision.[45]

More generally, we do not have a ubiquitous social movement mobilizing for recognition of a right to plural marriage, whether for Mormons or for everyone. Well, what do we have? To be sure, we had a Mormon presidential candidate in 2012, Mitt Romney, but he obviously did not practice or advocate polygamy. He did not argue for a pro-polygamy plank in the Republican Party Platform. Nor indeed did the leaders of the main branches of the Church of Jesus Christ of Latter-Day Saints. We had an HBO series, *Big Love*, and then a reality television show, *Sister Wives*. In May 2020, Utah decriminalized polygamous cohabitation among consenting adults, changing it from a third-degree felony, punishable by up to five years in prison, to an infraction with a fine of up to $750 and community service. (It remains a second-degree felony, punishable by up to fifteen years in prison, if made by threats, fraud, or force or if it involves abuse.)[46] Relatedly, there is now a hashtag: #familiesnotfelons![47] But decriminalizing polygamous "cohabitation" is still a considerable distance from recognizing a right to plural marriage. All of this does not add up to anything like a broad social movement underway seeking to show us that polygamists are folks just like the rest of us—or your friends and neighbors—as there had been with respect to gays and lesbians before *Obergefell*.

Admittedly, states like Utah and Montana may under-enforce laws concerning polygamy—and they may generally leave Mormons practicing polygamous cohabitation alone—presumably out of a live-and-let-live attitude. But that form of live-and-let-live attitude falls far short of moving beyond (1) grudging toleration to (2) appreciation and respect and ultimately to (3) full social acceptance of those who practice polygamy. These were the steps down the road of what Scalia characterized as the "homosexual agenda" in his dissent in *Lawrence*.[48] Or the steps down the road of what we should call social and constitutional change toward securing the status and benefits of equal citizenship for gays and lesbians. Scalia and Roberts surely knew that polygamists have made little progress down the parallel road. And I should observe that in recent years some western states have criminally prosecuted some of the more extreme polygamist Mormon sects, for example, for child abuse, food stamp fraud, and failure to pay property taxes, rather than simply leaving them alone.[49]

In his dissent in *Obergefell*, Chief Justice Roberts also mentioned polyamory, another significant form of plural union. He asked: "If not having the opportunity to marry 'serves to disrespect and subordinate' gay and lesbian couples, why wouldn't the same 'imposition of this disability' serve to disrespect and subordinate people who find fulfillment in polyamorous relationships?"[50] Although Roberts mentioned polygamy and polyamory in the same breath, they represent quite different practices. Many polyamorists seem to be engaging in what Mill called an "experiment in living,"[51] not seeking a right to plural marriage. Polyamory has been receiving increasing attention in the media. The *New York Times* now includes coverage of polyamorous unions in its style section. Those unions typically involve polyamorous relationships in which two of the partners have legally married without foreswearing all others in the relationship; they are not seeking legal recognition of a polyamorous marriage.[52] *Time* recently published an article concerning what monogamous couples can learn from polyamorous unions.[53] Still more recently, the *New Yorker* published an article on how polyamorists and polygamists, from opposite sides of the culture, are challenging family norms.[54]

What is more, in some liberal and progressive communities, including college campuses, one finds increasing discussion and practice of polyamory, along with the beginnings of legal recognition of and protection for polyamorous relationships. On June 29, 2020, the City Council of Somerville, Massachusetts, a progressive community next to Cambridge, unanimously adopted an ordinance broadening the definition of domestic partnership to include relationships between three or more adults. This is believed to be the first such ordinance in the country. Spurred by the COVID-19 pandemic, Somerville extended to polyamorous relationships the rights previously held by spouses in marriage, in particular the right to confer health insurance benefits or make hospital visits.[55] The ordinance permits "persons in committed relationships"—those who are in a "relationship of mutual support, caring and commitment and intend to remain in such a relationship," who also "reside together" and "consider themselves to be a family"—to register as domestic partnerships.[56] On March 8, 2021, the City Council of Cambridge, Massachusetts became the second city in the US to adopt an ordinance expanding domestic partnerships to recognize and protect polyamorous relationships. But in Cambridge, the partners do not have to reside together.[57] Next, on April 28, 2021, the town of Arlington, Massachusetts, which adjoins Somerville and Cambridge, adopted a bylaw offering legal recognition to domestic partnerships of "two or more" people.[58]

The efforts in these three neighboring communities were supported by the Polyamory Legal Advocacy Coalition (PLAC), which describes itself as "a multi-disciplinary coalition of academic and legal professionals" supported by the American Psychological Association Division 44 Committee on Consensual Non-Monogamy, the Chosen Family Law Center, and the Harvard Law School LGBTQ+ Advocacy Clinic. On its website, PLAC describes its mission as follows:

> PLAC seeks to advance the civil and human rights of polyamorous individuals, communities, and families through legislative advocacy, public policy, and public education. These rights include the legal recognition of diverse relationship structures, such as multi-partner/multi-parent families, diverse family structures, and relationships involving consensual non-monogamy, and the end of discrimination based on relationship status.[59]

Thus, we can see the beginnings of a social movement to recognize and protect polyamorous relationships. Notably, these three communities have used the legal structure of domestic partnerships and PLAC does not state that it seeks a right to plural marriage. Domestic partnerships provide many of the rights and protections of marriage but do not carry all the baggage of marriage, and campaigns for domestic partnerships typically do not provoke as much resistance and backlash as do those for a right to marry. It will be fascinating to observe the development of this emerging movement. Perhaps in the next few years we will see a state such as Massachusetts, California, or Vermont adopt a statewide domestic partnership law recognizing partnerships of three or more persons. (Organizations like PLAC may follow a path similar to that taken by proponents of rights for same-sex couples, who began in the mid-1980s by seeking domestic partnership ordinances in progressive communities including Berkeley, California and Cambridge, Massachusetts before pursuing passage of state laws, with California becoming the first state to adopt a statewide domestic partnership law in 1999.[60]) But none of these developments yet puts us anywhere near nationwide recognition and protection of polyamorous domestic partnerships, much less marriages.

And so, contrary to Chief Justice Roberts's assertions, a court making the decision to extend the right to marry to encompass plural marriage (whether polygamy or polyamory) would be taking a big leap—a much bigger one than the Supreme Court took in *Obergefell*. Doing so also would be far more adventurous than *Roe*—before that opinion, we had a women's movement and a reproductive rights movement seriously underway and at the forefront of national political and constitutional deliberation. We also had precedents like *Griswold* and *Eisenstadt v. Baird* (1972) protecting the right of the individual, married or single, to decide whether to bear or beget a child.[61] A court recognizing a right to plural marriage would be making its own judgment from abstract principles, without regard for the processes of constitutional change, including social movements, desuetude, and demo-cratic repeal of laws prohibiting it. All of this goes to show that there is no evidence of an evolving contemporary consensus in favor of a right to plural marriage, much less of a sudden embrace of polygamy or polyamory by the courts.

Testing Slippery Slope Arguments through Comparative Constitutional Inquiry

Next, I want to invoke the tool of comparative constitutional inquiry to sug-gest that we are not on the verge of sliding down a slippery slope to polyg-amy. In *Lawrence* (as noted above), notwithstanding his general opposition to comparative constitutional inquiry in judicial decisions, Justice Scalia engaged in such an inquiry to substantiate his worries that recognizing a right to same-sex intimate association would lead down the slippery slope to protecting a right to same-sex marriage—he pointed out that that very development had already occurred in Canada in *Halpern v. Toronto* (2003).[62]

Let's follow Scalia's logic further: To test Scalia's and Roberts's worry that recognizing a right to same-sex marriage in turn will take us down the slippery slope to protecting a right to plural marriage, let's check and see whether that has happened in Canada since the *Halpern* decision in 2003. Canada considered this very question of plural marriage in 2011, and the Supreme Court of British Columbia handed down a major decision reaffirming the prohibition of bigamy: *The British Columbia Reference Case*.[63] I want to emphasize, too, that this decision was no *Baker v. Nelson*. That was the first US Supreme Court decision to consider the question of same-sex marriage, back in 1972: a cursory one-sentence dismissal of the case for want of a substantial federal question.[64] By contrast, the Supreme Court of British Columbia in *The British Columbia Reference Case* issued a lengthy opinion based on the most comprehensive judicial assessment of polyg-amy—in light of constitutional principles of gender equality and evidence of harm to children—in the history of the world. That opinion credited the evidence concerning harm to children in deciding not to protect a right to plural marriage. It also credited the claim that polygamy undermines gender equality.

The fact that *The British Columbia Reference Case* came out the way it did confirms my claim that, contrary to Scalia's and Roberts's implications, recognizing a right to same-sex marriage does not lead inexorably to protecting a right to plural marriage. It also supports my contention that recognizing plural marriage would be a bigger step (from precedents protecting a right to intimate association, including for both opposite-sex and same-sex couples) than was recognizing same-sex marriage.

Limiting the Extension of Liberty through Harm Arguments

Finally, let's consider harm arguments as a limit on the supposed slippery slope to plural marriage. Research shows that the fears of Justice Scalia in *Lawrence* and Chief Justice Roberts in *Obergefell* about the slippery slope from recognizing a right of same-sex couples to marry to a right to polygamy are ill-founded: there are rational bases for not recognizing polygamy, at least in political and constitutional cultures such as those of the US and Canada. One basis is rooted in the concern that polygamy in its traditional form (one husband with multiple wives, or polygyny) subordinates women to men, a result offensive to the constitutional commitment to securing gender equality. Another concern is preventing harm to children in polygamy: not only the harm from the practice of adult male polygamists taking child brides, but also documented evidence of much higher rates of child abuse and conflict in polygamous households. And yet a third concern is that polygamy in its traditional form (virtually the only form known outside of desperately poor circumstances) disadvantages lower-status males, contributing to social conflict. This includes the so-called "lost boys" phenomenon resulting from powerful polygamous males expelling lower-status males from the community (in part, to eliminate the competition).[65] Hence, there are good reasons not to extend marriage beyond same-sex couples to polygamy.

We know from Scalia's dissent in *Romer* that he believes that Kennedy would distinguish same-sex intimate association from polygamy on the basis of harm. Scalia scoffed at that distinction there.[66] But it is a sound distinction. Raising such harm arguments makes it necessary to consider another argument that Roberts made in dissent in *Obergefell*. Roberts charges that Kennedy's majority opinion illegitimately reads the Fourteenth Amendment's protection of liberty to "enact" John Stuart Mill's "harm principle."[67] (I will rebut that charge in chapter 7.)

To be sure, Kennedy does say that same-sex marriage "pose[s] no risk of harm to [the couples] themselves or third parties."[68] But he is not saying—in the spirit of Mill—that the only ground for government to restrict individual liberty is to prevent harm to others. Indeed, if he were enacting Mill, he would not have mentioned that same-sex marriage poses no risk of harm to the couples themselves. For the only harm that would be relevant would be harm to others.

Instead, Kennedy pens this line to reject the argument behind the Defense of Marriage Act (invalidated in *Windsor*)—that extending marriage to same-sex couples will harm the institution of marriage, leading straight couples not to marry.[69] Kennedy's statement is one way of saying that no evidence whatever supports the claim of harm to opposite-sex marriage. He does not imply that the Fourteenth Amendment "enacts" Mill's comprehensive harm principle.

To recall our distinction above, Kennedy does not use Mill's harm principle as a *sword* to attack all traditional morals legislation and to extend liberties—to protect all self-regarding conduct and to limit the jurisdiction of government to regulating only other-regarding acts. Instead, in *Obergefell*, just as in *Lawrence*, Kennedy uses harm arguments to draw distinctions to avert the slippery slope—as a *shield* against extending liberties to activities that *do* threaten to impose harm on others or on institutions worth protecting, like marriage.

What kinds of harm to others or to the institution of marriage might count as a sufficient reason for not extending the right to marry to polygamy? Precisely the kinds of palpable, empirical harm I mentioned above—which studies of polygamy have documented—and which the Supreme Court of British Columbia credited in upholding the prohibition of bigamy in *The British Columbia Reference Case*. To begin with, these harms would include child abuse through adult polygamous males taking child brides. Less sensationally, they also would include other harmful outcomes for children alluded to above: less attention from parents; higher conflict within families; poorer performance in school or less success in life; and the "lost boys" phenomenon. If these are demonstrated empirical harms—and there are good reasons to accept that they are—they may be good grounds for not extending the right to marry to polygamy.

Furthermore, these concerns for palpable empirical harms to children and to the institution of the family do not simply reflect outmoded stereotypes rooted, for example, in animus against Mormons as a despised religious minority practicing polygamy, or stem from judgments that demean their existence. Nor does the commitment to securing the status of equal citizenship for women through establishing or maintaining a formally egalitarian structure for the institution of marriage reflect such animus or demeaning judgments. I am not going to undertake a thorough assessment of these harm arguments or gender equality arguments against protecting a right to plural marriage. I have been persuaded that these arguments are credible by the careful assessment of Stephen Macedo in his book, *Just Married: Same-Sex Couples, Monogamy & the Future of Marriage*,[70] as well as by that of the Supreme Court of British Columbia in *The British Columbia Reference Case*.

Finally, to suggest that we are on a slippery slope from same-sex marriage to polygamy is fundamentally to misunderstand the evolution in the institution of marriage in recent years. Marriage (at least in its formal structure) has been evolving away from an unequal, patriarchal institution toward a more egalitarian institution. Those developments made it a small step from contemporary opposite-sex marriage to same-sex marriage, which has no history of patriarchy and holds promise for being more egalitarian in structure than was traditional opposite-sex marriage. But those developments in an egalitarian direction have made it a larger step to recognizing polygamy, with its patriarchal structure. Indeed, Macedo suggests in *Just Married* that same-sex marriage and plural marriage, far from being on a slippery slope from one to the other, have been on "entirely different historical trajectories": the former toward a more egalitarian structure for marriage, the latter toward a more patriarchal structure.[71] (By contrast, polyamory, at least as practiced in progressive communities in the US, may be compatible with—and indeed a product of—egalitarian commitments. At any rate, it is a more egalitarian institution than polygamy as traditionally practiced.) In fact, *Obergefell* may contribute to a more egalitarian future for marriage.

To be clear: I am not arguing that the US Supreme Court will never recognize a constitutional right to plural marriage, nor am I arguing against its doing so. Instead, I am suggesting that we are not there yet, and there are good reasons to let the processes of social and constitutional change take their course, to look before we leap. Contrary to Chief Justice Roberts's implication, recognizing a right to plural marriage would be a much greater leap than was protecting a right of same-sex couples to marry in *Obergefell*. In short, *Obergefell* does not get us to a right to plural marriage.

Conclusion

The moral of the story is that the five tools I have sketched can help us get traction on Scalia's slippery slope from *Lawrence* to "the end of all morals legislation" and Roberts's slippery slope from *Obergefell* to plural marriage. Using such tools should help steady the course of common law constitutional interpretation, engaging in the principled development of the line of substantive due process cases without being frightened away from this responsibility by fallacious slippery slope arguments.

FIVE

Is Moral Disapproval Enough to Justify Traditional Morals Legislation?

In chapter 4, I assessed Justice Scalia's warning in dissent in *Lawrence v. Texas* (2003) that protecting constitutional rights of gays and lesbians to intimate association and to marry puts us on a slippery slope to "the end of all morals legislation." Some defenders of Scalia object that he was not really making a classic slippery slope argument. I interpret the objection to be that he was not claiming that protecting such rights would lead, causally, to sliding down a slope to legalizing the other traditionally immoral practices on his list: "bigamy, adult incest, prostitution, masturbation, adultery, fornication, bestiality, and obscenity." They argue that Scalia instead was contending that if moral disapproval alone is not an adequate reason to justify such traditional morals legislation—if the Supreme Court is going to put any "bite" into its rational basis scrutiny of such legislation, as it did in *Lawrence*—then, as he put it, "[e]very single one of these laws is called into question." In other words, any requirement of a good reason to justify traditional moral prohibitions "effectively decrees the end of all morals legislation."[1]

In this chapter, I assess this alternative interpretation by doing a "take two" on Scalia's warning in *Lawrence*. I also analyze Justice White's similar warning in *Bowers v. Hardwick* (1986) that protecting a right of gays and lesbians to intimate association would entail that any law "based on notions of morality" would be unconstitutional.[2] I sketch a number of versions of the claim that moral disapproval alone is not an adequate justification for traditional morals legislation. And I develop several types of (nontraditional) arguments beyond moral disapproval that—contrary to Scalia's warning—do provide good reasons to justify prohibitions of most of the types of conduct on his list. These include arguments about preventing harm to others, prohibiting conduct where we have good reason to fear lack of consent, protecting institutions worth protecting because they perform valuable civic and social functions, and securing the status and benefits of equal citizenship for all.

I argue that Kennedy's majority opinion in *Lawrence*, on this second interpretation, does not entail the end of all morals legislation. Nor do his majority opinions in *Romer v. Evans* (1996) and *Obergefell v. Hodges* (2015). The plaintiffs in *Bowers, Romer, Lawrence,* and *Obergefell* were not calling for invalidation of all laws based on morality in the broad sense of reflecting normative judgments. Nor were the dissenters in *Bowers* or Kennedy's majority opinions in *Romer, Lawrence,* and *Obergefell*. Instead, they were making moral arguments for (1) securing significant basic liberties (to intimate association and to marry) for gays and lesbians analogous to those already recognized for straights and (2) securing equal dignity and respect along with the status and benefits of equal citizenship for them. What is more, they were making decidedly moral arguments for protecting those basic liberties on the ground that doing so would promote moral goods (like commitment, fidelity, and security) and public values (like equal citizenship, mutual respect, and stability). They were arguing that the Due Process Clause requires a good reason (1) to restrict a significant basic liberty that promotes such moral goods and public values or (2) to withhold the status and benefits of equal citizenship from gays and lesbians, a group leading a morally worthy way of life. Thus, notwithstanding Scalia's warning in dissent in *Lawrence*, the majority opinions in *Romer, Lawrence,* and *Obergefell* embody, and entail continuation of, these types of moral arguments and normative judgments in constitutional interpretation. Indeed, these decisions reflect nontraditionalist moral projects that compete with and limit the traditionalist morals project Scalia defends.

A Preview of Adequate (Nontraditional) Reasons beyond Moral Disapproval

Conservative Justifications for Traditional Morals Legislation

How have moral conservatives typically justified traditional morals legislation? I shall sketch several kinds of moral disapproval they have expressed in justifying prohibitions of the types of conduct on Scalia's list.

· *Our traditions* proscribe the conduct. Moral conservatives have contended that, from time immemorial, we have prohibited the conduct and therefore we are justified in continuing to do so. For example, consider the traditional argument against same-sex intimate association on the ground that proscriptions against it have "ancient roots" in "millennia of moral teaching," as in Justice White's majority opinion and Chief Justice Burger's concurrence in *Bowers*.[3] Another example is the traditional definitional argument against same-sex marriage on the ground that marriage *just is* and *always has been* the union of one man and one woman.

· *Religious authority* forbids the conduct. For example, the Bible, in Leviticus 18:22, states that "thou shalt not lie with mankind, as with womankind: it is abomination."[4] Or, as Chief Justice Burger put it in concurrence in *Bowers*: "Condemnation of those practices is firmly rooted in Judeao-Christian moral and ethical standards."[5]

· *Public morality* condemns the conduct. Lord Patrick Devlin famously argued that it was permissible to criminalize conduct that arouses "intolerance, indignation, and disgust" in the mind of the ordinary person in the street. In another formulation, he argued for criminalizing certain conduct which disintegrates the moral fabric of the society.[6] Similarly, in advancing a conception of public morality, Robert P. George justified forbidding conduct that pollutes the "moral ecology" of the society.[7]

· *Decency*. Engaging in the conduct is indecent, degrading, or depraved.

· *Straightness or cleanliness*. We forbid the conduct because indulging in it is twisted or unclean. Being "morally straight" and "clean" forbid doing it (for example, Chief Justice Rehnquist's interpretation of the "Scout Oath" and "Scout Law" in *Boy Scouts of America v. Dale* [2000]).[8]

· Natural law, reason, and truth condemn it.[9]

These familiar and overlapping formulations succinctly and vividly express the spirit of such moral disapproval underpinning traditional morals prohibitions.

Justifications Not Resting on Traditional Moral Disapproval

Before returning to assessing Scalia's warning that *Lawrence* "effectively decrees the end of all morals legislation," I should acknowledge that some libertarians and progressives actually might welcome the end of all traditional morals legislation as justified on grounds of moral disapproval such as the foregoing. I have in mind: (1) libertarians who hate government and want to be free from traditional governmental regulations and (2) progressives who hate traditional governmental regulations that have subordinated or oppressed minorities or failed to protect them. These libertarians and progressives would not call for the end of prohibition of all the types of conduct on Scalia's list. But they would justify the prohibitions on different grounds than those which moral conservatives traditionally have offered. To the libertarians and progressives under consideration, none of these traditional moral justifications (or forms of moral disapproval) provides an adequate reason to justify the laws on Scalia's list.

First, some libertarians might welcome the end of all (or much) traditional morals legislation on two primary grounds: (1) that government has no business regulating such conduct in the first place (a jurisdictional argument) or (2) that protection of individual liberty, including personal autonomy and bodily integrity, entails that individuals have the right to decide for themselves whether to engage in (at least some of) the forms of traditionally immoral conduct on the list (a liberty or autonomy argument). We see the first ground illustrated by libertarian versions of John Stuart Mill's harm principle from *On Liberty* (1859): that the only legitimate ground for government to restrict individual liberty is to prevent harm to others.[10] We see the second ground illustrated by libertarian arguments that government must have a good reason for restricting individual liberty. For example, Randy Barnett argues for a presumption in favor of individual liberty and against governmental regulation. And Tara Smith argues that restrictions on individual liberty are presumptively unconstitutional and trigger strict judicial scrutiny.[11] Granted, some libertarians might justify prohibiting some of the types of conduct on Scalia's list, but they would do so on grounds that libertarians acknowledge to be legitimate (not traditional moral disapproval). They might justify prohibiting certain conduct on the ground of (1) preventing harm to others or (2) protecting individuals who may not have the capacity to give or withhold consent to such conduct.

Second, some progressives likewise might welcome the end of all (or much) traditional morals legislation on parallel, but different, grounds. Such progressives resemble the libertarians in their rejection of traditional morals legislation as such: they reject traditionalism and the forms of moral disapproval that conservatives typically have expressed to justify such legislation. But these progressives might offer progressive justifications for laws prohibiting many of the types of conduct on Scalia's list, for example: (1) that government should protect vulnerable, subordinate, or oppressed persons from harm; (2) that government should prohibit conduct where we have good reason to believe that vulnerable, subordinate, or oppressed persons lack the capacity to give or withhold meaningful consent; or (3) that government should outlaw practices that undermine the status or deny the benefits of equal citizenship to historically subordinate or oppressed groups.

Moreover, progressives might differ from libertarians with respect to some of the items on Scalia's list. For example, progressives might justify restrictions on obscenity, not on traditional moral grounds of prohibiting indecency, but on the progressive ground that it subordinates and harms women.[12] Whereas libertarians might oppose obscenity laws on grounds of protection of individual liberty or fear of governmental censorship.[13] Or progressives might oppose extending the right to marry to polygamy, not on traditional moral grounds—as the Supreme Court once put it, that polygamy is an "odious" form of promiscuity that is "almost exclusively a feature of the life of Asiatic and of African people" and that offends Christianity[14]— but on grounds of preventing child abuse and other harm to children and promoting the public value of gender equality.[15] Whereas libertarians might advocate extending the right to marry to plural unions on grounds of respecting individual autonomy.[16] Some libertarians and progressives, however, advocate abolishing marriage altogether in favor of private contracts.[17]

Thus, these progressives and libertarians, from different perspectives, might argue that moral disapproval alone is not an adequate reason to justify the traditional morals legislation on Scalia's list. That is, they might argue that laws prohibiting the types of conduct on his list can be justified, if at all, on (nontraditional) grounds of the sort previewed in this section.

By comparison with libertarians and progressives, why do liberals typically argue that moral disapproval alone is insufficient to justify such legislation? They too argue that government has no proper business regulating certain types of conduct. They too argue that government must respect individual rights to personal autonomy and bodily integrity. Yet they credit many of the types of (nontraditional) justifications libertarians and progressives might support for prohibiting (or permitting) certain types of conduct on Scalia's list, such as:

· *Harm*: preventing harm to others
· *Lack of consent*: prohibiting conduct where we have good reason to fear lack of meaningful consent
· *Protecting institutions*: protecting institutions worth protecting because they perform valuable civic and social functions
· *Securing status as equals*: securing the status and benefits of equal citizenship for all, including (1) promoting public values like gender equality and (2) inculcating civic virtues like toleration and mutual respect in circumstances of moral pluralism (for example, for gays and lesbians)

Liberals typically have thinner conceptions of liberty than libertarians do, and thinner conceptions of projects of securing the status and benefits of equal citizenship than progressives do. But many liberals have affinities to both libertarians and progressives in that they credit the sorts of reasons sketched in this section—beyond moral disapproval—for prohibiting some of the types of conduct on Scalia's list. Obviously, some conservatives might make these types of arguments as well. The point is that such arguments go beyond moral disapproval of the kind typically expressed in conservative justifications for traditional morals legislation.

Justice Kennedy's majority opinion in *Lawrence* deploys most of these types of nontraditional argument in distinguishing (1) protecting the rights of same-sex couples to intimate association from (2) prohibiting most of the types of conduct on Scalia's list. At the end of his opinion in *Lawrence*, as discussed in chapter 4, Kennedy articulated some limits on the scope of the liberty being recognized there, presumably in response to Scalia's warnings in dissent about "the end of all morals legislation."[18] Kennedy wove together arguments from the facts that: (1) the sexual intimacy did not inflict harm on others; (2) it was between consenting adults; (3) it did not abuse any institution the law protects; and (4) the prohibition on sexual intimacy demeaned the existence of gays and lesbians, who are entitled to the status and benefits of equal citizenship. Hence, his opinion extended the right of intimate association already recognized for straights to gays and lesbians.

The Due Process Clause requires an adequate reason for government to restrict liberty, especially basic liberties.[19] Some traditional morals legislation may not survive *Lawrence*-style rational basis scrutiny with "bite" (requiring a good reason to restrict a basic liberty, not just any old reason). In fact, I argue below that traditional prohibitions of "fornication" and "masturbation" cannot be justified by adequate reasons today. But the four kinds of arguments just previewed would provide good reasons to support prohibiting the other types of conduct on Scalia's list.

What Do People Mean When They Say That Moral Disapproval Alone Is Not an Adequate Reason to Justify Traditional Morals Legislation?

I enumerate eight (!) familiar formulations of the idea that moral disapproval alone is not an adequate reason to justify traditional morals legislation. We see these formulations in substantive due process cases as well as in scholarship concerning these cases. Sketching these formulations will enable us to assess whether any of them is embodied in *Lawrence* in a manner that entails "the end of all morals legislation."

1. One thing people *do not* mean is that any law based on morality—in the broad sense of reflecting normative judgments—is unconstitutional. This may sound like a reductio ad absurdum argument that no one would make and therefore that we need not address. Yet Justice White in the majority opinion in *Bowers* did address and reject this very argument—as if he believed Michael Hardwick's attorneys were making it. White wrote: "The law, however, is constantly based on notions of morality, and if all laws representing essentially moral choices are to be invalidated under the Due Process Clause, the courts will be very busy indeed." Furthermore, in rejecting "the right pressed upon us here," he warned: "Its limits are also difficult to discern." White expressed worries about not being able to distinguish between (1) gays' and lesbians' asserted right to intimate association and (2) "possession and use of illegal drugs," "adultery, incest, and other sexual crimes" committed in the home, and "victimless crimes" generally. Accordingly, he wrote: "We are unwilling to start down that road."[20] Here we see White's slippery slope forerunner to Scalia's warning about the end of all morals legislation.

In an undergraduate philosophy class, I suppose, we could imagine an immoralist, relativist, or skeptic arguing that any legislation based on "notions of morality" is illegitimate and even unconstitutional. But any such argument in US constitutional law would be utterly sophomoric. No Supreme Court justice writing an opinion or a dissent supporting protection of a right in a substantive due process case—and no plaintiff hoping to win their case—has ever disputed the proposition that law is "constantly based on notions of morality" in the broad sense of reflecting normative judgments; nor have they argued that a law is unconstitutional for that reason. Indeed, White, after rejecting the claim that any law based on "notions of morality" is unconstitutional, conceded that "even respondent [Hardwick] makes no such claim."[21]

Nonetheless, Justice Scalia in dissent in *Lawrence* charged Justice Kennedy with making that very claim.[22] If Kennedy in fact were making such a claim, *Lawrence* indeed would "effectively decree[] the end of all morals legislation." But he was not. Nor was Stevens in dissent in *Bowers*—whom Kennedy invoked for support[23]—notwithstanding White's implication.

What is more, in *Bowers*, White did not even require the state of Georgia to show that there was contemporary moral disapproval supporting the traditional morals legislation being challenged (a law dating back to 1816 prohibiting sodomy by both same-sex and opposite-sex persons, as applied to that between same-sex persons). Instead, White simply deferred to the "presumed belief of a majority of the electorate in Georgia that homosexual sodomy is immoral and unacceptable" as establishing that the law was rationally related to a legitimate governmental objective.[24] "Presumed" evidently signifies either deference to tradition or deference to majoritarian political processes. White's formulation in terms of the "presumed belief" demonstrates that the Court is applying *Williamson*-style highly deferential rational basis scrutiny.[25] Thus, the Court is not requiring a good reason to justify a law applied to prohibit same-sex sexual activity that is analogous to other sexual activity already protected for straights.

This "presumption" is problematic, given that the law being challenged manifested old moral disapproval (dating back to 1816) at a time when there was good evidence that moral views were changing. As White's majority opinion and Powell's concurrence acknowledged, twenty-six states had repealed their criminal laws prohibiting sodomy between 1961 and 1986, the year *Bowers* was decided.[26] For White in *Bowers* and Scalia in dissent in *Lawrence*, these changes were irrelevant to constitutional interpretation.

Given these changes, which may suggest that there was no longer majority moral support for the old morals laws being challenged in *Bowers* and *Lawrence*, Cass Sunstein makes an argument from desuetude for the unconstitutionality of those laws (as discussed in chapter 4). Indeed, in analyzing *Lawrence*, which rejected *Bowers*'s view that these changes were irrelevant to constitutional interpretation, Sunstein argued that desuetude actually *is* the ground for the decision. Again, he encapsulates the desuetude ground thus: "Without a strong justification, the state cannot bring the criminal law to bear on consensual sexual behavior if enforcement of the relevant law can no longer claim to have significant moral support in the enforcing state or the nation as a whole."[27] On his view, courts should strike down old morals laws in circumstances where there is good reason to believe that there is no longer contemporary majority support for them. In such circumstances of change, we should not "presume" that old morals laws, such as those prohibiting sodomy, have adequate contemporary justification. And there are good reasons why we should not defer to "presumed" moral beliefs of a majority.

In dissent in *Lawrence*, Scalia took the view that what White had called the "presumed" moral disapproval of a majority, under highly deferential rational basis scrutiny, was all that was necessary to justify the law prohibiting same-sex "deviate sexual intercourse."[28] Kennedy in *Lawrence* (and Stevens in dissent in *Bowers*) argued instead that "presumed" traditional moral disapproval is not an adequate justification for a law. Kennedy thought that these changes (repealing sodomy laws and, even where retaining them, not enforcing them) were significant for constitutional interpretation. He thought that the relevant tradition was not that of old laws and attitudes from Blackstone's time (as quoted in Burger's concurrence in *Bowers*), but that of the "emerging awareness," "in the past half century," "that liberty gives substantial protection to adult persons in deciding how to conduct their private lives in matters pertaining to sex."[29]

I have previewed several types of argument that might count as adequate justifications for prohibitions of the types of conduct on Scalia's list. As we have seen, Kennedy concluded that none of them justified prohibiting same-sex sexual intimacy. Moreover, he argued that in circumstances like those presented in *Lawrence* and *Obergefell*—where the question was whether to extend to gays and lesbians the rights to intimate association and to marry already recognized for straights—rational basis scrutiny with more "bite" than highly deferential rational basis scrutiny is required.[30] The Court should not "presume" that such laws resting on such "presumed" moral disapproval are constitutional. But such a requirement of a good reason hardly entails that government may not prohibit most of the kinds of conduct on Scalia's list.

2. People sometimes say that the fact that there has been a long-standing history of moral disapproval is not enough to justify a law. We see appeal to the fact of a long-standing history of moral disapproval as conclusively establishing the constitutionality of a law in White's opinion in *Bowers*, Burger's concurrence in *Bowers*, and Scalia's dissents in a number of cases (not only Due Process cases like *Lawrence* and *Obergefell* but also Equal Protection cases like *Romer* and *United States v. Virginia* [1996]—the *VMI* case).[31] For Scalia, there evidently can be no better justification for a law than the fact that we have a long-standing history of having such a law.

The first problem with such appeals to the bare fact of a long-standing practice is that they are traditionalist without more. The traditionalists talk as if all they have to do to justify a law is to say, well, that's the way we have always done things around here, as long as anyone can remember. To the contrary, critics argue, the fact of a long-standing practice, without an argument justifying the practice or its continuation, is not an adequate reason to justify a law. We see this argument in Blackmun's and Stevens's dissents in *Bowers*. Blackmun wrote: "Like Justice Holmes, I believe that '[i]t is revolting to have no better reason for a rule of law than that so it was laid down in the time of Henry IV. It is still more revolting if the grounds upon which it was laid down have vanished long since, and the rule simply persists from blind imitation of the past.'"[32] He continued: "I believe we must analyze Hard-wick's claim in the light of the values that underlie the constitutional right to privacy. If that right means anything, it means that, before Georgia can prosecute its citizens for making choices about the most intimate aspects of their lives, it must do more than assert that the choice they have made is an 'abominable crime not fit to be named among Christians.'"[33]

Similarly, Stevens wrote: "Our prior cases make two propositions abundantly clear. First, the fact that the governing majority in a State has traditionally viewed a particular practice as immoral is not a sufficient reason for upholding a law prohibiting the practice; neither history nor tradition could save a law prohibiting miscegenation from constitutional attack."[34] He continued: "Second, individual decisions by married persons, concerning the intimacies of their physical relationship, even when not intended to produce offspring, are a form of 'liberty' protected by the Due Process Clause of the Fourteenth Amendment. Moreover, this protection extends to intimate choices by unmarried as well as married persons."[35]

Kennedy's majority opinion in *Lawrence* likewise made this argument, quoting these two propositions from Stevens's dissent in *Bowers*.[36] Kennedy also wrote: "[H]istory and tradition are the starting point but not in all cases the ending point of the substantive due process inquiry."[37] His majority opinion in *Obergefell* similarly argued that history is the beginning, not the end, of the inquiry.[38]

The second problem is that when traditionalists go beyond the fact of a long-standing practice, they typically offer justifications rooted in traditionalist ideas of immorality, indecency, and disgust like those sketched above— along with repudiated science—that do not enjoy widespread acceptance today. Again, consider Chief Justice Burger's justifications for prohibiting same-sex sexual intimacy as expressed in his concurrence in *Bowers*. He made arguments sounding in traditionalist moral disapproval—invoking "millennia of moral teaching" which had condemned such intimacy and proclaiming that "Blackstone described 'the infamous crime against nature' as an offense of 'deeper malignity' than rape, a heinous act 'the very mention of which is a disgrace to human nature,' and 'a crime not fit to be named.'"[39] At the time *Bowers* was decided, it was still common for moral conservatives also to invoke relatively recent (but by then repudiated) science: that the first *Diagnostic and Statistical Manual of Mental Disorders* (1952) had classified "homosexuality" as a "mental disorder."[40] And when they acknowledged that the American Psychiatric Association had revised the second *Diagnostic and Statistical Manual of Mental Disorders* in 1973, eliminating that classification, they objected that the change was political, not scientific.[41] In short, neither the fact of moral disapproval embodied in long-standing practice nor the traditionalist moral disapproval that underlies such long-standing practice is an adequate justification for laws of the sort on Scalia's list. Due process of law requires adequate reasons—reasons with widespread contemporary acceptance—to justify the prohibitions today. *Lawrence* and *Obergefell* hold that there are no such reasons justifying refusing to extend the rights to intimate association and to marry to same-sex couples, but (as we shall see below) there are good reasons to continue to prohibit most of the other kinds of conduct on Scalia's list.

3. Some argue that moral disapproval alone—without being a reasoned moral position—is not enough to justify a law. In 1966, Ronald Dworkin made a sophisticated version of this argument in his criticism of Lord Patrick Devlin's famous argument for the legal enforcement of morals: that a majority has a right to prohibit conduct that arouses "intolerance, indignation, and disgust" in the mind of "the [person] in the Clapham omnibus" (or the ordinary person in the street).[42] (What prompted Devlin's argument was the 1957 Wolfenden Report's recommendation to decriminalize "homosexual offences.") Dworkin argued: "What is shocking and wrong is not [Devlin's] idea that the community's morality counts, but his idea of what counts as the community's morality."[43] Dworkin argued that certain attitudes—including "intolerance, indignation, and disgust" as well as "prejudices, rationalizations, matters of personal aversion or taste, arbitrary stands, and the like"—should not count as a moral position at all (and certainly not as an adequate justification for legal enforcement of traditional morals). He distinguished an "anthropological sense" of morality—whatever attitudes are displayed in the community—from a "discriminatory" sense of morality—which would filter out attitudes that do not count as a moral position that the community may enforce.[44]

Dworkin illustrated four criteria for filtering out the sorts of reasons which do not count:

1. *Prejudice*: "If I tell you that homosexuals are morally inferior because they do not have heterosexual desires, and so are not 'real men,' you would reject that reason as showing one type of prejudice. Prejudices, in general, are postures of judgment that take into account considerations our conventions exclude."
2. *Mere emotional reaction*: "If I base my view about homosexuals on a personal emotional reaction ('they make me sick') you would reject that reason as well."
3. *Rationalization*: "If I base my position on a proposition of fact ('homosexual acts are physically debilitating') which is not only false, but is so implausible that it challenges the minimal standards of evidence and argument I

generally accept and impose upon others, then you would regard my belief,
even though sincere, as a form of rationalization, and disqualify my reason
on that ground."

4. *Parroting*: "If I can argue for my own position only by citing the beliefs of
others ('everyone knows homosexuality is a sin') you will conclude that I am
parroting and not relying on a moral conviction of my own."[45]

To recapitulate, Dworkin argues that such prejudice, mere emotional reaction, rationalization, and parroting do not count as adequate reasons to justify traditional morals legislation. For the sake of argument, Dworkin does not rule out legal enforcement of adequately justified moral positions.[46]

I interpret Kennedy in *Romer* as making an argument along the lines of Dworkin's argument against Devlin: that prejudice or emotional reactions like "animus" against or a "bare desire to harm a politically unpopular group" like gays and lesbians do not count as a legitimate governmental objective.[47] Kennedy also concludes that the justifications the state of Colorado offered were rationalizations: "The breadth of the amendment [prohibiting laws protecting gays and lesbians against discrimination on the basis of their sexual orientation] is so far removed from these particular justifications that we find it impossible to credit them."[48] Finally, I interpret Kennedy in *Lawrence* as arguing that parroting long-standing practice or authority is not sufficient to justify traditional morals legislation.[49]

4. A related formulation in US constitutional law is that moral disapproval alone—in the form of prejudice, "animus" against, or a "bare desire to harm a politically unpopular group," to quote *Romer*—is not an adequate reason to justify a law.[50] A famous articulation of this view is the Supreme Court's statement in *Palmore v. Sidoti* (1984): "[T]he Constitution cannot control such prejudice, but neither can it tolerate it." The Court continued: "Private biases may be outside the reach of the law, but the law cannot, directly or indirectly, give them effect."[51] That is, even if government may not outlaw private prejudices, giving them effect through law does not count as a legitimate governmental objective. *City of Cleburne v. Cleburne Living Center, Inc.* (1985), an important case in this line of decisions leading up to *Romer*, involved discrimination against developmentally disabled persons. The Court stated that the "negative attitude of the majority of property owners," based on prejudice against such persons, was not an adequate reason to deny a permit to establish a home for them in a residential neighborhood.[52] *Department of Agriculture v. Moreno* (1973), a case upon which *Cleburne* built, involved denying food stamps to needy individuals who were living together but were "unrelated persons." The law, the Court held, was

intended to prevent "hippies" and "hippie communes" from participating in the food stamp program. The Court held that a "bare congressional desire to harm a politically unpopular group cannot constitute a legitimate governmental interest."[53]

Cases like *Palmore, Moreno,* and *Cleburne,* along with *Romer* and *Lawrence,* have established the requirement of an adequate reason—what is sometimes called rational basis scrutiny with "bite"—when laws treat certain classes of persons as "strangers to our law," "pariahs," or "outlaws"[54] or when laws demean the existence of a group entitled to equal dignity and respect. When courts analyze forms of moral disapproval such as those reflected in these cases, they do not apply highly deferential rational basis scrutiny, deferring to any old reason the government conceivably might put forward to justify the law. Not just any old reason is good enough. This formulation is a constitutional law analogue to Dworkin's argument: not all forms of moral disapproval count as reasoned moral positions or legitimate governmental objectives adequate to justify traditional morals legislation. The argument does not entail that majorities may not pass laws that are based on morality in the broad sense that they reflect normative judgments. It does entail, however, that "private prejudices," "animus," and "a bare desire to harm a politically unpopular group" are not legitimate moral positions that government may enforce.

5. Still another common formulation is that moral disapproval of a group is insufficient to justify a law. As stated, the formulation is incomplete. I would offer two available specifications to complete it: (a) moral disapproval of a group on the basis of a morally irrelevant characteristic is not an adequate justification for a law or (b) moral disapproval of a group that is worthy of equal dignity and respect—that deserves not to have its existence demeaned because it is entitled to the status and benefits of equal citizenship—is not an adequate justification.

Justice O'Connor made a well-known version of this argument in concurrence in *Lawrence*:

> Moral disapproval of this group, like a bare desire to harm the group, is an interest that is insufficient to satisfy rational basis review [with "bite"] under the Equal Protection Clause. See, e.g., *Moreno; Romer.* Indeed, we have never held that moral disapproval, without any other asserted state interest, is a sufficient rationale under the Equal Protection Clause to justify a law that discriminates among groups of persons.[55]

She elaborated:

Moral disapproval of a group cannot be a legitimate governmental interest under the Equal Protection Clause because legal classifications must not be "drawn for the purpose of disadvantaging the group burdened by the law." Texas' invocation of moral disapproval as a legitimate state interest proves nothing more than Texas' desire to criminalize homosexual sodomy. But the Equal Protection Clause prevents a State from creating "a classification of persons undertaken for its own sake." And because Texas so rarely enforces its sodomy law as applied to private, consensual acts, the law serves more as a statement of dislike and disapproval against homosexuals than as a tool to stop criminal behavior. The Texas sodomy law "raise[s] the inevitable inference that the disadvantage imposed is born of animosity toward the class of persons affected."[56]

I read O'Connor as taking a version of the first position sketched above. The passages quoted seem to imply that sexual orientation is a morally irrelevant characteristic for purposes of equal protection analysis. Hence, moral disapproval of gays or lesbians on the basis of their sexual orientation is not an adequate justification for a law. Of course, there is disagreement over what is a morally relevant characteristic and what is not. Scalia in dissent in *Romer* as well as in *Lawrence* and *Obergefell* is saying that sexual orientation—unlike race—*is* a morally relevant characteristic. He is insisting that majorities may criminalize same-sex sexual intimacy and refuse to recognize same-sex marriage on the ground that it is immoral and always has been immoral.[57]

I read Kennedy as also taking the second position. He argues that gays and lesbians are worthy of equal dignity and respect. They deserve not to have their existence or way of life demeaned by being denied the rights already extended to straights or denied the status and benefits of equal citizenship. They deserve not to be treated as strangers to our law, pariahs, or outlaws.

We might test this fifth position by asking whether moral disapproval of a group like burglars is an adequate justification for a law prohibiting burglary. Here I am alluding to a challenge Paul Brest put many years ago to John Hart Ely regarding the latter's arguments in his important book, *Democracy and Distrust* (1980). Ely insisted that, in arguing that laws discriminating against groups like gays and lesbians were unconstitutional, he was not making substantive moral judgments.[58] Brest challenged Ely to explain the difference between discrimination against burglars and that against groups like gays and lesbians. Brest suggested that one could draw such a distinction only on the basis of moral disapproval of burglars and moral approval of gays and lesbians.[59] In response to Brest's challenge, we might say (1) that being a burglar is not a morally irrelevant characteristic and (2) that burgling is not a morally worthy way of life deserving of equal dignity and respect. We would not justify prohibiting burglary simply by pointing to the fact that we have always had laws prohibiting burglary. We would justify the prohibition on the grounds of protecting people's rights to their property and more generally their rights to be secure in their persons, homes, and possessions.

And so, to return to Brest's question, what differentiates a group like burglars from a group like gays and lesbians? Gays and lesbians, in seeking rights to intimate association and to marry, are not violating other people's rights. No one has a right that gays and lesbians follow conventional gender roles, or that they have the "courage" not to act on their natural desires for sexual intimacy with persons of the same sex.[60] No one has a right that government forbid gays and lesbians from engaging in intimate sexual contact or from marrying. Again, moral disapproval of a group on the basis of a morally irrelevant characteristic is not an adequate justification for a law. Gays and lesbians, moreover, are entitled to the status and benefits of equal citizenship and therewith to the same basic liberties as straights—including the rights to intimate association and to marry. They have these rights in virtue of our moral judgment that they are entitled to equal dignity and respect: not to be demeaned in their existence or way of life. We recognize that they are pursuing the same moral goods through intimate association and marriage as straights do (for example, commitment, fidelity, and support). Accordingly, we extend to them the same rights to intimate association and to marry that straights already have.

If burglars were to launch a social movement seeking to show that laws prohibiting burglary demean their existence and way of life and deny them equal dignity and respect, we would not be moved. The reason, at bottom, is because of our moral judgments that they are not leading a morally worthy way of life and because they are violating other people's rights. Even if we might refrain from demeaning them—and we might attempt to "rehabilitate" them rather than merely to punish them for their moral failures—we would have no hesitation in criticizing ways of life that include burglary. In short, there are good reasons to outlaw burglary, just as there are good reasons to continue to prohibit most of the sorts of conduct on Scalia's list.

6. Moral disapproval alone—growing out of comprehensive religious, moral, or philosophical conceptions of the good—is not enough to justify a law in circumstances of moral pluralism such as our own. As we might put it, using John Rawls's well-known formulation, such moral disapproval

alone is not an adequate justification for a law if it runs afoul of the limits of "public reason": if government is imposing comprehensive religious, philo-sophical, or moral conceptions of the good. At least where constitutional essentials and matters of basic justice are at stake, Rawls argues, political decisions should be justifiable on the basis of public reasons: on grounds that citizens generally can reasonably be expected to accept, whatever their particular conceptions of the good.[61]

In US constitutional law, at least on some interpretations, an idea of public reason is embodied in the First Amendment's prohibition of an es-tablishment of religion.[62] But the idea of public reason does not preclude prohibitions of the types of conduct on Scalia's list that are justifiable on the basis of arguments of the sort we have sketched: harm arguments, consent arguments, arguments for protecting institutions worth protecting because they perform valuable civic and social functions, or arguments for securing the status and benefits of equal citizenship.

In US politics and constitutional law, we see religious individuals and groups complain about Rawls's idea of public reason—that they should frame their arguments regarding constitutional rights on grounds that citizens gen-erally can reasonably be expected to accept rather than on sectarian religious grounds—but we also see them largely operate within its limits.[63] For exam-ple, religious individuals and groups did not argue in court that same-sex marriage is not holy in the eyes of God and therefore must be prohibited. Instead, they made definitional or traditionalist arguments such as that mar-riage just is and always has been the union of one man and one woman. Or they made social scientific arguments, for example, (1) that the optimal set-ting for child-rearing is the intact, two-parent family with a biological father and mother who model gender complementarity, or (2) that marriage (and only opposite-sex marriage) solves the "marriage problem." Chief Justice Roberts, in dissent in *Obergefell*, quotes James Q. Wilson's well-known argu-ment on this point: "Marriage is a socially arranged solution for the problem of getting people to stay together and care for children that the mere desire for children, and the sex that makes children possible, does not solve."[64]

We also see the Supreme Court operating within the limits of public reason. It does not give religious grounds for its decisions. As Rawls put it, the Supreme Court is an "exemplar of public reason."[65] This is as it should be in our morally and religiously pluralistic constitutional democracy. This generic requirement of reasons that citizens generally can reasonably be ex-pected to accept, whatever their particular conceptions of the good, hardly rules out (nontraditional) arguments of the kind which I claim can justify most of the prohibitions on Scalia's list.

7. Another meaning is encapsulated in the statement in the joint opinion in *Planned Parenthood v. Casey* (1992), repeated in Justice Kennedy's majority opinion in *Lawrence*: "Our obligation is to define the liberty of all, not to mandate our own moral code." *Obergefell* expresses a similar view.[66] That is, justices may not let their own moral disapproval justify upholding traditional morals legislation if doing so would deny basic liberties. In this statement, *Casey* echoes Governor Mario Cuomo's famous speech at Notre Dame concerning the right to abortion. Cuomo stated that, as a Roman Catholic, he personally opposed abortion. But he stated further that, as a citizen and the Governor of New York, he accepted the constitutional right of a woman to decide whether to terminate her pregnancy as recognized in *Roe v. Wade* (1973).[67] At the time *Casey* came down, some people read the quoted passage from the joint opinion as making a similar point—that, even if Justice O'Connor, Kennedy, or Souter might personally oppose abortion (and indeed at least O'Connor and Kennedy had expressed reservations about it), they had come to the conclusion that the Constitution protected the right of a woman to decide whether to terminate her pregnancy and therefore they reaffirmed the central holding of *Roe*. More generally, the Court is saying that an individual justice's moral disapproval is not an adequate reason to uphold traditional morals legislation and to reject an asserted constitutional right. What matters is whether the Constitution protects the right in question. This formulation clearly does not entail the unconstitutionality of prohibiting the types of conduct on Scalia's list.

8. A final, related proposition—which hovers around arguments about moral disapproval as a ground for legislation—is that government may not "legislate morality." As observed in chapter 1, this formulation means different things to liberals than it does to conservatives. Liberals typically mean that there are limits on government's authority to use the criminal law to enforce traditional morality (that is, conservative morality). As we have seen, these limits typically stem either from a conception of the proper business of government or from a conception of the rights of individuals to make their own decisions concerning certain matters significant for personal self-government which have been the subject of traditional morals legislation. And so, liberals emphasize the limits on a conservative project of "legislating morality."

By contrast, when conservatives object to government legislating morality, they typically mean that there are limits on the propriety or efficacy of government using the civil law to promote public values like equality or to pursue liberal and progressive ends like securing the status and benefits of equal citizenship for all (that is, liberal or progressive morality). These limits typically stem from (1) a conception of the limits on the authority of government to engage in liberal or progressive moralizing to begin with; (2) a conception of the rights of individuals (like free exercise of religion or freedom of association) to resist such moralizing; or (3) a belief that such moralizing is likely to be ineffective. For example, in *Plessy v. Ferguson* (1896), Justice Brown echoed the classical liberal sociologist William Graham Sumner's slogan that "stateways cannot change folkways." He asserted: "Legislation is powerless to eradicate racial instincts . . . and the attempt to do so can only result in accentuating the difficulties of the present situation." He continued: "If one race be inferior to the other socially, the constitution of the United States cannot put them upon the same plane."[68] In our own time, Justice Thomas has echoed this conviction in concurring and dissenting opinions criticizing affirmative action (and many libertarians have made similar arguments). Thomas wrote in concurrence in *Adarand Constructors, Inc. v. Pena* (1995): "Government cannot make us equal; it can only recognize, respect, and protect us as equal before the law." Furthermore, Thomas clearly believes that governmental attempts to "make us equal" through affirmative action programs have accentuated the difficulties of race relations in the US.[69] Thus, conservatives invoke the slogan against "legislating morality" in opposition to liberal or progressive moralizing: projects of securing the status and benefits of equal citizenship for all, or promoting the public value of equality, or even merely teaching tolerance and respect for people who are different.[70] In short, each side objects to the other's "legislating morality": to its enforcement or promotion of morals and public values.

The point of all this is that *Lawrence* does not embody any of these eight ideas—that moral approval alone is inadequate to justify traditional morals legislation—in a manner that requires the end of all legislation of the kinds on Scalia's list. But to justify such legislation, one must be able to offer good nontraditional reasons of the sort I have discussed.

Would the Prohibitions of the Types of Conduct on Scalia's List Survive Rational Basis Scrutiny with "Bite"?

Again, Scalia argues or implies that if moral disapproval alone is not sufficient to justify prohibiting the types of conduct on his list—if the Court requires an adequate reason in applying rational basis scrutiny with "bite," as in *Lawrence*—then none of these prohibitions would be constitutional. It does not speak well of these types of traditional morals laws to suggest that one cannot provide good reasons beyond moral disapproval to justify them.

But his argument is not persuasive. For one thing, more than moral disapproval actually justifies prohibiting most of the types of conduct on his list. There are good reasons for prohibiting them, as I show below. Not so with same-sex intimate association or marriage, as shown in Justice Kennedy's majority opinions in *Lawrence* and *Obergefell*. For another, most of the activities on Scalia's list do not implicate significant basic liberties, whereas *Bowers*, *Lawrence*, and *Obergefell* did. Hardwick, Lawrence, and Obergefell were asking the Court to reason by analogy from the rights to intimate association and to marry already protected for straights to their analogues for gays and lesbians. By contrast, there is no close analogue between already protected rights and most of the activities on Scalia's list. Hence, there is no good argument that recognizing a right to engage in such activities would require only a small step through the ordinary processes of common law constitutional interpretation, reasoning by analogy from one case to the next. By contrast, there were good arguments to that effect in *Bowers*, as Justice Kennedy recognized in *Lawrence*, just as there were in *Obergefell*.

Furthermore, the preconditions for constitutional change are not in place for most of those types of conduct. (Recall the discussion of these preconditions in chapter 4 as providing traction on Scalia's slippery slope.) Whatever people might argue for—from abstract principles of liberty or autonomy—in political philosophy and constitutional theory seminars, we don't have to worry about the Supreme Court recognizing rights until these preconditions are in place. To be sure, there may be some libertarians somewhere who would argue for a right to engage in some of the activities on Scalia's list, but the Supreme Court is highly unlikely to recognize such rights. What is more, there is no good argument from desuetude that there is no longer majority support for the laws prohibiting most of the activities. Finally, there is no substantial social movement underway to secure recognition of rights to engage in the activities.

It is time to work through Scalia's list of types of conduct prohibited by traditional morals legislation to see whether such prohibitions can be justified by good reasons beyond moral disapproval alone. Let's recall Scalia's list: "bigamy, same-sex marriage, adult incest, prostitution, masturbation, adultery, fornication, bestiality, and obscenity." I shall discuss each of these in turn, briefly encapsulating how one might attempt to justify prohibiting them (or not) on the basis of the four types of good reasons I have previewed.

1. Bigamy: As previously discussed in chapter 4 and to be discussed further in chapter 7, there are good arguments against polygamy rooted in protecting against child abuse and other harm to children, protecting against nonconsensual sexual conduct, and promoting the public value of gender equality.

2. *Same-sex marriage*: As discussed extensively in chapters 2 and 4, there are no good arguments for denying same-sex couples the right to marry. Indeed, as *Obergefell* recognized, securing the status and benefits of equal citizenship for them requires extending this right to them.

3. *Adult incest*: There are good arguments for not extending the rights to intimate association and to marry so as to strike down prohibitions on adult incest. Notwithstanding Scalia's myth of two rigidly policed tiers of scrutiny, as discussed in chapter 3, many cases surrounding the legal regulation of the family demonstrate the following two-step framework:

· Determine that the right in question—for example, the right to marry, the right to decide one's family living arrangements, or the right to parental liberty—is fundamental.
· Conclude that even though the right is fundamental, it does not require strict scrutiny or entail that reasonable regulations are unconstitutional.[71]

Moreover, the regulations analyzed under such a two-step framework typically are justified on the ground of protecting people (for example, spouses and children) from harm or protecting the institution of the family.

Let's apply this two-step approach to adult incest. (1) Even if there are fundamental rights to intimate association and to decide whom to marry, that does not entail that the state may not prohibit adult incest. (2) For the adequate reasons justifying prohibiting it include protection of the integrity of the family, an institution worth protecting because of its role in a formative project of inculcating civic virtues and developing in children the capacities for responsible democratic and personal self-government. It would threaten the integrity of the family to permit siblings or parents and children to view one another, even as adults, as potential sexual partners or marital partners. Moreover, there are reasons to doubt that there can be genuine consent, given prior dynamics of the parent-child relationship and even of sibling-sibling relationships, not to mention psychiatric or psychosocial consequences of such relationships.[72] Notwithstanding Scalia's warning, courts in a number of states have rejected his suggestion that *Lawrence* entails the unconstitutionality of prohibitions of adult incest. Those courts have justified the prohibition on grounds like those I have sketched.[73]

4. *Prostitution*: One certainly can imagine someone arguing, from the right to intimate association, that prohibitions on prostitution are unconstitutional. We should observe that some arguments for decriminalizing prostitution are

policy arguments rather than constitutional arguments. Arguments for continuing to prohibit prostitution include protecting against harm to members of the client's family (spouses and children) as well as protecting sex workers against exploitation (in particular, in the context of sex trafficking, protecting individuals who may not be able to give or withhold meaningful consent). These arguments have force—perhaps not enough force to persuade every libertarian and every sex worker, but enough to satisfy the standard of rational basis scrutiny with "bite." Government also legitimately might wish to promote the public value of avoiding the commodification of sex. Besides, prostitution does not come within "intimate association" as articulated in cases like *Griswold*, *Roberts v. United States Jaycees* (1984),[74] *Lawrence*, and *Obergefell*, for it does not further the moral goods invoked to justify such intimate association in those cases—for example, protecting the intimate relationship of marriage, promoting commitment toward and nurture and mutual support of one another, developing bonds to impart values, and the like.

5. *Adultery*: Let us apply the family law two-step approach here. (1) The fact that there is a fundamental right to intimate association does not entail that there are no adequate reasons for forbidding adultery. (2) In fact, there are good reasons, including protecting an institution, the family, worth protecting. And protecting against harm to third parties, for example, spouses and children. Even if bans on adultery are not enforced, the bans send an important message about the significance of marital commitment and fidelity. These values are justified by good reasons, not mere long-standing practice or moral disapproval alone.

6. *Bestiality*: As stated in chapter 4, the good reasons for prohibiting it include preventing harm to animals and the animals' lack of the capacity to consent.

7. *Obscenity*: As mentioned above, some progressives might support restricting it, whereas some libertarians might support permitting it (at least absent evidence of lack of consent on the part of the models or performers). In any case, this traditional category of low-value speech or unprotected messages has been considerably narrowed over time by Supreme Court doctrine.[75] The fact that most obscenity is no longer visible on newsstands, but rather is available online, has undercut the "offensive to community standards" traditional moral justification for prohibition rooted in concern to prevent its public display.

Besides same-sex marriage, the only items on Scalia's list that would be in clear doubt—under rational basis scrutiny with "bite" or a requirement of an adequate reason—are fornication and masturbation. Indeed, there are no good arguments for continuing to outlaw them.

8. Fornication: In *Eisenstadt v. Baird* (1972), the Supreme Court invalidated a law prohibiting the distribution of contraceptives to unmarried persons under the Equal Protection Clause. The Court wrote: "It is true that in *Griswold* the right of privacy in question inhered in the marital relationship. . . . If the right of privacy means anything, it is the right of the *individual*, married or single, to be free from unwarranted governmental intrusion into matters so fundamentally affecting a person as the decision whether to bear or beget a child."[76] That case clearly entails the right of single persons to engage in sex outside of marriage, that is, "fornication." Any law prohibiting fornication surely would be an old law. It surely would lack majority support today.

Imagine a state legislature deciding to crack down on nonmarital sex and to revive the prohibition of fornication. The prohibition either would not be enforced or, if challenged, likely would be declared unconstitutional. Even if we could imagine someone offering the types of reasons I have canvassed in attempting to justify the prohibition of fornication—preventing harm to others, protecting against abuse of individuals who may not be able to give or withhold meaningful consent, protection of the institution of marriage—it is likely that a court would not find these to be adequate reasons today (other than in certain contexts like statutory rape).

9. Masturbation: It is even harder to imagine coming up with an adequate contemporary reason to justify a law prohibiting masturbation. It is difficult to conceive of justifications that would not run afoul of the limits of what Rawls called public reason. Such a prohibition would seem to reflect the imposition of a comprehensive religious conception of the good not acceptable to most people. To be sure, laws against masturbation are not enforced, just as laws against adultery are not. In some instances where a law is not enforced, yet is unlikely to be repealed, we can say with a straight face that the law sends an important message (and arguably should not be repealed for that reason). For example, the prohibition of adultery, even if it is not enforced, sends an important message about fidelity and trust within the institution of marriage. It is hard to say with a straight face that a prohibition of masturbation sends any analogous worthwhile message. For example, a message that sexual activity must be limited to coitus, with the possibility of/for the purpose of procreation, would impermissibly stem from a particular comprehensive religious conception.

We can repeat some of the justifications for forbidding masturbation that historically have been offered. Traditionalist moral and religious justifications included: The Bible condemns "onanism" and says that "it is a sin to spill or waste seed."[77] Just a generation ago, one could have imagined people offering "scientific" or health justifications: "[i]ndulging" in masturbation causes one to go blind. Or, doing so enervates one's sex drive for coitus and procreation, the only proper sexual activity and the only proper purpose for engaging in it. Such traditionalist moral and "scientific" justifications would ring oddly in most contemporary ears. In fact, they sound like good material for Monty Python movies or political television shows like John Oliver's *Last Week Tonight* or Samantha Bee's *Full Frontal*. These "justifications" certainly would be better material for those programs than for a Supreme Court opinion upholding a traditional morals prohibition of masturbation.

We would require a plausible contemporary justification to ban masturbation, and to most people today there is no acceptable moral reason and no plausible scientific or health justification for doing so. One can imagine some people still affirming some of the above justifications, but mostly if not entirely from within certain controversial comprehensive religious conceptions of the good. None can stand up to the bar of public reason. It is difficult to imagine reasons for such a prohibition being widely affirmed by people with different comprehensive conceptions of the good. Imagine trying to articulate any of these reasons with a straight face in front of a general audience or in a legislative debate or in an argument in court. In short, none of the nontraditional arguments I have canvassed here would be adequate to justify a prohibition on masturbation.

In sum, the foregoing justifications for prohibiting most of the items on Scalia's list provide adequate reasons—they could readily withstand rational basis scrutiny with "bite" of the type applied in *Lawrence*. Therefore, the requirement of an adequate reason does not "effectively decree the end of all morals legislation."

Competing Moral Projects: Civic Liberal and Progressive Moral Projects versus a Traditionalist Morals Project

To hear Scalia's warning in dissent in *Lawrence*, you would think that a gang of immoralists had hijacked the Supreme Court to bring about the end of all morals legislation. That is, you would think that the cases leading up to *Lawrence* and *Obergefell* were animated by an immoralist, relativist, or postmodernist project of liberating our political and constitutional culture from morality (indeed Justice Alito makes a groundless charge that *Obergefell* reflects a "postmodern" conception of liberty[78]). Yet Scalia's recurring talk about "culture war" seems to imply a war between competing moral projects. What has animated the cases has not been such an immoralist project but a number of overlapping civic liberal and progressive moral projects that compete with the traditionalist morals project Scalia defends. These include:

· A project of securing basic liberties significant for enabling people to make certain decisions fundamentally affecting their destiny, identity, or way of life free of compulsion by the state—what I elsewhere have called delibera- tive autonomy, to enable people to apply what I (following Rawls) called their second moral power, their capacity for a conception of the good, to pursuing their conception of a good life (see chapter 2).[79]

· A project of securing equal dignity and respect together with the status and benefits of equal citizenship for everyone, not only through protecting constitutional rights but also through adopting antidiscrimination laws (see chapters 4 and 9).[80]

· A project of justifying constitutional rights in part on the grounds of the moral goods and public values promoted by protecting them (see chapters 2 and 4).[81]

· A project of defending a moral reading of the Constitution as embodying commitments to abstract moral principles of liberty and equality—to be built out over time on the basis of moral judgments concerning the best understanding of those commitments (see chapters 2 and 7).[82]

In fact, if Scalia had read my account of all the nontraditional moral rea- sons liberals and progressives might give to justify prohibitions of most of the types of conduct on his list, he no doubt would have objected to liberal moralizing (or to liberals "legislating morality").

Furthermore, Scalia's warning about *Lawrence* "effectively decree[ing] the end of all morals legislation" exacts a considerable cost—it corrodes, even explodes, the very possibility of reasoning in constitutional interpretation (including reasoning about the implications of our commitments to moral principles). In turn, it contributes to the circumstances in which slippery slope arguments become prevalent, as discussed in chapter 4. Yet we do rea- son about the meaning and scope of liberty. We reason about what liberties are significant for personal self-government or essential to ordered liberty. We reason about what asserted liberties are analogous to liberties already protected in prior decisions. We do so through the familiar processes of common law constitutional interpretation, reasoning by analogy from one case to the next. This is a familiar form of moral reading.[83] We reason about the best understanding of our constitutional commitments, making norma- tive judgments about their meaning and application. And we reason about the adequacy of reasons for prohibiting the types of conduct on Scalia's list.

In *Ordered Liberty*, Linda C. McClain and I argued that the success of the US constitutional order depends upon a civic liberal formative project of inculcating civic virtues, encouraging responsible exercise of rights, and fostering the capacities of persons for responsible democratic and personal self-government. We conceived this project as a mild form of perfectionism.[84] A traditional conception of a perfectionist formative project was that government should promote good lives for its citizens. Part of this traditional conception was that government should enforce morals through traditional morals prohibitions of the types on Scalia's list. Crucial components of this traditionalist morals project included enforcing conventional sex lives and gender roles and limiting sexual intimacy to procreation within marriage.

But in the US constitutional order, pursuit of the constitutional commitments to liberty and equality have undermined some of the conservative justifications for such traditional morals legislation. Liberals and progressives celebrate the protection of these rights as important achievements of our constitutional practice. Scalia saw these achievements, not as fulfilling our constitutional commitments to moral principles of liberty and equality, but as "effectively decree[ing] the end of all morals legislation," indeed, as "destruction" and "rot."

In closing, I want to make clear that it has been the foregoing nontraditionalist moral projects that have made it imperative to limit the traditionalist morals project. These are moral projects no less than the traditionalist morals project, and are far more worthy and defensible in a constitutional order aspiring to realize liberty and equality for all in circumstances of moral pluralism. When we carry out such civic liberal and progressive moral projects of securing basic liberties and the status and benefits of equal citizenship for all, the moral traditionalists object to liberals and progressives "legislating morality." So it all comes down to a battle between competing moralities, not one between those who are for morality and those who would end it.

Clearly, the protection of the rights of same-sex couples to intimate association and to marry does not "effectively decree the end of all morals legislation." Indeed, we have seen that the gay and lesbian rights debate points to the appropriate scope of the legal enforcement and promotion of morals and public values in our morally pluralistic constitutional democracy. In chapters 6 and 7, I turn to arguments that substantive due process cases like *Obergefell* illegitimately read a controversial moral theory into the Constitution in the guise of interpreting it. I rebut arguments by Justice Scalia and

Chief Justice Roberts that such cases repeat the "grave errors" of *Lochner v. New York* (1905) or interpret the Constitution to "enact" John Stuart Mill's *On Liberty*. In short, I turn from conservative justices' arguments that *Lawrence* and *Obergefell* decree the end of all morals legislation to these same justices' arguments that such cases illegitimately impose moral theories!

PART THREE

Substantive Due Process Does Not Enact a Utopian Economic or Moral Theory

SIX

The Ghost of *Lochner v. New York*

A specter is haunting constitutional law—the specter of *Lochner v. New York* (1905).[1] Since *West Coast Hotel v. Parrish* (1937) repudiated the *Lochner* era's heightened judicial protection for substantive economic liberties through the Due Process Clauses, that ghost has manifested itself in charges that judges are "Lochnering" by imposing their own visions of utopia or "philosophical predilections" in the guise of interpreting the Constitution.[2] For example, in dissent in *Obergefell v. Hodges* (2015), Chief Justice Roberts charged the Court with repeating the "grave errors" of *Lochner*.[3]

You may ask, why do I speak so dramatically of the "ghost" of *Lochner* "haunting" constitutional law? Because that is the only way to capture the spookiness and dread surrounding the invocations of *Lochner*. The "ghost of *Lochner*" is an apparition that constitutional law professors have been conjuring to frighten law students since 1973—especially, but not only, in teaching *Roe v. Wade* (1973), *Planned Parenthood v. Casey* (1992), and *Obergefell*. It is a phantom that dissenters have been summoning to demonize the majority opinions in such cases protecting basic liberties under the Due Process Clauses.

In this chapter, I ask: "What was it that the Supreme Court did in *Lochner* that was so horrible?" My analysis proceeds through four questions:

· What did the Supreme Court do in *Lochner*?
· What did the dissenters in *Lochner* (in 1905) and the majority in *West Coast Hotel*, which repudiated *Lochner* (in 1937), say was wrong in that case?
· What have contemporary critics of *Roe*, *Casey*, and *Obergefell* said (from 1973 to the present) was wrong in *Lochner*?
· What is the best account of what was wrong in *Lochner*?

I contend that the dissents in *Lochner* and the majority in *West Coast Hotel* were largely right about what the Supreme Court actually did in *Lochner* in 1905 that was wrong. You will notice that I said "wrong," not "horrible." Whatever it was that the Supreme Court supposedly did in *Lochner* that was so "horrible" it did not do until 1973, when dissenters reinterpreted *Lochner* in *Roe*. The ghost of *Lochner* is an apparition that critics of substantive due process have been summoning since *Roe* revived the doctrine, though for personal liberties. Like all ghosts, this *Lochner* that is so horrible is a fabrication—by those who conjure it to frighten us away from the salutary practice of protecting basic liberties essential to personal self-government.

Thus, it is important to understand that criticism of Lochnering is less about *Lochner* itself than about *Roe, Casey,* and *Obergefell.* It is criticism of theories of constitutional interpretation that support and justify the practice of protecting substantive personal liberties through the Due Process Clauses. *Lochner* is a prism through which people refract their criticisms of *Roe, Casey,* and *Obergefell.*

I aim to vanquish the ghost of *Lochner* by showing that *Roe, Casey,* and *Obergefell* do not embody the "grave errors" of *Lochner*. Instead, these cases grow out of a coherent and worthy practice of protecting basic liberties which are essential to securing ordered liberty and the status and benefits of equal citizenship for all (here, women as well as gays and lesbians). The practice of substantive due process, contrary to the cries of Lochnering, is legitimate in our system of constitutional self-government. After all, our system is not a majoritarian representative democracy but a constitutional democracy in which basic liberties related to personal self-government prevent majorities from dictating how people make certain important decisions fundamentally affecting their destiny, identity, or way of life. Indeed, this practice is vital to securing the basic liberties which are preconditions for social cooperation on the basis of mutual respect and trust in a diverse constitutional democracy such as our own.[4]

I should state at the outset that my perspective on *Lochner* is decidedly presentist. I am not venturing a historical analysis of *Lochner* not only because doing so would be beyond my professional competence, but also because I am concerned with how invocations of the ghost of *Lochner* feature in contemporary opposition to protecting basic liberties in substantive due process cases.

What Did the Supreme Court Do in *Lochner*?

Justice Rufus Peckham's opinion for the majority in *Lochner* ranks as one of the most infamous opinions in Supreme Court history. This explains

Chief Justice Roberts's strenuous attempt to portray the majority opinion in *Obergefell* as a reprise of *Lochner*. The question in *Lochner* was whether New York could impose a maximum ten-hour day and sixty-hour week on bakers without violating the liberty to contract that the Court held was guaranteed by the Due Process Clause of the Fourteenth Amendment. The state legislature justified this legislation on the basis of the police power of the state: its power to legislate to provide for the safety, health, morals, and welfare of the public; and in particular, to protect the health of bakers by protecting them from overexposure to the dirty air of bakeries.[5]

The majority in *Lochner* framed the test for whether the law has transgressed the limits on the valid exercise of the police power by asking: "Is this a fair, reasonable, and appropriate exercise of the police power of the state?" Or is the invocation of the police power—and protecting the health of bakers—a "mere pretext" for "other motives," that is, *a phony reason*?[6] The latter formulation signaled that the Court was going to apply searching scrutiny of the ends that the state invoked to justify an economic regulation. It was not going to defer to the state's claim that it was appropriately exercising its police power to protect health.

After framing the question in this way, the Court answered: "There is no reasonable ground for interfering with the liberty of person or the right of free contract, by determining the hours of labor, in the occupation of a baker." The Court further held that bakers are "in no sense wards of the state" who "are not able to assert their rights and care for themselves without the protecting arm of the state." The Court also said that such statutes "are mere meddlesome interferences with the rights of the individual."[7] Here we see the Court's strong anti-paternalism—its indignant objection to the state protecting employees from economic oppression by employers rather than leaving them to fend for themselves. It clearly viewed such legislation as "meddlesome" and insulting to the employees, and took exception to what libertarians today would disparage as the "nanny state."

The Court pronounced the state's purported end, protecting the health of bakers, a "mere pretext" for "other motives." What is more, the Court seemed to fear that upholding such legislation under the police power would put the nation on a slippery slope that would ultimately permit "the supreme sovereignty of the state to be exercised free from constitutional restraint." The Court asked, rhetorically, "But are we all, on that account, at the mercy of legislative majorities?"[8] Now, if you believe that our scheme of government is a majoritarian democracy, your answer may be an emphatic "yes."[9] But the Court viewed our constitutional scheme as protecting substantive fundamental rights, including liberty of contract, against encroachment by legislative majorities.

What did the Court find was the "real object" of the maximum-hours statute? "[S]imply to regulate the hours of labor between the master and his employees . . . in a private business, not dangerous in any degree to morals, or . . . to the health of the employees."[10] To be sure, the New York law was probably motivated by the desire to achieve for the bakers the sixty-hour week they were unable to achieve for themselves at the bargaining table with management. The reason the bakers couldn't achieve a sixty-hour week by themselves was that management had greater bargaining power.

Peckham let it be known at the outset of his majority opinion in *Lochner* that the Court would not accept a "mere labor law"—that is, an act of the state legislature giving the bakers what they couldn't get on their own in the market. Peckham took this position because he believed with the free-marketeers of his day (and ours) that bargaining power amounted to property lawfully earned, and that using law to equalize bargaining power was using force to steal property from one party and give it to another. That, in short, was the illicit "other motive" the Court feared was at work here.

What Did the Court Do That Was Wrong in *Lochner*?

The two very famous dissents in *Lochner* provide contemporaneous answers to this question. Justice Harlan, in the first dissent, argued that the Court was wrong to doubt the state's motive. He contended that since a reasonable person could see the law as a good-faith effort to protect the bakers from overexposure to the dirty air of bakeries, the Court should uphold the law.[11]

Harlan argued for a more deferential test of constitutionality: "[T]he rule is universal that a legislative enactment, federal or state, is never to be disregarded or held invalid unless it be, beyond question, plainly and palpably in excess of legislative power." Harlan was very deferential in scrutinizing the *end* that the legislature claimed to be furthering: "It is plain that this statute was enacted in order to protect the physical well-being of those who work in bakery and confectionery establishments." He added: "Whether or not this be wise legislation it is not the province of the court to inquire. Under our systems of government the courts are not concerned with the wisdom or policy of legislation."[12]

Moreover, Harlan was quite deferential in scrutinizing the *fit* between that permissible legislative end and the means that the legislature has chosen to further it: "I find it impossible, in view of common experience, to say that there is here no real and substantial relation between the means employed by the state and the end sought to be accomplished by its legislation." He continued: "Nor can I say that . . . the regulation prescribed by the state is utterly unreasonable and extravagant or wholly arbitrary"—or, "beyond question, a plain, palpable invasion of rights secured by the fundamental law."[13] On Harlan's view, what was wrong in *Lochner* is simply that the Supreme Court did not defer to the legislature's judgment that the law was rationally related to a legitimate governmental interest in protecting the health of bakers.

Justice Holmes, in the second dissent, argued in effect that the Court was wrong to see the Constitution as committed to a free-market economic theory that regarded "mere labor laws" as a form of theft. He wrote: "This case is decided upon an economic theory which a large part of the country does not entertain." That economic theory was a libertarian theory of laissez-faire capitalism combined with anti-paternalism. Put another way, it was a libertarian social Darwinism, as espoused most prominently by Herbert Spencer in his book, *Social Statics*. Hence Holmes's famous line: "The Fourteenth Amendment does not enact Mr. Herbert Spencer's *Social Statics*." Its libertarian slogan or "shibboleth," as quoted by Holmes, was "[t]he liberty of the citizen to do as he likes so long as he does not interfere with the liberty of others to do the same."[14] If we fast forward from 1905 to 2022, we will see that the *Lochner* Court was interpreting the Constitution basically the way that many contemporary Republican legislators interpret it: viewing many forms of governmental regulation of the economy as unconstitutional socialism.

To the contrary, Holmes argued: "[A] constitution is not intended to embody a particular economic theory, whether of paternalism and the organic relation of the citizen to the State or of *laissez faire*."[15] Does he mean that the Constitution "says nothing about" economics—and makes no presuppositions about the economic system underlying it—and therefore that the legislature may pursue whatever economic theory it desires? Or does he mean simply that the Constitution does not embody a particular economic theory as among the many eligible economic theories of private property–owning democracy that it plausibly might presuppose?

To get at these questions, we should compare Holmes's statement in *Lochner*—"a constitution is not intended to embody a particular economic theory"—with Justice Black's statement for the majority in *Ferguson v. Skrupa* (1963)—"Whether the legislature takes for its textbook Adam Smith, Herbert Spencer, Lord Keynes, or some other is no concern of ours."[16] Even if the Constitution does not embody "a particular economic theory"—say, Smith's theory of laissez-faire capitalism as opposed to Keynes's theory of government-regulated capitalism—the Constitution surely does presuppose some form of private property–owning democracy. Otherwise, its protection of property rights would not make sense. On this view, the Constitution would forbid a legislature to take Karl Marx for "its textbook."

I do not read Holmes's dissent as incompatible with the view that the Constitution presupposes a commitment to some form of private property–owning democracy—rather than socialism or communism. Holmes's larger point seems to be a claim about *who should interpret the Constitution*: that the question of which particular economic theory—among the many available theories of private property–owning democracy—government may act upon is for legislatures rather than courts to decide.[17]

Holmes continued, in a famous line: the Constitution "is made for people of fundamentally differing views, and the accident of our finding certain opinions *natural and familiar, or novel, and even shocking*, ought not to conclude our judgment upon the question whether statutes embodying them conflict with the Constitution of the United States."[18] What does he mean by these statements? What is he charging the majority with doing? To determine this, we must examine what he means by "natural" and "familiar":

· *"Natural"*: As I read Holmes, he's charging the majority with assuming that the Constitution embodies laissez-faire economic theory as part of the natural order of things—and therefore that any "novel" governmental regulation of this natural economic ordering is presumptively unconstitutional.
· *"Familiar"*: He's also charging the majority with presuming that the Constitution requires the status quo of existing distributions of wealth and economic power—and therefore, again, that any governmental regulation of the market or redistribution of economic power is "shocking" and presumptively unconstitutional.[19]

Thus, on Holmes's view, what was wrong in *Lochner* was that the Court interpreted the Constitution to embody a particular economic theory rather than leaving it to the legislature to decide what understanding of private property–owning democracy to pursue. Holmes, however, evidently made a concession to substantive due process, for he contemplated the possibility that a law might be unconstitutional if it "would infringe fundamental principles as they have been understood by the traditions of our people and our law."[20]

In *West Coast Hotel* (1937)—at the height of the confrontation between President Franklin Roosevelt and the Supreme Court concerning the constitutionality of the New Deal—the Court repudiated the *Lochner* era and therewith aggressive judicial protection of economic liberties under the Due Process Clauses. The Court instead began to apply what has come to be known as deferential "rational basis scrutiny" in deciding the constitution-ality of economic regulations. Applying this standard, the Court upheld a state minimum-wage law against the challenge that it violated liberty of con-tract. In justifying this shift, the Court took judicial notice of "recent eco-nomic experience" during the Great Depression.[21]

In the majority opinion in *West Coast Hotel*, what did Chief Justice Hughes say was wrong in *Lochner*? He wrote: "The Constitution does not speak of freedom of contract." Rather, "[i]t speaks of liberty and prohibits the deprivation of liberty without due process of law."[22] Before you anach-ronistically jump to the conclusion that Hughes was prefiguring Scalia's objection to protecting "unenumerated" rights, I want to point out that he was actually saying that the Constitution protects abstract commitments to liberty and due process of law, not a particular right to freedom of contract.

To show this, we need to investigate what Hughes's conceptions of lib-erty and due process were. He wrote: "[T]he liberty safeguarded is liberty in a social organization which requires the protection of law against the evils which menace the health, safety, morals, and welfare of the people." He continued: "[R]egulation [A] which is reasonable in relation to its sub-ject and [B] is adopted in the interests of the community is due process."[23] Sound familiar? This is a version of deferential rational basis scrutiny as the test for what the Due Process Clause requires. [A] contemplates scrutiny of the fit between means and end and [B] contemplates that the law must further a legitimate, general governmental interest. He also observed that liberty and due process permit pervasive and manifold regulations of eco-nomic liberties to promote goods that are important to the general public.

Hence, according to Chief Justice Hughes's reasoning in *West Coast Hotel*, the stringent scrutiny that *Lochner* applied to such regulations is not war-ranted. Government need not have a compelling reason to justify economic regulations; a reason that can withstand the level of scrutiny contemplated in *West Coast Hotel* will do. The government most certainly had good rea-sons to support the economic regulations at issue in *Lochner* and *West Coast Hotel*. In fact, as Harlan pointed out in dissent in *Lochner*, the regulation was abundantly justified as a health regulation.[24] Hughes argued, in short, that the liberty safeguarded by our Constitution is ordered liberty—requiring adequate reasons for the regulation of liberty—not a libertarian conception of liberty with a presumption against the legitimacy of governmental regula-tion of the economy.

After *West Coast Hotel*, the Court left undisturbed the cases from the *Loch-ner* era protecting personal liberties (such as *Meyer v. Nebraska* [1923] and *Pierce v. Society of Sisters* [1925]) as distinguished from economic liberties.

Ultimately, as shown in chapters 2 and 3, the Court built upon these cases from 1965 to the present in protecting personal liberties, including those at issue in *Roe* and *Obergefell*.

A recurring issue surrounding judicial protection of substantive liberties is that of the so-called double standard concerning economic liberties as distinguished from personal liberties. The question is whether the Supreme Court can simultaneously justify its repudiation of *Lochner*'s aggressive judicial protection for economic liberties and its embrace of *Roe*'s, *Casey*'s, and *Obergefell*'s aggressive judicial protection for personal liberties. This question brings us to consider how dissenters today invoke the ghost of *Lochner* in criticizing *Roe*, *Casey*, and *Obergefell*.

What Have Critics of *Roe*, *Casey*, and *Obergefell* Said Was Wrong in *Lochner*?

In considering this issue, I shall begin with the most famous scholarly account of what was wrong in *Lochner* (and the related charge that *Roe* engaged in Lochnering). In 1973, in *The Wages of Crying Wolf*, John Hart Ely advanced a famous criticism of *Roe* by analogy to the fable of the boy who cried "wolf." The wolf, of course, is *Lochner*.[25] The point of Ely's fable is that judges and commentators should not have cried "*Lochner*" so indiscriminately between *West Coast Hotel* (1937) and *Roe* (1973). He offers a discriminating account:

> What is frightening about *Roe* is that [this] super-protected right is not inferable from the language of the Constitution, the framers' thinking respecting the specific problem in issue, any general value derivable from the provisions they included, or the nation's governmental structure. Nor is it explainable in terms of the unusual political impotence of the group judicially protected vis-à-vis the interest that legislatively prevailed over it. . . . [That is, it does not come within *Carolene Products* footnote four, to be explained below.] And that, I believe . . . is a charge that can responsibly be leveled at no other decision [since *West Coast Hotel* in 1937]. . . . The Court continues to disavow the philosophy of *Lochner v. New York*. Yet . . . it is impossible candidly to regard *Roe* as the product of anything else.[26]

(That is the moral of Ely's famous fable as of 1973. But that is not the end of his story, as we shall see in chapter 8.)

I interpret Ely's fable as follows: Since *West Coast Hotel* repudiated *Lochner*'s special judicial protection for substantive economic liberties, every time the Supreme Court has given heightened judicial protection to any constitutional value in any decision, dissenting judges and commentators alike have cried *"Lochner."* These critics have done so frequently and indiscriminately, regardless of whether the decisions in question could be justified—on the basis of inferences from the text, history, or structure of the Constitution—as being within the *Carolene Products* paradigm and its underlying theory of representative democracy. Therefore, Ely contends, when a real case of Lochnering came along, in the form of *Roe*, judges and commentators ignored the cry of *"Lochner."* They had heard that cry too often.

When I teach *Lochner*, I ask my students, why is *Lochner* infamous? What does it mean to summon the ghost of *Lochner*? My answer is that it means to charge someone with doing whatever it was that the Court did in *Lochner* that was so horrible! The response may seem vacuous, but it is not. The point is that constitutional scholars and judges have used *Lochner* as a rhetorical club to criticize their opponents. It is part of what Jamal Greene has called the "anticanon" of constitutional law.[27] I seek to avoid indiscriminate charges of Lochnering by showing that each theory of constitutional interpretation and judicial review has different implications for what, if anything, was wrong with *Lochner*—as well as for the relationship between *Lochner* (i.e., judicial protection of economic liberties) on the one hand, and *Roe* and *Obergefell* (i.e., judicial protection of personal liberties) on the other. Below, I shall offer my own account of what was wrong in *Lochner* and how it differs from *Roe* and *Obergefell*.

I shall sketch several theories' views concerning *Lochner* in relation to *Roe* and *Obergefell*.

· *Deferring to the Representative Process*: For those who believe that courts should defer to legislatures in all types of cases, *Lochner* was wrong simply because the Court did *not defer* to the legislature's interpretation of the Constitution as permitting the regulation of weekly working hours as a valid exercise of the police power. Justice Harlan's dissent in *Lochner* reflects this theory, as does Justice Holmes's dissent.[28] On this view, what was wrong with *Lochner* is also wrong with *Roe* and *Obergefell*. In *Roe*, the Court should have deferred to the state legislature's interpretation of the Constitution as permitting it to ban abortion. In *Obergefell*, the Court should have deferred to the state legislatures' interpretation of the Constitution as permitting it to limit marriage to opposite-sex couples.

· *Originalism*: For those who profess the version of originalism that entails that courts should enforce only the rights enumerated in the text of the Constitution, *Lochner* was wrong because the Court protected "unenumerated" fundamental rights through the Due Process Clause. Justice Scalia espoused this view, as did Robert Bork in his book, *The Tempting of America*.[29] From this standpoint, what was wrong with *Lochner* is also wrong with *Roe* and *Obergefell*. As Scalia put it, *Roe* is wrong because the Constitution doesn't "say anything" about abortion and therefore the states may prohibit it if they choose. And *Obergefell* is wrong because the Constitution doesn't "say anything" about marriage and therefore the states may limit it to opposite-sex couples.

· *Reinforcing the Representative Process*: For those who believe that the Constitution protects only process-oriented rights, what was wrong with *Lochner* is not that the Court protected "unenumerated" fundamental rights through the Due Process Clause, but that it protected "unenumerated" *substantive* fundamental rights, rights that are not essential to the *process* of representative democracy. Justice (later Chief Justice) Stone's footnote four in *United States v. Carolene Products Co.* (1938)—as articulated by Ely's influential book, *Democracy and Distrust*—reflects this vision.[30] On this view, what was wrong with *Lochner* is also wrong with *Roe* (as a matter of substantive due process). But, because he viewed sexual orientation as a "suspicious" classification,[31] Ely would have viewed *Obergefell* as rightly decided (though under the Equal Protection Clause, not the Due Process Clause) because denying the fundamental right to marry to same-sex couples denies them the status and benefits of equal citizenship.

· *Protecting Substantive Fundamental Rights: Personal Liberties*: For those who believe that the Constitution protects not only process-oriented rights, but also substantive fundamental rights essential to personal autonomy, the problem with *Lochner* is that the Court protected the *wrong* substantive fundamental rights, that is, economic liberties as distinguished from personal liberties. Justices Douglas, Brennan, Blackmun, and Stevens, among others, took this view, as did the joint opinion of Justices O'Connor, Kennedy, and Souter in *Casey*.[32] From this standpoint, the Court was wrong to protect substantive *economic* liberties in *Lochner*, but right to protect substantive *personal* liberties in *Roe*, *Casey*, and *Obergefell*. Here we see the most common version of the "double standard" as explained above. On this view, economic liberties in an unregulated marketplace are not fundamental, but being able to make personal decisions such as whether to terminate a pregnancy and whom to marry are.

· *Reinforcing Deliberative Democracy/Status Quo Neutrality*: For those who believe that the Constitution establishes a scheme of deliberative democracy, what was wrong with *Lochner* has nothing to do with protecting "unenumerated" substantive fundamental rights: it was *status quo neutrality*. That is, the

Court took the status quo of existing distributions of wealth and political power as neutral and presumptively justified, such that any governmental regulation of them was presumptively partisan and unconstitutional. Cass Sunstein has articulated the best-known version of this view.[33] This formulation tracks my analysis above of the language of Holmes's dissent in *Lochner* regarding "natural and familiar." From this viewpoint, what was wrong with *Lochner* is unrelated to *Roe* and *Obergefell* because, far from evincing status quo neutrality, the latter cases are justified on the basis of an anti-caste principle of equality that is critical of the status quo. That is, the status quo of traditional restrictions on reproductive freedom and the right to marry denies the status and benefits of equal citizenship for women and for gays and lesbians. Indeed, *Roe* and *Obergefell* are tantamount to a *Brown v. Board of Education* (1954) for women and for gays and lesbians, respectively, vital to securing that status for them. Here we see another version of the "double standard," that is, deferential protection for economic liberties but stringent protection for personal liberties essential to the status and benefits of equal citizenship.

It is striking that on three out of five of these understandings—specifically, the third (Ely's), fourth, and fifth (Sunstein's)—the "grave errors" of *Lochner* are not present in *Obergefell* (nor in *Casey*). It is also striking that Justices Harlan and Holmes in dissent in *Lochner* and Chief Justice Hughes for the majority in *West Coast Hotel* did not make the objections to *Lochner* that are most common in today's criticisms of Lochnering—the most common criticisms of *Roe*, *Casey*, and *Obergefell*. No one objected to the Court's protecting "unenumerated" rights as such. To be sure, Hughes says that "the Constitution does not speak of freedom of contract."[34] But he is arguing that the Constitution does not protect a particular right to freedom of contract; instead, it protects a more abstract right to ordered liberty and due process. No one objected that protecting substantive liberties under the Due Process Clause was a "contradiction in terms" or an "oxymoron"—or that the Due Process Clause is the due *process* clause and therefore that it protects only procedural rights. According to Jamal Greene, that objection takes hold only in 1980 with Ely.[35] And Scalia followed with a version of it.[36]

Finally, no one in *Lochner* or *West Coast Hotel* objected that protecting liberty of contract was not faithful to the original meaning of the Constitution. To the contrary, Justice Sutherland, in dissent in *West Coast Hotel*, forcefully argued that protecting liberty of contract stringently as in *Lochner* is *required* to be faithful to the original meaning of the Constitution.[37] Many contemporary libertarians make similar claims. And so, the invocation of the ghost of *Lochner* in contemporary constitutional law may tell us more about what frightens people today in *Roe*, *Casey*, and *Obergefell* than about what was wrong (or even horrible) in *Lochner* itself!

Lochner's Rehabilitation and Revenge

Notwithstanding the criticisms directed at *Lochner* all this time, some conservatives have argued in recent years that *Lochner*, properly understood or reconstructed, was rightly decided after all. Here we see a split between the "new right" originalist conservatives like Robert Bork and Justice Scalia (who criticize *Lochner*) and the "old right" libertarian conservatives like Bernard Siegan, Richard Epstein, Randy Barnett, David Bernstein, and Ilya Somin (who defend or reconstruct *Lochner*).[38] The new right originalists have argued for "judicial restraint," while the old right libertarians have argued for aggressive judicial protection of what they see as constitutionalist limitations upon majorities (in particular, limitations protecting economic liberties).

Some of the old right libertarians argue that *Lochner* was decided rightly, and the Court should revive aggressive judicial protection of economic liberties as well as continue such protection of personal liberties through the Due Process Clause. In short, on this view, the Court should abandon the "double standard" between these two types of liberties. This view would entail that *Lochner*, along with cases like *Roe* and *Obergefell*, were decided rightly—all involved judicial protection of liberties that are fundamental.[39]

Other old right libertarians argue that *Lochner* was decided rightly, and the Court should revive aggressive judicial protection of economic liberties, but should abandon aggressive judicial protection of personal liberties. In other words, the Court should invert the "double standard." On one version of this view, *Lochner* would have been decided correctly if the maximum-hours law had been struck down on the basis of the Takings Clause of the Fifth Amendment and/or the Contracts Clause of Article I, Section 10, not the Due Process Clause. That is, the Court should aggressively protect economic liberties that are "enumerated" in the Takings Clause and/or the Contracts Clause; but it should not aggressively protect "unenumerated" personal liberties under the Due Process Clause.[40] On such views, *Lochner* was decided rightly, but *Roe* and *Obergefell* were decided wrongly.

These types of argument amount to calls for *Lochner*'s rehabilitation and revenge. Such conservative scholars have sought in various ways to rehabilitate *Lochner* and aggressive judicial protection for economic liberties. And the ghost of *Lochner* has sought revenge on *West Coast Hotel* for forsaking aggressive judicial protection of such liberties. I shall distinguish two phases, corresponding to the two camps of contemporary conservative constitutional theory I just distinguished: the old right libertarians and the new right originalists. (These "phases" are analytical, not chronological; indeed, many of the former come along after many of the latter.) *Lochner's* revenge, phase one, is incarnate in Bork and Scalia. Phase two is embodied in Siegan, Epstein, Barnett, Bernstein, and Somin.[41]

Starting with *Roe*, we see the revenge of *Lochner*, phase one. As noted above, *West Coast Hotel* repudiated aggressive judicial protection of economic liberties, but time would tell that the Supreme Court did not therewith repudiate aggressive judicial protection of personal liberties that are "implicit in the concept of ordered liberty" (to recall the formulation from *Palko v. Connecticut*, decided the same year, 1937).[42] *Lochner's* revenge, phase one, is the cry by conservatives like Bork and Scalia against liberals: if, after *West Coast Hotel*, we conservatives can't have the economic liberties we hold dear (*Lochner*), you liberals can't have the personal liberties you cherish (*Roe* and *Obergefell*). It is commonplace for such conservatives to invoke or echo Justice Holmes's famous line in dissent in *Lochner*: "The Fourteenth Amendment does not enact Mr. Herbert Spencer's *Social Statics*."[43]

Why do I call this *Lochner's* revenge? It is the revenge of conservative champions of economic liberty protected in *Lochner* against the liberals who repudiated *Lochner* in *West Coast Hotel*. First, these conservatives basically have said, although we as conservatives hold economic liberties dear—and under our perfect Constitution there would be aggressive judicial protection of them as in the *Lochner* era—we are pillars of virtue and "judicial restraint," and so we renounce such aggressive judicial protection of economic liberties under our actual Constitution.

Second, these conservatives accordingly have demanded that liberals who cherish personal liberties—and under whose perfect Constitution there would be aggressive judicial protection of such liberties—must likewise show virtue and "judicial restraint" by abnegating such aggressive judicial protection of personal liberties under our actual Constitution. In other words, the new right originalists have purported to demonstrate their virtue by spurning *Lochner*, and they demand that liberals likewise be virtuous by repudiating *Roe*. Bork and Scalia are the most conspicuous illustrations. You can see why it becomes important for such conservatives to vilify *Lochner* in order to take the high ground in vilifying *Roe* and liberal constitutional theory more generally. They oppose a "double standard" of deferential judicial review where economic liberties are concerned but aggressive judicial review where personal liberties are at issue.

During the Reagan administration, we saw the emergence of the revenge of *Lochner*, phase two. Phase two is more radical than phase one. The old right libertarians—who had championed aggressive judicial protection for economic liberties during the *Lochner* era—rise again. Their contemporary successors seek revenge on *West Coast Hotel* by claiming that *Lochner* was rightly decided after all and indeed should be rehabilitated or resurrected.

I should sharpen the distinction between the two varieties of the old right libertarians sketched above. The first is epitomized by Bernard Siegan, the second by Richard Epstein. Siegan would revive *Lochner* and abolish the double standard, in favor of aggressive judicial protection of not only economic liberties but also personal liberties. Put bluntly, conservatives get *Lochner* and liberals get *Roe*.[44] Epstein, on the other hand, would revive *Lochner* but invert the double standard, in favor of aggressive judicial protection of economic liberties but not personal liberties. Put bluntly, conservatives get *Lochner*, but liberals do not get *Roe*.[45]

How does Chief Justice Roberts's dissent in *Obergefell* relate to these camps of conservative constitutional theory? Roberts's dissent embodies *Lochner*'s revenge, phase one (with Bork and Scalia). He blasts *Obergefell*, charging it with repeating the "grave errors" of *Lochner*, just as Bork and Scalia would. Roberts ignores or rejects *Lochner*'s revenge, phase two. Indeed, his dissent is curiously out of step with some contemporary conservative constitutional theory concerning *Lochner*.[46]

An entire generation of libertarian scholars has labored long and hard in rehabilitating *Lochner*. They are representatives of the old right libertarians who seek *Lochner*'s revenge, phase two. Scholars such as Barnett, Somin, and Bernstein have rejected the new right originalists' understanding of what was wrong in *Lochner* and its professed commitment to "judicial restraint." Their rehabilitations of *Lochner* have embodied a newer generation's version of the old right libertarian understanding that *Lochner* was rightly decided—and they are committed to reviving aggressive judicial enforcement of what they conceive as constitutionalist limitations upon majorities. They represent "the return of Justice George Sutherland"—to quote the title of Hadley Arkes's book.[47] As noted above, Justice Sutherland dissented in *West Coast Hotel* from its repudiation of the *Lochner* era. Some seek to restore a jurisprudence of what they (like Justice Sutherland) conceive as natural rights—in particular, economic liberties—in the form of an originalism. Many such libertarian conservatives must have been dismayed by Roberts's dissent in *Obergefell*, which spoke of the "grave errors" of *Lochner*. For it strongly suggested that the long-awaited rehabilitation of *Lochner* had not yet reached the Supreme Court.

What Is the Best Account of What Was Wrong in *Lochner*?

Now, I shall sketch my own account of what was wrong in *Lochner*. It is a synthesis of the views sketched above under *Protecting Substantive Fundamental Rights: Personal Liberties* and *Reinforcing Deliberative Democracy/Status Quo Neutrality*. On this variation, economic liberties and property rights, like personal liberties, are fundamental liberties secured by the Constitution. In fact, economic liberties and property rights are so fundamental in the constitutional scheme, and so sacred in the constitutional culture, that there is neither need nor good argument for aggressive judicial protection of them. Rather, such liberties are understood properly as "judicially underenforced norms," to use Lawrence G. Sager's term.[48] As Cass Sunstein would put it, their fuller enforcement and protection is secure with legislatures and executives in "the Constitution outside the courts."[49]

On this view, the Court was wrong to fear that basic *economic* liberties needed heightened protection in *Lochner*, but right to see that basic *personal* liberties—those significant for personal self-government—warrant more searching judicial protection in *Roe*, *Casey*, and *Obergefell*.[50] For, unlike economic liberties, personal liberties like reproductive freedom and freedom to marry are vulnerable in the political process. Specifically, these personal liberties are vulnerable to majoritarian efforts (1) to coerce conceptions of the good life upon pregnant women, such as how best to respect the sanctity of life in *Roe* and *Casey*, and (2) to deny the status and benefits of equal citizenship to some, such as gays and lesbians in *Obergefell*.

The fact that economic liberties are fundamental by itself does not justify aggressive judicial review protecting them, for there is every indication that they can and do fend well enough for themselves in the political process. It is important to distinguish between (1) the partial, judicially enforceable Constitution and (2) the whole Constitution that is binding outside the courts upon legislatures and executives in our constitutional democracy.[51] *Constitutional* theory is broader than theory of *judicial review*. I fear that many libertarian proponents of aggressive judicial protection for economic liberties do not recognize this distinction. Apparently, these libertarians assume that if economic liberties are not stringently enforced judicially, they have no protection in our constitutional scheme!

What turns on this distinction—between the partial, judicially enforceable Constitution and the whole Constitution that is binding outside the courts—is whether protection of constitutional rights is to be conceived as confined to judicial enforcement or to also include enforcement by legislatures and executives. A right that is not judicially enforceable nonetheless imposes obligations upon legislatures and executives to respect it or indeed to protect it affirmatively. We need to remember that legislatures and executives, as well as courts, have responsibilities to interpret the Constitution conscientiously so as to secure our basic liberties.

I realize that in our current court-centered constitutional culture and practice, this argument may be incomprehensible to court-lovers. Many disparage and fear legislatures, especially when it comes to protecting fundamental rights, while glorifying and trusting courts. At any rate, many trust courts more than legislatures to protect rights. Let me work up to the idea that some basic liberties are properly judicially underenforced and are secure in the Constitution outside the courts.

Here, I would recall 1938, not 1937, and relate my argument to *Carolene Products*. In the aftermath of the Court's repudiation of *Lochner* in *West Coast Hotel* (1937), *Carolene Products* (1938) presumed that deferential rational basis judicial review is appropriate in general, and in particular where legislation touching upon economic liberties is concerned. But footnote four, in its three paragraphs, intimates three exceptions where a "more searching judicial scrutiny" may be appropriate—namely, regulations implicating: (1) specific prohibition of the Constitution; (2) restrictions on the political process; and (3) corruption of the political process through prejudice against discrete and insular minorities.[52]

In *Democracy and Distrust*, Ely famously elaborated footnote four as presenting situations of "distrust": that is, situations where we could not trust the outcomes of the political process to be legitimate. In those situations, more searching judicial scrutiny may be justifiable. He argued—and he was right—that the regulation of economic liberties and property rights does not come within any of the situations of distrust of the *Carolene Products* framework that would warrant more searching judicial protection.[53]

I shall consider briefly two arguments to the contrary. One has been made by the libertarian Richard Epstein (*Lochner*'s revenge, phase two), and the other might be attributed to James Madison (though Madison himself did not make the argument). Neither is persuasive. First, Epstein has argued for bringing the "politics of distrust," which has operated in the scrutiny of restrictions upon and regulations of freedom of speech (the second paragraph of *Carolene Products*), to bear in justifying aggressive judicial scrutiny of regulations of economic liberties and property rights.[54] That is, he believes that we should not trust governmental regulation of economic liberties and property rights any more than we should trust governmental restrictions upon freedom of speech. In response, Frank Michelman argued cogently that there are "functional differences between expressive liberties on the one hand, and proprietary and economic liberties on the other, [that] can amply explain and justify a practice of exceptionally strict judicial scrutiny of laws directly infringing expressive liberties" but not proprietary and economic liberties. He argued further that distrust of lawmakers should not be exaggerated into a universal solvent that corrodes the legitimacy of all legislation.[55] As I would put Michelman's argument rebutting Epstein, *Carolene Products* does not stem from a libertarian theory of limited government that carries a presumption in favor of liberty and entails distrust of all governmental regulation.

Second, Madison might be invoked in support of an argument that the regulation of economic liberties and property rights constitutes a situation of distrust and poses dangers of a tyranny of the majority.[56] There are three responses to this line of argument. One, in response to his worry about a tyranny of the majority regarding property rights, Madison did not argue for aggressive judicial protection of such rights; instead, he argued for an "extended republic" (as contrasted with a small republic) as affording the best security against a tyranny of the majority over property rights and, for that matter, rights in general.[57] Two, William Treanor has argued persuasively that the original understanding—including Madison's understanding—supports deference to the political process where regulation of economic liberties and property rights is concerned. Treanor advocates judicial underenforcement of such liberties, except in situations of *Carolene Products*–style distrust, as for example in environmental racism.[58] Three, in any event, Madison presumably contemplated a situation more like class warfare, and a tyranny of the majority of non-wealthy over the minority of wealthy. It strains credulity to think that the regulation of economic liberties and property rights that we see today in the US involves anything like class warfare of this sort. There are few countries on earth where economic liberties and property rights are more secure than in ours—even without aggressive judicial protection of them, they are secure in the Constitution outside the courts. The only economic phenomenon in the US approaching class warfare is "the war against the poor,"[59] which is waged not just by the rich but also by the middle class and the working class. In short, it is waged by the non-poor against the poor.

To be sure, libertarians like Epstein, Barnett, or Somin will not be persuaded by my distinction between economic liberties and personal liberties and my argument that there is neither need nor good argument for aggressive judicial protection of economic liberties. With all due respect, whether I can persuade such libertarian scholars should not be the criterion for a successful argument, any more than whether I could persuade Justice

Scalia that *Roe* and *Obergefell* were rightly decided would be an appropriate criterion for success. It should be enough to make a coherent, sustained argument showing the practice of substantive due process in its best light and fairly grappling with the objections to it.

The reader may ask whether I have heard of *Kelo v. City of New London* (2005) and the enormous controversy it generated about the jurisprudence of eminent domain, one form of regulation of economic liberties. In that case, the Supreme Court upheld a city's condemnation of privately owned real property so that it could be used as part of a "comprehensive redevelopment plan" by a private developer.[60] Proponents of aggressive judicial protection for property rights might argue that it shows that such rights are not secure in the US.[61] In fact, the controversy over *Kelo* confirms my argument rather than undermining it: for *Kelo* prompted the "property rights movement," including forty-five state legislatures passing laws forbidding the very kind of "taking" of property for economic development upheld in that case.[62] Clearly, *Kelo* supports my arguments that economic liberties fend quite well for themselves through the political process and that there is no need for aggressive judicial protection of them.

Indeed, I daresay we need aggressive judicial protection for economic liberties about as much as we need aggressive judicial protection for my right to eat apple pie and my right to fly my flag on my front porch on the Fourth of July. Let me explain. Suppose I take the view that unless there is aggressive judicial protection for a right, there is no protection for the right. Suppose I decry the state of things in the US, in which there is no Supreme Court decision protecting my right to eat apple pie and my right to fly my flag on my front porch on the Fourth of July—while there are decisions protecting the right to decide whether to terminate a pregnancy and the right of same-sex couples to marry. Suppose I denounce this as an outrage—an inversion of any proper ordering of constitutional values. How should you respond to me? You should say that there is no need for aggressive judicial protection of my right to eat apple pie or my right to fly my flag on my front porch. To be sure, there might be background regulations concerning the food ingredients of a pie and the fabric of a flag. But we would think that those regulations are justified by adequate reasons—health and safety reasons—and that these reasons are not "mere pretexts," notwithstanding *Lochner*. And we should have no fear that the rights to eat apple pie and to fly a flag are endangered by such regulations. We can trust that any serious attempt to restrict eating apple pie and flying flags would trigger swift and sure outrage and legislative protection—these rights would not require judicial protection.

So it is with economic liberties in the US. Thus, despite the views of economic libertarians, the opportunity for consenting adults to perform capitalistic acts in private without governmental regulation is not among the stringently judicially enforced fundamental rights.[63] Much regulation that would be, as *Lochner* put it, "meddlesome interferences with the rights of the individual"[64] in a libertarian, private society is legitimate, important, or even compelling in a constitutional democracy such as our own.

To recapitulate: the fact that a right is fundamental by itself does not justify aggressive judicial review protecting it. We still need an argument that we cannot trust the ordinary political process to respect and protect it and therefore that aggressive judicial review is warranted. And the fact that there is not aggressive judicial protection for economic liberties by itself does not mean that there is no protection for such liberties. Can anyone say with a straight face that there is no protection for economic liberties in the US? Or can anyone say with a straight face that there is less protection for property rights than for reproductive rights or gay and lesbian rights?

The regulation of economic liberties does not present a situation of distrust of the ordinary political process that would warrant more searching judicial protection. Instead, it is appropriate to trust the political process and apply the deferential rational basis scrutiny of economic regulations Hughes contemplated in *West Coast Hotel*: there generally is an adequate reason for economic regulations in the common interest and for the common good. Even if we put some bite into rational basis scrutiny of economic regulations, they would be justified.

A question lurking in the background of this chapter concerns how the Supreme Court would view regulations of businesses during the COVID-19 pandemic. As discussed above, the *Lochner* Court was dubious about "health" as a justification for regulations touching upon economic liberties. But the same year that the Court decided *Lochner*, it decided *Jacobson v. Massachusetts*, upholding a compulsory vaccination for smallpox to promote the public health.[65] In any case, in the *West Coast Hotel-Williamson* era, during a pandemic like COVID-19, courts rightly would not be terribly suspicious of a public health justification for regulations of economic liberties like those of stay-at-home orders, especially given the limited duration of such orders. Understandably, proponents of economic liberties have been emboldened since the 2016 election of Donald Trump as President and his transformation of the federal judiciary in a hard-right conservative direction (not to mention his politicization of the COVID-19 pandemic). But even in such an era, courts generally have not accepted economic liberty arguments as grounds for invalidating COVID-19 pandemic regulations. The courts that invalidated such regulations typically did so on the ground that the government had exceeded its emergency powers. Whether the new 6-3 conservative majority of the Supreme Court might strike down such regulations in the future remains to be seen. We already have seen that that new majority has accepted religious liberty arguments as a ground for doing so.[66]

Vanquishing the Ghost of *Lochner*

My aim is not to vilify *Lochner* but to justify our practice of substantive due process, including cases like *Roe*, *Casey*, and *Obergefell*. In chapter 2, I listed the basic liberties the Court has protected through that practice and that list bears repeating: "liberty of conscience and freedom of thought; freedom of association, including both expressive association and intimate association, whatever one's sexual orientation; the right to live with one's family, whether nuclear or extended; the right to travel or relocate; the right to marry, whatever the gender of one's partner; the right to decide whether to bear or beget children, including the rights to procreate, to use contraceptives, and to terminate a pregnancy; the right to direct the education and rearing of children, including the right to make decisions concerning their care, custody, and control; and the right to exercise dominion over one's body, including the right to bodily integrity and ultimately the right to die (at least to the extent of the right to refuse unwanted medical treatment)."

I ask you: Does that list look like spooky, subjective "philosophical predilections" or "moral intuitions" that some rogue justices made up as rights and imposed upon the rest of us in the guise of interpreting the Constitution, as Justice Scalia asserts?[67] Or does the list represent a coherent practice of protecting basic liberties significant for personal self-government: securing the preconditions for people to make certain basic decisions fundamentally affecting their destiny, identity, or way of life, whatever their own moral or religious views, without compulsion from the state? In chapters 2 and 3, I argued that the practice of substantive due process—protecting the basic liberties on this list through common law constitutional interpretation—stems from reasoned judgment about the best understanding of our commitments to ordered liberty and such personal self-government. This list of basic liberties has nothing to do with *Lochner*. *Lochner* was not concerned with protecting the right to make such decisions; rather, it reflected status quo neutrality.

My related aim is to show that the ghost of *Lochner* is an apparition fabricated by opponents of modern substantive due process. The Supreme Court did not do anything *horrible*—as a matter of constitutional interpretation—in *Lochner*. (I concede, though, that what the Court did in the *Lochner* era was horrible in its impact upon our social and economic world: disabling the federal and state governments from protecting against human suffering.) To be sure, the Court was *wrong* to treat liberty of contract as being in need of aggressive judicial protection. And it was wrong to treat the status quo of existing distributions of wealth and political power as neutral and presumptively justified, such that any governmental regulation of them was presumptively partisan and unconstitutional. But I would distinguish being horrible from simply being wrong. Furthermore, in *Lochner*, the Court was wrong to fear the slippery slope concerning the police power and constitutional limitations. It was wrong not to appreciate that economic liberties—though basic—are subject to regulation for the common good. It was wrong to overlook that protection of economic liberties is secure in the Constitution outside the courts.

But none of these errors in *Lochner* has anything to do with the basic liberties protected in *Roe*, *Casey*, and *Obergefell* or with the practice of substantive due process as such. That *Lochner* was wrongly decided does not justify demonizing or throwing out the whole practice of protecting such basic liberties.

Fidelity in constitutional interpretation does not require the same level of judicial protection for economic liberties as for personal liberties. We should not let the ghost of *Lochner* frighten us away from substantive due process, this noble practice of protecting rights to make certain decisions significant for personal self-government. These rights shield persons from majoritarian compulsion concerning such decisions and help secure for them the status and benefits of equal citizenship. Extending basic liberties like the right to intimate association and to marry, already recognized for straights, to gays and lesbians is not analogous to reading the Constitution to embody a libertarian economic theory.

I shall close with an invocation of Shakespeare's *Henry IV, Part 1* concerning the summoning of ghosts. Justice Scalia and Chief Justice Roberts, like Glendower, warned: "I can call spirits from the vasty deep." Translation: I can call the ghost of *Lochner* and warn that it will destroy the Supreme Court and the Constitution. This chapter, like Hotspur, has given a rejoinder: "Why, so can I, or so can any man, But will they come when you do call for them?"[68] Translation: calling the ghost of *Lochner* is hot air. Put another way, calling the ghost of *Lochner* is like crying "wolf" in Ely's fable. But there is no real ghost and no real wolf, just our practice of securing the basic liberties that are preconditions for social cooperation on the basis of mutual respect and trust in our diverse constitutional democracy. Cases like *Roe*, *Casey*, and *Obergefell* secure such basic liberties and, contrary to Justice Scalia's assertion in *Casey* and Chief Justice Roberts's assertion in *Obergefell*, do not repeat the "grave errors" of *Lochner*.

Does Substantive Due Process Enact Mill's *On Liberty*?

As observed in chapter 6, it is commonplace for critics of substantive due process to invoke Justice Holmes's famous dissent in the infamous case of *Lochner v. New York* (1905): "The Fourteenth Amendment does not enact Herbert Spencer's *Social Statics.*"[1] These critics are charging the Supreme Court with reading its own favored economic or moral theory into the Constitution in the guise of interpreting it. Another common move is to echo Holmes's dissent by objecting: "The Constitution does not enact John Stuart Mill's *On Liberty* any more than it enacts Herbert Spencer's *Social Statics.*"[2] In *On Liberty* (1859), as discussed in chapters 4 and 5, Mill argued that the only justification for government to restrict individual liberty is to prevent harm to others.[3] Both the invocation and the echo of Holmes's dissent dramatically appeared in Chief Justice Roberts's scolding dissent in *Obergefell v. Hodges* (2015), the case holding that the fundamental right to marry, already recognized for opposite-sex couples, extends to same-sex couples as well.[4]

This move of echoing Holmes's dissent—with the line about Mill—passes for sophistication and many think it clever and dispositive. But Roberts's move may be more a rhetorical trope than a rigorous substantive critique of the line of cases culminating in *Obergefell*. Indeed, I argue, Roberts's echo of Holmes's dissent represents an attempt to imitate the cleverness of Holmes. In *Yankee from Olympus: Justice Holmes and His Family*, Catherine Drinker Bowen reports that Holmes's father motivated his children to be clever by rewarding the child who made the cleverest remark at the evening tea table with a spoonful of jam.[5] In his dissent in *Lochner*, Holmes is seeking to be clever and, for his line about Herbert Spencer, the legal profession has rewarded him with innumerable spoonfuls, if not vats, of jam. What is more, Holmes notoriously valued being clever and quotable over being rigorous, fair, or clear.[6]

In his dissent in *Obergefell*, Roberts is likewise substituting cleverness for rigor. Repeating the lines about Spencer and Mill, he says something clever that bypasses rigorous substantive argument and cannot withstand careful substantive analysis, yet is nonetheless rhetorically effective in blasting the practice of substantive due process. Roberts could simply have objected to protecting the right to autonomy or the right of same-sex couples to marry. Or he might even have protested, "Where in the Constitution does it say that government may not regulate conduct unless it poses a risk of harm to others?" But such utterances would not be clever enough to deserve the jam. The jam goes to the child of Holmes who utters the line: "The Fourteenth Amendment does not enact Mill's *On Liberty*."

Does Roberts's echo of Holmes's dissent simply replicate the charge of Lochnering? The objection regarding Mill may add something to and be more effective than the charge of Lochnering. As observed in chapter 6, people may have heard the cries of *Lochner* too often and so they may no longer respond with alarm to it.[7] If so, charging the Court with reading Mill's *On Liberty* into the Constitution may concern people more. Moreover, people nowadays probably have no familiarity with Spencer's *Social Statics* (beyond Holmes's dissent), but many have a general familiarity with Mill's *On Liberty* (quite apart from Roberts's dissent). If so, they may find it more intelligible and more plausible to charge the Court with reading Mill's harm principle into the Constitution whenever it strikes down traditional morals legislation.

What exactly do critics mean when they protest that "the Fourteenth Amendment does not enact Mill's *On Liberty*"? First, they may be objecting literally to what they see as the Court's reading Mill's (or a Millian) conception of liberty (including his harm principle) into the Constitution. Second, they may be objecting more generally to the Court's protecting a conception of liberty that includes a right of autonomy—whether or not the cases really do reflect Mill's (or a Millian) conception of liberty. Third, they may be objecting still more generally to the Court's substantive due process jurisprudence—protecting substantive basic liberties central to many liberal conceptions—rather than to its protecting Mill's (or a Millian) conception of liberty.

Or fourth, critics may be objecting yet more abstractly to moral readings of the Constitution as such.[8] For example, they may reject conceptions of liberty as embodying an abstract moral principle as opposed to enacting a concrete historical rule or practice. And they may reject conceptions of the Constitution as a charter of abstract moral and political principles to be built out over time on the basis of normative judgments about the best understanding of our constitutional commitments—as opposed to conceptions of it as a code of concrete historical rules or practices whose meaning is to be determined by historical research to discover relatively specific original meanings of the framers and ratifiers. And so, they may slam moral readings of the Constitution by asserting that they entail reading the Constitution to "enact" a particular text of moral theory and thereby to displace the authority of the framers and ratifiers with that of a foreign author (both Spencer and Mill were British).

Perhaps we should forget all of the foregoing possible meanings, which assume that critics who object that the Constitution does not enact Mill's *On Liberty* are trying to make coherent substantive arguments. Instead, they may simply be repeating the line as a piece of rhetoric that seeks to delegitimate substantive due process altogether. The line gives conservative critics of our practice of protecting substantive liberties, including the right of autonomy, a quotable slogan for a put-down. It makes substantive due process look ridiculous. It makes it look like the Court is illegitimately imposing external authority (and foreign external authority at that). It makes it sound like the Court is imposing a particular comprehensive moral conception of the good life—Mill's perfectionist conception of individuality—and thereby subverting the Constitution, which is said to be "made for people of fundamentally differing views" (to return to Holmes's dissent in *Lochner*).[9]

In this chapter, I inquire whether *Obergefell* and the line of substantive due process cases leading up to it illegitimately interpret the Fourteenth Amendment to enact Mill's *On Liberty*, as Chief Justice Roberts asserts. I begin by analyzing Roberts's assertion as a substantive argument about the content of our constitutional commitment to liberty, asking whether Justice Kennedy's majority opinion in *Obergefell* and prior cases in fact read anything like Mill's conception of liberty—in particular, his harm principle—into the Fourteenth Amendment's protection of liberty. I also examine Roberts's assertion as a substantive argument about the nature of constitutional interpretation, considering (1) whether the substantive due process cases involve anything like reading the Constitution to enact a particular comprehensive moral conception such as Mill's; (2) whether they more generally reflect a moral reading of the Constitution; and (3) what the differences are between these two. The cases do protect a right to autonomy, but it is very different from Mill's perfectionist conception of cultivating individuality and his harm principle. Moreover, the cases do embody a moral reading, but that is quite different from, and more defensible than, reading Mill's comprehensive moral conception into the Constitution. I conclude the chapter by returning to polygamy.

In chapter 4, I analyzed Roberts's argument that *Obergefell*'s protection of a right of same-sex couples to marry puts us on a slippery slope to a right to plural marriage. In this chapter, I assess his argument that *Obergefell* interprets the Constitution to enact Mill's *On Liberty*. Jonathan Turley has made a Millian argument, rooted in the harm principle, for a right to polygamy. I reject his argument together with his contention that opposition to polygamy stems from objectionable legal enforcement of liberal morals.

My general contention is that Roberts's echo of Holmes's dissent—the line about Mill—is unsound as an account of our actual line of cases protecting substantive liberties and of the actual nature of constitutional interpretation manifested in those cases. It ignores the rationales for protecting basic liberties that the Court has developed. It also ignores the practice of common law constitutional interpretation—building out our constitutional commitments to liberty through reasoning by analogy from one case to the next rather than through imposing an abstract moral theory—that the Court has applied. In short, Roberts's line about Mill is not true to our practice of substantive due process. It is a substantively fallacious rhetorical move aimed at damning the enterprise of protecting basic liberties under the Due Process Clause.

Roberts's Echo of Holmes's Dissent

In assessing Roberts's echo of Holmes's dissent, I shall distinguish two versions of the charge that the Supreme Court is reading the Constitution to enact Mill's *On Liberty*. The first is that the Court is reading the Constitution to enact Mill's (or a Millian) "harm principle." The second is that it is reading the Constitution to enact (what John Hart Ely called) a Millian "right to be different."[10] Let me preview my argument regarding each of these versions.

- *Harm principle*: Harm arguments have appeared in constitutional law cases protecting substantive liberties under the Due Process Clause, but they have not operated as a Millian harm principle.
- *Right to be different*: Autonomy arguments are central in constitutional law cases protecting substantive liberties, but they have not protected a Millian right to be different. That is, the cases have not been animated by a Millian cultivation of individuality.

The Supreme Court Has Not Read the Constitution to Enact Mill's Harm Principle

The development of substantive due process jurisprudence in US constitutional law has not been the unfolding of Mill's (or a Millian) harm principle. Most of the cases protecting substantive liberties have nothing to do with harm to others—and the liberties are not justified on the Millian ground (1) that they do not inflict harm on others but are merely self-regarding and therefore (2) that government has no business regulating them. I shall go through some of the most prominent cases leading up to *Obergefell* to support my claim (and to rebut Roberts's assertion).

Let's begin with *Griswold v. Connecticut* (1965), the first case explicitly to protect a constitutional right to privacy. That case invalidated traditional morals legislation, from the era of Anthony Comstock, prohibiting the use of contraceptives by married couples. It had nothing to do with the harm principle (or no harm to others). One could imagine plaintiffs in that case making a harm principle argument: that married couples' use of contraceptives imposes no harm on others, therefore the government may not regulate it, and indeed married couples have a right to use contraceptives. But the Court did not make such an argument. To be sure, the Court was concerned that permitting government to outlaw married couples' use of contraceptives, or to break into the "sacred precincts of the marital bedroom" to search for evidence of the use of contraceptives, would harm the "intimate relation" of husband and wife in the privacy of the home.[11] That violation of marital privacy—not the idea that married couples using contraceptives were not harming anyone else—was the ground for invalidating the law. And Justice Douglas's majority opinion defended the right of marital privacy on the basis of the moral goods or noble purposes furthered by the institution of marriage, not on any ground that celebrated cultivating or realizing the individuality of the people who were using contraceptives.[12]

Eisenstadt v. Baird (1972) extended the right of privacy from the intimate relation of husband and wife to the individual, married or single. It did not protect that right because receiving contraceptives and using them would not inflict harm on others. Rather, the Court protected the right of the individual, married or single, to make certain important decisions such as whether to bear or beget a child.[13]

Moreover, Mill's harm principle is neither explicit nor implicit in *Roe v. Wade* (1973). There, the Court protected the right of a woman to decide whether to terminate her pregnancy. The opinion is grounded in a right of privacy, understood as a right of autonomy to make a decision so fundamentally affecting one's destiny as whether to bear or beget a child. The Court in *Roe* did not justify that right on the ground that a woman's getting an abortion imposes no harm on others. Indeed, the only way that harm comes into the opinion is in the Court's acknowledgment that denying the right would impose distress or harm upon pregnant women.[14] That is not Mill's harm principle.

Yet critics of *Roe*, including Judge Henry Friendly, have argued that interpreting the Constitution to protect a woman's right to decide whether to terminate her pregnancy illegitimately interprets the Constitution to enact Mill's
On Liberty. Judge Randolph of the US Court of Appeals for the DC Circuit,
who was Friendly's law clerk at the time, has told the story of Friendly's draft-
ing an unpublished opinion to that effect in a case the Second Circuit Court
of Appeals decided just before *Roe*.[15] Randolph reports that Friendly went on
a cruise with his wife to Panama but was so agitated about the case that he
drafted an opinion, without any of the record or briefs or precedents in front
of him, while on the cruise. It shows: Friendly was responding to an argument
that no one was making and that was not implicit in the precedents. And he
did so in a gratuitous way wholly unnecessary to resolve the case before him.
Randolph should have been a loyal law clerk and protected Friendly's reputa-
tion by not telling the story rather than presenting it as an illustration of the
great wisdom of the great judge. This misguided and unfounded interpretation passes for great wisdom among Friendly's law clerks, including Chief
Justice Roberts, who invoked Friendly's argument in his dissent in *Obergefell*.[16]

In *Bowers v. Hardwick* (1986), the Court rudely dismissed Michael Hardwick's arguments for a right to intimate association for gays and lesbians as
"facetious"—as if he were making libertarian arguments against the legal
enforcement of morals as such or harm principle arguments.[17] In their brief
for Hardwick, Laurence Tribe and Kathleen Sullivan specifically denied that
they were making such arguments: "Respondent obviously does not contend that the Fourteenth Amendment enacted John Stuart Mill's *On Liberty*, any more than it enacted Herbert Spencer's *Social Statics*."[18] The Court
nonetheless may have assumed that something like Mill's harm principle
must underlie a challenge to the legal enforcement of traditional morals.
The amicus brief of the Rutherford Institute certainly encouraged the Court
to make that assumption, asserting: "The manner in which American courts
have been influenced by Mill is astounding."[19] In any case, the dissenters in
Bowers do not rest upon the harm principle in arguing for a right of gays and
lesbians to privacy or autonomy with respect to their intimate associations.
Justice Blackmun in dissent quotes H. L. A. Hart's famous criticism of Lord
Patrick Devlin, *Immorality and Treason*, not for Hart's reworking of Mill's
harm principle, but for his argument that it is preposterous to think that
same-sex sexual intimacy is analogous to treason and threatens the disintegration of the moral fabric of society.[20]

Lawrence v. Texas (2003) does mention harm—stating that sexual intimacy between consenting adults of the same sex does not inflict harm on
others or on an institution worth protecting.[21] But, as we saw in chapter 4,

the Court makes a harm argument as a shield to limit the extension of liberty, not a harm principle argument as a sword to invalidate all morals legislation punishing victimless crimes.

How do harm arguments operate in *Obergefell?* To be sure, as discussed in chapter 4, Justice Kennedy does say that same-sex marriage "pose[s] no risk of harm to [the couples] themselves or third parties."[22] But, again, he is not saying—in the spirit of Mill—that the only ground for government to restrict individual liberty is to prevent harm to others. Indeed, if he were enacting Mill, he would not have mentioned that same-sex marriage poses no risk of harm to the couples themselves. For the only harm that would be relevant would be harm to others. Instead, Kennedy pens this line to reject the argument that extending marriage to same-sex couples will harm the institution of marriage, leading straight couples not to marry.[23] Kennedy does not use Mill's harm principle as a *sword* to attack all traditional morals legislation and to extend liberties—to protect all self-regarding conduct and to limit the jurisdiction of government to regulating only other-regarding acts. Instead, he uses harm arguments to draw distinctions to avert the slippery slope—as a *shield* against extending liberties to activities that *do* threaten to impose harm on others or on institutions like marriage.

Notwithstanding Mill's harm principle, we see references to harm in constitutional law and in law generally in arguments that rights *do* permit persons to inflict irremediable harm upon others as well as against the common good. Here the two main ideas are that (1) as Ronald Dworkin famously put it, "[a] right against the Government must be a right to do something even when the majority thinks it would be wrong to do it, and even when the majority would be worse off for having it done," which seems to imply that a right permits one to inflict harm as against the common good,[24] and (2) as Jack Balkin put it in developing a more general conception of rights, "a legal right is a privilege to inflict harm that is either not legally cognizable or is . . . without legal remedy," which seems to imply that a right permits one to inflict harm upon others.[25] The First Amendment's protection of freedom of speech is a clear case of a right to inflict irremediable harm upon others as well as against the common good.[26] These understandings of rights as permitting persons to inflict such irremediable harm hardly presume that the Constitution enacts Mill's harm principle. In fact, they are contrary to it.

In sum, the decisions from *Griswold* to *Obergefell* striking down traditional morals legislation have not been animated by Mill's harm principle. More generally, it is hardly the case that Mill has a trademark on the term "harm" and that every time anyone uses that word in a constitutional law case they are invoking or evoking Mill.

The Supreme Court Has Not Protected a Millian "Right to Be Different"

Even if not to enact Mill's harm principle, has the Supreme Court interpreted the Constitution to enact a Millian "right to be different"? Writing
in 1981, Ely mocked the right to autonomy protected in substantive due
process cases as "the right to be different," belittling it as being an "upper-
middle-class right"—"the right of my son to wear his hair as long as he
pleases"—or as reflecting the values of the "reasoning class." Moreover, because the best-known liberal conception of autonomy or individuality is
that of Mill, Ely rolled out the inevitable paraphrase of Justice Holmes's dissent in *Lochner*: "If the Constitution does not enact Herbert Spencer's *Social
Statics*, does it enact John Stuart Mill's *On Liberty?*"[27]

The substantive due process cases leading up to *Obergefell* have protected
rights of autonomy, but such rights are hardly peculiarly Millian. Mill did
not hold a trademark on autonomy arguments any more than on harm
arguments. Cases protecting rights of autonomy are not necessarily protecting a Millian "right to be different." "Mill's defense of liberty rested on the
assumption that human beings were diverse in their nature and needed diverse circumstances within which to develop and flourish. He also appealed
to the value to society of being able to observe different 'experiments in living' and learn from them."[28] Our substantive due process cases, unlike Mill's
perfectionist conception of promoting human flourishing, do not cultivate
individuality, "experiments in living," the higher faculties, or "being different"
as a comprehensive moral conception of the good life. Instead, the cases ask:
what basic liberties are essential to ordered liberty?

Consider the right to wear one's hair as long as one pleases (which Ely
mocks) or the right to loaf. Although Justices Marshall (in dissent) and
Douglas (in concurrence) argued during the early years of the Burger Court
that the Constitution does protect such rights, I fear that they may have extended the idea of autonomy too far, well beyond constitutional essentials
to a romantic ideal of self-fulfillment or the development of one's individuality, tastes, and personality[29]—that is, to a Millian "right to be different."
But no majority opinion of the Supreme Court has ever adopted such an
idea. Our actual practice of substantive due process from *Meyer v. Nebraska*
(1923) through *Griswold* (1965) on up to *Obergefell* (2015) has tethered
constitutional rights of autonomy to the structure of basic liberties that are
essential to ordered liberty or, as I have argued, significant for personal self-
government or deliberative autonomy.[30] It has not tried to secure, as constitutional rights, whatever liberties are entailed by comprehensive moral
views of individuality or autonomy like Mill's.

I do not mean to trivialize the significance of hair length or loafing in any particular conception of the good or ideal of self-fulfillment, or to deny that there may be good arguments against regulations that encroach on such liberty claims. But advancing such claims as constitutional rights has provided fodder for those who would trivialize the more significant basic liberties our practice of substantive due process has protected, making it too easy to caricature arguments for such rights. Perhaps notions of individuality or self-fulfillment like those expressed by Justices Marshall and Douglas frightened the conservative Burger, Rehnquist, and Roberts Courts and fueled their flight to narrow the Due Process inquiry (as discussed in chapter 2) from aspirational principles in cases like *Planned Parenthood v. Casey* (1992) to historical practices in cases like *Washington v. Glucksberg* (1997)—and more generally fueled their anxiety about protecting rights under the Due Process Clause.[31] We see similar anxiety in Justice Alito's wrongheaded disparagement of *Obergefell* as expressing a "postmodern" conception of liberty.[32]

However substantive due process may have looked to Ely in 1981—with a few strands of 1960s romantic self-fulfillment liberalism still kicking around in some dissents and appearing occasionally in plaintiffs' and scholars' arguments—substantive due process took a pronounced conservative turn in leading cases like *Moore v. City of East Cleveland* (1977), *Casey*, *Lawrence*, and *Obergefell*: to protecting rights on the ground that doing so promoted noble purposes and moral goods.[33] As discussed in chapter 2, I mean conservative in the manner of Justice Harlan as illustrated in his famous dissent in *Poe v. Ullman* (1961). After all, as discussed in chapter 3, the primary opinions in all of these cases were written by conservative justices in the mold of Harlan: Powell, O'Connor, Kennedy, and Souter.

Thus, these cases are not animated by a project of securing a right to be different in the sense of being eccentric or idiosyncratic or realizing one's individuality. Rather, the cases engage in a project of extending rights already protected for some to others in order to enable them to pursue the same noble purposes and moral goods. For example, in *Moore*, the plurality opinion of Justice Powell extended the right of a family to live together from the context of the nuclear family to that of the extended family, observing that the extended family "has roots equally venerable," and equally promotes the moral goods of "inculcat[ing] and pass[ing] down many of our most cherished values, moral and cultural," as the nuclear family.[34]

And cases like *Lawrence* and *Obergefell* extend rights to gays and lesbians to be like the straights who already have those rights, not a right to be different. *Lawrence* protected the right of gays and lesbians to intimate association to enable them to pursue the same purposes that straights do.[35] And

Obergefell protected the right of same-sex couples to marry in order to enable them to pursue the same noble purposes and moral goods of marriage that opposite-sex couples do.[36] In these cases, Kennedy says gays and lesbians are similar to straights and so they deserve the same rights, protections, and benefits with respect to intimate association and marriage that straights have. One certainly could imagine quite different justifications for these rights, formulations sounding more in a Millian right to be different—for example, a right of gays and lesbians to be outlaws to smash gender norms. But, seen in light of Kennedy's conservative moral goods arguments for extending rights already recognized for straights to gays and lesbians, *Lawrence* and *Obergefell* hardly protect a right to be different.

It should come as no surprise that many substantive due process cases from 1973 through *Obergefell* have such a conservative, moral goods cast—given that it was a conservative court that decided them, with conservative justices writing most of the opinions. As Thomas Grey insightfully observed, even *Roe* reflects not liberal concerns for autonomy and the sexual revolution of the 1960s and 1970s, but conservative concerns for family stability and family planning.[37] Similar conservative themes are even more pronounced in *Obergefell*, as discussed in chapter 2. That is why some queer theorists (as well as some feminists and progressives) are ambivalent about (1) the right to marry in general and (2) *Obergefell*'s justification for it on the basis of the moral goods it furthers in particular.[38] (I return to such criticisms in chapter 8.)

Roberts's dissent in *Obergefell* totally misses or ignores the character of Kennedy's majority opinion in that case. He recasts it from the conservative moral goods argument Kennedy actually makes into his quotable line that Kennedy is reading the Constitution to enact a classic work of liberalism, Mill's *On Liberty*. Even if it would be understandable that critics of *Lawrence* might object that it was reading Mill's harm principle into the Constitution, it is far less understandable or even plausible to object that *Obergefell* is doing so. After all, *Obergefell* is not concerned with limiting the authority of government with respect to victimless crimes or with permitting gays and lesbians to be *different*—to do whatever they want in pursuing their individuality as long as they do not harm others. Instead, *Obergefell* is concerned with extending the status and benefits of civil marriage to same-sex couples so they can be *like* opposite-sex couples, who already enjoy this status and these benefits.

In sum, the substantive due process cases are not animated by a Millian right to be different any more than by a Millian harm principle.

Is Roberts Right that *Obergefell* Converts the Shield of Negative Liberty into a Sword of Positive Liberty?

After charging the majority in *Obergefell* with repeating the "grave errors" of *Lochner*, Chief Justice Roberts suggests that the majority claims to rely primarily on "'other, more instructive precedents' informing the right to marry"—in particular, those involving the "right of privacy" as a "right to be let alone."[39] Roberts argues that such a right is inapt here because laws forbidding same-sex couples to marry *do* leave them alone in private. They are free to have sexual intimacy together and free to live together; the government will not come after them with criminal prosecutions for engaging in these activities.[40] But Roberts ignores that Kennedy's majority opinion in *Obergefell*, instead of arguing from a right of same-sex couples to privacy as a right to be let alone, specifically argues for the opposite, a right *not* to be let alone—a right to intimate association with others including a right to join in marriage with them.[41]

Roberts further makes the predictable move invoking *DeShaney v. Winnebago County's* (1989) conception of the Constitution as a charter of negative liberties, not positive benefits. He argues that Kennedy is trying to convert the "shield" of negative liberties to be free from governmental interference into a "sword" to demand positive entitlements from the state.[42] This argument may sound superficially plausible, especially to libertarians who hate government and want to be free from it. Indeed, his argument might have force if states had no laws creating civil marriage and same-sex couples were demanding that the states create an institution of civil marriage affirmatively providing them with benefits and imposing responsibilities upon them. But that is not the case here. The states already have created the institution of civil marriage with all of its benefits and responsibilities. And they have made that institution available to opposite-sex couples but not to same-sex couples. The question is, are the states denying same-sex couples the positive benefits surrounding marriage which they themselves already have provided to opposite-sex couples? The answer is that they unquestionably are. That is a denial of, in Kennedy's formulation, "equal dignity."[43]

Moreover, the Supreme Court already has recognized a fundamental right to marry. That right is not merely a negative right: a right to be let alone or to be free from government. It is in part an affirmative right: a right to equal liberty with respect to the status and benefits the state provides through its civil marriage laws. As the Massachusetts Supreme Judicial Court put it in *Goodridge v. Department of Public Health* (2003), the right to marry is not only *freedom from* (in the sense that you have a right to decide whom to marry without governmental interference) but also *freedom to* (in the sense that you have a right to whatever positive benefits the state laws creating civil marriage afford to others).[44] Indeed, more generally, state constitutions are charters of positive benefits, not merely negative liberties (whatever may be the character of the US Constitution according to *DeShaney*).[45] Thus, the fundamental right to marry is hardly merely a negative liberty: it is a right to whatever benefits the state has provided in creating the institution of civil marriage.

Thus, the right to marry protected in *Obergefell* is not a positive liberty in the sense that the state has an affirmative obligation in the state of nature to create the civil institution of marriage to provide certain positive benefits for same-sex couples. Plaintiffs are not arguing for that in *Obergefell*, though Roberts contorts their arguments to make it appear that they are. Instead, they are simply arguing that, where the state already has created an institution of civil marriage to further certain moral goods and to afford certain benefits and protections, it is obligated to extend the benefits and protections of that institution to same-sex couples just as to opposite-sex couples.

If we step back for a moment, we can see just how scattershot Roberts's attacks are. He is simultaneously charging the Court with (1) wrongly reading the Constitution to enact Mill's *On Liberty*, which on his understanding is a conception of *negative liberty* (requiring government to leave same-sex couples alone), and (2) wrongly reading the Constitution to enact a conception of *positive liberty* (requiring government to create certain benefits for them). Roberts is thus talking out of both sides of his mouth at once. To make matters worse, at the same time that Roberts objects that the Constitution *does not* enact Mill's *On Liberty*, he (and even more explicitly Justice Thomas) in effect argues that the Constitution *does* enact John Locke's *Second Treatise of Civil Government*![46] Roberts even cites Locke for his understanding of marriage and attributes that understanding to the founders of the US Constitution.[47] Justice Thomas, making an argument about negative versus positive liberty similar to Roberts's, quotes Locke for his supposed understanding of liberty as negative liberty and then reads the Constitution to enact such an understanding.[48]

Therefore, Roberts does not seem to rule out recourse to political theory in constitutional interpretation in general or in interpreting our commitment to liberty in particular (not even to British political theory at that!). This recognition invites the rhetorical question: if the Constitution does not enact Mill's *On Liberty*, does it enact Locke's *Second Treatise*?

The Distinction between Reading the Constitution to Enact a Particular Moral Theory and a Moral Reading of the Constitution

Chief Justice Roberts's echo of Justice Holmes's dissent in *Lochner*—the line about Mill—may encapsulate a more general criticism of substantive due process cases' presuppositions about the nature of constitutional interpretation. In *Obergefell*, Kennedy makes a moral argument from constitutional principles of liberty, equality, and fairness. Roberts misconceives this argument and accuses Kennedy of applying extra-constitutional authority, that of Mill's *On Liberty*. The lesson here is that the Constitution does embody a morality of its own and that explicating and applying that morality is the function of constitutional interpretation. More fundamentally, *Obergefell* poses a long-standing interpretive issue that turns on the relationship between law and morality: Does constitutional interpretation involve determining the original meaning of the Constitution, conceived as historical facts (originalism)? Or does it involve moral and philosophic judgments in constructing the best understanding of our constitutional commitments (moral reading)? As shown in chapter 2, *Obergefell* plays out this clash, with Justice Kennedy's majority opinion exemplifying a moral reading (as seen in the *Casey* framework) and the dissents more or less reflecting originalism (as seen in the *Glucksberg* framework). Chief Justice Roberts articulates a general view that the Constitution does not "enact" a particular moral theory but is "made for people of fundamentally differing views" (invoking Justice Holmes's dissent in *Lochner*). He maintains that, where there is deep moral disagreement concerning a right, and recognizing a right would depart from historical practices, the courts should leave the matter to the democratic process.[49] In chapter 2, I criticize Roberts's assertions that Kennedy's moral reading has no basis in the Constitution or judicial precedents and is undemocratic. I defend Kennedy's moral reading of the Constitution and show that Roberts's democratic objections are overstated and misplaced, given the best understandings of constitutional interpretation (moral reading) and of the form of democracy embodied in our constitutional practice (a constitutional democracy in which basic liberties associated with personal self-government limit majority rule). Here I shall focus on the implications of Roberts's assertions for the nature of constitutional interpretation.

To begin, consider Holmes's and Roberts's formulations that the Constitution does not "enact" a particular economic or moral theory. These formulations reflect the positivism of Holmes and of all those who invoke or echo him, including Roberts. "Enact" bespeaks a positivist conception of lawmaking, including constitutional lawmaking: that law includes only specific "enacted" norms. It also signifies a positivist conception of the "enacted" Constitution as being a specific, authoritative text, perhaps analogous to a statute or code. It also evidently presupposes a positivist approach to the interpretation of such a text.

Furthermore, consider the authoritarianism reflected in Holmes's charge and Roberts's echo of it. They presuppose that the Court is substituting an external authority (Mill's or Spencer's authoritative text) to displace the authority of the founders of the Constitution. They further presuppose that the Court is reading that external authoritative text to decide our questions for us instead of following the Constitution and letting the founders decide our questions for us. That is not the character of our Constitution, and that is not the nature of our practice of constitutional interpretation. The Constitution embodies a charter of abstract moral principles, including commitments to liberty and equality. It does not "enact" a code of detailed rules and concrete historical practices, such as the specific original meanings and expectations of the framers and ratifiers. And constitutional interpretation requires making moral judgments about the best understanding of our constitutional commitments. It does not involve discovering historical facts about the founding or invoking external authorities to decide our questions for us. We have to make moral judgments to decide those questions for ourselves.

To be sure, the Constitution does not "enact" a particular authoritative text of moral theory, but it does embody a charter of abstract moral principles to be built out over time on the basis of experience, new insight, moral progress, and evolving consensus concerning the best understanding of our constitutional commitments. That is how our practice of substantive due process has conceived the Constitution and constitutional interpretation in cases from *Meyer* (1923) and *Pierce* (1925) through *Griswold* (1965) and *Casey* (1992) and beyond to *Lawrence* (2003) and *Obergefell* (2015).

More abstractly, Roberts's echo of Holmes's dissent may simply object to moral readings of the Constitution as such. Roberts's echo may distort such readings as tantamount to importing a foreign normative moral theory into the Constitution. If so, it bespeaks a fundamental misunderstanding of the way a moral reading of the Constitution works. A moral reading does not read the Constitution as directly "enacting," incorporating, or applying the conception of liberty put forward in a classic text of moral theory—or even directly applying an abstract principle (like autonomy) that seems to underlie and justify a line of cases. Instead, it proceeds through common law constitutional interpretation—reasoning by analogy from one case to the next, building out our constitutional commitments, elaborating principles implicit in the precedents through making recourse to the basic reasons for protecting the rights recognized in the precedents and applying them to new situations. Thus, the principles that comprise a moral reading are implicit in and grow out of the practice of constitutional interpretation: We elaborate or construct the principles as we go along. We do not import them from external authority. Nor do we derive them from ready-made abstract theories. (Recall our archaeological excavation of the practice of substantive due process in chapter 2, in which the moral reader archaeologist has an obligation to construct principles that fit and justify the extant legal materials, to interpret them in their best light.)

Furthermore, as we build out our constitutional commitments through developing a line of precedents, we may reinterpret the precedents in order to make sense of them as fitting into and justifying that line—to make them better cohere with the other decisions. For example, initially, *Griswold* protected a right of privacy within the intimate relation of husband and wife.[50] Subsequently, *Griswold* combined with *Eisenstadt* protected a right of the individual, married or single, to decide whether to bear or beget a child.[51] At yet a later point, *Griswold* together with *Lawrence* protected a right of intimate association that includes not only nonprocreative sexual intimacy of straights but also that of gays and lesbians.[52] Still farther down the line, *Griswold* combined with *Obergefell* is fundamentally about promoting noble purposes and moral goods like commitment, stability, and fidelity through protecting the right to intimate association and to marry, not only for opposite-sex couples but also for same-sex couples.[53] At no point in this moral reading of the Constitution, through common law constitutional interpretation, does the Court put aside the line of cases it must fit and justify and import an external authority like a classic text of moral theory to resolve our questions for us.

All down the line in this process, moreover, the Court moves from particular to general in constructing the general principles or rights embodied in the cases and articulating criteria common to the rights already recognized in order to guide further development of those principles. For example, *Roe* begins by listing the "roots" of the right of privacy recognized in prior cases, then lists the subjects to which that right has been applied, and finally offers a general criterion for deciding what liberties the Due Process Clause protects: those "'fundamental' or 'implicit in the concept of ordered liberty.'"[54] In dissent in *Bowers*, Justice Stevens generalizes from the cases, arguing that the Due Process Clause protects "the individual's right to make certain unusually important decisions that will affect his own, or his family's, destiny."[55] The joint opinion in *Casey* offers a similar abstract formulation concerning its conception of liberty: "These matters, involving the most intimate and personal choices a person may make in a lifetime, choices central to personal dignity and autonomy, are central to the liberty protected by the Fourteenth Amendment."[56] These understandings of liberty embody what I previously have termed a general criterion of significance for deliberative autonomy that is implicit in the practice of substantive due process.[57] As I discussed in chapter 2, this criterion makes sense of and shows the coherence and structure of the line of substantive due process cases protecting basic personal liberties.

The justices who are opposed to this whole line of cases, or extension of the line in general, or recognition of a particular right asserted in a case before the Court—or all of the above—typically resist this process of generalization in favor of limiting cases to protecting specific activities. For example, Justice White's majority opinion in *Bowers* reduces the basic liberties protected in previous cases to a list of particular activities, over and against Blackmun's and Stevens's attempts in dissent to generalize from the cases, elaborating and extending the principles animating them.[58] Chief Justice Rehnquist in *Glucksberg* rejects *Casey*'s abstract conception of liberty and its framework of "reasoned judgment" for deciding what liberties the Due Process Clause protects—instead construing the precedents narrowly, limiting them to their specific holdings, and reducing the basic liberties protected in previous cases to a list of particular activities.[59] And Roberts in dissent in *Obergefell* argues for the narrow, positivist framework of *Glucksberg* over the abstract, moral reading framework of *Casey*.[60]

What is more, in building out the line of cases, the Court develops the principles incrementally and conservatively. Admittedly, any extension may seem like a small incremental step to some and a big unanticipated and unjustifiable leap to others. For example, the move from *Griswold* to *Eisenstadt*—from the intimate relation of husband and wife to the individual, married or single—seemed like a small incremental step to Justice Brennan in *Eisenstadt*, whereas it seemed like a significant, fateful wrong turn to conservative communitarian scholars like Mary Ann Glendon.[61] Furthermore, the move from *Griswold* and *Eisenstadt* to *Roe* seemed like a small incremental step to Justice Blackmun in *Roe*, whereas it seemed like a bridge too far, with "not a single sentence qualifying as legal argument," to Robert Bork and Justice Scalia.[62] And the move from *Griswold*, *Eisenstadt*, and *Roe* to protecting a right of privacy or intimate association for gays and lesbians seemed like an incremental step to the four dissenters in *Bowers*, yet none of those precedents "bears any resemblance" to a right of intimate association for gays and lesbians according to White for the majority in *Bowers*.[63]

Finally, courts do not generally extend a line of cases simply on the basis of the elaboration of an abstract principle like privacy or autonomy. Typically they do not make such extensions until preconditions for constitutional change like those elaborated in chapter 4 are in place. Some think *Roe* is an exception in this regard. But *Lawrence* and *Obergefell* certainly substantiate this claim, as argued in chapter 4.

In sum, the story of substantive due process from *Meyer* (1923) to the present is not a story of the Court imposing authoritative texts of economic or moral theory sprung full grown from the brow of Herbert Spencer or John Stuart Mill in nineteenth-century England upon US constitutional law. It is instead a story of a moral reading of the Constitution through common law constitutional interpretation, building out our constitutional commitments to liberty and equality through reasoning by analogy, one case at a time. Roberts's repetition of the line that the Constitution does not enact Mill's *On Liberty* is nothing more than a rhetorical put-down in opposition to the practice of substantive due process and more generally to a moral reading of the Constitution.

Does Mill's Harm Principle Support a Right to Polygamy?

In chapter 4, I analyzed Chief Justice Roberts's argument that *Obergefell's* protection of a right of same-sex couples to marry puts us on a slippery slope to a right to plural marriage. In this chapter, I am assessing his argument that *Obergefell* interprets the Constitution to enact Mill's *On Liberty*. Combining two similar moves, Jonathan Turley, who litigated and won the Kody Brown–*Sister Wives* polygamy case at the federal district court level, builds upon Mill's harm principle in arguing for a right to polygamy.[64] In order to assess his argument, I have to revisit a classic debate in jurisprudence concerning the legal enforcement of morals and the harm principle—namely, the Hart-Devlin debate from the 1960s. I will paint with a very broad brush here.

The Hart-Devlin Debate Concerning the Legal Enforcement of Morals

In 1957, in the UK, the Wolfenden Report recommended decriminalizing "homosexual offenses."[65] Patrick Devlin, a prominent Law Lord at the time, gave a famous 1959 Maccabean Lecture in response to that recommendation. In that lecture and his subsequent book, *The Enforcement of Morals* (1965), Lord Devlin defended the legal enforcement of traditional morals—including the prohibition of "homosexual offences"—on majoritarian grounds. He argued that a people have the right to enact into the criminal law prohibitions of anything that arouses "intolerance, indignation, and disgust" in the mind of "the [person] in the Clapham omnibus." In short, he argued that the moral outrage of the ordinary person in the street against certain traditionally immoral offenses provided sufficient ground for criminalization of those practices. Devlin also argued that traditional morality was a seamless web that constituted a society—and that actions violating that morality were analogous to treason because they threatened the subversion and very disintegration of the society.[66]

H. L. A. Hart, Professor of Jurisprudence at Oxford at the time, famously rebutted Devlin's arguments, reworking Mill's conception of liberty and his harm principle. Hart argued that the intolerance, indignation, and disgust—the moral outrage—of the ordinary person in the street were not sufficient justifications for the legal enforcement of traditional morality and, in particular, for the traditional prohibition of same-sex intimacy. And he argued that the analogy between immorality and treason was far-fetched and too destructive of liberty to be accepted as a ground for outlawing such intimacy.[67]

A generation later, in *The Tempting of America* (1990), Robert Bork made arguments similar to those of Devlin in favor of legal enforcement of traditional morality. He argued that nothing more than the moral outrage of ordinary people was necessary to justify laws seeking to preserve traditional morality.[68] In dissents in *Romer* and *Lawrence*, Justice Scalia seemed to credit similar arguments in presupposing that government may seek to preserve traditional morality by outlawing what the majority views as immoral acts.[69]

As against Devlin (as well as Bork and Scalia), US constitutional law and practice has rejected a number of forms of traditional morals legislation. Since the Hart-Devlin debate was ongoing around the time that the Supreme Court decided *Griswold* in 1965, one might have expected the opinion in that case to take the route of Mill and Hart by invoking some version of the harm principle. But the Court did not do so, as shown above. The only echo of Hart's jurisprudence in Justice William Douglas's majority opinion in *Griswold* is Douglas's use of the word "penumbra," a word Hart made famous in his 1961 classic, *The Concept of Law*. But Douglas views "penumbras" or "emanations" from particular constitutional provisions basically as the spirit emanating from the letter of those provisions, whereas Hart views a penumbra as the shadow of uncertainty in the application of a general rule.[70] This has nothing to do with the harm principle or with liberal criticism of traditional morals legislation.

Turley's Argument That Opposition to Polygamy Stems from Objectionable Legal Enforcement of Liberal Morals

Let's fast forward fifty years from the Hart-Devlin debate to Turley's 2015 article arguing for a right to polygamy. Turley observes that liberals, feminists, and progressives who argue that recognizing same-sex marriage does not imply that we must recognize polygamy typically make arguments rooted in concern to prevent harm to children and to secure gender equality to distinguish the two. But he contends that such arguments are overstated and insufficient to justify the bans on polygamy. He says that they are based on extreme cases like that of polygamist Warren Jeffs (who was convicted of child abuse through taking child brides and having sex with them) and should not apply to folks like Kody Brown of *Sister Wives* fame (who do not take child brides and do not subordinate their wives).[71] He argues that polygamous unions like the latter are more typical and impose no harm on others. In fact, he basically contends that the harm arguments opponents make to defend the prohibition of polygamy are pretexts for the intolerance, indignation, and disgust that liberals, feminists, and progressives feel toward the decidedly illiberal, unfeminist, and unprogressive Mormons who wish to practice polygamy. He presents such liberals, feminists, and progressives as analogous to the Devlin-type moral conservatives who were morally outraged—felt intolerance, indignation, and disgust—at the very idea of "homosexual offenses." Whereas Devlin advocated a compulsive conservatism, Turley argues that many of today's opponents of polygamy advocate a compulsive liberalism. In other words, Turley believes liberals, feminists, and progressives opposed to polygamy are trying to impose a liberal morality under the guise of protecting against harm to children and women.[72]

But are liberal, feminist, and progressive arguments for securing the status of women as equal citizens and for protecting children from abuse and harm really analogous to Devlin's arguments for enforcing traditional sexual morality? I think there are two significant differences. First, the harms that critics of polygamy point to are concrete, palpable harms to real people living real lives. They are nothing like the moral outrage experienced by moral conservatives who felt intolerance, indignation, and disgust at the very idea of "homosexual offenses" being committed in the privacy of gays' and lesbians' homes. To be sure, moral conservatives in Devlin's time persuaded themselves that there were harms both to the people having same-sex sex and to the society—for example, Devlin's claim that their violation of traditional sexual norms caused the moral fabric of the society to disintegrate and thus was analogous to treason.[73] In our own time, some fundamentalist rabbis argued that gay and lesbian sex caused the 2010 earthquakes in Haiti, and the Moral Majority leader Jerry Falwell and conservative televangelist Pat Robertson suggested that our nation's tolerance of same-sex sex caused the 9/11 terrorist attack on the World Trade Center and the Pentagon.[74] But these claims were completely implausible, with no basis in fact. In 2003, the year *Lawrence* was decided, there were no credible arguments that gay and lesbian sex harmed other people. And in 2015, the year *Obergefell* was decided, there were no credible arguments that same-sex marriage harmed children, the institution of marriage, or straights who were married or were considering getting married. By contrast, the arguments that polygamy harms children and undermines the public value of gender equality are plausible and empirically grounded, not merely ideological moral outrage.

Second, we should distinguish between (1) government seeking to preserve traditional sexual morality and (2) government promoting the public value of gender equality through the structure of its basic institutions like marriage. Securing the status of equal citizenship for women is one of our deepest constitutional commitments. And protecting children from harm is one of our most compelling governmental objectives. Both are far more compelling governmental objectives than is expressing moral outrage against those who refuse to conform to traditional sexual morality (or simply preserving traditional sexual morality). Thus, promoting the public value of gender equality and preventing harm to children are not compulsive liberalism analogous to compulsive conservatism supporting criminalization of traditional morals offenses. Turley's argument from Mill's harm principle for a right to polygamy fails.

I want to emphasize that my concerns about polygamy are not moralistic but are empirical and systemic. The empirical concerns are that the evidence regarding harm to children in polygamy seems credible—more credible than was the corresponding evidence with respect to harm to children from being reared in interracial marriages (in 1967, say, just before *Loving v. Virginia*) or in same-sex marriages (in 2015, just before *Obergefell*).[75] It seems far less likely that such concern about harm to children in polygamous unions merely reflects prejudice or moral outrage. In fact, as discussed in chapter 4, the Supreme Court of British Columbia in *The British Columbia Reference Case*[76] credited the evidence concerning harm to children in deciding not to protect a right to polygamy. It also credited the claim that polygamy undermines gender equality.

The systemic concerns are more complex. In our book, *Ordered Liberty*, Linda C. McClain and I develop a civic liberalism, defending a formative project of government and the institutions of civil society (including the family) inculcating civic virtues in children and developing their capacities for responsible democratic and personal self-government in our constitutional democracy. Within such a formative project, we aspire to, or at least hope for, some congruence between the structures and values of the basic institutions of civil society and the public values of our constitutional democracy.[77] Those public values include securing the status of equal citizenship for women. From this vantage point, an egalitarian institution of marriage is likely to be more congruent with the public values of equal citizenship than is a patriarchal institution of marriage; and so, the evolution of marriage from a patriarchal institution to a more egalitarian institution has been a good thing. Indeed, as discussed in chapter 4, that evolution has made the institution of marriage more hospitable, and more attractive, to same-sex couples. Likewise, an inegalitarian institution of marriage like polygamy would raise concerns: it would be a structure with systemic inequality built into it, and so it would be in deep conflict with, rather than congruent with, the public value of equal citizenship for women.

I am not saying that this is a definitive argument against recognizing a right to polygamy. Indeed, I acknowledge that some basic liberties protect rights in conflict with the public value of securing equal citizenship for women or for gays and lesbians. For example, protecting freedom of speech, free exercise of religion, and due process liberty to direct the upbringing and education of children may foster individuals and families who reject the constitutional commitments to gender equality and marriage equality. What I am saying is that an egalitarian institution of marriage recognizing same-sex marriage *is* congruent with the public value of securing equal citizenship for all; by contrast, an inegalitarian institution of marriage recognizing polygamy would be in conflict with that public value.

Thus, Mill's harm principle does not support recognizing a right to polygamy. And not recognizing such a right does not stem from objectionable legal enforcement of liberal morals.

Conclusion

Chief Justice Roberts's echo of Justice Holmes's dissent in *Lochner* illustrates the meming of "the Fourteenth Amendment does not enact John Stuart Mill's *On Liberty*."[78] It is more a repetition of a quotable line or rhetorical trope than a rigorous substantive critique of the line of cases protecting basic liberties leading up to *Obergefell*. Roberts's assertion is simply grist for the mill of those who oppose substantive due process. I have acknowledged that—even though it is fallacious as a substantive critique—it nonetheless may be rhetorically effective in persuading readers that the enterprise of substantive due process is illegitimate and should be narrowly limited or even abandoned. My hope is that by exposing Roberts's criticism as a rhetorical trope shot through with fallacies, I might contribute to making it less effective in the face of our actual practice of protecting basic liberties under the Due Process Clause. That practice, stemming from a moral reading of the Constitution, has not illegitimately interpreted the Constitution to enact Mill's *On Liberty*.

In the next two chapters, I turn to conflicts between liberty and equality. In chapter 8, I consider whether certain basic liberties protected under the Due Process Clause would be on firmer ground if they instead were based on the Equal Protection Clause. In chapter 9, I ask whether securing basic liberties and the status and benefits of equal citizenship for gays and lesbians, including the right to marry and the right not to be discriminated against, has imperiled the religious liberty of opponents of such rights.

PART FOUR

Conflicts between Liberty and Equality

EIGHT

The Grounds for Protecting Basic Liberties: Liberty Together with Equality

Constitutional law scholars are a fussy bunch of people and, worse yet, we are cocky. We commonly criticize landmark Supreme Court opinions, saying things like: "Well, I believe the case was rightly decided, but the majority opinion is flawed. Here's how I would have written it." In this vein, some argue that leading substantive due process cases like *Roe v. Wade* (1973) and *Obergefell v. Hodges* (2015) reached the right result, but that we need to "rewrite" the opinions. That is, we need to develop a better justification for the rights protected in those cases than the Court provided. Indeed, there is a whole genre of critics rewriting landmark opinions like *Brown v. Board of Education* (1954), *Roe*, and *Obergefell*. Such critics entertain the questions "What *Brown* Should Have Said," "What *Roe* Should Have Said," and "What *Obergefell* Should Have Said."[1]

With substantive due process cases, the answer rewriters commonly give to the question of what the case should have said is that the Court should have grounded the right in the Equal Protection Clause (equality) instead of the Due Process Clause (liberty). In assessing arguments of this sort, I examine the relationship between these two clauses. I argue that the Due Process and Equal Protection Clauses, rather than being opposed to one another, overlap and are intertwined: both provide sound grounds for protecting these basic liberties, which are essential to securing ordered liberty and the status and benefits of equal citizenship.

I begin by explicating the joint opinion's and concurrences' own rewriting of *Roe* in *Planned Parenthood v. Casey* (1992). Then I argue that *Casey* and *Obergefell*, while officially grounded primarily in due process, are also rooted in equal protection; indeed, the opinions intimate the very concerns for the status of equal citizenship which the rewriters articulate. Thus, we need not rewrite *Casey* and *Obergefell*—those opinions already contain and intertwine the best liberty arguments and threads of the best equality arguments needed to justify them adequately.

Furthermore, even though both liberty and equality provide good grounds for these decisions, I develop criteria for deciding which might seem to the Court to provide a sounder ground in certain circumstances. I then apply these criteria to the circumstances of *Roe*, *Casey*, and *Obergefell*. I also bring out what might have seemed to the Court to be advantages of grounding the rights at issue in *Roe*, *Casey*, and *Obergefell* in liberty, advantages the rewriters have overlooked. For example, in *Obergefell*, the conservative Justice Kennedy might have thought that rooting the right of same-sex couples to marry in liberty rather than equality would enable him to avoid drawing analogies between discrimination on the basis of sexual orientation and that on the basis of race, and thus to sidestep the dissenters' arguments that he was equating opposition to same-sex marriage with racial prejudice and bigotry. He also might have thought that through taking the liberty route instead of the equality route he could avoid deciding (or implying an answer to) the question of whether all forms of discrimination on the basis of sexual orientation are unconstitutional. To be sure, some liberals and progressives might see the latter as a disadvantage of the liberty ground, but to Kennedy, a conservative, it might have seemed to be an advantage. More generally, I suggest below, Kennedy's majority opinion in *Obergefell* makes the types of arguments more likely to persuade conservatives who are not already persuaded. After all, as shown in chapter 2, his opinion is conservative in the mold of Justice Harlan.

What Should *Roe* Have Said?

Unlike some of the cases where critics have called for rewriting a controversial opinion, the Supreme Court itself actually has rewritten *Roe*—in *Casey*. If I were to rewrite *Roe*'s explication of the grounds for the constitutional right to decide whether to terminate a pregnancy, I would write an opinion encompassing what the joint opinion of Justices O'Connor, Kennedy, and Souter together with the concurrences of Justices Blackmun and Stevens articulated in *Casey*. Everything we need for an adequate justification is in those three opinions. We have not only the explication of liberty—personal autonomy and bodily integrity—but also equality justifications.

And so, my answer to the question "What should *Roe* have said?" is basically "What *Casey* said." I should make clear that I am speaking here only of the basic justification for the right. For I am quite critical of *Casey* for adopting the more deferential undue burden standard and for upholding several restrictions upon reproductive freedom, restrictions which presumably would have been invalidated under *Roe*.

How Does Casey *Rewrite* Roe?

In what senses has the Supreme Court itself rewritten *Roe* in *Casey*? Does *Casey* provide a different justification for the right to abortion than did *Roe*? Or simply a fuller explication of the same basic rationale? The joint opinion recasts the privacy argument of *Roe* as a personal autonomy argument and intimates an equality argument not present in *Roe*, while the concurrences develop the equality argument more fully. To elaborate: *Casey* invokes two lines of constitutional doctrine interpreting the Due Process Clause to justify reaffirming the "central holding" in *Roe*. First, "*Griswold* liberty": cases protecting "liberty relating to intimate relationships, the family, and decisions about whether or not to beget or bear a child." The joint opinion encapsulates this line of cases in terms of "personal autonomy." Second, bodily integrity: "cases recognizing limits on governmental power to mandate medical treatment or to bar its rejection." The joint opinion cites *Cruzan v. Director, Missouri Department of Health* (1990) to illustrate this line.[2]

Casey also includes a gender equality ground for the right. The joint opinion mentions the role of *Roe* in securing "[t]he ability of women to participate equally in the economic and social life of the Nation."[3] Also, in striking down the requirement that a married woman seeking an abortion must notify her husband, the joint opinion concludes: "A State may not give to a man the kind of dominion over his wife that parents exercise over their children."[4] But it does not officially ground the right in the Equal Protection Clause.

The concurrences of Justices Stevens and Blackmun more fully develop equal protection justifications. Stevens argues that "*Roe* is an integral part of a correct understanding of both the concept of liberty and the basic equality of men and women." He writes that "[t]he authority to make such traumatic and yet empowering decisions is an element of basic human dignity" and that protecting that right is necessary to afford equal respect and dignity to women. He condemns the twenty-four-hour waiting period on the ground that it "appears to rest on outmoded and unacceptable assumptions about the decision-making capacity of women." It "denies women . . . equal respect."[5] Thus, Stevens would ground the right in both the Equal Protection and the Due Process Clauses.

Blackmun also justifies the right on the basis of liberty together with gender equality. He writes:

A State's restrictions . . . also implicate constitutional guarantees of gender equality. . . . By restricting the right to terminate pregnancies, the State conscripts women's bodies into its service, forcing women to continue their pregnancies, suffer the pains of childbirth, and in most instances, provide years of maternal care. The State does not compensate women for their services; instead, it assumes that they owe this duty as a matter of course. This assumption—that women can simply be forced to accept the "natural" status and incidents of motherhood—appears to rest upon a conception of women's role that has triggered the protection of the Equal Protection Clause. See, *e.g.*, *Mississippi Univ. for Women v. Hogan* (1982); *Craig v. Boren* (1976). The joint opinion recognizes that these assumptions about women's place in society "are no longer consistent with our understanding of the family, the individual, or the Constitution."[6]

Blackmun drops a footnote including citations to Reva Siegel, Cass Sunstein, and Catharine MacKinnon, all of whom have famously pressed the gender equality justification.[7]

In sum, the joint opinion in *Casey* together with the concurrences of Justices Stevens and Blackmun rewrite *Roe*, both by recasting its privacy justification in terms of personal autonomy and by suggesting or developing equality arguments. They give us all the ingredients we need to rewrite *Roe* so as to make its arguments more persuasive.

Privacy versus Equality or Privacy Together with Equality in Justifying Reproductive Freedom?

In scholarship rewriting *Roe*, many feminists and other progressives disparage liberty or privacy and praise equality as a ground for reproductive freedom. Two leading, though distinct, examples are MacKinnon and Sunstein. Put simply, they frame the issue as *privacy versus equality*: privacy is bad, equality is good. Substantively, MacKinnon and Sunstein offer similar antisubordination or anti-caste conceptions of equal protection, and provide similar justifications for the right to abortion. But their criticisms of privacy differ. MacKinnon criticizes it as bad *substantively* for women: as a "right of men 'to be let alone' to oppress women" and as a "hellhole" of sanctified isolation.[8]

Sunstein, on the other hand, criticizes privacy as bad *institutionally*: he rejects the argument that privacy is bad substantively for women, but he makes the argument that equality is better, institutionally, for courts. One, he states that privacy is an "unenumerated" right, and the ghost of *Lochner v. New York* (1905) haunts any attempt by courts to protect such rights under the Due Process Clause. But who is Sunstein of all people to make this criticism? After all, as we saw in chapter 6, he is the one who told us that what was wrong with *Lochner* had nothing to do with "unenumerated" rights and everything to do with status quo neutrality (taking the status quo of existing distributions of wealth and power as presumptively justified, such that any law interfering with them is presumptively unconstitutional).[9] The latter certainly is not present in *Roe* and *Casey*, which are critical of the status quo regarding reproductive freedom. Two, Sunstein claims that privacy is more "adventurous" or more intrusive on the political process than is equal protection.[10] But is this really so? To be sure, some equal protection arguments are less intrusive on the political process than substantive due process arguments would be. For example, in *Skinner v. Oklahoma* (1942), the case invalidating a law sterilizing criminals like chicken thieves but not criminals like embezzlers, the Court's equal protection holding left it to the Oklahoma legislature to decide whether to sterilize both classes of criminals or to sterilize neither. By contrast, a substantive due process holding would have required that the legislature sterilize neither.[11] But the equal protection argument for reproductive freedom does not leave a legislature with an analogous choice: it says that the legislature may not subject pregnant persons to the restriction on abortion in question. Thus, any decision invalidating a restriction on abortion on grounds of equality would be every bit as intrusive on the political process as a decision justified on the basis of substantive due process. Moreover, a decision rooted in an anti-caste or anti-subordination principle of equality would require normative judgments no less ambitious and controversial (no less "adventurous") than one grounded in substantive due process.[12]

By contrast to MacKinnon and Sunstein, Ronald Dworkin argues that there is overlap between the Due Process and Equal Protection Clauses, and that most of the basic rights that we can justify on the basis of liberty we can also justify on the basis of equality.[13] Where the right to reproductive freedom is concerned, the due process and equal protection justifications are not opposed to one another. Rather, the two justifications overlap and reinforce one another. Dworkin argues that MacKinnon confuses the right of privacy as "territorial privacy" with the right as "sovereignty over personal decisions" or personal autonomy.[14] The latter is the right at issue in *Roe* and *Casey*. (As a matter of fact, contrary to MacKinnon's worries, courts have not used the right to privacy precedents to shield domestic violence or uphold marital rape exemptions.[15])

In *Casey*, Blackmun and Stevens, like Dworkin, presuppose that the liberty and equality justifications overlap and reinforce one another. They make both types of argument, and treat each as equally fundamental and persuasive. They see the relationship as *privacy together with equality*, not *privacy versus equality*: both provide good justifications for the right to decide whether to terminate a pregnancy.

The Development of the Equality Justification between Roe and Casey

All of this raises the larger question of the relationship between the Due Process and Equal Protection Clauses in grounding rights: do arguments from equality provide a firmer basis for the right to reproductive freedom than do arguments from liberty or privacy? I want to address the choice at two different points in time. First, in 1973, when Blackmun wrote the majority opinion in *Roe*; and second, in 1992, when the Court decided *Casey*.

In 1973, I do not believe that the gender equality argument for the right to terminate a pregnancy was yet available in our constitutional culture. I do not deny that it was in the early stages of formulation; I mean that it was not available in the sense that it would seem plausible to a mainstream lawyer like a justice of the Supreme Court or indeed to mainstream scholars. In 1973, the equality argument was at best an incipient aspiration of feminist litigators seeking to vindicate equality for women, notably Ruth Bader Ginsburg.[16] Indeed, as discussed below, Ginsburg had just begun to litigate and win gender discrimination cases in the Supreme Court, though not abortion cases. Yet by 1992, the equality argument for reproductive freedom was clearly available and fully developed. I offer anecdotal evidence centering on John Hart Ely, a pro-choice liberal law professor.

In 1973, as discussed in chapter 6, Ely wrote one of the most famous criticisms of Blackmun's opinion in *Roe*, "The Wages of Crying Wolf: A Comment on *Roe v. Wade*."[17] Like Sunstein, Ely disparaged the privacy ground institutionally. He invoked the ghost of *Lochner* in criticizing *Roe*'s revival of substantive due process to protect personal liberties, including the right of a woman to decide whether to terminate her pregnancy. The crying "wolf" in his title is of course crying "*Lochner*"! Here was a man who was incredibly imaginative at coming up with equality and process justifications for rights that others justified on grounds of privacy or substantive liberty. For example, in his book, *Democracy and Distrust*, he justified the First Amendment's religion clauses in general on structural or process grounds and free exercise of religion in particular on equal protection grounds.[18] Yet, try as he might, Ely just couldn't see an equality justification for the right of a woman to decide whether to terminate her pregnancy—at least in 1973. He thought you had to begin by asking whether restrictions on pregnancy reflected, in *Carolene Products* footnote four terms, "prejudice" against women as a "discrete and insular minority." He famously ridiculed the idea that women were either "insular" or even a "minority." He quipped that fetuses would more readily satisfy these criteria than women.[19] As he saw it, those were the only equal protection arguments conceivable at the time: one had to jump through these hoops to get the argument going, and the equal protection argument for women's reproductive freedom was a nonstarter.

In 1992, however, after the Supreme Court decided *Casey*, Ely wrote a "fan letter" to the authors of the joint opinion praising their opinion as "excellent": "not only reaching what seem to me entirely sensible results, but defending the refusal to overrule *Roe* splendidly." He published this letter, along with commentary on it, in his book, *On Constitutional Ground*. He added: "*Roe* has contributed greatly to the more general move toward equality for women, which seems to me not only good but also in line with the central themes of our Constitution." In his commentary, he said that he now sees that *Casey* is rightly decided, not just as a matter of stare decisis, but as a matter of constitutional principle, our commitment to equality for women. But, speaking of *Roe* as of 1973, he added: "I don't think a principled opinion along these lines could have been written at the time."[20]

As I read him, Ely is saying that the equality argument just wasn't fully developed in our constitutional culture when *Roe* was decided in 1973 (in the sense that it would seem compelling to a mainstream lawyer like a justice of the Supreme Court). By 1992, though, equality arguments had evolved to the point where one did not have to jump through the hoops on which Ely stumbled in 1973. One no longer had to run the analysis through the *Carolene Products* formulation, "prejudice against discrete and insular minorities," and the like. Instead, one could argue directly from an anti-caste or anti-subordination principle of equality: women are entitled to the status and benefits of equal citizenship, including reproductive freedom. In short, by 1992, the kinds of equal protection arguments made by Siegel, MacKinnon, Sunstein, and Dworkin, as well as by the joint opinion along with concurring opinions of Stevens and Blackmun in *Casey*, were fully developed and compelling.

Criteria for Deciding Whether Due Process or Equal Protection Provides the Better Ground for Reproductive Freedom

Again, even when both due process and equal protection arguments are available, it might seem to the Court that one ground is more persuasive

than the other for certain rights in certain circumstances. I sketch four criteria for choosing between these two grounds:

· One ground may involve a smaller step in existing doctrine than the other.
  This is a criterion of Occam's razor or elegance.
· One ground may avoid or overcome doctrinal obstacles faced by the other
  ground. Indeed, the other ground may be doctrinally foreclosed or at
  least more problematic. Alternatively, one ground may avoid or postpone
  doctrinal problems or implications raised by the other. For example, it may
  sidestep problems or implications which the Court may not be ready to face.
  Or one ground may be harder to limit, or it may press the Court to go in a
  direction where it does not wish to go.
· One ground may better capture the heart of the matter, what is at stake in
  protecting the right.
· One ground may be more likely to persuade people not already persuaded
  to protect the right (this criterion may be especially important in situations
  of impasse or standstill).

Next, I apply these four criteria to see whether they would have favored the
Due Process Clause or the Equal Protection Clause in 1973, when the Court
decided *Roe*.

First, Occam's razor or elegance. Which way does it cut with respect to *Roe*?
Well, how would things have looked to a mainstream lawyer like Blackmun
at the time? On the due process side, we had *Griswold v. Connecticut* (1965),
holding that the Constitution protects a right of privacy that includes the
right to decide whether to use contraceptives within the marital relationship.[21] We also had *Eisenstadt v. Baird* (1972), extending that right to unmarried individuals. Justice Brennan wrote: "If the right of privacy means
anything, it is the right of the *individual*, married or single, to be free from
unwarranted governmental intrusion into matters so fundamentally affecting a person as the decision whether to bear or beget a child."[22] Understandably, it might have seemed to Blackmun to be a small step, doctrinally, from
these cases holding that the right of privacy includes (1) the right of an individual to decide whether to bear or beget a child to holding that it includes
(2) the right of a woman to decide whether to terminate her pregnancy.[23]

On the equal protection side, how would things have looked in 1973?
There were no immediate criticisms of *Roe* on the ground that the Court
should have based the decision on the Equal Protection Clause. Twelve
years later, in 1985, Ginsburg published an article arguing that the equal
protection justification for *Roe* is superior to the due process justification.[24]

Before becoming a judge, she was a feminist law professor and litigator who brought many of the equal protection cases that became building blocks in gender equality jurisprudence.

Where did things stand in equal protection jurisprudence regarding gender in 1973? Ginsburg herself had just begun to litigate gender equality cases, and she had won *Reed v. Reed* in 1971, in which the Supreme Court held for the first time that classifications based on gender were "subject to scrutiny" under the Equal Protection Clause.[25] Note well: the Court did not say "strict scrutiny" or "intermediate scrutiny," but simply "scrutiny." In that case, for the first time in its history, the Court invalidated a gender classification, a law that said that if there were two competing applicants to be appointed as administrators of an estate when a person died intestate, a male was to be preferred over a female. With all due respect to Ginsburg, I believe that mainstream lawyers in 1973 would have thought that, even to get an equal protection argument going, there would have to be a law treating men and women differently. And so, they would have thought, for there to be gender discrimination involved in restrictions on abortion, there would have to be a law treating pregnant women differently from pregnant men. If you are quizzical about this 1973 mindset—putting aside our more fluid conceptions of gender identity today—you must not have heard of *Geduldig v. Aiello*, decided in 1974, in which the Burger Court said exactly that.[26] In fact, the 6-3 majority included Justice Blackmun and three other justices who were in the majority in *Roe*. We'll call this the *Geduldig* problem with the equal protection argument circa 1973 or 1974. (In 1978, Congress in effect overruled the particular outcome in *Geduldig* when it enacted the Pregnancy Discrimination Act, defining sex discrimination to include discrimination on the basis of pregnancy.[27])

The radical gulf between Ginsburg's arguments and *Geduldig*'s holding prompts me to observe that as of 1973, there were two kinds of people when it comes to the Equal Protection Clause and restrictions on abortion. One kind, like Ginsburg, believes or assumes that if only women can get pregnant, it is very likely that any restriction on abortion reflects gender discrimination in violation of the Equal Protection Clause. The other kind, like the majority in *Geduldig*, believes or assumes that if only women can get pregnant, no restriction on abortion can be gender discrimination in violation of the Equal Protection Clause. On the latter view, to constitute gender discrimination, a law would have to treat pregnant women differently from pregnant men. In 1973, when the Court decided *Roe*, the *Geduldig* (1974) mindset clearly would have dominated Supreme Court thinking about challenges to pregnancy regulations under the Equal Protection Clause.

Furthermore, Ginsburg seemed to imply that it was a smaller step from equal protection cases prohibiting discrimination between male and female applicants to administer an estate (*Reed*) to *Roe* than from privacy cases involving reproductive freedom (*Griswold* and *Eisenstadt*) to *Roe*. Again, with all due respect, I think that in 1973, most people would have been puzzled by that idea. They would have thought it would be a very large step from the holding that the Equal Protection Clause forbids a state to prefer a male to a female administrator of an estate to a holding that it also forbids restrictions on abortion. They would have asked, what does the former holding have to do with women's reproductive freedom? It bears noting that the earliest published scholarly articles Ginsburg cited for the equal protection justification for *Roe*, those by Kenneth Karst and Sylvia Law, came out several years after *Roe*, in 1977 and 1984.[28]

In sum, as of 1973, Occam's razor cuts clearly in favor of the due process argument over the equal protection argument. To Justice Blackmun, it would have been a considerably smaller step from *Griswold* and *Eisenstadt* to *Roe* than from *Reed* to *Roe*.

Second, one ground avoids or overcomes doctrinal obstacles faced by the other ground. Scholars like Ely and Sunstein would argue that equal protection is superior to due process as far as this criterion is concerned. They would say that the equal protection route avoids the charge of Lochnering that is sure to arise on the due process route. But the people who cried *Lochner* in the due process cases leading up to *Roe* (those whom Ely said had cried wolf too often) also invoked *Lochner* in criticizing most of the equal protection cases protecting fundamental rights between 1937 (when the Court repudiated substantive due process for economic liberties in *West Coast Hotel v. Parrish*) and 1973 (when the Court revived substantive due process for personal liberties in *Roe*). For example, dissenters cried *Lochner* when the Court held that malapportionment and a poll tax denied the right to vote in violation of the Equal Protection Clause, just as they did when the Court held that durational residency requirements to receive welfare benefits were invalid under the Equal Protection Clause.[29] As Ely himself acknowledged in "The Wages of Crying Wolf," critics complained about Lochnering whenever the Warren Court "was aggressive in enforcing its ideals of liberty and equality," not just liberty.[30] And so, going with equal protection instead of due process in *Roe* would not have avoided the charge of Lochnering.

Moreover, let's not forget that the due process argument in 1973 avoided a considerable doctrinal obstacle that would have faced the equal protection argument at that time: the *Geduldig* problem, which would have blinded people to the equal protection argument. The problem is not insurmountable today, but I believe it would have seemed so to mainstream lawyers in 1973 or 1974, when *Roe* and *Geduldig* were decided. It bears repeating that Blackmun, the author of the 7-2 majority opinion in *Roe*, was in the majority in *Geduldig*, as were three other justices from the majority in *Roe*.

Furthermore, we should bear in mind that the early Burger Court feared that, in Archibald Cox's famous formulation, "equality is an idea that is not easily cabined."[31] Accordingly, in 1973, in *San Antonio v. Rodriguez*, the Court shut down the expansion of equal protection jurisprudence, in both its fundamental rights and its suspect classifications strands.[32] That same year, in *Roe*, the Court revived substantive due process.[33] As observed in chapter 2, rarely is history so tidy: the Court shut down the use of the Equal Protection Clause to protect "new" fundamental rights or to recognize "new" suspect classifications at the very moment that it revived use of the Due Process Clause to protect basic liberties. Perhaps the early Burger Court was wary of and wanted to curb what it saw as the Warren Court's egalitarian revolution, but was comfortable with protecting rights of privacy or autonomy developed in a line of decisions through common law constitutional interpretation. To such a Court, in 1973, an equality justification for women's reproductive freedom was not on the table.

And so, on this second criterion, the Due Process Clause would have seemed a superior ground in 1973.

Third, one ground better captures the heart of the matter, or better gets at what is at stake in protecting the right. On this criterion, as of 1973, I would give the nod to liberty for the reason just stated: it was more intelligible to mainstream lawyers, while the equal protection argument was not yet fully developed and comprehensible to them. In that context, defenders of the right would have believed that what was at stake in striking down restrictions on abortion was protecting women's privacy or autonomy in making an important decision. In the grips of the *Geduldig* mindset, they would not have comprehended the argument that the denial of equal protection to women was the heart of the matter.

But, as of 1992, when *Casey* was decided, we might have a tie between liberty and equality as grounds with respect to this criterion. Based on understandings available by that time, defenders of the right would have seen that both capture the heart of the matter. For one thing, the right to decide whether to terminate a pregnancy is a right to make an important decision fundamentally affecting one's destiny, identity, or way of life. That's the due process heart of the matter. For another, denial of the right certainly reflects constitutionally problematic assumptions about the role of women as naturally being mothers and denies them the status of equal citizenship. That's the equal protection heart of the matter. Hence, as of 1992, Justices Blackmun and Stevens could forcefully and clear-headedly articulate both the due process and the equal protection arguments for reproductive freedom. Hence, they recognized that the denials of both a basic liberty and the status of equal citizenship were at stake when states restrict abortion.

Fourth, one ground is more likely to persuade people not already persuaded. This criterion would come into play when the debates concerning the right to decide whether to terminate a pregnancy were very far along, as by 1992, rather than when they were near the beginning, as in 1973. Rewriters might claim that this is a virtue of equal protection arguments for the right over due process arguments, at least as of 1992. They might say that, by 1992, we had reached an impasse or standstill in gaining support for the right. Those people not already persuaded by the due process argument over the previous nineteen years, they might contend, were not likely ever to be persuaded by it. They might think that we could make new headway with the equal protection argument. Maybe people will see the right in a new light and finally be persuaded to support it.

So let's ask, as of 1992 and thereafter, is the equal protection argument likely to persuade people not already persuaded by the due process argument? I grant that some people who support the right have doubts about the privacy argument in *Roe*. They have heard all the criticisms that it is vulnerable. Maybe they will be fortified in their support for the right once they hear and grasp the equal protection argument, especially in the powerful and well-developed form in which it was available as of 1992. But firming up the positions of those already persuaded is not the same thing as persuading people not already persuaded. You may charge me with forgetting my own example of Ely. I mentioned that in 1973, before the equal protection argument was available in our constitutional culture, Ely thought *Roe* was wrongly decided as a matter of due process. But, as of 1992, when the equal protection argument was available, he thought *Casey* was rightly decided. Let's remember, though, that Ely was already a pro-choice liberal with a great gift for recasting arguments others made in terms of privacy or liberty into equal protection arguments. That is a far cry from an equal protection argument persuading someone who was not already persuaded or at least predisposed to being persuaded.

Would the development of the equal protection argument persuade ordinary people who were not already persuaded by the due process argument? I am dubious. I don't believe that people who oppose the right to decide whether to terminate a pregnancy are likely to say, oh, I never considered the fact that restrictions on pregnancy violate an anti-caste or anti-subordination principle of equality—and therefore deny women the status of equal citizenship. I guess *Roe* and *Casey* were rightly decided after all.

What is more, as of 1992, I believe that *Casey*'s due process justification—which stresses a woman's "right to make the ultimate decision, not a right to be insulated from all others in doing so," and allows the state greater latitude to encourage what it views as women's responsible exercise of the right than did *Roe*'s justification[34]—was more likely to persuade people not already persuaded than would any equal protection justification. Indeed, at the time *Casey* was decided, there were analyses suggesting that it better captured and matched public opinion on the proper scope of a woman's right to decide whether to terminate her pregnancy than did *Roe*, which seemed to be more "absolutist" and to entail that governmental regulations seeking to encourage what the government views as women's responsible exercise of the right were unconstitutional.[35] At least some people who were uncomfortable with *Roe*'s more absolutist protection of the right evidently were more persuaded by *Casey*'s less stringent protection under its "undue burden" test. And so, this criterion does not cut in favor of equal protection over due process.

In sum, applying these four criteria suggests that in 1973, due process arguments would have seemed to mainstream lawyers like Justice Blackmun to be a more available and persuasive ground than equal protection arguments. And it becomes easier to understand why the Supreme Court would have grounded *Roe* in due process rather than equal protection. But by 1992, strong arguments sounding in both due process and equal protection were available and were cogently articulated in the joint opinion and the concurrences in *Casey*.

Conflict or Overlap: Liberty versus Equality or Liberty Together with Equality?

With this analysis in mind, we should return to the question posed above: should we view the relationship between the due process and equal protection arguments as *liberty versus equality* or *liberty together with equality*? I urge the latter approach: we should make both liberty arguments under the Due Process Clause and equality arguments under the Equal Protection Clause in justifying reproductive freedom. *Casey* itself rewrote *Roe* through the ordinary processes of common law constitutional interpretation over a period of nineteen years. We don't need fully to rewrite *Roe* beyond making the liberty and equality arguments in the joint opinion together with the concurrences of Stevens and Blackmun in *Casey*. Doing so gives us everything we need adequately to justify the right to decide whether to terminate a pregnancy.

This is not to say that *Casey*'s undue burden test adequately values liberty or equality, or that the Court correctly applied that test in *Casey* when it upheld several restrictions on abortion. But unfortunately, we are not likely to do any better with the Supreme Court for the foreseeable future—especially not after Justice Kennedy retired and was succeeded by Justice Kavanaugh and Justice Ginsburg died and was succeeded by Justice Barrett.

What Should *Obergefell* Have Said?

Just as with *Roe*, so with *Obergefell*, critics call for rewriting the opinion by recasting it from its official primary ground of the Due Process Clause to the Equal Protection Clause. But the situation of these two cases is different. If you had polled every constitutional law professor in the country on June 25, 2015, the day before *Obergefell* was decided, I daresay most would have predicted that the decision would be grounded in the Equal Protection Clause rather than the Due Process Clause. After all, in 2013, in *United States v. Windsor*, the Court had just invalidated the federal Defense of Marriage Act (DOMA)—defining marriage for purposes of federal law as the union of one man and one woman—on the ground that it violated the Equal Protection Clause.[36] Thus, the equal protection argument for a right of same-sex couples to marry was well developed as of 2015 (unlike the situation with the equal protection argument for *Roe* as of 1973). Nonetheless, in *Obergefell*, the Court officially used the Due Process Clause as the primary ground, though as intertwined with the Equal Protection Clause.

Obergefell has been celebrated by many liberals and progressives and condemned by many conservatives. Yet Justice Kennedy's majority opinion is hardly the opinion that many liberals or progressives would have written. (To oversimplify ideas: liberals typically support strong autonomy and right-to-choose arguments, while progressives characteristically advance equality arguments aimed at securing the status and benefits of equal citizenship for groups historically oppressed or marginalized.) Many liberals and progressives would like to rewrite *Obergefell*. To be sure, the dream liberal decision, like Kennedy's opinion, would have recognized a fundamental right to marry under the Due Process Clause that extends to same-sex couples. But, doctrinally, it would have held that this fundamental right triggers "strict scrutiny"—requiring that laws regulating the right promote a compelling governmental interest and be narrowly tailored to furthering that interest. The dream liberal opinion would have clearly articulated and applied this framework, giving the most stringent protection to the fundamental right to marry. Instead, Kennedy's opinion is minimalist with respect to doctrinal framework. It does not articulate a level of scrutiny or a doctrinal test. And so, some liberals worry about how clearly articulated and stringent the protection for the right is. But, as seen in chapter 3, this opinion is vintage Kennedy: he took a similarly minimalist approach in all three of his previous landmark decisions protecting gays and lesbians under the Due Process Clause (*Lawrence v. Texas* [2003]) as well as the Equal Protection Clause (*Romer v. Evans* [1996] and *Windsor*).[37]

Nor is Kennedy's opinion the opinion that many progressives would have written. The dream progressive decision would have been squarely grounded in the Equal Protection Clause, not the Due Process Clause. It would have condemned laws denying marriage to same-sex couples for denying them the status and benefits of equal citizenship rather than for denying them liberty. What is more, the dream progressive decision would have held that discrimination on the basis of sexual orientation, by analogy to that on the basis of race, embodies a "suspect classification." It would have held that such discrimination triggers "strict scrutiny," with the stringent protection that it entails—requiring that the law promote a compelling governmental interest and be narrowly tailored to doing so. Alternatively, another sort of dream progressive decision would have held that laws prohibiting same-sex couples to marry reflect discrimination on the basis of gender and therefore warrant the relatively stringent protection of "intermediate scrutiny." But again, Kennedy's opinion is characteristically minimalist regarding doctrinal framework and level of scrutiny, whether under the Equal Protection Clause or the Due Process Clause.

Thus, Kennedy's opinion did not give liberals or progressives everything they hoped for, though I want to acknowledge its liberal and progressive strands. The liberal elements include concern for individual autonomy in making certain intimate decisions that fundamentally affect one's identity, destiny, or way of life. The progressive elements include reference to sexual orientation as "immutable"—though many progressives hold a more fluid conception of sexual orientation and gender identity than Kennedy did in 2015—and concern that laws denying recognition and benefits to same-sex couples demean their existence and humiliate them and their children.[38]

All things considered, it is no surprise that Kennedy took the liberty route he took rather than the liberty route liberals would have favored or the equality route progressives would have taken. For one thing, most obviously, he is not a liberal or a progressive but a conservative. For another, the opinion he wrote is more understandable and persuasive in the context of his battles with the four movement conservatives to the right of him dissenting in *Obergefell* than those liberals and progressives who would rewrite his majority opinion have recognized.

In chapter 2, I argued that Justice Kennedy's majority opinion in *Oberge-fell* is best understood as a conservative opinion in the mold of Justice John Marshall Harlan II, the most conservative member of the Warren Court. Kennedy's opinion in *Obergefell*—like the joint opinion of Justices O'Connor, Kennedy, and Souter in *Casey*—invokes and evokes Harlan's conservative constitutional jurisprudence as manifested famously in his dissenting opinion in *Poe v. Ullman* (1961) and his concurring opinion in *Griswold*.[39] The dissenters in *Obergefell*—like those in *Casey*—are a new breed of culture war conservatives who have rejected Harlan's conservative jurisprudence. The battle in *Obergefell*—like that in *Casey*—is between these two types of conservatives, whom I have called, respectively, preservative conservatives and counterrevolutionary conservatives.[40]

I elaborated five characteristics of Harlan's (and Kennedy's) substantive due process jurisprudence in contradistinction from that of the four dissenters in *Obergefell*. Here I repeat the fifth. In elaborating the basic reasons underlying our constitutional commitments and our precedents interpreting them, Kennedy like Harlan makes recourse to the moral goods promoted by protecting our freedoms. I drew a stylized distinction between *liberal* choice arguments and *conservative* moral goods arguments. Applied to marriage, the liberal argument stresses my right as an individual to choose whom to have sex with, to decide whom to marry, and to do whatever I please with my body—a right to choose without regard for the moral good of what is chosen. By contrast, the conservative argument emphasizes the moral goods promoted by protecting that right and the institution of marriage. In *Oberge-fell*, Kennedy quotes *Griswold*'s stirring language about the noble purposes of marriage: promoting intimacy, harmony, and loyalty within a worthy relationship.[41] He also quotes the formulations of the Massachusetts Supreme Judicial Court in *Goodridge v. Department of Public Health* (2003) concerning the moral goods of "commitment" along with "mutuality, companionship, intimacy, fidelity, and family."[42] On Kennedy's and Harlan's view, we protect the fundamental right to marry because marriage is an intimate association for furthering such noble purposes and promoting such moral goods. Kennedy justifies extending the fundamental right to marry to same-sex couples on the ground that doing so not only respects their basic liberty, but also promotes these moral goods, just as opposite-sex marriage does.

In justifying rights, liberals typically are more comfortable with strong personal autonomy arguments than with such moral goods discourse. Historically, they have distrusted the latter, fearing that it is inherently conservative and that it will too narrowly limit the scope of liberty. They fear that rights justified on the ground that they promote moral goods will be extended only to those people whom conservatives judge to be morally good! For analogous reasons, progressives typically are more comfortable with strong equal citizenship arguments than with such moral goods discourse. Some progressives have worried that, in "emphasizing the exalted status of marriage in our society, the dignity and respectability attached to that status, and the harm and humiliation suffered by same-sex couples and their children due to restrictive marriage laws," the majority opinion may "suggest that those who choose *not* to marry and to form nonmarital family relationships lack dignity and are less worthy."[43]

Should we rewrite *Obergefell* so as to ground it primarily in the Equal Protection Clause instead of the Due Process Clause? Later in this chapter, I apply the four criteria for deciding between these two available grounds (just as I applied them above to *Roe*). As I see it, there are good reasons to stick with liberty intertwined with equality. And there are good reasons to combine moral goods arguments with personal autonomy and equal citizenship arguments. Moral goods arguments are especially apt when we are talking about rights related to an institution like marriage, which is a status and package of benefits and responsibilities with important civic purposes, not merely rights involving personal choices. Furthermore, as argued in chapter 4, moral goods arguments are effective in rebutting slippery slope arguments like those of Scalia in dissent in *Lawrence*. Justice Kennedy's opinion may not be as elegant as some would hope. And it is easier to ridicule than an opinion by Justice Harlan would be. After all, Harlan was a much-admired legal craftsman (and even the liberals and progressives who disagreed with his conservative views typically respected him and his opinions). But all in all there is a "mad genius" in Kennedy's opinion.[44] And so, to the liberals and progressives who wish to rewrite *Obergefell* along the lines of the above dream liberal and progressive opinions, I caution: "You can't always get what you want / But if you try sometimes / Well, you just might find / You get what you need."[45] *Obergefell* contains every argument we need fully to justify it.

From *Romer* to *Obergefell*: The Court's Own Rewriting of the Grounds for Protecting Gay and Lesbian Rights

Over a period of twenty years, the Supreme Court's analysis of the constitutional flaws in laws denying liberty or equality to gays and lesbians underwent a significant shift—from forbidding illegitimate emotions to rejecting inadequate reasons. In that sense, the Court engaged in its own rewriting. I sketch that shift through examining three leading decisions culminating in *Obergefell*. In *Romer* (1996), the Court held that a state constitutional amendment—barring protection of gays and lesbians from discrimination on the basis of sexual orientation—reflected unconstitutional "animus" against and a "bare . . . desire to harm [them as] a politically unpopular group." Therefore, the Court held that the amendment violated the Equal Protection Clause.[46] In *Lawrence* (2003), by contrast, the Court concluded that a law banning intimate sexual conduct between same-sex persons unconstitutionally "demean[ed] the lives" of gays and lesbians. The law officially violated the Due Process Clause and implicitly violated the Equal Protection Clause.[47] *Windsor* (2013), which struck down the federal DOMA under the Equal Protection Clause, is the third of Justice Kennedy's important decisions protecting gay and lesbian rights. Here I will leave *Windsor* out of the analysis, viewing it as a ladder from *Romer* and *Lawrence* to *Obergefell*. (Below I shall discuss *Windsor's* federalism strands and consider whether, because of its equal protection holding, we might have expected the Court to decide *Obergefell* on equal protection grounds.) Finally, in *Obergefell* (2015), the Court ruled that laws not extending the fundamental right to marry to same-sex couples unconstitutionally denied equal dignity and respect to gays and lesbians and failed to afford them and their children the status and benefits of equal citizenship. The primary ground was the Due Process Clause, also intertwined with the Equal Protection Clause.[48]

Thus, in *Romer*, emotions animating the denials of rights to gays and lesbians evidently played a central role, whereas in *Lawrence* and *Obergefell*, it was the social meaning of the denials that was crucial. I shall argue that the focus in *Romer* on emotions—"animus" and the "bare desire to harm," which Justice Scalia's dissent equated with "racial or religious bias" or "bigotry"[49]—is unnecessary and unfortunate. I shall also contend that the shift, in *Lawrence* and *Obergefell*, to concluding that laws denying rights to gays and lesbians demean their existence and deny them the status and benefits of equal citizenship puts gay and lesbian rights on firmer ground and better deflects Scalia's and other dissenters' allegations that the Court is charging opponents of gay and lesbian rights with bigotry. Let us begin at the beginning, with *Romer*, and then trace the shift in the ground for rights—the Court's own rewriting—through *Lawrence* and *Obergefell*.

Romer: "Animus" against and a "Bare Desire to Harm a Politically Unpopular Group" Denies Equal Protection to Gays and Lesbians

Romer involved a challenge, under the Equal Protection Clause, to a Colorado state constitutional amendment forbidding the protection of gays, lesbians, and bisexuals from discrimination on the basis of sexual orientation.

The state had adopted this amendment after several progressive cities had passed local ordinances protecting them from such discrimination.[50]

In *Romer*, decided in 1996, the Court does not even consider certain familiar equal protection arguments that were available at the time. First, it does not consider whether discrimination on the basis of sexual orientation, like that on the basis of race, embodies a "suspect classification" that would trigger "strict scrutiny." Relatedly, the Court does not inquire whether the legal measure being challenged, like measures discriminating on the basis of race, reflects "prejudice" against a "discrete and insular minority." Under conventional analysis, such prejudice reflects bigotry or irrational hostility toward such minorities.[51]

Second, the Court does not address whether discrimination on the basis of sexual orientation is impermissible discrimination on the basis of gender that would call for "intermediate scrutiny." On this view, the constitutional flaw in laws discriminating against gays and lesbians is that they aim to enforce traditional gender roles or "compulsory heterosexuality" upon gays and lesbians and therefore represent a form of discrimination on the basis of gender.

Why did Justice Kennedy's opinion of the Court in *Romer* not take either of these two available doctrinal approaches? My view is that Kennedy was not about to take the first: he wanted not only to avoid taking what he would have viewed as the big and controversial step to holding that sexual orientation is a "suspect classification" analogous to race, but also to avoid implying that opposition to gay and lesbian rights is analogous to prejudice or bigotry against "discrete and insular minorities" like racial minorities. Kennedy presumably also was not prepared to take the second approach: not only because he did not wish to take what he would have seen as the big and controversial step to holding that sexual orientation discrimination is a somewhat suspicious classification on the basis of gender, but also because he wanted to avoid resting the holding upon a complex and controversial normative theory about sexual orientation discrimination and the enforcement of gender roles not likely to have been acceptable (or even comprehensible) to many people in 1996.

These were the two main doctrinal roads to protecting gay and lesbian rights not taken in *Romer* in 1996. Were there any other roads available at the time? There was an emerging line of cases dealing with classifications that were not quite "suspect classifications" but toward which the Court was somewhat suspicious, out of concern that majorities might be treating disfavored minorities unequally out of lack of concern for, fear of, or hostility toward them. *Department of Agriculture v. Moreno* (1973) involved denying food stamps to needy individuals who were living together but were "unrelated persons." The law, the Court held, was intended to prevent "hippies" and "hippie communes" from participating in the food stamp program. The Court further held that a "bare congressional desire to harm a politically unpopular group cannot constitute a *legitimate* governmental interest."[52] *City of Cleburne v. Cleburne Living Center, Inc.* (1985), a prominent case building upon *Moreno* in this line of decisions leading up to *Romer*, involved discrimination against developmentally disabled persons. The Court stated that "mere negative attitudes" of the majority of property owners, based on "prejudice" against such persons, was not an adequate reason to deny a permit to establish a home for them in a residential neighborhood.[53]

In *Romer*'s majority opinion, Justice Kennedy argued that the state constitutional amendment being challenged, which discriminated on the basis of sexual orientation, likewise reflected illegitimate "animus" and "bare . . . desire to harm."[54] Thus, in the first case to protect gay and lesbian rights in US constitutional law, Kennedy invoked cases involving discrimination, not on the basis of race or gender—which might have seemed analogous to sexual orientation—but against needy "hippies" and developmentally disabled persons. Taking this route, the Court did not have to reach the controversial decision that sexual orientation is like race or gender and warrants "strict scrutiny" or "intermediate scrutiny." On the other hand, the Court did not simply defer to and uphold the legislation because one might reasonably conclude that it was rationally related to a legitimate governmental objective. Instead, the Court applied rational basis scrutiny with "bite." That is, it put some teeth into the requirement that a law be rationally related to a legitimate governmental objective and it found the state constitutional amendment unconstitutional under that standard.[55]

Thus, Justice Kennedy's majority opinion in *Romer* took a doctrinal approach that he quite reasonably might have thought would avoid the controversial insinuation that opposition to gay and lesbian rights was as objectionable as racial bigotry. Yet his opinion nevertheless prompted Justice Scalia to object in dissent that the Court was "equating the moral disapproval of homosexual conduct with racial and religious bigotry." By giving a central role to "animus" and a "bare desire to harm," Kennedy's opinion may, instead of avoiding the charge that he is implying that opponents of gay and lesbian rights are bigots, practically invite that charge. We should apply a principle of interpretive charity to Kennedy's opinion: he did the best he could with the doctrinal tools available at the time. Like a good common law constitutional interpreter, he reached for the precedents available—*Cleburne* and *Moreno*—and, since they used the terms "animus" against and a "bare desire to harm a politically unpopular group," he applied that formulation to the denial of rights to gays and lesbians.[56]

Was there an alternative route that Kennedy could have taken in *Romer* that might have averted Scalia's accusation that the majority was tarring the opponents of gay and lesbian rights with the brush of bigotry? In fact, there was another route—which provides a bridge to *Lawrence*—and Kennedy arguably took it as well in *Romer*! He quoted Justice John Marshall Harlan's famous dissent in *Plessy v. Ferguson* (1896) that the Constitution "neither knows nor tolerates classes among citizens."[57] This principle—the core of an anti-caste principle—forbids government to "deem a class of persons strangers to its laws" by branding them as pariahs, outlaws, or outcasts.[58] The state constitutional amendment had done precisely that to gays and lesbians. It was a "status-based . . . classification of persons" that was not rationally related to a legitimate governmental purpose.[59]

Under this principle, the constitutional flaw in the state amendment was that it denied the status of equal citizenship, including the benefits and protections afforded to others, to a group of persons who are worthy of those benefits and protections. Taking this approach, what matters is not the illegitimate emotions animating the denial of equal citizenship— "animus" against and a "bare desire to harm [them as] a politically unpopular group"—but the social meaning of the denial—that gays and lesbians are pariahs, outlaws, or outcasts. And what undergirds the holding that the state amendment is unconstitutional is the normative judgment that gays and lesbians are worthy of the status, benefits, and protections of equal citizenship. Thus, normative judgments that there are no adequate reasons for denying these protections to gays and lesbians are an alternative—and superior—basis for protecting gay and lesbian rights.

Lawrence: *Laws Denying the Right to Intimate Association to Gays and Lesbians Demean Their Existence*

In *Lawrence*, the Supreme Court held that laws criminalizing intimate sexual conduct between same-sex persons denied basic liberty in violation of the Due Process Clause. The Court shifted from the inquiry into "animus" and a "bare desire to harm" to an inquiry into the social meaning of a practice— whether laws that deny the right of intimate association to gays and lesbians "demean their existence."[60] In previous decisions, the Court had recognized a right to autonomy and intimate association for straights.[61] According to Justice Kennedy, same-sex intimate association is analogous to opposite-sex intimate association. And gays and lesbians engage in intimate association for the same purposes and to pursue the same moral goods as straights. Thus, Kennedy concluded that gays and lesbians are entitled to "respect for their private lives" and that the state may not "demean their existence or control their destiny by making their private sexual conduct a crime."[62] Kennedy implicitly judged gays' and lesbians' sexual intimacy and way of life to be as morally worthy and entitled to respect as that of straights. This normative judgment underpins the conclusion that laws prohibiting sexual intimacy between same-sex persons demean the existence of gays and lesbians. At the time, Kennedy wrote *Lawrence* as a due process holding rather than an equal protection holding (although there were unmistakable expressions of a concern for equality in his due process arguments). In *Obergefell*, Kennedy looked back and interpreted *Lawrence* as intertwining due process and equal protection.[63]

With this better justification for gay and lesbian rights on hand, we can see that Scalia's objections that the majority tarred the opponents of the right to same-sex intimate association with the brush of bigotry are overwrought and inapt. Holding that the laws forbidding same-sex couples from engaging in intimate sexual conduct deny such couples equal dignity and respect in no way impugns the motivations or character of opponents of gay and lesbian rights. It does not charge opponents with "animus" against or a "bare desire to harm a politically unpopular group." It simply recognizes that the social meaning of such laws—even if based on sincerely and conscientiously held religious convictions—is to deny equal dignity and respect to gays and lesbians. The fact that opponents act out of sincerely and conscientiously held religious views is not an adequate reason to deny gays and lesbians the basic liberties and status and benefits of equal citizenship already afforded to straights. The recognition of this fact became central in *Obergefell*.

Obergefell: *The State May Not Deny Equal Dignity or the Status and Benefits of Equal Citizenship to Gays and Lesbians*

In *Obergefell*, ruling that the fundamental right to marry extends to same-sex couples, Justice Kennedy writes the majority opinion in the same vein as in *Lawrence* rather than in the style of *Romer*. *Obergefell* completes *Lawrence*'s shift away from illegitimate emotions and toward a more fully articulated justification for why laws denying basic liberties to gays and lesbians lack any adequate justification. Here I briefly encapsulate the reasoning of *Obergefell*.

Gays and lesbians are entitled to the rights to autonomy, to intimate association, and to marry, all of which are already protected for straights.

The state may not demean their existence—their morally legitimate way of life—by denying them these rights. They are entitled to equal dignity and respect. The state has created an important institution—civil marriage—to promote certain noble purposes and moral goods. Here, Kennedy quotes the stirring language from *Griswold* and *Goodridge* about these purposes and goods. Same-sex couples are similarly situated to opposite-sex couples with respect to the pursuit of such moral goods and the need for the benefits of marriage. There is no adequate reason for denying them this right and these benefits. Not extending the fundamental right to marry to same-sex couples demeans their existence and humiliates them and their children, denying them the status and benefits of equal citizenship.

Justice Kennedy's majority opinion in *Obergefell* was based primarily on the ground that the law denied the fundamental right to marry in violation of the Due Process Clause rather than on the ground that it violated the Equal Protection Clause. As suggested above, Kennedy may have taken this route to avoid the need to draw analogies between discrimination on the basis of sexual orientation and that on the basis of race and to avoid implying that opponents of gay and lesbian rights are analogous to racial or religious bigots. Nonetheless, Chief Justice Roberts and Justices Scalia and Alito in their dissents in *Obergefell* contended that the majority opinion had portrayed those who did not share its understanding of marriage as bigoted.[64] For example, Justice Alito warned that the majority's decision would be "used to vilify Americans who are unwilling to assent to the new orthodoxy," and that, while "those who cling to old beliefs will be able to whisper their thoughts in the recesses of their homes . . . if they repeat those views in public, they will risk being labeled as bigots and treated as such by governments, employers, and schools."[65]

These charges ignore what Kennedy's opinion in *Obergefell* said and did. In fact, Kennedy nowhere referred to those who oppose allowing same-sex couples to marry as bigots. To the contrary, he stressed that he does not doubt the sincerity of opponents of same-sex marriage. Moreover, he emphasized that he was not disparaging their conscientious religious convictions: "Many who deem same-sex marriage to be wrong reach that conclusion based on decent and honorable religious or philosophical premises, and neither they nor their beliefs are disparaged here."[66] He also stated: "religions, and those who adhere to religious doctrines, may continue to advocate with utmost, sincere conviction that, by divine precepts, same-sex marriage should not be condoned."[67] But he explained that "when that sincere, personal opposition becomes enacted into law and public policy, the necessary consequence is to put the imprimatur of the State itself on an exclusion that soon demeans or stigmatizes those whose own liberty is denied."[68]

This passage reflects important constitutional limits upon the legal enforcement of morality in a morally pluralistic constitutional democracy: however sincere their beliefs, citizens may not use the vehicle of the law to exclude others from basic civil institutions. Saying that a law which is sincerely defended by people of conscience denies gays and lesbians equal dignity by denying them the status and benefits of equal citizenship where a basic civil institution like marriage is concerned is hardly equivalent to branding those people as bigots. In any case, nothing in Kennedy's opinion precludes states from enacting measures or using existing laws to protect (their conception of) religious liberty, provided they do not run afoul of the Court's holding that same-sex couples must be allowed to exercise the fundamental right to marry in all states and that states must allow them to marry on the same terms and conditions as opposite-sex couples. In chapter 9, I will examine conflicts between gay and lesbian rights and religious liberty and briefly consider religious exemptions to accommodate such conflicts.

Applying the Criteria for Deciding whether Due Process or Equal Protection Provides the Better Ground for *Obergefell*

It is time to apply the four criteria (sketched above) to deciding whether the Due Process Clause or the Equal Protection Clause provides the better ground for justifying the right recognized in *Obergefell*.

First, Occam's razor or elegance. Is it a smaller step from *Lawrence* (Due Process Clause) to *Obergefell* or from *Romer* and *Windsor* (Equal Protection Clause) to *Obergefell*? It certainly seems a small step from *Lawrence*'s due process ruling. *Lawrence*'s formulation of gays' and lesbians' right to intimate association, with its analogy to the rights recognized for straights and its reference to moral goods, paved the way for the moral goods landscape in *Goodridge* and *Obergefell*. *Lawrence*'s articulation that denial of the right "demeans the existence" of gays and lesbians likewise paved the way for *Obergefell*. Despite Kennedy's disclaimer in *Lawrence* that the Court was not deciding the issue of same-sex marriage, Scalia warned that protecting a right to same-sex intimate association would lead to recognizing a right to same-sex marriage.[69] And so it did, though (as argued in chapter 4) by the working out of constitutional principle through common law constitutional interpretation, not (as Scalia warned) by plummeting down a slippery slope toward "the end of all morals legislation."

Yet *Obergefell* also seems a short step from *Windsor's* equal protection holding. *Romer's* inquiry into "animus" and "bare desire to harm" traveled to *Windsor* and certainly could have traveled through to *Obergefell*. *Windsor* introduces the argument that states create marriage and by doing so confer dignity upon the marital relationship; therefore, the federal government may not deny that dignity through denying the right of same-sex couples to marry where the states have recognized it.[70] In that sense, *Windsor* represents a move from the "negative" liberty involved in *Lawrence* to evidently "positive" liberty stemming from the state creating the institution of marriage and then being obligated to confer the benefits of that institution with equal respect and dignity. Once there, it may seem a smaller step from *Windsor* to *Obergefell* than it would be from *Lawrence* to *Obergefell*. As in *Lawrence*, so in *Windsor*, Scalia warns in dissent that the next step will be a right to same-sex marriage everywhere.[71]

Thus, it may seem that we have a draw: it is a small step to *Obergefell* through either the due process or the equal protection route. However, the due process approach in *Obergefell* is a better fit with Kennedy's gay and lesbian rights jurisprudence. Kennedy generally uses the Equal Protection Clause to strike down new laws or amendments adopted specifically to limit or deny rights to gays and lesbians, as in *Romer* (Amendment 2) and *Windsor* (DOMA). By contrast, he uses the Due Process Clause to strike down long-standing laws or prohibitions—old laws adopted long before anyone may have thought of how they might apply to gays and lesbians—that we now understand demean the existence of or deny the status and benefits of equal citizenship to them. He would have seen laws limiting marriage to opposite-sex couples as the latter. With this distinction in mind, it becomes easy to understand why Kennedy might have seen the due process ground as a smaller step or better ground in *Obergefell*.

Second, one ground avoids or overcomes doctrinal obstacles faced by the other ground. On this criterion, two arguments cut in favor of the Due Process Clause over the Equal Protection Clause. One, as discussed above, Kennedy might have wished to go due process rather than equal protection to avoid deciding or implying that all classifications on the basis of sexual orientation are unconstitutional. Indeed, the very reason progressives wanted an equal protection holding may be the reasons why he avoided making one. He may want to take the evidently larger–but actually smaller step to marriage through the Due Process Clause and go no farther for now. Furthermore, as discussed above, he might have hoped that the due process route would better avoid or deflect the charge that he is branding opponents as bigots.

Two, *Windsor* stressed federalism, and the Court in striking down the federal DOMA emphasized that marriage is a subject of state control, which might throw up doctrinal obstacles to arguments from it for a federal constitutional right to same-sex marriage everywhere. In dissent in *Windsor*, Chief Justice Roberts took Kennedy at his word, stressing the federalism part of the opinion, striving to interpret the holding narrowly as not leading to any such federal right.[72] But Scalia warned, don't be fooled, this is not a federalism opinion, this analysis leads straightaway to a federal constitutional right to same-sex marriage everywhere.[73]

The equal protection precedent of *Baker v. Nelson* (1972) did not really pose a doctrinal obstacle. In that early case, the Minnesota Supreme Court had rejected the argument that the limitation of marriage to opposite-sex couples denied equal protection of the laws.[74] The US Supreme Court simply dismissed the case "for want of a substantial federal question."[75] Opponents of same-sex marriage wanted to treat *Baker* as having definitively resolved the matter, but a one-sentence opinion in a case decided forty-three years prior—when the gay and lesbian rights movement was just getting started, and long before *Romer*, *Lawrence*, and *Windsor* protected rights of gays and lesbians under the Due Process and Equal Protection Clauses—hardly counts as an authoritative resolution. In any case, *Baker* would be a greater doctrinal obstacle for the equal protection argument than for the due process argument. The linchpin of the Minnesota Supreme Court's opinion was that *Loving* did not support a right to same-sex marriage because it was confined to "patent racial discrimination," which entails a rejection of the equal protection argument.[76]

Third, one ground better captures the heart of the matter, or better gets at what is at stake in protecting the right. Here too there seems to be a draw between the Due Process and Equal Protection Clauses. With the due process argument, we have the right to decide whom to marry as the heart of the matter. With the equal protection argument, we have the failure to extend the status and benefits of equal citizenship as the heart of the matter. We also have demeaning the existence of a morally worthy group as the heart of the matter. While this sounds like an equal protection argument, Kennedy characteristically utters this pronouncement in the name of due process. Thus, one can articulate the heart of the holding to sound equally in the Due Process Clause or the Equal Protection Clause.

Fourth, one ground is more likely to persuade people not already persuaded. A generation ago, a famous Yale law professor said to me that his students were more persuaded by equal protection arguments than by due process arguments for *Roe*. He added that they were more persuaded by the equal protection arguments against *Bowers v. Hardwick* (1986) than by the due process arguments. He said further that the only people who thought the due process arguments were superior to the equal protection arguments were older generation liberals like Ronald Dworkin and Laurence Tribe. He argued that the wave of the future was equal protection arguments.

I was dubious about the argument at the time. I would be even more dubious about any such argument with respect to the current generation. In my experience with students at Boston University and Princeton University, this generation is more libertarian than the last and is more persuaded by liberty arguments than by equality arguments when it comes to rights like reproductive freedom and LGBTQ+ rights. More broadly, in my experience, the arguments that typically persuade people not already persuaded to accept same-sex marriage are the moral goods arguments Kennedy made, not equal protection arguments about animus and a bare desire to harm a politically unpopular group (nor even more general anti-caste arguments). People do not want to be told that their attitudes express prejudice, animus, or a bare desire to harm. But they may be persuaded to accept gays and lesbians if they come to understand that some of their family, friends, and neighbors are gay or lesbian, and that those folks are pursuing moral goods (for example, through marriage) analogous to those they (as straights) pursue. They also come to see that gays and lesbians need the same protections for their children, along with stability, commitment, fidelity, and the other moral goods mentioned in *Obergefell*. As acknowledged above, many progressives are wary of such moral goods arguments. Indeed, the reasons some progressives don't like Kennedy's opinion derive from the reasons it is most likely to be persuasive to other people: its arguments sounding in moral goods and in liberal or libertarian rights to choose.

All things considered, I conclude that these criteria weigh in favor of the Due Process Clause arguments over the Equal Protection Clause arguments for justifying *Obergefell*. But, as does *Obergefell* itself, I acknowledge and insist on intertwining liberty arguments together with equality arguments. Therefore, I disagree with those who insist that equality arguments are superior to liberty arguments and therefore that we must rewrite the latter to become the former. Furthermore, as does *Obergefell*, I stress the wisdom and prudence of intertwining moral goods arguments with these arguments. Such eclectic opinions may not satisfy liberals' and progressives' desires for clarity or stringency, but they may be more persuasive in circumstances of moral pluralism and as products of a multi-member court (where an eclectic opinion may be necessary to build a majority).

Conclusion

There is no compelling need to rewrite *Casey* and *Obergefell*. Some liberals and progressives might want more than these decisions give them, but I conclude that the cases give us what we need to justify them. There may be underappreciated benefits of going with the Due Process Clause. Indeed, I have hypothesized that Justice Kennedy might have thought there were such benefits, like avoiding the implication that opponents of the right of same-sex couples to marry were analogous to racist bigots. Ironically, given all the worries critics have expressed about substantive due process being unbounded, it might have seemed to Kennedy easier to limit a due process holding than an equal protection holding, since the latter might imply that all discrimination on the basis of sexual orientation violates the Equal Protection Clause.

In sum, *Casey* and *Obergefell* intertwine the best Due Process Clause arguments and threads of the best Equal Protection Clause arguments. To be sure, these arguments are inflected through the lens of conservative justices, not liberals or progressives. For the foreseeable future, that is likely to be the best liberals and progressives can hope for. Besides, the joint opinion of Justices O'Connor, Kennedy, and Souter in *Casey* as well as Kennedy's majority opinion in *Obergefell* make the types of arguments more likely to persuade conservatives who are not already persuaded. After all, these opinions are conservative in the mold of Justice Harlan.

NINE

Accommodating Gay and Lesbian Rights and Religious Liberty

In this chapter, I focus on another type of conflict between equality and liberty: conflicts between equal rights for gays and lesbians (protected through antidiscrimination laws together with judicial decisions like *Obergefell v. Hodges* [2015][1]) and religious liberty. Such conflicts are bound to arise in a morally pluralistic constitutional democracy such as the US, which is committed to pursuing both ideals. Recent developments have dramatically posed the question whether laws recognizing same-sex marriage and protecting against discrimination on the basis of sexual orientation or gender identity (including in the marketplace) should grant exemptions to businesspeople who disapprove of such rights on religious grounds. The four justices who dissented in *Obergefell* have warned that protecting the right of same-sex couples to marry threatened the religious liberty of those who oppose that right.[2] Yet Chief Justice Roberts, in dissent, acknowledged that every state that had recognized same-sex marriage had created religious exemptions.[3] Nothing in *Obergefell* implies that the state statutes already granting such exemptions were unconstitutional, nor would it prohibit legislatures prospectively from creating exemptions as long as they do not impose a substantial burden on the rights of others. *Obergefell* leaves room for the democratic processes to continue to operate as before in creating religious exemptions. To be sure, exemptions will not satisfy those who oppose same-sex marriage altogether. Nor will they satisfy many supporters of equal rights. Yet limited exemptions seem to some to be a reasonable approach to ameliorating clashes between gay and lesbian rights and religious liberty.[4]

In *Ordered Liberty*, Linda C. McClain and I argued for conceiving religious exemptions concerning same-sex marriage as a prudential remedy, rooted in recognition of religious and moral objections to extending marriage to same-sex couples. Recognizing these exemptions stops just short of affording full, equal citizenship to gays and lesbians, for the time being, out of respect for and deference to those religious objections. We acknowledged that there may be pragmatic reasons for creating such religious exemptions during periods of rapid cultural and constitutional change. Doing so, we observed, might help to minimize backlash against gay and lesbian rights. But we tendered the hope that the prudential, mutual adjustment by granting religious exemptions concerning same-sex marriage would follow the path of same-sex civil unions in Vermont: that religious exemptions will prove to be a ladder to full, equal citizenship through acceptance of same-sex marriage. Going forward, we hope that the need for such exemptions will wither away along with religious objections to such marriage.[5] After all, in our morally pluralistic constitutional democracy, the aspiration is to social cooperation on the basis of mutual respect and trust, not the absolutist vindication of the rights claims of one group over those of another. Furthermore, we should recognize that religious exemptions undermine the government's formative project of inculcating civic virtues like tolerance and promoting the public value of securing the status and benefits of equal citizenship for all, including gays and lesbians. Religious exemptions are sites of resistance to such virtues and values.[6]

In a perceptive article, Christopher L. Eisgruber asked: "Is the Supreme Court an Educative Institution?" He argued that in some cases the Court may teach by offering lessons capable of inspiring Americans to live up to their constitutional ideals.[7] I sketch several senses in which the Court might be a civic educative institution (though I hardly mean to glorify it). I then explore one of these senses in action in two recent cases involving conflicts between gay and lesbian rights and religious liberty.

First, a Supreme Court opinion might exhort the government and the people themselves to live up to their constitutional commitments in cases where it holds that the government has violated those commitments. Think of Justice Robert Jackson's majority opinion in *West Virginia v. Barnette* (1943), which struck down a compulsory flag salute on the ground that "no official . . . can prescribe what shall be orthodox in politics."[8]

Second, an opinion might proclaim our constitutional ideals even while it upholds governmental actions. Consider Justice Louis Brandeis's concurrence in *Whitney v. California* (1927), upholding a restriction on advocacy of radical change while proclaiming: "Those who won our independence by revolution were not cowards. They did not fear political change. They did not exalt order at the cost of liberty."[9]

Third, a Supreme Court opinion might bring out the civic dimension of constitutional commitments, perhaps highlighting their role in a civic educative project or emphasizing their significance for performing civic duties. For example, in interpreting the First Amendment's guarantee of freedom of speech, the opinion might emphasize protecting speech that is essential to democratic self-government and elaborate the responsibilities of citizens. Consider again Brandeis's concurrence in *Whitney*: "[F]reedom to think as you will and to speak as you think are means indispensable to the discovery and spread of political truth . . . the greatest menace to freedom is an inert people . . . public discussion is a political duty."[10] Unfortunately, this civic dimension is largely absent in recent freedom of speech decisions, which appear to be grounded in distrust of government and a deregulatory rather than civic conception of the First Amendment.[11]

Fourth, a Supreme Court opinion might underscore each governmental institution's roles and responsibilities in maintaining the successful functioning of the constitutional order. For example, the Court might articulate its own responsibilities, such as: (1) safeguarding the rule of law even in times of crisis, for example, during the "war on terror" (*Boumediene v. Bush* [2008][12]); (2) upholding the obligation of the Court to decide cases as a matter of principle and build out lines of decisions with coherence and integrity, rather than overruling precedents simply because of a change in personnel (*Planned Parenthood v. Casey* [1992][13]); and (3) extending our constitutional commitments, on the basis of moral progress and new insights, to fulfill the Constitution's promise of liberty and equality to all (*Obergefell*[14]). Furthermore, as against arguments by dissenters that democratic majorities should be free to decide matters such as how to inculcate patriotism, regulate abortion, or define marriage, a Supreme Court opinion might seek to educate concerning the form of self-government embodied in the Constitution: it is not a majoritarian democracy but a constitutional democracy, with certain basic liberties limiting what majorities may do to people (*Barnette*, *Casey*, and *Obergefell*). Through such opinions, the Court also articulates some of the roles and responsibilities of executives and legislatures within such a constitutional democracy.

I focus on a fifth sense of civic educative institution: Supreme Court opinions, in attempting to resolve conflicts between rights in "culture war" controversies—in particular, between gay and lesbian rights and religious liberty—might teach lessons to citizens concerning how to accommodate such conflicts. Court opinions might model how to secure the central range of application of each conflicting right rather than vindicating one right absolutely to the exclusion of the other, with one side winning it all. They also might teach how to speak with respect concerning both gay and lesbian rights and religious liberty.

I primarily analyze the US Supreme Court's decision in *Masterpiece Cake-shop, Ltd. v. Colorado Civil Rights Commission* (2018),[15] but I also discuss the New Mexico Supreme Court's decision in *Elane Photography, LLC v. Willock* (2013).[16] Such cases teach (1) that antidiscrimination laws properly exact a commitment to nondiscrimination in the marketplace as "the price of citizenship" (to invoke a phrase from *Elane Photography*) and (2) that it is an obligation of government to afford equal respect both to gays and lesbians and to religious opponents of gay and lesbian rights.

At first glance, *Masterpiece Cakeshop* and *Elane Photography* seem quite different. *Elane Photography* holds for the same-sex couple and against the photographers (the Huguenins) who declined to photograph a same-sex ceremony on the basis of religious objections. *Masterpiece Cakeshop*, by contrast, holds for the baker (Jack Phillips), who refused to bake a wedding cake to celebrate a same-sex couple's marriage (that of Charlie Craig and David Mullins). Justice Kennedy's majority opinion chastises a Colorado civil rights commissioner's "hostility" toward Phillips's religious beliefs, holding that it "was inconsistent with the First Amendment's guarantee that our laws be applied in a manner that is neutral toward religion."[17] On closer examination, these cases prove to be quite similar.

I should say at the outset that I believe that *Masterpiece Cakeshop* was wrongly decided. Still, if we view the decision in its best light, we see that Justice Kennedy clearly believes that he is accommodating the conflict in a way that affords equal respect both to gays and lesbians and to religious opponents of gay and lesbian rights.

Two Cases Teaching Respect and "the Price of Citizenship"

Elane Photography

In his concurring opinion in *Elane Photography*, Justice Richard C. Bosson stressed that the New Mexico antidiscrimination law is broader than Title II of the Civil Rights Act of 1964, which prohibited discrimination in public accommodations (hotels, restaurants, gas stations, and entertainment venues) on the basis of race, color, religion, or national origin.[18] New Mexico's law has expanded to "preclude invidious discrimination in most every public business" (including photography businesses). It also has extended the "prohibited classifications" from "the historical classes"—those in Title II, as well as sex (or gender)—to include sexual orientation. Bosson interpreted this expansion of New Mexico's law in terms of evolving understanding of what forms of discrimination are "intolerable." He wrote: "The Huguenins today can no more turn away customers on the basis of sexual orientation . . . than they could refuse to photograph African-Americans or Muslims."[19] He treated racial, religious, and sexual-orientation discrimination as intolerable, without saying that the Huguenins are bigots for the sincere beliefs they hold. To the contrary, Bosson stated, "their religious convictions deserve our respect."[20]

But are the Huguenins, as conservative critics have charged, being unjustly driven from the public square? Bosson acknowledged that they are "compelled by law to compromise the very religious beliefs that inspire their lives"—a "sobering" result. Nonetheless, he would tell the Huguenins, "with the utmost respect," that this is part of the "price of citizenship" that we all have to pay in "our civic life."[21] Civic life in a "multicultural, pluralistic society" requires some "compromise" with and accommodation of the "contrasting values of others." The Huguenins retain the constitutional protection "to think, to say, to believe, as they wish," and to "follow [their God's] commandments in their personal lives," but in "the smaller, more focused world of the marketplace of commerce, of public accommodation," they "have to channel their conduct . . . to leave space for other Americans who believe something different." Notably, Bosson concluded that such compromise "is part of the glue that holds us together as a nation, the tolerance that lubricates the varied moving parts of us as a people."[22] This concurrence is a prime example of the lessons a judicial opinion can teach about living up to our constitutional commitments.

Masterpiece Cakeshop

Masterpiece Cakeshop teaches similar lessons. Many contend that *Masterpiece Cakeshop* was a narrow holding. Maybe so, in the sense that the Supreme Court did not accept the baker's broad arguments regarding religious liberty and freedom from compelled expression (for a right not to be compelled to express antidiscrimination laws' message of equality for gays and lesbians):[23] arguments which, if accepted, would have imperiled the very structure of antidiscrimination laws. The Court only set aside the Colorado Civil Rights Commission's (CCRC) order against Phillips, postponing to "later cases" how best to resolve the many "difficult" and "delicate" questions the case raised. It stated that "the Commission's consideration of Phillips's case was neither tolerant nor respectful of Phillips's religious beliefs."[24] Basically, the Court held that the baker was entitled to a hearing before the CCRC that was neutral and free from hostility toward his religious views.

But in reaching that narrow holding, the Supreme Court taught some broad lessons about antidiscrimination laws, clashes of rights, and the price of citizenship. These lessons are best summed up by Justice Ruth Bader Ginsburg's vigorous dissent, which opened by quoting passages from Justice Kennedy's majority opinion. Ginsburg began: "There is much in the Court's opinion with which I agree." (1) "'[I]t is a general rule that [religious and philosophical] objections do not allow business owners and other actors in the economy and in society to deny protected persons equal access to goods and services under a neutral and generally applicable public accommodations law.'" (2) "'Colorado law can protect gay persons, just as it can protect other classes of individuals, in acquiring whatever products and services they choose on the same terms and conditions as are offered to other members of the public.'" (3) "'[P]urveyors of goods and services who object to gay marriages for moral and religious reasons [may not] put up signs saying 'no goods or services will be sold if they will be used for gay marriages.'" (4) "Gay persons may be spared from 'indignities when they seek goods and services in an open market.'" Ginsburg concluded: "I strongly disagree, however, with the Court's conclusion that Craig and Mullins should lose this case. All of the above-quoted statements point in the opposite direction."[25] In a nutshell, the Court made broad pronouncements about the legitimacy of antidiscrimination laws in seeking to secure the status of equal citizenship for gays and lesbians by promoting nondiscrimination and even equal dignity and respect for them in the marketplace.

Another way to bring out how narrow (and broad) the ruling was is to focus on how the Supreme Court conceived the baker's right to free exercise of religion. Let us notice several available conceptions of religious liberty articulated in the US culture wars which the Court declined to endorse.

1. Some religious opponents of same-sex marriage assert or presuppose that, to respect their religious liberty, the state must define marriage in accordance with their religious beliefs, as the union of one man and one woman. Put another way, they assert or presuppose a right that same-sex marriage not be recognized. You may think no one argues this. Yet the dissents in the Supreme Court's gay and lesbian rights decisions from *Romer v. Evans* (1996) through *Obergefell* make clear that Justices Antonin Scalia, Clarence Thomas, and Samuel Alito believe that recognition of gay and lesbian rights as such imperils religious liberty. Thomas and Alito recently reiterated that view in a concurrence in the decision turning down the appeal from Kim Davis, the Kentucky county clerk who had been sued for refusing to issue marriage licenses for same-sex couples.[26] And I have heard Ryan Anderson argue that antidiscrimination laws prohibiting discrimination on the basis of sexual orientation by their very existence deny religious liberty.[27]

2. Some religious opponents of same-sex marriage assert or presuppose a less ambitious right not to be compelled to be complicit in same-sex marriage: for example, a right not to be compelled, by antidiscrimination laws, to bake a cake for a same-sex wedding ceremony. Perhaps this formulation is synonymous with the next.

3. A right to religious exemptions from laws protecting gay and lesbian rights. That is, if a state prohibits discrimination on the basis of sexual orientation or extends the right to marry to same-sex couples (as it must under *Obergefell*), religious opponents have a right to religious exemptions from such laws. Note that the assertion of a right to religious exemptions is a second-best solution. One argues for religious exemptions only when one has lost the larger battle against gay and lesbian rights under antidiscrimination laws or marriage equality laws. The religious opponents' ideal would be to "win it all" in these larger battles, as I have heard Matthew J. Franck of the Witherspoon Institute say, insisting that "a house divided against itself cannot stand."[28]

Masterpiece Cakeshop did not recognize any of these formulations. Instead, it endorsed a weaker formulation: a right that government, in any proceeding under a constitutionally permitted antidiscrimination law prohibiting discrimination on the basis of sexual orientation, not express hostility toward religious objections to gay and lesbian rights. Put another way, a right that government be neutral toward religion in such a proceeding.

In closing, Kennedy offered the following guidance to courts considering future cases: "[T]hese disputes must be resolved with tolerance, without undue disrespect to sincere religious beliefs, and without subjecting gay persons to indignities when they seek goods and services in an open market."[29] Arguably, the *Elane* concurrence is a model of respectful treatment and of "resolv[ing] with tolerance," since it explicitly says the Huguenins' beliefs "deserve our respect," even as it says they must follow New Mexico's law.

Jack Phillips, the baker in *Masterpiece Cakeshop*, argued that the CCRC showed hostility toward his religion. He cited a comment by an individual commissioner during a hearing on his case: "Freedom of religion and religion have been used to justify all kinds of discrimination throughout history, whether it be slavery, whether it be the [H]olocaust. . . . And to me it is one of the most despicable pieces of rhetoric that people . . . use their religion to hurt others."[30] This comment troubled Justice Kennedy, who concluded that it expressed hostility toward the baker's religious opposition to baking the wedding cake.

First, Kennedy thought that to compare Phillips's religious beliefs about marriage to religious defenses of slavery and the Holocaust was a "sentiment . . .

inappropriate" for someone charged with "neutral enforcement" of the Colorado Antidiscrimination Act (CADA), which protects "on *the basis of religion* as well as sexual orientation." Second, he found that the commissioner's "despicable piece of rhetoric" comment "disparaged" Phillips's religion in "at least two distinct ways": (1) by calling the appeal to religious beliefs "despicable" and (2) by "characterizing it as merely rhetorical—something insubstantial and even insincere." Another factor showing hostility, Kennedy said, was the disparity between the Commission's ruling in this case and its ruling in a different case, where it affirmed the right of three other bakers—on the basis of "conscience-based objections"—to decline to bake cakes bearing anti-same-sex marriage imagery and text requested by a customer named William Jack.[31]

Let us break down the commissioner's statement into two propositions. The first part: "Freedom of religion and religion have been used to justify all kinds of discrimination throughout history, whether it be slavery, whether it be the [H]olocaust." But this proposition is undeniably true as a matter of historical fact,[32] even if religious people today do not wish to be reminded of it. In concluding that this statement expressed hostility toward Phillips's religious beliefs, the Court in effect seems to be imposing a religious or conservative political correctness upon the commissioner by forbidding him to say what is indisputably true because it offends contemporary conservative religious sensibilities.

The second part: "And to me it is one of the most despicable pieces of rhetoric that people . . . use their religion to hurt others." Here Kennedy was nearer the mark in his interpretation that this remark expressed hostility toward Phillips's religious convictions. But Justice Ginsburg made good arguments that the Court was flawed in attributing the attitudes of this one commissioner to the entire CCRC and in turn to the Colorado Court of Appeals's decision upholding the CCRC.[33]

Is the majority in *Masterpiece Cakeshop* right that the Commission showed hostility toward Phillips's religious beliefs? In a process free from hostility, could the Commission still have ruled against Phillips and in favor of the three bakers who declined to make the cakes requested by William Jack? The justices disagreed with each other concerning whether these cases could be distinguished. Let us consider the following hypotheticals to test the majority's conception of hostility to religion.

1. Suppose that a baker refused to bake a cake for an interracial wedding, citing the Bible in support of segregation and religious objections to such marriage. (Recall that in *Loving v. Virginia* [1967], the trial judge had cited the Bible in opposition to interracial marriage.[34]) Suppose that a civil rights

commissioner quoted the Supreme Court's statement in *Newman v. Piggie Park Industries, Inc.* (1968), that such religious objections were "patently frivolous,"[35] and the Commission rejected the baker's claim. Does the majority in *Masterpiece Cakeshop* imply that such a statement would express unconstitutional hostility toward the baker's religious convictions?

2. Suppose that a baker refused to bake a cake for a same-sex wedding, citing the Bible in support of religious objections. Suppose that a commissioner quoted the Court's statements in *Romer* that traditional religious objections to gay and lesbian rights amounted to "animus" against and "a bare desire to harm a politically unpopular group."[36] Does the majority in *Masterpiece Cakeshop* imply that such a statement would express hostility toward the baker's religious convictions? (Bear in mind that Justice Scalia, in dissent in *Romer*, accused the majority of tarring the "seemingly tolerant Coloradans" with the brush of bigotry—that is, he accused the majority of expressing hostility toward their religious convictions.[37])

3. Suppose that a baker refused to bake a cake for an interfaith wedding between a Christian and a Muslim, citing religious objections. Suppose further that a commissioner argued the following in support of the baker (quoting President Trump's statements which these same five conservative justices who were in the majority in *Masterpiece Cakeshop* concluded did not express unconstitutional hostility toward Muslims in *Trump v. Hawaii* [2018], the travel ban case): "Islam hates us," Muslims "do not respect us at all," we need a "total and complete shutdown of Muslims entering the United States."[38] Does the majority in *Masterpiece Cakeshop* imply that such statements would express hostility toward the Muslim's religion (notwithstanding that same majority's decision in *Trump*)?

4. What if, in the previous three hypotheticals, the commissioner in question had simply observed, as a matter of historical fact, that people have asserted religious beliefs as a reason to discriminate on various bases, including race, religion, and sexual orientation, and that there is no absolute protection to act on religious beliefs in the marketplace? Does the majority in *Masterpiece Cakeshop* imply that even that factual observation would signal hostility toward religion?

As suggested above, I initially feared that the Court was in effect imposing a religious or conservative political correctness upon civil rights commissioners by forbidding them to recognize undeniable facts—that religion has been used to justify the Holocaust and slavery, not to mention denial of civil rights in the United States—because those facts offend contemporary conservative religious sensibilities. I feared that Scalia had bludgeoned Kennedy into this finding over the years with his pugnacious, overwrought culture-warrior dissents in all the gay and lesbian rights cases from *Romer* through *Obergefell*.

The students in my seminar, "Jurisprudence: Contemporary Controversies over Law and Morality," however, argued that even if what the commissioner said was undeniably true historically, bringing up these general facts in the context of the baker's particular hearing might imply hostility toward his particular religious convictions. From this perspective, it might have been perfectly appropriate to say these very same things in a legislative proceeding concerning whether to establish religious exemptions from antidiscrimination laws prohibiting discrimination on the basis of sexual orientation. But it would not be appropriate to do so in an administrative proceeding concerning whether a particular religious person, here the baker, had discriminated on the basis of sexual orientation in violation of the CADA. On this view, the case is teaching an important civics lesson about respect for religious liberty in a particular case, together with respect for gays' and lesbians' rights in general to be secure in the status of equal citizenship through acknowledging the legitimacy of antidiscrimination laws prohibiting discrimination on the basis of sexual orientation.

Seen in this light, Justice Kennedy, in *Masterpiece Cakeshop*, implicitly acknowledges what Justice Bosson in *Elane Photography* called "the price of citizenship." Government must respect religious convictions: it must be neutral and may not express hostility toward a particular person's religious convictions when determining whether that person has violated an antidiscrimination law. But when one operates a business—a public accommodation—engaging in commerce, one likewise must tolerate and even respect gays and lesbians. Recall the passages from Kennedy's opinion quoted above and emphasized in Ginsburg's dissent.

Furthermore, *Masterpiece Cakeshop* does not entail that, after a neutral proceeding, Phillips may not be held to have violated the CADA. Nor does the decision entail that he has any right to a religious exemption from the act's prohibition of discrimination on the basis of sexual orientation. Justice Kagan's concurrence, joined by Justice Breyer, emphasizes these important points. She offers a blueprint to guide civil rights commissioners in future controversies, showing how it could have been possible to apply Colorado's law against Phillips "untainted by any bias against a religious belief."[39]

To recapitulate: Kennedy's majority opinion in *Masterpiece Cakeshop* models how to resolve conflicts between gay and lesbian rights and religious liberty in a manner respectful to both sides in the culture war: (1) Accept the structure and aspirations of antidiscrimination laws. (2) Make clear that antidiscrimination laws may protect gays and lesbians from discrimination that denies their equal dignity and undermines their status as equal citizens. (3) Yet, also make clear that government in applying antidiscrimination laws must be respectful toward, and not express hostility against, religious convictions that are critical of antidiscrimination laws' aspirations. Through it all, do not imperil antidiscrimination laws with broad holdings regarding rights to religious exemptions or rights not to be compelled to express antidiscrimination laws' message of equality for gays and lesbians.

Religious Exemptions and the Moralization of Commerce in a Large Commercial Republic

Stepping back from these judicial opinions, I want to reflect on antidiscrimination laws and arguments for religious exemptions more generally. In *Ordered Liberty*, McClain and I defend government's role in a formative project of inculcating civic virtues, developing the capacities of citizens for self-government in a morally pluralistic constitutional democracy, and promoting public values like securing the status of equal citizenship for all, including gays and lesbians. We view antidiscrimination laws as playing a vital role in such a formative project, as mechanisms for promoting the public value of equality.[40] Public accommodations laws, for example, are not just about protecting the right to procure a hamburger or a hotel room when traveling in interstate commerce. More importantly, they are about securing equal dignity for all, whatever one's race, religion, sexual orientation, or gender identity.

Antidiscrimination laws are not simply negative: protecting minorities against denials of equal dignity. They also are affirmative: part of a formative project of government promoting the public value of securing the status of equal citizenship for all. Through antidiscrimination laws, government is implicitly aiming to change the attitudes of the discriminators themselves: it is aspiring to teach the discriminators that their discrimination is intolerable. I believe it is the recognition of this that drives the discriminators to object, invoking *Barnette*, that government through antidiscrimination laws is "prescrib[ing] what shall be orthodox"[41] or compelling them to express a message with which they disagree. This is also what fuels Justice Thomas's and Justice Gorsuch's acceptance of the "compelled expression" argument in concurrence in *Masterpiece Cakeshop*.[42]

Elsewhere, I along with my coauthors elaborate a conception of the US constitutional democracy as a "large commercial republic."[43] Here I want to invoke one aspect of that conception. The large commercial republic is religiously and morally diverse. In such a diverse society, the hope is that even though people disagree about religion and morality, they should be able to engage in commerce with one another. The further hope is that such commercial interactions may moderate their religious and moral differences. Perhaps people will see that, despite their religious and moral disagreements, they can trade with, get along with, and maybe even come to appreciate other, different people.

I conceive the large commercial republic as a mechanism of a formative project of inculcating civic virtues like tolerance and promoting public values like equal citizenship for all, including gays and lesbians. (To avoid misunderstanding, I wish to make clear that I do not conceive commerce itself as a moral or civic virtue, nor do I celebrate the morality of trade or capitalism.) The aspiration is that trade will moderate religious and moral disagreements and differences and will promote social cooperation on the basis of mutual respect and trust. For trade facilitates contact with people who are different from us and promotes at least toleration of them if not appreciation and respect for them. For this mechanism to work, people have to trade, come to see and even appreciate their commonalities and their differences, and come to accept, even to respect, others with whom they disagree on religious and moral grounds.

From this standpoint, religious exemptions for businesses—including wedding photographers and bakers—undercut the formative influences of the large commercial republic. They undermine the salutary civic function of trade in moderating difference, promoting tolerance and respect, and securing the status of equal citizenship for all. They balkanize trade and, in doing so, balkanize the polity. And so, if we are to keep in view this larger formative project of promoting social cooperation on the basis of mutual respect and trust, we should be cautious about creating broad exemptions. From this vantage point, it may be that Justice Bosson in *Elane Photography* and Justice Kennedy in *Masterpiece Cakeshop* model a better course: according respect both to gay and lesbian rights and to religious beliefs in opposition to such rights, while yet acknowledging that antidiscrimination laws exact the price of citizenship.

What is more, we should acknowledge forthrightly that the moralized commerce that comes with religious exemptions is a double-edged sword. Religious exemptions from antidiscrimination laws moralize commerce in a divisive way and in doing so undercut the aspirations and operation of the large commercial republic in promoting the moral objective of securing the status of equal citizenship for all. In a culture war, both sides can moralize commerce in divisive ways. For example, when a state declines to prohibit discrimination on the basis of sexual orientation, or creates broad religious exemptions for businesses with religious objections to marriage equality, corporations sympathetic to gay and lesbian rights can take their business to other states. The same goes for sports leagues and associations supportive of such rights. In turn, customers who support such rights can boycott businesses asserting or exercising religious exemptions. For example, you can be sure that many opposite-sex couples in Colorado who are committed to gay and lesbian rights are not going to order wedding cakes from Masterpiece Cakeshop. They probably will not buy cookies or cupcakes there either (even though Phillips offered to sell such baked goods to gays and lesbians). Moralizing commerce is easy in the era of Twitter, Facebook, Yelp, Google reviews, TripAdvisor, and other sources of reputational information and sanction.

Recognizing all of this, I hope, may give us pause before we head down this road of moralizing and balkanizing trade in these divisive ways. Proponents of religious exemptions (and thus moralized commerce) commonly cry foul when supporters of gay and lesbian rights engage in such boycotts (and thus moralized commerce) against businesses with religious opposition to gay and lesbian rights. But this is exactly what is to be expected when proponents of religious exemptions moralize commerce.

And so, in *Ordered Liberty*, McClain and I adopted a prudential attitude toward granting religious accommodations, at least in periods of rapid cultural and constitutional change. Yet we tendered the hope that the need for them would wither away.[44] We must acknowledge that prudence also may counsel against granting broad or long-standing exemptions in a large commercial republic that aspires to secure the status of equal citizenship for all, for they undercut the salutary civic function of trade.

Conclusion

Justice Kennedy's majority opinion in *Masterpiece Cakeshop* and Justice Bosson's concurrence in *Elane Photography* serve a valuable civic educative function: they model how to resolve conflicts between gay and lesbian rights and religious liberty. These opinions teach valuable civics lessons concerning the price of citizenship. They recognize the importance of respect on both sides. Importantly, *Masterpiece Cakeshop* did not accept the compelled expression argument (the argument urged by the culture warriors Thomas and Gorsuch). That would have been a winner-take-all victory in the culture wars. That would have imperiled antidiscrimination laws and the quest for securing the status of equal citizenship for all in our morally pluralistic constitutional democracy.

PART FIVE

The Future

TEN

The Future of Substantive Due Process

The practice of substantive due process is seriously vulnerable now, due to recent judicial appointments. In concluding, I reflect upon the future of the Supreme Court, focusing on substantive due process. I begin by analyzing where we are in constitutional law today and what is likely to change with respect to substantive due process after the replacement of Justice Kennedy with Justice Kavanaugh and of Justice Ginsburg with Justice Barrett. I close, not with a forecast of gloom and doom concerning the future, but with some constructive thoughts: a pep talk for dismayed liberals and progressives and some words of caution for jubilant conservatives.

Where We Are in Constitutional Law Today

It is 2022, and it seems we are on the verge of a conservative transformation of constitutional law. I have the feeling that we have been here before. In fact we were, in 1987. That year, Justice Lewis Powell—the swing vote on the Supreme Court at the time—announced his retirement. The Burger Court, thanks in part to the moderate, preservative conservatism of Powell, had proven to be "the counter-revolution that wasn't," to use Vincent Blasi's apt formulation.[1] President Ronald Reagan nominated Robert Bork to fill Powell's seat, and conservatives believed that Bork would provide the fifth vote for a conservative counterrevolution to reverse the Warren Court's liberal revolution. Moreover, they thought it would be an *originalist* counterrevolution, with two powerhouse originalists, Bork and Scalia, working together to fundamentally remake constitutional law.

But the Senate rejected the nomination of Bork, 58-42, with five Republicans voting against him. Indeed, it rejected Bork in no small part because of his originalism, which entailed that many landmark decisions of constitutional law, including substantive due process cases, were wrongly decided and should be overruled. Eventually, Reagan nominated, and the Senate confirmed, a more moderate conservative, Justice Anthony Kennedy, which forestalled the conservative counterrevolution for thirty years. Ironically, Kennedy's retirement in 2018 may have ushered in the very conservative counterrevolution that his appointment in 1988 had thwarted.

Many understandably predicted that the confirmation of Justice Brett Kavanaugh would cement a five-justice conservative bloc—and the confirmation of Justice Amy Coney Barrett undoubtedly does cement a six-justice conservative bloc—which has been the dream of conservatives since the failed nomination of Bork in 1987. The truth of the matter is that the Supreme Court has been very conservative for quite some time now, in particular since the moderately conservative Justice O'Connor retired and was succeeded by the considerably more conservative Justice Alito in 2006. In fact, in 2010, after the Court's decision in *Citizens United* overturned one of Justice O'Connor's campaign finance opinions, she lamented her retirement, saying, "Gosh, I step away for a couple of years and there's no telling what's going to happen."[2] Will the replacement of Kennedy with Kavanaugh lead the Court to make a hard right turn? Will Kennedy end up lamenting his retirement just as O'Connor did hers? Perhaps all of this is academic anyway, because the replacement of Ginsburg with Barrett may eventually bring about such a turn. Nonetheless, we must understand the past, and specifically the appointment and retirement of Kennedy, to understand the significance of the appointments of Kavanaugh and Barrett.

Kennedy was decidedly not the originalist Bork would have been. Indeed, Kennedy is best known for substantive due process decisions that were the bane of Justices Scalia's and Thomas's originalist existences. As discussed in prior chapters, *Planned Parenthood v. Casey* (1992) reaffirmed the central holding of *Roe v. Wade* (1973) protecting the right to decide whether to terminate a pregnancy.[3] *Lawrence v. Texas* (2003) overruled the infamous originalist decision, *Bowers v. Hardwick* (1986), and extended the right of intimate association already protected for straights to gays and lesbians.[4] *Casey* and *Lawrence* paved the way for Kennedy's landmark decision in *Obergefell v. Hodges* (2015) extending the right to marry already protected for opposite-sex couples to same-sex couples.[5]

To an originalist like Scalia, all of these decisions reflect a "new mode of constitutional interpretation" made up by liberal justices and consisting of nothing more than their "philosophical predilections" or "moral intuitions."[6] But to the authors of the joint opinion in *Casey*—the preservative conservative Justices O'Connor, Kennedy, and Souter—our practice of substantive due process, including these decisions, gives "full meaning" to the Constitution's "promise of liberty": "The inescapable fact is that adjudication of substantive due process claims may call upon the Court in interpreting the Constitution to exercise that same capacity which by tradition courts always have exercised: reasoned judgment."[7] The joint opinion in *Casey* retorts to Scalia that originalist approaches to substantive due process have been "inconsistent with our law"—that is, they cannot fit and justify our leading decisions interpreting the Due Process Clause, which stem from a practice of constructing basic liberties through common law constitutional interpretation.[8]

These decisions, this book has argued, have been among our most worthy achievements in constitutional law. They have vindicated basic liberties essential to securing the promise of ordered liberty and the status and benefits of equal citizenship for all. Yet, according to originalists like Scalia and Thomas, and now Gorsuch and Barrett, these cases are wrongly decided and presumably should be overruled.

What Is Likely to Change in Substantive Due Process?

What is likely to change in our practice of substantive due process after the replacement of Justice Kennedy with Justice Kavanaugh and of Justice Ginsburg with Justice Barrett? As observed in chapter 1, Donald Trump ran for President on a Republican Party platform committed to appointing to the Supreme Court justices like Scalia who would vote to overrule *Roe/Casey* and *Obergefell*—in short, two cornerstones of Justice Kennedy's legacy.[9]

I have written extensively about theories of constitutional interpretation—in defense of moral readings and against originalisms—and I believe such scholarship is important. But I do not believe that originalism had anything to do with the nomination and confirmation of Kavanaugh. I think that his substantive conservative vision of the Constitution had everything to do with it. Kavanaugh's commitments to narrowing the rights liberals and progressives support, limiting the administrative state, using the First Amendment to protect businesses from regulation, expanding presidential powers, narrowing congressional powers, broadening the individual right to bear arms, and the like were the basis for his nomination and confirmation to the Supreme Court.

Originalism presumably had more to do with the nomination and confirmation of Barrett. Barrett evidently generally shares Kavanaugh's substantive conservative vision but, unlike Kavanaugh, she *is* an avowed originalist and is viewed as a protégé of Scalia. While her confirmation hearings were deliberately uninformative, her record as an academic makes her views on substantive due process clear. It would be an understatement to say that she is a critic who in all likelihood would not have decided cases like *Casey*, *Lawrence*, and *Obergefell* as the Court did.

The idea of a moral reading looms large in my assessment of what we lost when Kennedy retired. The decisions at the center of his legacy—*Casey*, *Lawrence*, and *Obergefell*—all embody a moral reading and set their face against originalisms. More particularly, they embody the *Casey* framework for substantive due process over and against the *Washington v. Glucksberg* (1997) framework (as discussed in chapters 2 and 3). The *Glucksberg* framework advocated by the dissents in *Lawrence* and *Obergefell* and foreshadowed by the dissents in *Casey* limits the Due Process Clause to protecting only those liberties enumerated in the Constitution or which we have a long-standing historical practice of protecting, and interprets precedents protecting liberties narrowly, confining them to their specific holdings or factual contexts rather than building them out with coherence and integrity in future cases.

What approach(es) might we expect Kavanaugh and Barrett to take to interpreting the Due Process Clause? Are they likely to vote to overrule the substantive due process cases at the core of Kennedy's legacy? At his initial confirmation hearings, Kavanaugh said that *Glucksberg* provides the proper framework for the Due Process inquiry.[10] And again, Barrett is a professed originalist who is viewed as a disciple of Scalia. On that basis, we might expect both to side with the dissenters' approach in *Obergefell* and against that of Kennedy in any future cases involving claims to basic liberties under the Due Process Clause. In *Obergefell*, Chief Justice Roberts said in dissent that *Glucksberg* is the "leading modern case" on substantive due process.[11] As I showed in chapters 2 and 3, *Glucksberg* is the leading modern case on substantive due process only for those who oppose and wish to shut down the practice of substantive due process. It provided a method of damage control for conservatives who opposed these cases but did not have the votes to overrule them and therefore had to settle for narrowing them. Only time will tell whether the conservatives who oppose these cases now do have the votes to overrule them when the opportunity to do so arises.

For the time being, we can expect Kavanaugh and Barrett, under the *Glucksberg* approach, not to extend any substantive due process precedents, by analogy, to cutting-edge claims of previously unrecognized rights. And even if the *Glucksberg* framework itself does not dictate overruling any of those precedents, it drains them of any generative vitality in future cases that might provide occasions for extending them. For example, after *Obergefell* recognized the right of same-sex couples to marry, some states resisted its implications concerning the parenthood of same-sex spouses. In a per curiam order in *Pavan v. Smith* (2017), the Court reversed an Arkansas Supreme Court decision which had concluded that *"Obergefell* did not necessarily require the State to issue birth certificates listing the nonbiological mother as a parent when her same-sex spouse gives birth."[12] That stands to reason, since Kennedy's majority opinion in *Obergefell* emphasized extending the rights, responsibilities, and protections of marriage to same-sex couples and their children: "civil marriage on the same terms and conditions as opposite-sex couples." His opinion even "expressly identified 'birth and death certificates'" as among those "rights, benefits, and responsibilities."[13] Kennedy was concerned that the state not deny equal respect to and humiliate those children by denying them the protections of marriage, understood as a status and package of benefits.

Nonetheless, in *Pavan,* in a dissenting opinion in a *Glucksbergian* vein, Justice Gorsuch distinguished between *Obergefell*—which he said "'addressed the question whether a State must recognize same-sex marriages'"—and the issue of parental recognition, to which he said "nothing in *Obergefell* spoke."[14] Gorsuch seemed to accept Arkansas's implausible characterization of its birth certificate law as a biology-based registration scheme, even though, under it, husbands with no biological connection to their wife's child were listed as the father as long as they consented to the wife's alternative insemination. Fortunately, Douglas NeJaime observes, the majority "made clear that *Obergefell* reaches questions of nonbiological parental recognition."[15] Thomas and Alito joined Gorsuch's dissent.[16] But Roberts notably did not. Hopefully, this signals that he does not wish to revisit *Obergefell* or to resist its clear implications. It is unclear which way Kavanaugh or Barrett would have gone here, but we reasonably might fear that they would have agreed with Gorsuch, Thomas, and Alito.

More generally, under the *Glucksberg* approach, even if the Supreme Court does not overrule precedents protecting reproductive freedom or the rights of same-sex couples to intimate association and to marry, we should not be surprised if today's Court "never finds another restriction on abortion to impose an undue burden [and] never extends the rights of gays and lesbians beyond where they are now."[17]

I acknowledge that in a recent case involving a clash between the rights of same-sex couples and religious liberty, *Fulton v. City of Philadelphia* (2021), Kavanaugh and Barrett joined Chief Justice Roberts—along with the three liberal justices—in a narrow opinion that rejected the arguments in concurrence by Justices Alito, Thomas, and Gorsuch that the Court should overrule *Employment Division, Department of Human Resources v. Smith* (1990), which might have opened the door to broad religious exemptions, even from neutral and generally applicable laws. That was a relief, but in *Fulton* the Court still did rule in favor of a Catholic social services agency that refused to work with same-sex couples who apply to take in foster children.[18] Hence, that case is consistent with the possibility that the Court will not extend the rights of gays and lesbians beyond where they are now. Speaking not only of the *Fulton* decision but more generally of the 2020–21 term, Michael C. Dorf said: "More than in most recent terms, Chief Justice Roberts was able to present a credible picture of a nonpartisan court, with Justices Breyer, Kagan, Kavanaugh and Barrett in particular seeming to go out of their way to forge centrist alliances." "However," Dorf continued, "the justices appear to have reached a truce rather than a lasting peace. With high-profile abortion and gun control cases already on the docket for the next term, the ideological disagreements will likely re-emerge sooner rather than later." Indeed, we will see soon enough.[19]

Thoughts Concerning the Future

Finally, I want to offer some thoughts concerning the future. I have overcome the temptation to say, to liberals and progressives, quoting Dante's *Inferno*: "Abandon all hope, you who enter here."[20] That is, abandon hope (for at least the next generation) that the Supreme Court will protect basic liberties essential to securing ordered liberty or the status and benefits of equal citizenship for gays, lesbians, women, and Black Americans, to say nothing of others, including transgender persons; abandon hope that the Court will not strike down a wide range of liberal and progressive legislation promoting social justice, racial justice, gender justice, and the common good. Instead, I offer some more constructive thoughts about concrete actions liberals and progressives can take to make the best they can of a bad situation.

Liberals and Progressives: Don't "Get Over It," but Do Move On

The late Justice Scalia used to go around the country giving speeches. Whenever anyone asked him about the illegitimacy of *Bush v. Gore* (2000)—in which the Republican majority cut off the counting of the votes in Florida and handed the Presidency to George W. Bush, thereby "packing itself" with Republican successors[21]—Scalia would retort: "Get over it!"[22] Similarly, whenever anyone asked Senator Mitch McConnell about the illegitimacy of his stealing the Supreme Court seat that ultimately went to Gorsuch or the illegitimacy of his "plow[ing] right through" the allegations against Kavanaugh to confirm him, or the illegitimacy of his stealing the Supreme Court seat that went to Barrett eight days before the 2020 presidential election, he basically said: "Get over it."[23] Well, I urge liberals and progressives, never forget *Bush v. Gore*, never forget the stolen seats, never forget the "plowing through," and never forget Republicans' hardball hypocrisy when refusing to adhere to their own professed standard about not confirming Supreme Court Justices in a presidential election year—never "get over" these wounds to the legitimacy of the Supreme Court and of our practice of constitutional law. At the same time, we have to acknowledge the fact that we are stuck with a packed Republican Supreme Court for the foreseeable future. The hard truth is that we have to move on. In the rough-and-tumble world of a fiercely partisan and polarized constitutional democracy—one frayed almost beyond repair by Trump and McConnell—we have to be resilient. In that spirit, I shall offer a pep talk for dismayed liberals and progressives—or proposals for what to do next—and some words of caution for jubilant conservatives.

Pep Talk for Dismayed Liberals and Progressives: What to Do Next

First, I urge liberals and progressives finally to open their eyes and stop harboring "hollow hopes" (in Gerald Rosenberg's famous formulation) that courts will protect their rights or pursue (or even enable) liberal or progressive change.[24] Admittedly, Kennedy more than anyone else in the past generation kept liberals' and progressives' hollow hopes alive by occasionally "swinging" to vote with the more liberal justices on the Court. That he did so in high-profile culture war cases involving abortion and gay and lesbian rights obscured his very conservative voting record on almost every other issue.

Relatedly, I urge liberals and progressives finally to stop disparaging and eschewing legislatures. I would exhort liberals and progressives finally to turn more to legislatures than to courts—not only to protect their rights but more generally to promote their substantive constitutional visions or political conceptions of justice. Here I include not only the national legislature but also state and local governments. For the foreseeable future, these are going to be the best institutions through which liberals and progressives might effectively pursue justice and the common good. Liberals and progressives must take hope from the fact that time and demography may be on their side when it comes to emerging (more) progressive majorities, at least in blue states and purple states. At the same time, they must recognize that Republicans will seek through courts to entrench their substantive constitutional vision despite these democratic developments (just as they will attempt to limit voting rights, especially in states that are turning from red to blue). Ran Hirschl's classic work, *Towards Juristocracy: The Origins and Consequences of the New Constitutionalism*, warned about the global trend toward "juristocracy," including in the US, whereby elites—especially when they are losing power in the democratic processes—seek through courts to insulate policy-making from the vicissitudes of liberal and progressive democratic politics.[25]

Second, I encourage liberals and progressives to learn from and emulate what the conservatives did over the past two generations in resisting the Supreme Court decisions with which they vigorously disagreed. When you have political power—whether in state legislatures or in Congress or the Presidency—pass laws that challenge or undermine objectionable Supreme Court holdings and provide occasions to narrow those holdings. For example, after *Roe*, conservatives passed federal and state laws granting exemptions. They also passed laws challenging *Roe* at the margins, leading to later decisions narrowing it. Emboldened by Trump's appointments of Gorsuch, Kavanaugh, and Barrett, conservatives now pass ever more restrictive laws implicitly urging the Court to overrule *Roe*. After *Obergefell*, conservatives have done similar things, passing laws granting religious exemptions for those who oppose same-sex marriage and bringing legal challenges to civil rights laws protecting gays and lesbians against discrimination on the basis of sexual orientation, as in *Masterpiece Cakeshop* (discussed in chapter 9) and in the recent *Fulton* case (discussed above). They make not only religious liberty arguments but also freedom of association and freedom of speech arguments against civil rights protections for gays and lesbians. Liberals and progressives need to learn to chip away at objectionable conservative precedents in analogous ways. Furthermore, they need to attempt to protect reproductive freedom on the state level in the event *Roe* and *Casey* are overturned or narrowed further, just as they need to strive to protect gay and lesbian rights, along with other gender identity rights, at the state level in case *Lawrence* and *Obergefell* are overturned or are the end of the line for such federal constitutional rights rather than the beginning. Nevada, Virginia, and Massachusetts provide three instructive recent illustrations. In November 2020, Nevada voters approved a constitutional amendment, the "Marriage Regardless of Gender Amendment," which repealed its earlier "defense of marriage" act. This made Nevada the first state to adopt a constitutional amendment *affirming* civil marriage equality.[26] In April 2020, Virginia passed comprehensive non-discrimination protections adding sexual orientation and gender identity to its human rights law.[27] And in December 2020, the Massachusetts legislature passed the so-called *Roe* Act, securing expanded access to abortion by allowing the procedure after twenty-four weeks of pregnancy in cases of a fatal fetal anomaly and if "necessary, in the best medical judgment of the physician, to preserve the patient's physical or mental health."[28]

Liberals and progressives also need to learn from conservative examples of fundamentally moving the constitutional culture in their direction through tireless advocacy over a generation or longer. Think, for example, of conservatives' successful movement of the constitutional culture from the state militia reading of the Second Amendment's protection of the right to bear arms to the individual rights reading, culminating in *District of Columbia v. Heller* (2008).[29] Required reading for liberals and progressives should be Adam Winkler's book *Gunfight: The Battle over the Right to Bear Arms in America* and David Cole's book *Engines of Liberty: The Power of Citizen Advocates to Make Constitutional Law*. Both explicitly or implicitly urge liberals and progressives to learn from the National Rifle Association's successful advocacy and to apply those lessons to furthering justice and the common good.[30]

Third, as the conservatives did, liberals and progressives should learn to appreciate the virtues of federalism in our circumstances of disagreement and polarization. We may aspire to *e pluribus unum* and national unity. But the fact remains that we as a people are deeply divided on many fundamental moral and political questions. Federalism is a structural mechanism for accommodating pluralism in circumstances of disagreement. If you are a liberal or progressive, and you live in a blue state, appreciate the fact that you do (instead of focusing on how disappointing, frustrating, and dysfunctional our national politics are). Or, if you are more adventurous, move to a purple state or a red state with some potential to turn blue.[31] Liberals and progressives should learn from the successful political mobilization carried on by Stacey Abrams and other Black women through years of hard work to protect voting rights and mobilize voters to help turn Georgia from red to blue in the 2020 presidential election (as well as in the Senatorial elections in that state).[32]

Fourth, liberals and progressives should learn that federalism is also a mechanism for resistance to the national government by states that disagree with the party in control of the Presidency, Congress, and/or Supreme Court. Just as conservatives of the past generation have practiced culture war federalism, it is time for liberals and progressives to practice blue states' federalism for the left.[33] Use the national government, when you have power there, to advance your substantive constitutional vision and political conception of justice. Use the state governments, when you lack national power, to resist the national government (or otherwise to advance your aims). Breathe a sigh of relief that the blue state governments may be able to shelter you somewhat from the injustices of Republican administrations, Republican Congresses, and the Republican-controlled Supreme Court.

Most Republicans who sing the glories of federalism take a similar approach, especially in the context of culture war federalism. Just consider the actions of Jeff Sessions, formerly a Senator from Alabama and then Attorney General in the Trump administration (until November 7, 2018, the day after the midterm elections, when Trump ingloriously fired him) in fighting the culture war through the US Department of Justice. When the Democrats control the national government, the Republicans praise the virtues of federalism: of limiting the powers of the national government and devolving power to the state and local governments. They also call for state governments to resist national power. But when the Republicans control the national government, they attempt to crush resistance by state and local governments in blue states: for example, cracking down on state laws permitting medical and recreational use of marijuana, permitting aid in dying, protecting sanctuary cities, and addressing climate change.

Fifth, to continue with federalism, I encourage liberals and progressives to turn to state courts as well as state legislatures to pursue constitutional justice. Given the racist history surrounding federalism and the states' rights tradition, liberals and progressives understandably have been wary of them. But over the past thirty-six years—since *Bowers v. Hardwick* (1986)—proponents of gay and lesbian rights have effectively used state courts together with state legislatures to secure such rights in circumstances of national disagreement, at a time when the prospects for victory in places like Vermont and Massachusetts were greater than in the US Supreme Court or Congress. Gay and lesbian rights proponents assiduously avoided federal court initially and were prudent to do so. They brought lawsuits and passed legislation in states where circumstances were more propitious for attaining constitutional justice— most notably, Vermont and Massachusetts, whose decisions in *Baker v. State* (Vt. 1999) and *Goodridge v. Department of Public Health* (Mass. 2003) got the ball rolling toward *Lawrence* and *Obergefell*.[34] But one might also mention a number of other states. Only after a mostly successful run in state courts and state legislatures for over a decade did gay and lesbian rights proponents take the issue of the right of same-sex couples to marry to the US Supreme Court.

More generally, as the political scientist Emily Zackin has put it, liberals and progressives have been "looking for rights in all the wrong places."[35] Instead of looking exclusively to the federal Constitution, they should be looking primarily to state constitutions, especially for the next generation. Whereas the US Supreme Court in *DeShaney v. Winnebago County* (1989) has erroneously interpreted the US Constitution as a charter of negative liberties (simply protecting people from government),[36] state supreme courts have interpreted state constitutions as charters of positive benefits imposing affirmative obligations upon state governments to provide for people's basic needs.[37] Conceiving constitutions as such charters of positive benefits is crucial to promoting liberal and progressive constitutional visions and political conceptions of justice. For the foreseeable future, with a conservative-dominated US Supreme Court, liberals and progressives need to engage with state constitutions to seek justice.

Some Words of Caution for Jubilant Conservatives

For years, conservative judges and scholars have been calling for restoring the "Constitution in exile" or for "restoring the lost [libertarian] Constitution."[38] These wishes—for a Supreme Court restoration of the conservative Constitution that has been in exile since the New Deal liberal revolution in 1937—may be about to come true. But conservatives should beware that such a Court may come to live in infamy. What I have called (in chapter 6) *Lochner*'s rehabilitation and revenge may wreak havoc on the Supreme Court and the republic.

To explain: for generations, judges and scholars have vilified the Supreme Court of the *Lochner* era (roughly 1887 to 1937) for reading its own economic and political theory into the Constitution. Its own economic and political theory was basically a free-market–libertarian precursor to recent Republican Party platforms. The current conservative 6-3 majority may well read such a theory into the Constitution. It has largely been doing so for quite some time now—over the objections of dissenting moderate and liberal justices that the Court is resurrecting doctrines and repeating errors from the *Lochner* era. For example, Justice Souter made this argument in dissent in federalism cases limiting Congress's power to regulate interstate commerce.[39] Justice Stevens made similar arguments in dissent in cases holding that the First Amendment prohibits the government from banning corporations from making expenditures advocating the election or defeat of a candidate.[40] And Justice Breyer charged the Court with resurrecting *Lochner* in his dissent in a case holding that the First Amendment prevents California from requiring "crisis pregnancy centers" to notify pregnant women who come to them of true factual information that the state has "public programs that provide immediate free or low-cost access to comprehensive family planning services (including all FDA-approved methods of contraception), prenatal care, and abortion for eligible women."[41]

This time around, the Court's reading its own economic and political theory into the Constitution would likely be worse—more delegitimating—than during the *Lochner* era. For one thing, doing so would likely be worse because the people nowadays expect far more from their governments than the people did during the *Lochner* era. The people are likely to chafe far more at the Court's limitations on government's power to pursue justice and the common good, for example, to use the administrative state to promote the general welfare or to use state governments to pursue liberal and progressive ends.[42] Moreover, after (1) the Republican majority of the Supreme Court "packed itself" through *Bush v. Gore*; (2) the Republican Party stole a seat from President Obama to get Gorsuch on the Court; (3) the Republican Party "plowed through" the accusations against Kavanaugh to get him confirmed; and (4) the Republican Party pushed through the nomination of Barrett eight days before the presidential election repudiated the president who nominated her—people are understandably more dubious about any claim that the Supreme Court today is just an umpire calling balls and strikes, not a partisan tool of the Republican Party.[43]

After the confirmation of Kavanaugh, Barry Friedman made similar points concerning "the coming storm over the Supreme Court." As he put it, "an extremely conservative majority now is fully in control of the court, which, at some point in the future—perhaps five or 10 years from now—could lead to another crisis much like the one in 1937." He added: "If the country moves left in the next few years, as the court moves right, we have the makings for a serious collision." With the confirmation of Barrett, the possibility of such a collision is greater. Furthermore, I agree with Friedman that it is likely that "any future attack from the left will include claims that the court's current majority is illegitimate" for reasons like those I have stated.[44] By contrast, in the 1930s, the primary attack from the left was that the members of the Court—the "nine old men"—were old and out of touch with a changing world.[45] They were thwarting popular reforms aimed at addressing economic problems in this new world. Here is Friedman's punch line: "Historically, when big collisions between public opinion and the Supreme Court have occurred, the justices lose and the public gets its way."[46]

In closing, I caution jubilant conservatives who hope the long-awaited conservative counterrevolution is nigh, and with it the restoration of the Constitution that has been in exile since the New Deal liberal revolution in 1937: Be careful what you wish for. It may come back to haunt you and doom the Court to an infamy even worse than that of its prior incarnation, the *Lochner* Court. In fulfilling such conservative wishes, rather than protecting basic personal liberties in substantive due process cases culminating in *Obergefell*, the Court would truly repeat the "grave errors" of *Lochner*.

ACKNOWLEDGMENTS

In this book, I defend the embattled yet venerable and worthy practice of substantive due process—the protection of substantive liberties such as privacy or autonomy under the Due Process Clauses of the US Constitution—at a time when it is vulnerable. I argue that substantive due process reflects an attractive moral reading of the Constitution—a conception of it as embodying abstract moral and political principles, not codifying concrete historical rules or practices—and is justifiable on the basis of constitutional imperatives—protecting the basic liberties significant for personal self-government and securing the status and benefits of equal citizenship for all.

Three invitations kickstarted this project. First, Mark Tushnet, Mark Graber, and Sandy Levinson invited Linda McClain and me to write the chapter on "Liberty" for *The Oxford Handbook of the U.S. Constitution*. In working on that chapter, I conceived the core of this book. Second, Justin Dyer of the University of Missouri's Kinder Institute on Constitutional Democracy invited Linda and me to give a Constitution Day Lecture. In preparing that lecture, we formulated our initial thoughts concerning a significant substantive due process decision, *Obergefell v. Hodges*, which protected the right of same-sex couples to marry. Third, Dean Maureen O'Rourke of Boston University School of Law invited me to give an inaugural lecture as The Honorable Paul J. Liacos Professor of Law, for which I presented my initial rebuttals of slippery slope arguments against substantive due process.

Next, a sabbatical year as a Visiting Research Scholar at Princeton University's Program in Law and Public Affairs provided a wonderful setting in which to make progress on this book. I am grateful to LAPA and Princeton's University Center for Human Values for generous financial and institutional support while I developed my ideas through writing as well as teaching an undergraduate seminar titled "Perfectionism and the Legal Enforcement of Morals." LAPA Director Paul Frymer and Associate Director Leslie Gerwin fostered an inviting intellectual community, and I greatly appreciated and benefited from the company of the other visiting scholars that year: Kathy Abrams, Nina Dayton, Melynda Price, David Rabban, and Sarah Schindler. The comments I received when presenting an early version of chapter 4 in a LAPA Seminar were invaluable, especially those by the assigned commentator, Keith Whittington. Dara Strolovitch and Ben Johnson, through their questions from opposing progressive and conservative viewpoints, made me realize the need to write what became chapter 5. I benefited from presenting a draft of that chapter in a LAPA Works-in-Progress Workshop as well as in Professor Steve Macedo's course on Ethics and Public Policy. Conversations with many friends in the Princeton community, including David Bernhardt, Dirk Hartog, Des Jagmohan, Melissa Lane, Steve Macedo, and Alan Patten, were as valuable as they were enjoyable.

I am indebted to several scholars for inviting me to write pieces (now incorporated in this book) for various scholarly occasions: Imer Flores invited me to prepare an essay for a conference on Linda McClain's book, *Who's the Bigot?* (Oxford University Press, 2020), at the National Autonomous University of Mexico (UNAM); John Witte and Michael Welker asked me to write an essay for the University of Heidelberg Conference on The Impact of Law on Character Formation in Modern Pluralistic Societies; and Keegan Callanan invited me to take part in a public debate with John McGinnis at Middlebury College on Trump, constitutional interpretation, and the future of the Supreme Court.

Once I completed a draft of the entire book, Justin Dyer was gracious enough to include a symposium on it at the University of Missouri's Kinder Institute on Constitutional Democracy as part of the Fifth Annual Shawnee Trail Conference. Panelists Sot Barber, Ken Kersch, and Rigel Oliveri offered insightful remarks, as did other participants, including Justin himself. I also have gotten helpful comments through presenting drafts of chapters at a number of institutions in addition to those already mentioned: Boston College's Clough Center for the Study of Constitutional Democracy; Mark Graber's Schmoozes on Constitutional Law at the University of Maryland School of Law; the International Society of Family Law North American Regional Conference; Loyola University (Chicago) School of Law's Tenth Annual Constitutional Law Colloquium; and University of Notre Dame's Constitutional Studies Program.

Finally, I have learned from discussions with many friends and colleagues about this project as a whole as well as particular pieces of it: Jack Balkin,

Sot Barber, Sonu Bedi, Bob Davoli, Dick Fallon, Greg Keating, Ken Kersch, Linda McClain, Eileen McDonagh, Frank Michelman, Phillip Munoz, Doug NeJaime, Josh Rabinowitz, Alex Tsesis, and Emily Zackin. I have especially appreciated Josh's characteristically incisive and thorough comments.

At Boston University School of Law, I am grateful to Dean Maureen O'Rourke and Dean Angela Onwuachi-Willig for generous financial support, including summer research grants and support provided by The Honorable Paul J. Liacos Professor of Law fund. My BU colleagues made instructive criticisms in several faculty workshops—in particular, Jack Beermann, Khiara Bridges, Pnina Lahav, Gary Lawson, David Lyons, Tracey Maclin, Chris Robertson, and David Seipp. Most of all, I have learned through engagement with my BU students in teaching Constitutional Law and a seminar in Jurisprudence: Contemporary Controversies over Law and Morality.

I thank Chuck Myers, my initial editor at the University of Chicago Press, for encouragement of as well as patience with this project. I appreciate his successor, Sara Doskow, for shepherding the manuscript through to publication after Chuck's retirement. I also am indebted to Sandy Levinson and an anonymous reviewer for constructive comments on my original book proposal as well as to Mike Dorf and Mark Graber for generous and useful criticisms in reviewing the full manuscript.

Thanks finally to my research assistants, current or former BU Law students Kyle Angelotti, Lina Bader, Brad Baranowski, Jeremy Perlman, Emily Rothkin, and Emily Zheng, for their conscientious and careful work on research, cite-checking, and editing. Each of them read the full manuscript at various stages of completion, helping me clarify and sharpen my arguments. Another research assistant, Esther Miller, provided valuable creative advice. I am grateful to Stefanie Weigmann, Associate Director for Research and Faculty Services at BU Law's Fineman & Pappas Libraries, for providing prompt and expert help with research. I also want to acknowledge two Senior Program Coordinators at BU, Ben Morgan and Joseph Graham, for their highly capable and cheerful assistance.

This book partially incorporates but revises material from three published articles: "Liberty," in *The Oxford Handbook of the United States Constitution* 479 (Mark Tushnet, Mark A. Graber, and Sanford Levinson, eds., Oxford University Press, 2015) (with Linda C. McClain); "The Unnecessary and Unfortunate Focus on 'Animus,' 'Bare Desire to Harm,' and 'Bigotry' in Analyzing Opposition to Gay and Lesbian Rights," 99 *Boston University Law Review* 2671 (2019); and "Are Constitutional Courts Civic Educative Institutions? If So, What Do They Teach?" in *The Impact of the Law: On Character Formation, Ethical Education, and the Communication of Values in Late Modern*

Pluralistic Societies 95 (John Witte Jr. and Michael Welker, eds., Evangelische Verlagsanstalt, 2021). In addition, I draw on and rework passages from *Securing Constitutional Democracy: The Case of Autonomy* (University of Chicago Press, 2006).

I dedicate this book to Linda McClain, my sometime coauthor and full-time spouse, and our two incredible daughters, Sarah and Katherine. Their love, encouragement, and support have sustained me while writing this book.

NOTES

CHAPTER ONE

1. JOHN HART ELY, DEMOCRACY AND DISTRUST: A THEORY OF JUDICIAL REVIEW 18 (1980) [hereinafter ELY, DEMOCRACY].
2. United States v. Carlton, 512 U.S. 26, 39 (1994) (Scalia, J., concurring).
3. See Obergefell v. Hodges, 576 U.S. 644, 721 (2015) (Thomas, J., dissenting); see also Davis v. Ermold, No. 19-926, 2020 WL 5881537, at *1 (U.S. Oct. 5, 2020) (statement of Thomas, J., with whom Alito, J., joined, respecting the denial of certiorari).
4. See the sources cited below in note 53.
5. 576 U.S. at 646 (majority opinion).
6. Id. at 687, 704 (Roberts, C. J., dissenting).
7. See, e.g., Adkins v. Children's Hospital, 261 U.S. 525 (1923) (striking down a federal minimum-wage law for women and minors as in violation of the Due Process Clause of the Fifth Amendment); Lochner v. New York, 198 U.S. 45, 61 (1905) (invalidating, under the Due Process Clause of the Fourteenth Amendment, a state maximum-hours law).
8. 300 U.S. 379 (1937) (upholding a state minimum-wage law and signaling the demise of the *Lochner* era by overruling *Adkins*).
9. See, e.g., ROBERT H. BORK, THE TEMPTING OF AMERICA: THE POLITICAL SEDUCTION OF THE LAW 32, 111–16, 158, 209 (1990); Planned Parenthood v. Casey, 505 U.S. 833, 998, 1000 (1992) (Scalia, J., concurring in the judgment in part and dissenting in part); John Hart Ely, *The Wages of Crying Wolf: A Comment on* Roe v. Wade, 82 YALE LAW JOURNAL 920 (1973). Ely apparently coined the term "Lochnering" or "to *Lochner*." Id. at 944.
10. 410 U.S. 113, 153 (1973).
11. Id. at 152 (quoting Palko v. Connecticut, 302 U.S. 319, 325 [1937]).
12. *Casey*, 505 U.S. at 846 (joint opinion of Justices O'Connor, Kennedy, and Souter). For an earlier argument using this phrase, see Daniel O. Conkle, *The Second Death of Substantive Due Process*, 62 INDIANA LAW JOURNAL 215 (1987).
13. 576 U.S. at 663–64, 674, 681 (majority opinion).
14. *Casey*, 505 U.S. at 849; id. at 982 (Scalia, J., dissenting); see also *Obergefell*, 576 U.S. at 664.
15. See Aaron Blake, *Trump Says 17-Month-Old Gay Marriage Ruling Is "Settled" Law, but 43-Year-Old Abortion Ruling Isn't*, WASH. POST, Nov. 14, 2016, https://www

.washingtonpost.com/news/the-fix/wp/2016/11/14/trump-says-17-month-old-gay-marriage-ruling-is-settled-law-but-43-year-old-abortion-ruling-isnt/. On December 1, 2021, the Supreme Court heard arguments in a case—Dobbs v. Jackson Women's Health Organization, No. 19-1392—challenging a Mississippi law that banned abortions if "the probable gestational age of the unborn human" was determined to be more than fifteen weeks. The law included exceptions for medical emergencies or "a severe fetal abnormality." The lower federal courts ruled that the law was unconstitutional, with the United States Court of Appeals for the Fifth Circuit stating: "In an unbroken line dating to Roe v. Wade, the Supreme Court's abortion cases have established (and affirmed, and reaffirmed) a woman's right to choose an abortion before viability." (The point of fetal viability is around twenty-three or twenty-four weeks.) The specific question the Supreme Court agreed to decide was "whether all pre-viability prohibitions on elective abortions are unconstitutional." Id. On November 1, 2021, the Court heard arguments in two cases—Whole Woman's Health v. Jackson, No. 21-463, and United States v. Texas, No. 21-588—in which abortion providers and the Biden administration challenged an even more radical state law. The Texas Heartbeat Act, S.8, bans abortions once cardiac activity of a fetus is detected, usually about six weeks after a person's last menstrual period (before many know they are pregnant). It puts enforcement of the law in the hands of private persons, rather than the state government, in an attempt to evade review by federal courts. Under the statute, any individual can sue anyone who aids or abets prohibited abortions, with an award of at least $10,000 and legal fees for any successful lawsuit. The federal district court suspended the law as an "offensive deprivation" of an important constitutional right, but the United States Court of Appeals for the Fifth Circuit reversed and reinstated it. The arguments in the two cases before the Supreme Court focused on procedural questions concerning whether abortion providers and the United States government could challenge the law by suing state officials in federal court instead of on the constitutionality of the underlying restriction of abortions. As this book goes to press, the Court has not yet issued its decisions in these cases.

16. See Adam Liptak, *In Judge Neil Gorsuch, an Echo of Scalia in Philosophy and Style*, N.Y. TIMES, Jan. 31, 2017, https://www.nytimes.com/2017/01/31/us/politics/neil-gorsuch-supreme-court-nominee.html.

17. At his confirmation hearings, then-Judge Kavanaugh said "I think all roads lead to the *Glucksberg* test." CNN, http://www.cnn.com/TRANSCRIPTS/1809/05/cnr.08.html.

18. Michael Kranish, Robert Barnes, Shawn Boburg & Ann E. Marimow, *Amy Coney Barrett, a Disciple of Justice Scalia, Is Poised to Push the Supreme Court Further Right*, WASH. POST, Sept. 26, 2020, https://www.washingtonpost.com/politics/barrett-supreme-court-trump/2020/09/26/20863794-feac-11ea-830c-a160b331ca62_story.html.

19. For another recent book defending the practice of substantive due process, see MATTHEW W. LUNDER, THE CONCEPT OF ORDERED LIBERTY AND THE COMMON-LAW DUE-PROCESS TRADITION: *SLAUGHTERHOUSE CASES* THROUGH *OBERGEFELL V. HODGES* (1872–2015) (2021). Like my book, Lunder's book defends the practice of common law constitutional interpretation epitomized by Justice John Marshall Harlan II and Justice David Souter. Lunder, however, argues that not only modern conservative but also modern liberal approaches to protecting fundamental rights have strayed from the common-law concept of ordered liberty.

20. Some constitutional theorists have distinguished between "interpretation" and "construction." See, e.g., KEITH E. WHITTINGTON, CONSTITUTIONAL CONSTRUCTION: DIVIDED POWERS AND CONSTITUTIONAL MEANING (1999); Lawrence B. Solum, *Originalism*

and Constitutional Construction, 82 FORDHAM LAW REVIEW 453 (2013). In speaking of "constructing basic liberties," I do not employ any such notion of constructing as distinguished from interpreting. The terms "construction" and "interpretation" have been used as synonyms for each other throughout our constitutional history. One need only recall Chief Justice John Marshall's famous statement that resolution of the question whether Congress had the power to establish a national bank depended upon "a fair construction of the whole instrument." McCulloch v. Maryland, 17 U.S. 316, 406 (1819). As I use the term, "constructing" encompasses building out our scheme of constitutional self-government through making normative judgments about the best understanding of our constitutional commitments.

21. See Lawrence v. Texas, 539 U.S. 558, 599 (2003) (Scalia, J., dissenting).

22. Mark Twain ("Nothing so needs reforming as other people's habits").

23. JAMES E. FLEMING, FIDELITY TO OUR IMPERFECT CONSTITUTION: FOR MORAL READINGS AND AGAINST ORIGINALISMS 3 (2015) [hereinafter FLEMING, FIDELITY]. See also SOTIRIOS A. BARBER & JAMES E. FLEMING, CONSTITUTIONAL INTERPRETATION: THE BASIC QUESTIONS 155–70 (2007) (defending a "philosophic approach" to constitutional interpretation and criticizing all theories and approaches that aim and claim to avoid making such moral judgments in constitutional interpretation).

24. *Obergefell*, 576 U.S. at 687 (Roberts, C. J., dissenting).

25. JAMES E. FLEMING, SECURING CONSTITUTIONAL DEMOCRACY: THE CASE OF AUTONOMY (2006) [hereinafter FLEMING, SECURING] (arguing that basic liberties associated with autonomy, along with those related to participation in the political processes, fit together into a coherent scheme of basic liberties integral to our constitutional democracy).

26. In previous books, I have developed and applied normative theories of constitutional interpretation and of constitutional constructivism that aim, in the spirit of Ronald Dworkin and John Rawls, to fit and justify the US Constitution and underlying constitutional democracy. See id. at 61–64; FLEMING, FIDELITY, supra note 23, at 73–97. Some readers may find this book to be more "descriptive" of our constitutional practice and doctrine, and less normative, than those works. Moreover, some readers may find it to be more "common law constitutional interpretation," and less Dworkinian "moral reading," than my prior books. To be sure, this book offers an account of our practice of substantive due process and, accordingly, a defense of the conception of common law constitutional interpretation found, for example, in the joint opinion of Justices O'Connor, Kennedy, and Souter in *Casey*. But, as such, it is normative through and through in the sense that it aims to fit and justify our practice, even though it does not advance an ideal Dworkinian or Rawlsian theory. As I will show in chapters 6 and 7, Justice Scalia and Chief Justice Roberts fail to appreciate the distinction between accounts that fit and justify our practice of substantive due process and ideal liberal moral and political theory.

27. See FLEMING, SECURING, supra note 25, at 92 (distilling this list of basic liberties).

28. See *Casey*, 505 U.S. at 979–80, 982–84 (Scalia, J., dissenting); ELY, DEMOCRACY, supra note 1, at 43–72.

29. See *Casey*, 505 U.S. at 848, 851 (joint opinion); Poe v. Ullman, 367 U.S. 497, 543 (1961) (Harlan, J., dissenting); *Obergefell*, 576 U.S. at 666 (majority opinion).

30. Bowers v. Hardwick, 478 U.S. 186, 217 (1986) (Stevens, J., dissenting).

31. I present the practice of substantive due process as one of common law constitutional interpretation, and my account of such interpretation has affinities to that of DAVID A. STRAUSS, THE LIVING CONSTITUTION (2010). But I present common

law constitutional interpretation as engaging in a moral reading of the Constitution and as making decidedly normative judgments about the best understandings of our constitutional commitments as we have built them out over time. At a symposium on his book at Boston University School of Law, Strauss resisted my view of such interpretation as embodying a moral reading. And he has written instead as if common law constitutional interpretation mainly involves more pragmatic "judgments about good policy." Id. at 101. For fuller discussion of the affinities and differences between our views, see FLEMING, FIDELITY, supra note 23, at 108–15.

32. 521 U.S. 702, 720–21 (1997).
33. *Casey,* 505 U.S. at 901.
34. *Obergefell,* 576 U.S. at 664.
35. Id. at 702 (Roberts, C. J., dissenting).
36. For a previous argument along these lines, see FLEMING, SECURING, supra note 25, at 126–27.
37. *Lawrence,* 539 U.S. at 593–94.
38. For a famous and influential early formulation of the idea of rational basis scrutiny with "bite," in the context of equal protection, see Gerald Gunther, *Foreword: In Search of Evolving Doctrine on a Changing Court: A Model for a Newer Equal Protection,* 86 HARVARD LAW REVIEW 1, 12 (1972).
39. *Lawrence,* 539 U.S. at 574 (majority opinion).
40. Id. at 593–94 (Scalia, J., dissenting).
41. McClain and I previously developed a similar argument in JAMES E. FLEMING & LINDA C. MCCLAIN, ORDERED LIBERTY: RIGHTS, RESPONSIBILITIES, AND VIRTUES 237–72 (2013).
42. 410 U.S. at 155–56.
43. *Casey,* 505 U.S. at 851–53, 877.
44. *Glucksberg,* 521 U.S. at 702; Michael H. v. Gerald D., 491 U.S. 110 (1989); *Bowers,* 478 U.S. at 186.
45. *Lawrence,* 539 U.S. at 590, 599.
46. *Obergefell,* 576 U.S. at 705 (Roberts, C. J., dissenting).
47. Id. at 666–67 (majority opinion) (quoting Griswold v. Connecticut, 381 U.S. 479, 486 [1965]).
48. *Lawrence,* 539 U.S. at 590, 599.
49. See LAWRENCE G. SAGER, JUSTICE IN PLAINCLOTHES: A THEORY OF AMERICAN CONSTITUTIONAL PRACTICE 84–92 (2004) (judicial under-enforcement); CASS R. SUNSTEIN, THE PARTIAL CONSTITUTION 9–10 (1993) (Constitution outside the courts).
50. See JOHN STUART MILL, ON LIBERTY 10–11 (David Spitz ed., 1975) (1859).
51. *Obergefell,* 576 U.S. at 706 (Roberts, C. J., dissenting).
52. Thomas C. Grey, *Eros, Civilization and the Burger Court,* 43 LAW & CONTEMPORARY PROBLEMS 83 (1980).
53. See, e.g., WHAT *BROWN V. BOARD OF EDUCATION* SHOULD HAVE SAID (Jack Balkin ed., 2004); WHAT *ROE V. WADE* SHOULD HAVE SAID (Jack Balkin ed., 2007); WHAT *OBERGEFELL V. HODGES* SHOULD HAVE SAID (Jack Balkin ed., 2020).
54. *Obergefell,* 576 U.S. at 710 (Roberts, C. J., dissenting); id. at 733 (Thomas, J., dissenting); id. at 740 (Alito, J., dissenting). Justice Scalia had made such a warning in dissent in Romer v. Evans, 517 U.S. 620, 636, 646 (1996) (Scalia, J., dissenting).
55. *Obergefell,* 576 U.S. at 693, 710.
56. 138 S. Ct. 1719 (2018).
57. 309 P.3d 53 (N.M. 2013).

58. 517 U.S. 620 (1996).
59. 140 S. Ct. 1731 (2020).

CHAPTER TWO

1. 83 U.S. 36, 125 (1873) (Swayne, J., dissenting); id. at 92, 96, 97–98 (Field, J., dissenting). In this chapter I draw from previous work. James E. Fleming & Linda C. McClain, *Liberty*, in THE OXFORD HANDBOOK OF THE U.S. CONSTITUTION 479, 481–93 (Mark Tushnet et al. eds., 2015) [hereinafter Fleming & McClain, *Liberty*].
2. 83 U.S. at 79 (majority opinion).
3. Id. at 96 (Field, J., dissenting).
4. United States v. Carlton, 512 U.S. 26, 39 (1994) (Scalia, J., concurring); Obergefell v. Hodges, 576 U.S. 644, 721 (2015) (Thomas, J., dissenting).
5. CHARLES L. BLACK, JR., DECISION ACCORDING TO LAW 41–54 (1981); RONALD DWORKIN, LIFE'S DOMINION: AN ARGUMENT ABOUT ABORTION, EUTHANASIA, AND INDIVIDUAL FREEDOM 129–31, 143–44 (1993). See also GEORGE THOMAS, THE (UN) WRITTEN CONSTITUTION (2021).
6. 505 U.S. 833, 846 (1992).
7. 60 U.S. (19 How.) 393 (1857). (The US Reports misspelled Sanford's name as "Sandford.") See *Casey*, 505 U.S. at 979, 998 (Scalia, J., concurring in the judgment in part and dissenting in part) (analogizing *Casey* to *Dred Scott*).
8. *Dred Scott*, 60 U.S. at 450–52.
9. *Casey*, 505 U.S. at 980 (Scalia, J., dissenting).
10. Cruzan v. Director, Missouri Dept. of Health, 497 U.S. 261, 300 (1990) (Scalia, J., concurring).
11. 262 U.S. 390, 399 (1923) (some citations omitted).
12. For a discussion of the incorporation of certain basic liberties "enumerated" in the Bill of Rights to apply to the state governments through the Due Process Clause of the Fourteenth Amendment, and its relation to substantive due process, see Fleming & McClain, *Liberty*, supra note 1, at 482–83.
13. 262 U.S. at 399.
14. Palko v. Connecticut, 302 U.S. 319, 325 (1937); Loving v. Virginia, 388 U.S. 1, 12 (1967).
15. 262 U.S. at 402.
16. 268 U.S. 510, 534–35 (1925).
17. 198 U.S. 45, 52, 56, 64 (1905).
18. 300 U.S. 379, 391–92 (1937).
19. Id. at 391, 399.
20. 316 U.S. 535, 536–37 (1942).
21. Id. at 536, 541.
22. See, e.g., *Loving*, 388 U.S. at 12; Roe v. Wade, 410 U.S. 113, 152 (1973).
23. The fundamental rights protected through the Equal Protection Clause include not only the right to procreate but also the right to vote and to have one's vote counted equally, the right not to be denied the vote by reason of inability to pay a fee or poll tax, the right not to be denied appellate review solely on account of inability to pay for a transcript, and the right to travel. See Shapiro v. Thompson, 394 U.S. 618 (1969); Harper v. Virginia State Board of Elections, 383 U.S. 663 (1966); Reynolds v. Sims, 377 U.S. 533 (1964); Griffin v. Illinois, 351 U.S. 12 (1956).
24. 381 U.S. 479, 481–85 (1965).
25. Id. at 484.

26. Id. at 485.
27. Id. at 481, 485–86.
28. Id. at 500 (Harlan, J., concurring).
29. *Loving*, 388 U.S. at 12.
30. Id.
31. BRUCE ACKERMAN, WE THE PEOPLE: THE CIVIL RIGHTS REVOLUTION 305 (2014).
32. *Loving*, 388 U.S. at 12.
33. 411 U.S. 1 (1973).
34. Id. at 33.
35. *Roe*, 410 U.S. at 152–53.
36. Id. at 152 (quoting *Palko*, 302 U.S. at 325).
37. Moore v. City of East Cleveland, 431 U.S. 494, 503 (1977).
38. Snyder v. Massachusetts, 291 U.S. 97, 105 (1934).
39. Hebert v. Louisiana, 272 U.S. 312, 316 (1926).
40. In this section, I draw upon the fuller analysis in JAMES E. FLEMING, SECURING CON-STITUTIONAL DEMOCRACY 112–27 (2006) [hereinafter FLEMING, SECURING].
41. 491 U.S. 110, 141 (1989) (Brennan, J., dissenting).
42. *Michael H.*, 491 U.S. at 127 n.6 (1989) (Scalia, J., plurality); Washington v. Glucks-berg, 521 U.S. 702 (1997).
43. Poe v. Ullman, 367 U.S. 497, 542–43 (1961) (Harlan, J., dissenting).
44. Bolling v. Sharpe, 347 U.S. 497 (1954) (companion case to Brown v. Board of Educa-tion, 347 U.S. 483 [1954]). To be sure, *Bolling* and *Loving* involved equal protection as well as due process, but that supports my claim that the two clauses overlap and are intertwined. See chapter 8.
45. *Bolling*, 347 U.S. at 499.
46. *Loving*, 388 U.S. at 12.
47. 478 U.S. 186, 192–94 (1986).
48. *Michael H.*, 491 U.S. at 123–27, 127 n.6. Only Chief Justice Rehnquist joined the quoted formulation from n.6 of Justice Scalia's plurality opinion.
49. Id. at 125, 127.
50. 497 U.S. at 300–01 (1990) (Scalia, J., concurring).
51. Id. at 279 (majority opinion).
52. *Michael H.*, 491 U.S. at 141 (Brennan, J., dissenting).
53. *Casey*, 505 U.S. at 847–48.
54. Id. at 848–50, 901; *Poe*, 367 U.S. at 542–43 (Harlan, J., dissenting).
55. *Casey*, 505 U.S. at 849, 901.
56. *Glucksberg*, 521 U.S. at 720–21.
57. Lawrence v. Texas, 539 U.S. 558, 568–78 (2003).
58. Id. at 588 (Scalia, J., dissenting).
59. Id. at 578–79 (majority opinion).
60. Id. at 564–66, 573–76.
61. *Bowers*, 478 U.S. at 197 (Burger, C. J., concurring).
62. *Obergefell*, 576 U.S. at 687 (Roberts, C. J., dissenting).
63. Id. at 699.
64. Romer v. Evans, 517 U.S. 620 (1996); *Lawrence*, 539 U.S. at 558; United States v. Windsor, 570 U.S. 744 (2013).
65. See PRINCE, *1999, on* 1999 (Warner Bros. 1982).
66. See, e.g., West Virginia State Board of Education v. Barnette, 319 U.S. 624, 630, 642 (1943) (liberty of conscience, freedom of thought, and right to self-determination);

Roberts v. United States Jaycees, 468 U.S. 609, 617–18 (1984) (freedom of association, including both expressive association and intimate association); Lawrence, 539
U.S. at 574–75 (right to privacy or autonomy to engage in same-sex intimate association); Moore, 431 U.S. at 503–04 (right to live with one's family, whether nuclear or
extended); Crandall v. Nevada, 73 U.S. (6 Wall.) 35, 49 (1868) (right to travel); Shapiro,
394 U.S. at 629–30 (right to travel or relocate); Turner v. Safley, 482 U.S. 78, 95–96
(1987) (right to marry); Loving, 388 U.S. at 12 (right to marry); Skinner, 316 U.S. at 541
(right to procreate); Griswold, 381 U.S. at 485–86 (right within marital association to
use contraceptives); Eisenstadt v. Baird, 405 U.S. 438, 453 (1972) (right of individual,
married or single, to use contraceptives); Carey v. Population Services International,
431 U.S. 678, 694 (1977) (right to distribute contraceptives); Roe, 410 U.S. at 153 (right
of a woman to decide whether to terminate her pregnancy); Casey, 505 U.S. at 846, 857
(reaffirming "central holding" of Roe and emphasizing personal autonomy and bodily
integrity); Meyer, 262 U.S. at 400 (right to direct the education of children); Pierce, 268
U.S. at 534–35 (right to direct the upbringing and education of children); Troxel v.
Granville, 530 U.S. 57, 66 (2000) (right of parents to make decisions concerning the
care, custody, and control of children); Washington v. Harper, 494 U.S. 210, 221–22
(1990) (right to bodily integrity, in particular, to avoid unwanted administration of an-
tipsychotic drugs); Rochin v. California, 342 U.S. 165, 172–73 (1952) (right to bodily
integrity, in particular, to be protected against the extraction of evidence obtained by
"breaking into the privacy" of a person's mouth or stomach); Cruzan, 497 U.S. at 279
(assuming for purposes of the case a "right to die" that includes the "right to refuse lifesaving hydration and nutrition"); Stanley v. Georgia, 394 U.S. 557, 564 (1969) (right
to receive ideas and to be free from unwanted governmental intrusions into the privacy
of one's home). For a discussion of this list of substantive basic liberties, see FLEMING,
SECURING, supra note 40, at 92–98. I draw from that analysis here.

67. But see Glucksberg, 521 U.S. at 702 (declining to extend the right to die assumed in
Cruzan—the right to refuse unwanted lifesaving hydration and nutrition—to include
the right to "physician-assisted suicide" or aid in dying).

68. In speaking of the bones and shards as fitting into, and being justifiable within, a
coherent structure, I refer to Dworkin's formulation of the two dimensions of best interpretation: fit and justification. See RONALD DWORKIN, LAW'S EMPIRE 239 (1986).

69. I draw this account of an originalist archaeologist from several sources. See, e.g.,
Lawrence, 539 U.S. at 586 (Scalia, J., dissenting); Casey, 505 U.S. at 980, 999–1000
(Scalia, J., dissenting); Cruzan, 497 U.S. at 300 (Scalia, J., concurring); Michael H.,
491 U.S. at 123–27 & n.6 (Scalia, J., plurality opinion); Bowers, 478 U.S. at 194–95;
ROBERT H. BORK, THE TEMPTING OF AMERICA: THE POLITICAL SEDUCTION OF THE
LAW (1990); ANTONIN SCALIA, A MATTER OF INTERPRETATION: FEDERAL COURTS AND
THE LAW (Amy Gutmann ed., 1997).

70. I base this account of a moral reader archaeologist on several sources. See, e.g., RON-
ALD DWORKIN, FREEDOM'S LAW: THE MORAL READING OF THE AMERICAN CONSTITU-
TION (1996); RONALD DWORKIN, TAKING RIGHTS SERIOUSLY 159–68 (1977); FLEM-
ING, SECURING, supra note 40, at 93–94.

71. Bowers, 478 U.S. at 217 (Stevens, J., dissenting) (quoting Fitzgerald v. Porter Mem'l
Hosp., 523 F.2d 716, 719–20 [7th Cir. 1975] [Stevens, J.] [footnotes omitted], cert.
denied, 425 U.S. 916 [1976]).

72. Bowers, 478 U.S. at 202, 204 (Blackmun, J., dissenting).

73. Roberts, 468 U.S. at 618.

74. Id. at 619.

75. *Casey*, 505 U.S. at 916 (Stevens, J., concurring in part and dissenting in part); see also *Cruzan*, 497 U.S. at 339–45 (Stevens, J., dissenting) (arguing that choices about death are a matter of individual conscience).

76. *Casey*, 505 U.S. at 915, 919–20.

77. Id. at 927 (Blackmun, J., concurring in part, concurring in the judgment in part, and dissenting in part).

78. Id. at 927–28.

79. Id. at 851 (joint opinion).

80. See id. at 851, 856, 857, 897–98.

81. *Meyer*, 262 U.S. at 402 ("[The] ideas touching the relation between individual and state [in ancient Sparta and Plato's ideal commonwealth, which 'submerge the individual and develop ideal citizens'] were wholly different from those upon which our institutions rest").

82. *Pierce*, 268 U.S. at 535 ("The fundamental theory of liberty upon which all governments in this Union repose excludes any general power of the state to standardize its children by forcing them to accept instruction from public teachers only. The child is not the mere creature of the state").

83. *Griswold*, 381 U.S. at 486 ("We deal with a right of privacy older than the Bill of Rights. . . . Marriage is . . . intimate to the degree of being sacred. It is an association that promotes a way of life").

84. *Loving*, 388 U.S. at 12 ("The freedom to marry has long been recognized as one of the vital personal rights essential to the orderly pursuit of happiness by free men").

85. *Eisenstadt*, 405 U.S. at 453 ("If the right of privacy means anything, it is the right of the individual, married or single, to be free from unwarranted governmental intrusion into matters so fundamentally affecting a person as the decision whether to bear or beget a child").

86. *Moore*, 431 U.S. at 506 ("[T]he Constitution prevents [the city] from standardizing its children—and its adults—by forcing all to live in certain narrowly defined family patterns").

87. *Roe*, 410 U.S. at 153 ("Th[e] right of privacy . . . is broad enough to encompass a woman's decision whether or not to terminate her pregnancy").

88. *Carey*, 431 U.S. at 687–88 (stressing that prior decisions such as *Griswold, Eisenstadt,* and *Roe* protected the right to "[i]ndividual autonomy in matters of childbearing" and the individual's "right of decision" about procreation from unjustified intrusion by the government).

89. *Lawrence*, 539 U.S. at 562, 567, 574, 575, 578 (majority opinion) ("Liberty presumes an autonomy of self that includes freedom of thought, belief, expression, and certain intimate conduct").

90. *Obergefell*, 576 U.S. at 665 (majority opinion) ("A first premise of the Court's relevant precedents is that the right to personal choice regarding marriage is inherent in the concept of individual autonomy").

91. *Lawrence*, 539 U.S. at 567, 575, 578; *Obergefell*, 576 U.S. at 647.

92. *Casey*, 505 U.S. at 847.

93. See FLEMING, SECURING, supra note 40, at 3–4, 77, 89.

94. For a similar view, see DWORKIN, supra note 5, at 123.

95. *Obergefell*, 576 U.S. at 702 (Roberts, C. J., dissenting).

96. Id. at 671 (majority opinion).

97. *Griswold*, 381 U.S. at 499 (Harlan, J., concurring); *Poe*, 367 U.S. at 523 (Harlan, J., dissenting).
98. See FLEMING, SECURING, supra note 40, at 117, 123.
99. *Obergefell*, 576 U.S. at 671; *Poe*, 367 U.S. at 540.
100. *Obergefell*, 576 U.S. at 664; *Poe*, 367 U.S. at 540.
101. *Obergefell*, 576 U.S. at 657, 663–64, 669–70, 679; *Poe*, 367 U.S. at 542.
102. *Poe*, 367 U.S. at 542–43.
103. *Obergefell*, 576 U.S. at 657.
104. *Poe*, 367 U.S. at 545–46.
105. For extensive analysis of the relationship between autonomy arguments and moral goods arguments, see JAMES E. FLEMING & LINDA C. MCCLAIN, ORDERED LIBERTY: RIGHTS, RESPONSIBILITIES, AND VIRTUES 177–206 (2013).
106. *Obergefell*, 576 U.S. at 666–67 (quoting *Griswold*, 381 U.S. at 485).
107. Id. at 666 (quoting Goodridge v. Department of Public Health, 798 N.E.2d 941, 955 [Mass. 2003]); *Goodridge*, 798 N.E.2d at 945.
108. *Palko*, 302 U.S. at 325.
109. See FLEMING, SECURING, supra note 40, at 109–11. There I develop this idea more fully and I draw from that analysis here.
110. *Obergefell*, 576 U.S. at 677 (quoting *Barnette*, 319 U.S. at 638).
111. See FLEMING, SECURING, supra note 40, at 126–27.
112. *Palko*, 302 U.S. at 325.
113. *Loving*, 388 U.S. at 12.
114. *Casey*, 505 U.S. at 901.
115. *Lawrence*, 539 U.S. at 578.
116. *Obergefell*, 576 U.S. at 664.

CHAPTER THREE

1. In this chapter, I draw extensively from analysis in prior work. See JAMES E. FLEMING & LINDA C. MCCLAIN, ORDERED LIBERTY: RIGHTS, RESPONSIBILITIES, AND VIRTUES 237–72 (2013) [hereinafter FLEMING & MCCLAIN, ORDERED LIBERTY]. The focus there, however, was on the extent to which substantive due process cases leave latitude for government to inculcate civic virtues and promote responsible exercise of rights. Here, I focus on showing that these cases have not raised the bar for protection of basic liberties as high as Justice Scalia claims and confirming that they have embodied the *Casey* framework instead of the *Glucksberg* framework (as argued in chapter 2).
2. 539 U.S. 558, 593–94 (2003) (Scalia, J., dissenting).
3. For a famous and influential early formulation of the idea of rational basis scrutiny with "bite," in the context of equal protection, see Gerald Gunther, *Foreword: In Search of Evolving Doctrine on a Changing Court: A Model for a Newer Equal Protection*, 86 HARVARD LAW REVIEW 1, 12 (1972).
4. Romer v. Evans, 517 U.S. 620, 632–34 (1996); *Lawrence*, 539 U.S. at 574 (majority opinion); id. at 580, 582–83 (O'Connor, J., concurring).
5. *Lawrence*, 539 U.S. at 593–94 (Scalia, J., dissenting).
6. See, e.g., Adam Winkler, *Fatal in Theory and Strict in Fact: An Empirical Analysis of Strict Scrutiny in the Federal Courts*, 59 VANDERBILT LAW REVIEW 793 (2006); Richard H. Fallon Jr., *Strict Judicial Scrutiny*, 54 UCLA LAW REVIEW 1267 (2007).
7. 410 U.S. 113 (1973).
8. 505 U.S. 833, 847, 876 (1992).

9. Id. at 848–49; Obergefell v. Hodges, 576 U.S. 644, 663–64 (2015); Poe v. Ullman, 367 U.S. 497, 543, 549 (1961) (Harlan, J., dissenting).

10. 478 U.S. 186 (1986).

11. 491 U.S. 110 (1989).

12. 521 U.S. 702 (1997).

13. Laurence H. Tribe, *Lawrence v. Texas: The "Fundamental Right" that Dare Not Speak Its Name*, 117 HARVARD LAW REVIEW 1894, 1917 (2004).

14. For example, for analysis of the latitude *Casey* leaves the government to promote responsible exercise of rights, see FLEMING & MCCLAIN, ORDERED LIBERTY, supra note 1, at 50–80. For analysis of the latitude cases like *Moore* and *Troxel* leave for government to regulate the family, see infra text accompanying notes 31, 51, and 77 as well as James E. Fleming & Linda C. McClain, *Liberty*, in THE OXFORD HANDBOOK OF THE U.S. CONSTITUTION 479, 497 (Mark Tushnet et al. eds., 2015).

15. *Casey*, 505 U.S. at 848–50 (quoting *Poe*, 367 U.S. at 542–43).

16. Id. at 849.

17. Compare City of Cleburne v. Cleburne Living Center, 473 U.S. 432, 451 (1985) (Stevens, J., concurring) (arguing that, under the Equal Protection Clause, despite official doctrine, instead of having rigidly maintained tiers, we have a "continuum of judgmental responses") with San Antonio v. Rodriguez, 411 U.S. 1, 98 (1973) (Marshall, J., dissenting) (similarly arguing that Equal Protection doctrine consists not of rigidly maintained tiers but of a "spectrum of standards").

18. 262 U.S. 390 (1923).

19. Id. at 399–402.

20. Id. at 399–401.

21. Id. at 401–03.

22. Id. at 412.

23. 268 U.S. 510 (1925).

24. Id. at 534–35.

25. Id. at 535.

26. Id. at 534.

27. 321 U.S. 158, 160–61 (1944).

28. Id. at 165–66.

29. Id. at 165, 170.

30. Id. at 170 (emphasis added).

31. Id. at 166–67.

32. 381 U.S. 479, 480 (1965).

33. Id. at 485.

34. Id. (quoting NAACP v. Alabama, 357 U.S. 449, 462 [1964]).

35. Id. at 485–86.

36. 388 U.S. 1, 8 (1967).

37. Id. at 11 (quoting Korematsu v. United States, 324 U.S. 214, 216 [1944]).

38. Id. at 12 (citing Skinner v. Oklahoma, 316 U.S. 535, 541 [1942]).

39. Id.

40. See *Skinner*, 316 U.S. at 541.

41. See, e.g., GEOFFREY R. STONE, LOUIS MICHAEL SEIDMAN, CASS R. SUNSTEIN, MARK V. TUSHNET & PAMELA S. KARLAN, CONSTITUTIONAL LAW 536–38 (8th ed., 2017).

42. *Roe*, 410 U.S. at 118, 152–53.

43. Id. at 152 (quoting Palko v. Connecticut, 302 U.S. 319, 325 [1937]).

44. Id. at 155–56.

45. 431 U.S. 494 (1977) (Powell, J., plurality opinion).
46. Id. at 499 (quoting Cleveland Board of Education v. LaFleur, 414 U.S. 632, 639–40 [1974]).
47. Id. (citing, e.g., *Prince*; *Roe*; *Griswold*; *Poe*; compare *Loving*; *Skinner*).
48. Id.
49. Id. at 503 n.12 (quoting *Poe*, 367 U.S. at 551–52).
50. Id. at 502–03.
51. Id. at 499.
52. 429 U.S. 190, 197 (1976).
53. *Moore*, 431 U.S. at 499–500.
54. 497 U.S. 261 (1990).
55. Id. at 262, 279 n.7.
56. Id. at 279 (emphasis added) (quoting Youngberg v. Romeo, 457 U.S. 307, 321 [1982]).
57. 348 U.S. 483 (1955) (applying highly deferential rational basis scrutiny to economic regulations under both the Equal Protection and Due Process Clauses).
58. *Casey*, 505 U.S. at 872, 876.
59. Id. at 877.
60. Whole Woman's Health v. Hellerstedt, 136 S. Ct. 2292 (2016) (Texas); June Medical Services, LLC v. Russo, 140 S. Ct. 2013 (2020) (Louisiana).
61. *Hellerstedt*, 136 S. Ct. at 2323–24 (Thomas, J., dissenting); *June Medical Services*, 140 S. Ct. at 2181 (Thomas, J., dissenting).
62. 521 U.S. 702 (1997).
63. Id. at 720–21.
64. Id. at 723.
65. See Compassion in Dying v. Washington, 79 F.3d 790 (9th Cir. 1996) (en banc), *rev'd sub nom. Glucksberg*, 521 U.S. 702 (1997).
66. *Glucksberg*, 521 U.S. at 790 (Breyer, J., concurring).
67. Id. at 740, 743 (Stevens, J., concurring).
68. Id. at 721, 722 n.17.
69. See JAMES E. FLEMING, SECURING CONSTITUTIONAL DEMOCRACY: THE CASE OF AUTONOMY 120–23 (2006).
70. See *Bowers*, 478 U.S. at 199 (Blackmun, J., dissenting); id. at 217 (Stevens, J., dissenting); *Michael H.*, 491 U.S. at 139 (Brennan, J., dissenting); *Glucksberg*, 521 U.S. at 743 (Stevens, J., concurring); id. at 790 (Breyer, J., concurring).
71. 530 U.S. 57, 65 (2000).
72. Id. (citing *Glucksberg*, 521 U.S. at 720).
73. David Meyer, *Constitutional Pragmatism for a Changing American Family*, 32 RUTGERS LAW JOURNAL 711, 711 (2001).
74. *Troxel*, 530 U.S. at 80 (Thomas, J., concurring).
75. Id. at 58–59, 67–69, 72–73 (plurality opinion).
76. Id. at 86–89 (Stevens, J., dissenting).
77. This form of analysis bears some resemblance to "proportionality" analysis as articulated by European scholars and judges. See, e.g., AHARON BARAK, PROPORTIONALITY: CONSTITUTIONAL RIGHTS AND THEIR LIMITATIONS (2012).
78. *Lawrence*, 539 U.S. at 578.
79. Id. at 568–78 (criticizing *Bowers*, 478 U.S. at 191).
80. Id. at 562, 564; see *Bowers*, 478 U.S. at 204 (Blackmun, J., dissenting).
81. *Lawrence*, 539 U.S. at 571–72.

82. Id. at 572.
83. *Poe*, 367 U.S. at 550, 553.
84. CHARLES FRIED, ORDER AND LAW: ARGUING THE REAGAN REVOLUTION: A FIRSTHAND ACCOUNT 82–83 (1991).
85. LAURENCE H. TRIBE & MICHAEL C. DORF, ON READING THE CONSTITUTION 116–17 (1991).
86. 576 U.S. 644, 663–64 (2015).
87. Id. at 647.

CHAPTER FOUR

1. 539 U.S. 558 (2003); id. at 590, 599 (Scalia, J., dissenting).
2. 576 U.S. 644 (2015); id. at 704–05 (Roberts, C. J., dissenting).
3. See WARD FARNSWORTH, THE LEGAL ANALYST: A TOOLKIT FOR THINKING ABOUT THE LAW 172–81 (2007).
4. ALI ALMOSSAWI & ALEJANDRO GIRALDO, AN ILLUSTRATED BOOK OF BAD ARGUMENTS 36 (2014).
5. Edmund Burke, On Moving His Resolutions for Conciliation with the Colonies, Speech to Parliament, Mar. 22, 1775.
6. See GARRY WILLS, A NECESSARY EVIL: A HISTORY OF AMERICAN DISTRUST OF GOVERNMENT (2002).
7. ANTONIN SCALIA, A MATTER OF INTERPRETATION: FEDERAL COURTS AND THE LAW 9–14 (Amy Gutmann ed., 1997).
8. *Obergefell*, 576 U.S. at 716–20 (Scalia, J., dissenting); *Lawrence*, 539 U.S. at 586 (Scalia, J., dissenting); Planned Parenthood v. Casey, 505 U.S. 833, 979 (1992) (Scalia, J., concurring in the judgment in part and dissenting in part).
9. See ALBERT O. HIRSCHMAN, THE RHETORIC OF REACTION: PERVERSITY, FUTILITY, JEOPARDY (1991).
10. PATRICK DEVLIN, THE ENFORCEMENT OF MORALS 17 (1965).
11. United States v. Virginia, 518 U.S. 515, 570 (1996) (Scalia, J., dissenting) (asserting that the Supreme Court's requiring Virginia Military Institute to stop discriminating against female applicants "shuts down" or "destroys" it); SCALIA, supra note 7, at 40–41 ("rot").
12. James E. Fleming and Linda C. McClain, *Ordered Gun Liberty*, 94 BOSTON UNIVERSITY LAW REVIEW 849, 850, 852 (2014).
13. *Lawrence*, 539 U.S. at 567, 578 (majority opinion).
14. Id. at 578.
15. I take the term "libertarian revolution," but not this particular formulation of the idea, from Randy E. Barnett, *Justice Kennedy's Libertarian Revolution*: Lawrence v. Texas, 2002–2003 CATO SUPREME COURT REVIEW 21.
16. *Obergefell*, 576 U.S. at 666–67 (quoting Griswold v. Connecticut, 381 U.S. 479, 486 [1965]).
17. Id. at 666 (quoting Goodridge v. Department of Public Health, 798 N.E.2d 941, 955 [Mass. 2003]); *Goodridge*, 798 N.E.2d at 945.
18. JAMES E. FLEMING, FIDELITY TO OUR IMPERFECT CONSTITUTION: FOR MORAL READINGS AND AGAINST ORIGINALISMS (2015). See also SOTIRIOS A. BARBER & JAMES E. FLEMING, CONSTITUTIONAL INTERPRETATION: THE BASIC QUESTIONS 155–70 (2007) (defending a "philosophic approach" to constitutional interpretation and criticizing

all theories and approaches that aim and claim to avoid making such moral judgments in constitutional interpretation).

19. Cass R. Sunstein, *What Did Lawrence Hold? Of Autonomy, Desuetude, Sexuality, and Marriage,* 2003 SUPREME COURT REVIEW 27, 30.

20. *Bowers,* 478 U.S. 186, 190–91 (1986); *Lawrence,* 539 U.S. at 574.

21. *Lawrence,* 539 U.S. at 567.

22. See JOHN STUART MILL, ON LIBERTY 10–11 (David Spitz ed., 1975) (1859).

23. *Lawrence,* 539 U.S. at 598 (Scalia, J., dissenting).

24. Id.

25. Id. at 604.

26. *Obergefell,* 576 U.S. at 704–05 (Roberts, C. J., dissenting).

27. 771 F.2d 323, 328, 329 (7th Cir. 1985), *aff'd* mem., 475 U.S. 1001 (1986).

28. [1992], 1 S.C.R. 452 (Can. S.C.C.).

29. *Obergefell,* 576 U.S. at 704–05.

30. 431 U.S. 494, 503 (1977).

31. *Obergefell,* 576 U.S. at 688, 704.

32. Id. at 704.

33. No. 15-83-BLG-SPW-CSO, 2015 WL 12804521 (D. Mont. Dec. 8, 2018).

34. *Obergefell,* 576 U.S. at 686; *Windsor,* 570 U.S. 744, 778 (2013) (Scalia, J., dissenting); *Lawrence,* 539 U.S. at 586 (Scalia, J., dissenting). For lower court decisions citing Scalia's dissent in *Windsor* to support their recognition of a right of same-sex couples to marry, see, e.g., Bostic v. Rainey, 970 F. Supp. 2d 456, 476 (E.D. Va. 2014); Kitchen v. Hebert, 961 F. Supp. 2d 1181, 1194 (D. Utah 2013).

35. *Windsor,* 570 U.S. at 775 (Roberts, C. J., dissenting).

36. *Obergefell,* 576 U.S. at 686.

37. Interview by Nina Totenberg with Ruth Bader Ginsburg, Justice, Supreme Court (May 2, 2002), https://www.pbs.org/now/transcript/transcript116_full.html.

38. *Collier,* 2015 WL 12804521, at *1, 3.

39. *Obergefell,* 576 U.S. at 710 (quoting Ruth Bader Ginsburg, *Some Thoughts on Autonomy and Equality in Relation to* Roe v. Wade, 63 NORTH CAROLINA LAW REVIEW 375, 385–86 [1985]).

40. Ginsburg, supra note 39, at 382.

41. See, e.g., Governing: State and Local Government News and Analysis, *State Same-Sex Marriage State Laws Map: Thirty-Seven States Had Legalized Same-Sex Marriage Prior to the Supreme Court Ruling,* https://www.governing.com/gov-data/same-sex-marriage-civil-unions-doma-laws-by-state.html.

42. Pew Research Center, *Attitudes on Same-Sex Marriage,* May 14, 2019, https://www.pewforum.org/fact-sheet/changing-attitudes-on-gay-marriage/.

43. *Obergefell,* 576 U.S. at 711.

44. 947 F. Supp. 2d 1170, 1179–80 (D. Utah 2013) (citing Reynolds v. United States, 98 U.S. 145 [1878]), *rev'd* 822 F.3d 1151 (10th Cir. 2016).

45. 137 S. Ct. 828 (2017).

46. Christine Hauser, *Utah Lowers Penalty for Polygamy: No Longer a Felony,* N.Y. TIMES, May 13, 2020, https://www.nytimes.com/2020/05/13/us/utah-bigamy-law.html.

47. See Vanessa Romo, *Utah Bill Decriminalizing Polygamy Clears First Hurdle, Moves to State Senate,* NPR, Feb. 12, 2020, https://www.npr.org/2020/02/12/805455196/utah-bill-decriminalizing-polygamy-clears-first-hurdle-moves-to-state-senate (showing photo of Kody Brown carrying a sign bearing the hashtag).

48. *Lawrence*, 539 U.S. at 602.

49. See Fernanda Santos & Julie Turkewitz, *Fraud Arrests May Be Turning Point for Polyga-mist Sect*, N.Y. TIMES, Mar. 3, 2016, at A9, https://www.nytimes.com/2016/03/03/us/food-stamp-trial-may-be-turning-point-for-polygamist-sect.html.

50. *Obergefell*, 576 U.S. at 704 (Roberts, C. J., dissenting).

51. MILL, supra note 22, at 75.

52. See, e.g., *The Look: Polyamory Works for Them*, N.Y. TIMES, Aug. 8, 2019, https://www.nytimes.com/2019/08/03/style/polyamory-nonmonogamy-relationships.html; Jenny Block, *A Blue Moon Wedding for Two Goth Romantics*, N.Y. TIMES, Nov. 13, 2020, https://www.nytimes.com/2020/11/13/style/a-goth-wedding.html.

53. Samantha Cooney, *What Monogamous Couples Can Learn from Polyamorous Unions, According to Experts*, TIME, Aug. 27, 2018, https://time.com/5330833/polyamory-monogamous-relationships/.

54. Andrew Solomon, *The Shape of Love: How Polyamorists and Polygamists Are Challenging Family Norms*, THE NEW YORKER, March 15, 2021, https://www.newyorker.com/magazine/2021/03/22/how-polyamorists-and-polygamists-are-challenging-family-norms.

55. Ellen Barry, *A Massachusetts City Decides to Recognize Polyamorous Relationships*, N.Y. TIMES, July 1, 2020, https://www.nytimes.com/2020/07/01/us/somerville-polyamorous-domestic-partnership.html.

56. For fuller analysis, see Joanna L. Grossman & Lawrence M. Friedman, *The Chosen Few: Polyamory and the Law*, VERDICT, Apr. 6, 2021, https://verdict.justia.com/2021/04/06/the-chosen-few-polyamory-and-the-law.

57. Id.

58. Jesse Collings, *Town Meeting Approves Domestic Partnership for Relationships with More than Two People*, WICKED LOCAL, Apr. 30, 2021, https://www.wickedlocal.com/story/arlington-advocate/2021/04/30/arlington-approves-domestic-partnerships-polyamorous-relationships/7410640002/.

59. Polyamory Legal Advocacy Coalition, https://polyamorylegal.org/our-mission.

60. DOUGLAS E. ABRAMS, NAOMI R. CAHN, CATHERINE J. ROSS & LINDA C. MCCLAIN, CON-TEMPORARY FAMILY LAW 291–92 (5th ed. 2019).

61. 405 U.S. 438 (1972); *Griswold*, 381 U.S. at 479.

62. [2003] 65 O.R. 3d 161 (Can. Ont. C.A.).

63. See Reference re: Section 293 of the Criminal Code of Can., 2011 BCSC 1588, para. 256 (Can.).

64. 409 U.S. 810, 810 (1972).

65. See STEPHEN MACEDO, JUST MARRIED: SAME-SEX COUPLES, MONOGAMY & THE FU-TURE OF MARRIAGE 167–73 (2015).

66. 517 U.S. 620, 636 (1996) (Scalia, J., dissenting).

67. *Obergefell*, 576 U.S. at 705–06.

68. Id. at 679 (majority opinion).

69. Id.

70. See MACEDO, supra note 65, at 167–73.

71. See id. at 203.

CHAPTER FIVE

1. 539 U.S. 558, 590, 599 (2003) (Scalia, J., dissenting).

2. 478 U.S. 186, 196 (1986).

3. Id. at 192; id. at 196–97 (Burger, C. J., concurring).

4. Leviticus 18:22.
5. *Bowers*, 478 U.S. at 196.
6. See PATRICK DEVLIN, THE ENFORCEMENT OF MORALS 13 (1965).
7. Robert P. George, *The Concept of Public Morality*, 45 AMERICAN JOURNAL OF JURISPRU-DENCE 17, 17–19 (2000).
8. 530 U.S. 640, 641, 649 (2000).
9. See RYAN T. ANDERSON, TRUTH OVERRULED: THE FUTURE OF MARRIAGE AND RELI-GIOUS FREEDOM (2015).
10. JOHN STUART MILL, ON LIBERTY 10–11 (David Spitz ed., 1975) (1859).
11. RANDY E. BARNETT, RESTORING THE LOST CONSTITUTION: THE PRESUMPTION OF LIBERTY (2004); TARA SMITH, JUDICIAL REVIEW IN AN OBJECTIVE LEGAL SYSTEM (2015).
12. See, e.g., CATHARINE A. MACKINNON, ONLY WORDS (1993).
13. See, e.g., NADINE STROSSEN, DEFENDING PORNOGRAPHY: FREE SPEECH, SEX, AND THE FIGHT FOR WOMEN'S RIGHTS (1995).
14. Reynolds v. United States, 98 U.S. 145 (1878).
15. See, e.g., STEPHEN MACEDO, JUST MARRIED: SAME-SEX COUPLES, MONOGAMY & THE FUTURE OF MARRIAGE 167–73 (2015); Rose McDermott and Jonathan Cowden, *Polygyny and Violence against Women*, 64 EMORY LAW JOURNAL 1767 (2015); Maura I. Strassberg, *The Crime of Polygamy*, 12 TEMPLE POLITICAL AND CIVIL RIGHTS LAW RE-VIEW 353 (2003).
16. See, e.g., Jonathan Turley, *The Loadstone Rock: The Role of Harm in the Criminalization of Plural Unions*, 64 EMORY LAW JOURNAL 1905 (2015).
17. MARTHA ALBERTSON FINEMAN, THE AUTONOMY MYTH: A THEORY OF DEPENDENCY 123, 133–38 (2004) (progressive); David Boaz, *Privatize Marriage: A Simple Solution to the Gay Marriage Debate*, SLATE, April 25, 1997, https://slate.com/news-and-politics/1997/04/privatize-marriage.html (libertarian).
18. *Lawrence*, 539 U.S. at 578 (majority opinion).
19. See JAMES E. FLEMING, SOTIRIOS A. BARBER, STEPHEN MACEDO & LINDA C. MCCLAIN, GAY RIGHTS AND THE CONSTITUTION 63–86 (2016).
20. *Bowers*, 478 U.S. at 195–96 (majority opinion).
21. Id. at 196.
22. *Lawrence*, 539 U.S. at 599 (Scalia, J., dissenting).
23. Id. at 577–78 (majority opinion) (quoting *Bowers*, 478 U.S. at 215 [Stevens, J., dissenting]).
24. *Bowers*, 478 U.S. at 196.
25. See Williamson v. Lee Optical of Oklahoma, Inc., 348 U.S. 483 (1955).
26. *Bowers*, 478 U.S. at 193–94; id. at 198 n.2 (Powell, J., concurring).
27. Cass R. Sunstein, *What Did* Lawrence *Hold? Of Autonomy, Desuetude, Sexuality, and Marriage*, 2003 SUPREME COURT REVIEW 27, 30.
28. *Lawrence*, 539 U.S. at 599, 602 (Scalia, J., dissenting).
29. Id. at 571–72 (majority opinion); see also *Bowers*, 478 U.S. at 197 (Burger, C. J., concurring).
30. See *Lawrence*, 539 U.S. at 564 (majority opinion); Obergefell v. Hodges, 576 U.S. 644, 663–64 (2015).
31. See *Bowers*, 478 U.S. at 188 (majority opinion); id. at 196 (Burger, C. J., concurring); Romer v. Evans, 517 U.S. 620, 636 (1996) (Scalia, J., dissenting); United States v. Virginia, 518 U.S. 515, 567 (1996) (Scalia, J., dissenting); *Lawrence*, 539 U.S. at 589 (Scalia, J., dissenting); *Obergefell*, 576 U.S. at 715 (Scalia, J., dissenting).

32. *Bowers*, 478 U.S. at 199 (Blackmun, J., dissenting) (citing Oliver W. Holmes Jr., *The Path of the Law*, 10 HARVARD LAW REVIEW 457, 469 [1897]).

33. Id. at 199–200 (citing Herring v. State, 119 Ga. 709, 721 [1904]).

34. Id. at 216 (Stevens, J., dissenting) (citing Loving v. Virginia, 388 U.S. 1 [1967]).

35. Id. (internal citations omitted).

36. *Lawrence*, 539 U.S. at 560, 577–79 (majority opinion).

37. Id. at 572 (citing County of Sacramento v. Lewis, 532 U.S. 833, 857 [1998] [Kennedy, J., concurring]).

38. *Obergefell*, 576 U.S. at 656–57 (majority opinion).

39. *Bowers*, 476 U.S. at 197 (Burger, J., concurring) (internal citations omitted).

40. AMERICAN PSYCHIATRIC ASSOCIATION, DIAGNOSTIC AND STATISTICAL MANUAL OF MENTAL DISORDERS (1973) ("DSM II"), revising AMERICAN PSYCHIATRIC ASSOCIATION, DIAGNOSTIC AND STATISTICAL MANUAL OF MENTAL DISORDERS (1952) ("DSM I").

41. See, e.g., Benjamin Kaufman, *Why NARTH? The American Psychiatric Association's Destructive and Blind Pursuit of Political Correctness*, 14 REGENT UNIVERSITY LAW REVIEW 423, 423–24 (2002).

42. DEVLIN, supra note 6, at 17.

43. Ronald Dworkin, *Lord Devlin and the Enforcement of Morals*, 75 YALE LAW JOURNAL 986, 1001 (1966).

44. Id. at 994.

45. Id. at 996–97.

46. See id. at 994, 1000.

47. See *Romer*, 517 U.S. at 632, 634–35 (majority opinion).

48. Id. at 635.

49. See *Lawrence*, 539 U.S. at 571–72.

50. See *Romer*, 517 U.S. at 632, 634–35.

51. See Palmore v. Sidoti, 466 U.S. 429, 433 (1984) (involving racial prejudice).

52. 473 U.S. 432, 448 (1985).

53. 413 U.S. 528, 533–34 (1973).

54. *Romer*, 517 U.S. at 635 ("strangers to our law"); *Cleburne*, 473 U.S. at 473 (Marshall, J., concurring) ("pariah"); *Obergefell*, 576 U.S. at 667 ("outlaw").

55. *Lawrence*, 539 U.S. at 582 (O'Connor, J., concurring).

56. Id. at 583 (internal citations omitted).

57. See Linda C. McClain, *From Romer v. Evans to United States v. Windsor: Law as a Vehicle for Moral Disapproval in Amendment 2 and the Defense of Marriage Act*, 20 DUKE JOURNAL OF GENDER LAW & POLICY 351 (2013) (analyzing opposing briefs in *Romer*).

58. See JOHN HART ELY, DEMOCRACY AND DISTRUST: A THEORY OF JUDICIAL REVIEW 153–54 (1980).

59. Paul Brest, *The Substance of Process*, 42 OHIO STATE LAW JOURNAL 131, 134–37 (1981).

60. The group "Courage" counsels Catholics with "same-sex attractions" to live a life of chastity.

61. JOHN RAWLS, POLITICAL LIBERALISM 213–20, 223–30 (1993).

62. See, e.g., Edward B. Foley, *Political Liberalism and Establishment Clause Jurisprudence*, 43 CASE WESTERN RESERVE LAW REVIEW 963 (1993).

63. See, e.g., NATURAL LAW AND PUBLIC REASON (Robert P. George & Christopher Wolfe eds., 2000).

64. *Obergefell*, 576 U.S. at 690 (Roberts, C. J., dissenting).

65. RAWLS, supra note 61, at 240.

66. 505 U.S. 833, 850 (1992). See *Lawrence*, 539 U.S. at 571 (quoting *Casey*, 505 U.S. at 850); see also *Obergefell*, 576 U.S. at 679–80.
67. Mario Cuomo, *Religious Belief and Public Morality: A Catholic Governor's Perspective*, delivered Sept. 13, 1984 as the John O'Brien Lecture in the University of Notre Dame's Department of Theology, http://archives.nd.edu/research/texts/cuomo.htm.
68. 163 U.S. 537, 551–52 (1896). For analysis of Sumner's arguments in the context of resistance to government attempting to reduce prejudice, for example, through civil rights laws, see LINDA C. MCCLAIN, WHO'S THE BIGOT? LEARNING FROM CONFLICTS OVER MARRIAGE AND CIVIL RIGHTS LAW 36–38, 106–14 (2020).
69. 515 U.S. 200, 240 (1995) (Thomas, J., concurring). For analysis of the similarities between *Plessy*'s worldview and Thomas's in this respect, see James E. Fleming, *Rewriting Brown, Resurrecting Plessy*, 52 SAINT LOUIS UNIVERSITY LAW JOURNAL 1141, 1145–49 (2008).
70. See Harper v. Poway Unified Sch. Dist., 445 F.3d 1166, 1192 (9th Cir. 2006) (Kozinski, J., dissenting).
71. See James E. Fleming & Linda C. McClain, *Liberty*, in THE OXFORD HANDBOOK OF THE U.S. CONSTITUTION 479, 497 (Mark Tushnet et al. eds., 2015); see also JAMES E. FLEMING & LINDA C. MCCLAIN, ORDERED LIBERTY: RIGHTS, RESPONSIBILITIES, AND VIRTUES 263–65 (2013) [hereinafter FLEMING & MCCLAIN, ORDERED LIBERTY].
72. See MACEDO, supra note 15, at 194–97.
73. See, e.g., Beard v. State, 2005 WL 1334378 (Tenn. Crim. App. 2005); People v. McEvoy, 154 Cal. Rptr.3d 914 (Ct. App. 2013); State v. Freeman, 801 N.E.2d 906 (Ohio Ct. App. 2003).
74. 468 U.S. 609 (1984).
75. See, e.g., Miller v. California, 413 U.S. 15 (1973).
76. 405 U.S. 438, 453 (1972) (emphasis added).
77. Genesis 38:9.
78. *Obergefell*, 576 U.S. at 737 (Alito, J., dissenting).
79. See JAMES E. FLEMING, SECURING CONSTITUTIONAL DEMOCRACY: THE CASE OF AUTONOMY 67–69 (2006).
80. See FLEMING & MCCLAIN, ORDERED LIBERTY, supra note 71, at 146–76.
81. See id. at 177–206.
82. See JAMES E. FLEMING, FIDELITY TO OUR IMPERFECT CONSTITUTION: FOR MORAL READINGS AND AGAINST ORIGINALISMS (2015).
83. See id.
84. See FLEMING & MCCLAIN, ORDERED LIBERTY, supra note 71, at 4, 117–18, 209.

CHAPTER SIX
1. 198 U.S. 45 (1905); cf. KARL MARX & FRIEDRICH ENGELS, MANIFESTO OF THE COMMUNIST PARTY (1848), reprinted in THE MARX-ENGELS READER 469, 473 (Robert C. Tucker ed., 2d ed. 1978) ("A spectre is haunting Europe—the spectre of Communism"). In this chapter, I draw upon previous work. See JAMES E. FLEMING, SOTIRIOS A. BARBER, STEPHEN MACEDO & LINDA C. MCCLAIN, GAY RIGHTS AND THE CONSTITUTION 98–100 (2016); James E. Fleming & Linda C. McClain, *Liberty*, in THE OXFORD HANDBOOK OF THE U.S. CONSTITUTION 479, 493–95 (Mark Tushnet et al. eds., 2015); JAMES E. FLEMING, SECURING CONSTITUTIONAL DEMOCRACY: THE CASE OF AUTONOMY 7–8, 134–36 (2006) [hereinafter FLEMING, SECURING]; James E. Fleming, *Fidelity, Basic Liberties, and the Specter of Lochner*, 41 WILLIAM & MARY LAW REVIEW 147, 149–51, 167–71, 173–75 (1999).

2. See, e.g., Planned Parenthood v. Casey, 505 U.S. 833, 998 (1992) (Scalia, J., concurring in the judgment in part and dissenting in part); ROBERT H. BORK, THE TEMPTING OF AMERICA: THE POLITICAL SEDUCTION OF THE LAW 32, 111–16, 158, 209 (1990); John Hart Ely, *The Wages of Crying Wolf: A Comment on Roe v. Wade*, 82 YALE LAW JOURNAL 920 (1973) [hereinafter Ely, *Wages*].
3. 576 U.S. 644, 704 (2015) (Roberts, C. J., dissenting).
4. See FLEMING, SECURING, supra note 1, at 62–74.
5. *Lochner*, 198 U.S. at 52–53, 54, 59.
6. Id. at 56.
7. Id. at 57, 61.
8. Id. at 56, 59, 63.
9. See, e.g., BORK, supra note 2, at 49.
10. *Lochner*, 198 U.S. at 64.
11. Id. at 65 (Harlan, J., dissenting).
12. Id. at 68–69.
13. Id. at 69–70.
14. Id. at 74–75 (Holmes, J., dissenting).
15. Id. at 75.
16. Ferguson v. Skrupa, 372 U.S. 726, 732 (1963).
17. WALTER F. MURPHY, JAMES E. FLEMING, SOTIRIOS A. BARBER & STEPHEN MACEDO, AMERICAN CONSTITUTIONAL INTERPRETATION 1167 (6th ed. 2019).
18. *Lochner*, 198 U.S. at 76 (emphasis added).
19. See CASS R. SUNSTEIN, THE PARTIAL CONSTITUTION 45–62, 259–61 (1993) [hereinafter SUNSTEIN, PARTIAL]; Cass R. Sunstein, Lochner's Legacy, 87 COLUMBIA LAW REVIEW 873, 874–75, 882–83 (1987) [hereinafter Sunstein, *Legacy*].
20. *Lochner*, 198 U.S. at 76.
21. 300 U.S. 379, 399 (1937).
22. Id. at 391.
23. Id.
24. 198 U.S. at 69 (Harlan, J., dissenting).
25. Ely, *Wages*, supra note 2, at 935–36.
26. Id. at 939.
27. Jamal Greene, *The Anticanon*, 125 HARVARD LAW REVIEW 379 (2011).
28. 198 U.S. at 68–70; id. at 75–76 (Holmes, J., dissenting).
29. See, e.g., *Casey*, 505 U.S. at 998 (Scalia, J., dissenting); BORK, supra note 2, at 32, 111–16, 158, 209.
30. 304 U.S. 144, 152 n.4 (1938). Ely fully developed this understanding of a *Carolene Products* jurisprudence. JOHN HART ELY, DEMOCRACY AND DISTRUST: A THEORY OF JUDICIAL REVIEW 73–104 (1980) [hereinafter ELY, DEMOCRACY]. Some scholars, however, subsequently have developed a *Carolene Products*–like equal protection argument that protecting the right to abortion is necessary to secure the status of equal citizenship for women. See, e.g., SUNSTEIN, PARTIAL, supra note 19, at 143–44, 270–85.
31. ELY, DEMOCRACY, supra note 30, at 162–64.
32. See, e.g., Griswold v. Connecticut, 381 U.S. 479, 482 (1965) (Douglas, J., opinion of the Court); Poe v. Ullman, 367 U.S. 497, 517–18 (1961) (Douglas, J., dissenting); William Brennan, *The Constitution of the United States: Contemporary Ratification*, 27 SOUTH TEXAS LAW JOURNAL 433, 439–45 (1986) (contrasting contemporary understanding of what rights human dignity requires with a nineteenth-century

understanding that had emphasized economic liberties); *Casey*, 505 U.S. at 861–62 (joint opinion of Justices O'Connor, Kennedy, and Souter).

33. SUNSTEIN, PARTIAL, supra note 19, at 40–67; Sunstein, *Legacy*, supra note 19.

34. 300 U.S. at 392.

35. Jamal Greene, *The Meaning of Substantive Due Process*, 31 CONSTITUTIONAL COMMENTARY 253, 269 (2016) (discussing ELY, DEMOCRACY, supra note 30, at 18).

36. United States v. Carlton, 512 U.S. 26, 39 (1994) (Scalia, J., concurring).

37. *West Coast Hotel*, 300 U.S. at 402–3 (Sutherland, J., dissenting).

38. I draw this distinction from STEPHEN MACEDO, THE NEW RIGHT VERSUS THE CONSTITUTION (1987).

39. See, e.g., BERNARD SIEGAN, ECONOMIC LIBERTIES AND THE CONSTITUTION (1986).

40. See, e.g., RICHARD A. EPSTEIN, TAKINGS: PRIVATE PROPERTY AND THE POWER OF EMINENT DOMAIN (1985) [hereinafter EPSTEIN, TAKINGS]; Richard A. Epstein, *Substantive Due Process by Any Other Name: The Abortion Cases*, 1973 SUPREME COURT REVIEW 159; Richard A. Epstein, *Toward a Revitalization of the Contract Clause*, 51 UNIVERSITY OF CHICAGO LAW REVIEW 703 (1984).

41. In addition to Siegan's and Epstein's works cited supra notes 39 and 40, see RANDY E. BARNETT, RESTORING THE LOST CONSTITUTION: THE PRESUMPTION OF LIBERTY (2004); DAVID E. BERNSTEIN, REHABILITATING *LOCHNER*: DEFENDING INDIVIDUAL RIGHTS AGAINST PROGRESSIVE REFORM (2012); ILYA SOMIN, DEMOCRACY AND POLITICAL IGNORANCE: WHY SMALLER GOVERNMENT IS SMARTER (2013).

42. 302 U.S. 319, 325 (1937).

43. 198 U.S. at 75 (Holmes, J., dissenting).

44. See SIEGAN, supra note 39.

45. See EPSTEIN, TAKINGS, supra note 40; Epstein, *Substantive Due Process by Any Other Name*, supra note 40.

46. See, e.g., Steven G. Calabresi & Hannah M. Begley, *Justice Oliver Wendell Holmes and Chief Justice John Roberts's Dissent in* Obergefell v. Hodges, 8 ELON LAW REVIEW 1 (2016).

47. See HADLEY ARKES, THE RETURN OF GEORGE SUTHERLAND: RESTORING A JURISPRUDENCE OF NATURAL RIGHTS (1994).

48. LAWRENCE G. SAGER, JUSTICE IN PLAINCLOTHES: A THEORY OF AMERICAN CONSTITUTIONAL PRACTICE 84–92 (2004).

49. SUNSTEIN, PARTIAL, supra note 19, at 9–10.

50. See FLEMING, SECURING, supra note 1, at 135–36.

51. See SUNSTEIN, PARTIAL, supra note 19, at v–vi, 9–10, 139–40, 145–61, 350; MARK TUSHNET, TAKING THE CONSTITUTION AWAY FROM THE COURTS (1999); Paul Brest, *The Conscientious Legislator's Guide to Constitutional Interpretation*, 27 STANFORD LAW REVIEW 585, 586 (1975); SAGER, supra note 48, at 84–92.

52. 304 U.S. at 152 n.4.

53. ELY, DEMOCRACY, supra note 30, 87–104.

54. Richard A. Epstein, *Property, Speech, and the Politics of Distrust*, 59 UNIVERSITY OF CHICAGO LAW REVIEW 41 (1992).

55. Frank I. Michelman, *Liberties, Fair Values, and Constitutional Method*, 59 UNIVERSITY OF CHICAGO LAW REVIEW 91, 105–14 (1992).

56. See THE FEDERALIST NO. 10 (James Madison) (Clinton Rossiter ed., 1961).

57. See id.

58. William Michael Treanor, *The Original Understanding of the Takings Clause and the Political Process*, 95 COLUMBIA LAW REVIEW 782, 836–55, 887 (1995).

59. For discussion of "the war against the poor," see, e.g., RANDY ALBELDA ET AL., THE WAR ON THE POOR: A DEFENSE MANUAL (1996); HERBERT J. GANS, THE WAR AGAINST THE POOR: THE UNDERCLASS AND ANTIPOVERTY POLICY (1995).

60. Kelo v. City of New London, 545 U.S. 469, 488 (2005).

61. See ILYA SOMIN, THE GRASPING HAND: KELO V. CITY OF NEW LONDON AND THE LIMITS OF EMINENT DOMAIN (2016).

62. See Ilya Somin, *The Political and Judicial Reaction to* Kelo, WASH. POST, June 4, 2015, https://www.washingtonpost.com/news/volokh-conspiracy/wp/2015/06/04/the-political-and-judicial-reaction-to-kelo/.

63. But see ROBERT NOZICK, ANARCHY, STATE, AND UTOPIA 163 (1974) (stating that a hypothetical "socialist society would have to forbid capitalisti[c] acts between consenting adults").

64. 198 U.S. at 61.

65. 197 U.S. 11 (1905).

66. See, e.g., Adam Liptak, *Supreme Court Blocks New York's Virus-Imposed Limits to Religious Services*, N.Y. TIMES, Nov. 26, 2020, https://www.nytimes.com/2020/11/26/world/supreme-court-blocks-new-yorks-virus-imposed-limits-to-religious-services.html.

67. *Casey*, 505 U.S. at 998, 1000 (Scalia, J., dissenting).

68. WILLIAM SHAKESPEARE, HENRY IV, PART I, act III, sc. I, 52–54 (G. Blakemore Evans ed., Riverside 1974) (1597).

CHAPTER SEVEN

1. 198 U.S. 45, 75 (1905) (Holmes, J., dissenting).

2. See, e.g., John Hart Ely, *Democracy and the Right to Be Different*, 56 NEW YORK UNIVERSITY LAW REVIEW 397, 401 (1981) [hereinafter Ely, *Different*].

3. JOHN STUART MILL, ON LIBERTY 10–11 (David Spitz ed., 1975) (1859).

4. 576 U.S. 644, 686 (2015) (Roberts, C. J., dissenting).

5. CATHERINE DRINKER BOWEN, YANKEE FROM OLYMPUS: JUSTICE HOLMES AND HIS FAMILY 109–10 (1945).

6. See William Michael Treanor, *Jam for Justice Holmes: Reassessing the Significance of* Mahon, 86 GEORGETOWN LAW JOURNAL 813, 874 (1998).

7. John Hart Ely, *The Wages of Crying Wolf: A Comment on* Roe v. Wade, 82 YALE LAW JOURNAL 920, 943–45 (1973).

8. For the idea of moral readings of the Constitution, see JAMES E. FLEMING, FIDELITY TO OUR IMPERFECT CONSTITUTION: FOR MORAL READINGS AND AGAINST ORIGINALISMS 3 (2015).

9. 198 U.S. at 76.

10. See Ely, *Different*, supra note 2, at 401.

11. 381 U.S. 479, 485–86 (1965).

12. Id. at 486. Similarly, Justice Goldberg in concurrence feared that not protecting the right to privacy would enable government to harm the institution of marriage (as did Justice Harlan in dissent in *Poe v. Ullman*, the predecessor to *Griswold*). Id. at 499 (Goldberg, J., concurring); Poe v. Ullman, 367 U.S. 497, 546 (1961) (Harlan, J., dissenting).

13. 405 U.S. 438, 453 (1972).

14. 410 U.S. 113, 153 (1973).

15. A. Raymond Randolph, *Before* Roe v. Wade: *Judge Friendly's Draft Abortion Opinion*, 29 HARVARD JOURNAL OF LAW & PUBLIC POLICY 1035, 1037 (2006).

16. 576 U.S. at 705–06.

17. 478 U.S. 186, 194 (1986).
18. Brief for Respondent at 23 n.43, Bowers v. Hardwick, 478 U.S. 186 (1986) (No. 85-140), 1986 WL 720442.
19. Brief of the Rutherford Institute, and the Rutherford Institutes of Alabama, Connecticut, Delaware, Georgia, Minnesota, Montana, Tennessee, Texas, and Virginia, Amici Curiae, in Support of the Petitioner at 24 n.10, Bowers v. Hardwick, 478 U.S. 186 (1986) (No. 85-140), 1985 WL 667943.
20. *Bowers*, 478 U.S. at 212 (Blackmun, J., dissenting).
21. 539 U.S. 558, 578 (2003).
22. *Obergefell*, 576 U.S. at 679 (majority opinion).
23. Id.
24. RONALD DWORKIN, TAKING RIGHTS SERIOUSLY 269 (1977).
25. Jack M. Balkin, *The Hohfeldian Approach to Law and Semiotics*, 44 UNIVERSITY OF MIAMI LAW REVIEW 1119, 1129 (1990).
26. See, e.g., Snyder v. Phelps, 562 U.S. 443 (2011); R.A.V. v. St. Paul, 505 U.S. 377 (1992); New York Times v. Sullivan, 376 U.S. 254 (1964).
27. JOHN HART ELY, DEMOCRACY AND DISTRUST: A THEORY OF JUDICIAL REVIEW 59 ** (1980); Ely, *Different*, supra note 2, at 405, 401. In this section, I draw from my analysis in JAMES E. FLEMING, SECURING CONSTITUTIONAL DEMOCRACY 132–34 (2006) [hereinafter FLEMING, SECURING].
28. See LINDA C. MCCLAIN, THE PLACE OF FAMILIES: FOSTERING CAPACITY, EQUALITY, AND RESPONSIBILITY 31 (2006).
29. Kelley v. Johnson, 425 U.S. 238, 249–53 (1976) (Marshall, J., dissenting) (hair length); Doe v. Bolton, 410 U.S. 179, 213 (1973) (Douglas, J., concurring) (loafing).
30. *Obergefell*, 576 U.S. at 644; *Griswold*, 381 U.S. at 479; Meyer v. Nebraska, 262 U.S. 390 (1923). For analysis of such substantive due process cases in terms of a criterion of significance for deliberative autonomy, see FLEMING, SECURING, supra note 27, at 109–11.
31. *Glucksberg*, 521 U.S. 702 (1997); *Casey*, 505 U.S. 833 (1992).
32. 576 U.S. at 737 (Alito, J., dissenting).
33. Id. at 660 (majority opinion); *Lawrence*, 539 U.S. at 564–65; *Casey*, 505 U.S at 851; *Moore*, 431 U.S. 494, 503 (1977). For analysis of such substantive due process cases in terms of moral goods, see JAMES E. FLEMING & LINDA C. MCCLAIN, ORDERED LIBERTY: RIGHTS, RESPONSIBILITIES, AND VIRTUES 177–206 (2013) [hereinafter FLEMING & MCCLAIN, ORDERED LIBERTY].
34. 431 U.S. at 503–4.
35. 539 U.S. at 578.
36. 576 U.S. at 659.
37. Thomas C. Grey, *Eros, Civilization and the Burger Court*, 43 LAW & CONTEMPORARY PROBLEMS 83 (1980).
38. See, e.g., Nan Hunter, *Interpreting Liberty and Equality through the Lens of Marriage*, 6 CALIFORNIA LAW REVIEW CIRCUIT 107 (2015).
39. 576 U.S. at 700–702 (Roberts, C. J., dissenting).
40. Id. at 701.
41. Id. at 645–46 (majority opinion).
42. Id. at 702 (Roberts, C. J. dissenting) (citing DeShaney v. Winnebago County, 489 U.S. 189 [1989]).
43. Id. at 660 (majority opinion).
44. 798 N.E.2d 941, 959 (Mass. 2003).

45. See SOTIRIOS A. BARBER, WELFARE AND THE CONSTITUTION (2003) (arguing that the US Constitution is a charter of positive benefits, not negative liberties); EMILY ZACKIN, LOOKING FOR RIGHTS IN ALL THE WRONG PLACES: WHY STATE CONSTITUTIONS CONTAIN AMERICA'S POSITIVE RIGHTS (2013) (arguing that state constitutions are charters of positive rights, not negative liberties).

46. *Obergefell*, 576 U.S. at 690, 701 (Roberts, C. J., dissenting); id. at 727–30 (Thomas, J., dissenting).

47. Id. at 690 (Roberts, C. J., dissenting).

48. Id. at 726 (Thomas, J., dissenting).

49. Id. at 687 (Roberts, C. J., dissenting).

50. *Griswold*, 381 U.S. at 485–86.

51. *Eisenstadt*, 405 U.S. at 453.

52. *Lawrence*, 538 U.S. at 560.

53. *Obergefell*, 576 U.S. at 646–47, 681.

54. *Roe*, 410 U.S. at 152.

55. *Bowers*, 478 U.S. at 217 (Stevens, J., dissenting).

56. *Casey*, 505 U.S. at 851.

57. See FLEMING, SECURING, supra note 27, at 109–11, 116–19, 126–27.

58. *Bowers*, 478 U.S. at 187 (majority opinion); id. at 199 (Blackmun, J., dissenting); id. at 214 (Stevens, J., dissenting).

59. *Glucksberg*, 521 U.S. at 703, 725, 728.

60. *Obergefell*, 576 U.S. at 703 (Roberts, C. J., dissenting).

61. MARY ANN GLENDON, RIGHTS TALK: THE IMPOVERISHMENT OF POLITICAL DISCOURSE 57 (1990).

62. ROBERT H. BORK, THE TEMPTING OF AMERICA: THE POLITICAL SEDUCTION OF THE LAW 112 (1990); *Casey*, 505 U.S. at 983 (Scalia, J., concurring in the judgment in part and dissenting in part).

63. *Bowers*, 478 U.S. at 190–91 (majority opinion).

64. Jonathan Turley, *The Loadstone Rock: The Role of Harm in the Criminalization of Plural Unions*, 64 EMORY LAW JOURNAL 1905 (2015).

65. THE REPORT OF THE DEPARTMENTAL COMMITTEE ON HOMOSEXUAL OFFENCES AND PROSTITUTION (1957) (Wolfenden Report).

66. PATRICK DEVLIN, THE ENFORCEMENT OF MORALS 13–14, 15, 17 (1965).

67. H. L. A. Hart, *Immorality and Treason*, THE LISTENER, July 30, 1959, 162–63. Hart developed these arguments more fully in H. L. A. HART, LAW, LIBERTY, AND MORALITY (1963).

68. BORK, supra note 62, at 121–26.

69. *Lawrence*, 539 U.S. at 586 (Scalia, J., dissenting); *Romer*, 517 U.S. at 636 (Scalia, J., dissenting).

70. See *Griswold*, 381 U.S. at 484; H. L. A. HART, THE CONCEPT OF LAW 121–32 (1961).

71. Turley, supra note 64, at 1922.

72. Id. at 1929–35, 1942–72.

73. DEVLIN, supra note 66, at 13–14.

74. Jeffrey Goldberg, *Does Gay Sex Cause Earthquakes?* THE ATLANTIC, Feb. 16, 2010, https://www.theatlantic.com/international/archive/2010/02/does-gay-sex-cause-earthquakes/36039/; Laurie Goldstein, *After the Attacks, Finding Fault: Falwell's Finger-Pointing Inappropriate, Bush Says*, N.Y. TIMES, Sept. 15, 2001, at A15, https://www.nytimes.com/2001/09/15/us/after-attacks-finding-fault-falwell-s-finger-pointing-inappropriate-bush-says.html.

75. See LINDA C. MCCLAIN, WHO'S THE BIGOT? LEARNING FROM CONFLICTS OVER MAR-
RIAGE AND CIVIL RIGHTS LAW 130–35 (2020) (discussing the state of Virginia's arguments in *Loving* concerning alleged harm to children from interracial marriage);
Obergefell, 576 U.S. at 646 (rejecting arguments concerning supposed harm to children from same-sex marriage).

76. See Reference re: Section 293 of the Criminal Code of Can., 2011 BCSC 1588,
para. 256 (Can.).

77. See FLEMING & MCCLAIN, ORDERED LIBERTY, supra note 33, at 146–47.

78. Compare Jamal Greene, *The Meming of Substantive Due Process*, 31 CONSTITUTIONAL
COMMENTARY 253 (2016).

CHAPTER EIGHT

1. See, e.g., WHAT *BROWN V. BOARD OF EDUCATION* SHOULD HAVE SAID (Jack Balkin ed.,
2004); WHAT *ROE V. WADE* SHOULD HAVE SAID (Jack Balkin ed., 2007); WHAT *OBERGE-
FELL V. HODGES* SHOULD HAVE SAID (Jack Balkin ed., 2020).

2. 505 U.S. 833, 857 (1992).

3. Id. at 856.

4. Id. at 898.

5. Id. at 912, 916, 918, 920 (Stevens, J., concurring).

6. Id. at 928–29 (Blackmun, J., concurring) (internal citations omitted).

7. Id. at 928 n.4.

8. CATHARINE A. MACKINNON, *Privacy v. Equality: Beyond* Roe v. Wade, in FEMINISM
UNMODIFIED: DISCOURSES ON LIFE AND LAW 100, 102 (1987); Catharine A. MacKinnon,
Reflections on Sex Equality under Law, 100 YALE LAW JOURNAL 1281, 1311 (1991).

9. CASS R. SUNSTEIN, THE PARTIAL CONSTITUTION 45–62, 259–61 (1993); Cass R.
Sunstein, Lochner's *Legacy*, 87 COLUMBIA LAW REVIEW 873, 874–75, 882–93 (1987).

10. Cass R. Sunstein, *Liberal Constitutionalism and Liberal Justice*, 72 TEXAS LAW REVIEW
305, 312 (1993).

11. 316 U.S. 535, 543 (1942).

12. See JAMES E. FLEMING & LINDA C. MCCLAIN, ORDERED LIBERTY: RIGHTS, RESPONSI-
BILITIES, AND VIRTUES 224–28 (2013) [hereinafter FLEMING & MCCLAIN, ORDERED
LIBERTY]; JAMES E. FLEMING, SECURING CONSTITUTIONAL DEMOCRACY: THE CASE OF
AUTONOMY 56–57 (2006) [hereinafter FLEMING, SECURING].

13. RONALD DWORKIN, LIFE'S DOMINION: AN ARGUMENT ABOUT ABORTION, EUTHANA-
SIA, AND INDIVIDUAL FREEDOM 166 (1993).

14. Id. at 53–54.

15. FLEMING, SECURING, supra note 12, at 138.

16. See LINDA GREENHOUSE & REVA B. SIEGEL, BEFORE *ROE V. WADE*: VOICES THAT SHAPED
THE ABORTION DEBATE BEFORE THE SUPREME COURT'S RULING (2010).

17. John Hart Ely, *The Wages of Crying Wolf: A Comment on* Roe v. Wade, 82 YALE LAW
JOURNAL 920 (1973) [hereinafter Ely, *Wages*].

18. JOHN HART ELY, DEMOCRACY AND DISTRUST: A THEORY OF JUDICIAL REVIEW 94, 100
(1980).

19. Ely, *Wages*, supra note 17, at 933–35.

20. JOHN HART ELY, ON CONSTITUTIONAL GROUND 305 (1996).

21. 381 U.S. 479 (1965).

22. 405 U.S. 438, 453 (1972) (emphasis added).

23. Indeed, there is evidence that the Court, including Justice Blackmun, did not an-
ticipate that *Roe* would be an important or controversial decision. See LINDA

GREENHOUSE, BECOMING JUSTICE BLACKMUN 80 (2005); Nan D. Hunter, *Justice Blackmun, Abortion, and the Myth of Medical Independence*, 72 BROOKLYN LAW REVIEW 147, 170–71 (2006).

24. Ruth Bader Ginsburg, *Some Thoughts on Autonomy and Equality in Relation to* Roe v. Wade, 63 NORTH CAROLINA LAW REVIEW 375 (1985).

25. 404 U.S. 71, 75 (1971).

26. 417 U.S. 484 (1974). A similar case was Gilbert v. General Electric Co., 425 U.S. 989 (1976).

27. Pregnancy Discrimination Act, Pub. L. No. 95-555, 92 Stat. 2076 (1978).

28. Ginsburg, supra note 24, at 375 n.1.

29. See, e.g., Shapiro v. Thompson, 394 U.S. 618 (1969); Harper v. Virginia State Bd. of Elections, 383 U.S. 663 (1966); Reynolds v. Sims, 377 U.S. 533 (1964).

30. Ely, *Wages*, supra note 17, at 943.

31. Archibald Cox, *Foreword: Constitutional Adjudication and the Promotion of Human Rights*, 80 HARVARD LAW REVIEW 91, 91 (1966).

32. 411 U.S. 1 (1973).

33. 410 U.S. 113 (1973).

34. For extensive analysis, see FLEMING & MCCLAIN, ORDERED LIBERTY, supra note 12, at 53–68.

35. See, e.g., Carey Goldberg & Janet Elder, *Public Still Backs Abortion, but Wants Limits, Poll Says*, N.Y. TIMES, Jan. 16, 1998, at A1, https://www.nytimes.com/1998/01/16/us/public-still-backs-abortion-but-wants-limits-poll-says.html (reporting shift in public opinion from general acceptance of abortion to a "permit but discourage mode").

36. 570 U.S. 744 (2013).

37. Lawrence v. Texas, 539 U.S. 558 (2003); Romer v. Evans, 517 U.S. 620 (1996); *Windsor*, 570 U.S. at 744.

38. 576 U.S. 644, 658, 661 (2015).

39. 367 U.S. 497, 523 (1961) (Harlan, J., dissenting); *Griswold*, 381 U.S. at 499 (Harlan, J., concurring).

40. See FLEMING, SECURING, supra note 12, at 117, 123.

41. 576 U.S. at 666–67 (quoting *Griswold*, 381 U.S. at 485).

42. *Id.* at 666 (quoting Goodridge v. Department of Public Health, 798 N.E.2d 941, 955 [Mass. 2003]); *Goodridge*, 798 N.E.2d at 945.

43. See JAMES E. FLEMING, SOTIRIOS A. BARBER, STEPHEN J. MACEDO & LINDA C. MC-CLAIN, GAY RIGHTS AND THE CONSTITUTION 59 (2016).

44. Compare Heather Gerken, *Windsor's Mad Genius: The Interlocking Gears of Rights and Structure*, 95 BOSTON UNIVERSITY LAW REVIEW 587 (2015).

45. ROLLING STONES, *You Can't Always Get What You Want*, on LET IT BLEED (Decca Records 1969).

46. *Romer*, 517 U.S. at 632, 634 (quoting Department of Agriculture v. Moreno, 413 U.S. 528, 534 [1973]).

47. *Lawrence*, 539 U.S. at 564, 575.

48. *Obergefell*, 576 U.S. at 674, 681.

49. 517 U.S. at 632, 634 (majority opinion); id. at 646, 652 (Scalia, J., dissenting).

50. Id. at 623 (majority opinion).

51. FLEMING, BARBER, MACEDO & MCCLAIN, supra note 43, at 114.

52. 413 U.S. at 532–34 (emphasis added).

53. 473 U.S. 432, 435–37, 448 (1985).

54. 517 U.S. at 632, 634 (omission in original) (quoting *Moreno*, 413 U.S. at 534).
55. Id. at 635.
56. Id. at 632, 634; id. at 646 (Scalia, J., dissenting).
57. Id. at 623 (majority opinion) (quoting Plessy v. Ferguson, 163 U.S. 537, 559 [1896] [Harlan, J., dissenting]).
58. Id. at 635.
59. Id. ("We must conclude that Amendment 2 classifies homosexuals . . . to make them unequal to everyone else.").
60. *Lawrence*, 539 U.S. at 578.
61. Id. at 564–66; see e.g., *Griswold*, 381 U.S. at 486.
62. *Lawrence*, 539 U.S. at 574, 578.
63. *Obergefell*, 576 U.S. at 674–75 ("In *Lawrence* the Court acknowledge the interlocking nature of [due process and equal protection] in the context of the legal treatment of gays and lesbians.").
64. Id. at 712 (Roberts, C. J., dissenting) ("Perhaps the most discouraging aspect of today's decision is the extent to which the majority feels compelled to sully those on the other side of the debate"); id. at 719 (Scalia, J., dissenting) (criticizing majority opinion for implying that limiting marriage to one man and one woman "cannot possibly be supported by anything other than ignorance or bigotry"); id. at 741 (Alito, J., dissenting) ("In the course of its opinion, the majority compares traditional marriage laws to laws that denied equal treatment for African-Americans and women. The implications of this analogy will be exploited by those who are determined to stamp out every vestige of dissent").
65. Id. at 741 (Alito, J., dissenting).
66. Id. at 672 (majority opinion).
67. Id. at 679.
68. Id. at 672.
69. 539 U.S. at 601 (Scalia, J., dissenting).
70. 570 U.S. at 765–66.
71. Id. at 800–01 (Scalia, J., dissenting).
72. Id. at 775 (majority opinion); id. at 776 (Roberts, C. J., dissenting).
73. Id. at 800–801 (Scalia, J., dissenting).
74. 191 N.W.2d 185 (Minn. 1971).
75. Baker v. Nelson, 409 U.S. 810, 810 (1972).
76. *Baker*, 191 N.W.2d at 187.

CHAPTER NINE
1. 576 U.S. 644 (2015). This chapter is based on James E. Fleming, *Are Constitutional Courts Civic Educative Institutions? If So, What Do They Teach?* in THE IMPACT OF THE LAW: ON CHARACTER FORMATION, ETHICAL EDUCATION, AND THE COMMUNICATION OF VALUES IN LATE MODERN PLURALISTIC SOCIETIES 95 (John Witte Jr. and Michael Welker eds., 2021).
2. *Obergefell*, 576 U.S. at 711 (Roberts, C. J., dissenting); id. at 733 (Thomas, J., dissenting); id. 741–42 (Alito, J., dissenting). Justice Scalia had made such a warning in dissent in Romer v. Evans, 517 U.S. 620, 636, 646 (1996) (Scalia, J., dissenting).
3. *Obergefell*, 576 U.S. at 693, 711 (Roberts, C. J., dissenting).
4. On June 17, 2021, the Supreme Court, 6-3, rejected the arguments of Justices Alito, Thomas, and Gorsuch that the Court should overrule Employment Division, Department of Human Resources v. Smith, 494 U.S. 872 (1990), which might have opened

the door to broad religious exemptions, even from neutral and generally applicable laws. In the case, Fulton v. City of Philadelphia, No. 19-123, Chief Justice Roberts wrote a narrow opinion for a unanimous Court, ruling in favor of a Catholic social services agency that refused to work with same-sex couples who apply to take in foster children. Roberts's narrow opinion prompted Justice Alito to write a "caustic," "disappointed" concurrence, joined by Thomas and Gorsuch, criticizing the Court for passing up the opportunity to overturn *Smith*. See Adam Liptak, *Supreme Court Backs Catholic Agency in Case on Gay Rights and Foster Care*, N.Y. TIMES, June 17, 2021, https://www.nytimes.com/2021/06/17/us/supreme-court-gay-rights-foster-care.html.

5. JAMES E. FLEMING & LINDA C. MCCLAIN, ORDERED LIBERTY: RIGHTS, RESPONSI- BILITIES, AND VIRTUES 174–75 (2013) [hereinafter FLEMING & MCCLAIN, ORDERED LIBERTY].

6. Id. at 92, 146–47.

7. Christopher L. Eisgruber, *Is the Supreme Court an Educative Institution?* 67 NEW YORK UNIVERSITY LAW REVIEW 961 (1992).

8. 319 U.S. 624, 642 (1943).

9. 274 U.S. 357, 377 (1927) (Brandeis, J., concurring).

10. Id. at 375.

11. See, e.g., United States v. Alvarez, 567 U.S. 709 (2012) (holding that government may not forbid people to lie about military honors); National Institute of Family and Life Advocates v. Becerra, 138 S. Ct. 2361 (2018) (ruling that government may not regulate "crisis pregnancy centers" by requiring them to post true factual information about government-provided reproductive health care services).

12. 553 U.S. 723 (2008) (holding that the President and Congress had unconstitution- ally suspended the writ of habeas corpus).

13. 505 U.S. 833 (1992) (reaffirming the right to decide whether to terminate a pregnancy).

14. 576 U.S. at 644 (extending the right to marry to same-sex couples).

15. 138 S. Ct. 1719 (2018).

16. 309 P.3d 53 (N.M. 2013).

17. *Masterpiece Cakeshop*, 138 S. Ct. at 1723.

18. In this section, I have drawn extensively from LINDA C. MCCLAIN, WHO'S THE BIGOT? LEARNING FROM CONFLICTS OVER MARRIAGE AND CIVIL RIGHTS LAW 186–91 (2020).

19. *Elane Photography*, 309 P.3d at 79 (Bosson, J., concurring).

20. Id. at 78.

21. Id. at 78–80.

22. Id. at 80.

23. *Masterpiece Cakeshop*, 138 S. Ct. at 1728–29.

24. Id. at 1731–32.

25. Id. at 1748 (Ginsburg, J., dissenting).

26. Adam Liptak, *Justices Thomas and Alito Question Same-Sex Marriage Precedent*, N.Y. TIMES, Oct. 6, 2020, at A20, https://www.nytimes.com/2020/10/05/us/politics/thomas -alito-same-sex-marriage.html.

27. "Religious Liberty or a License to Discriminate?" Debate between Ryan T. Anderson and Linda C. McClain, sponsored by *Princeton Tory*, Princeton University, April 12, 2017; see also RYAN T. ANDERSON, TRUTH OVERRULED: THE FUTURE OF MARRIAGE AND RELIGIOUS FREEDOM (2015).

28. "Marriage and the Law," Murphy Lecture Roundtable Discussion, Princeton University Program in Law and Public Affairs, May 4, 2012 (colloquy between Matthew J. Franck and Linda C. McClain concerning religious exemptions, with Franck drawing an analogy to Abraham Lincoln's famous argument against slavery); see also Matthew J. Franck, *Can Religious Freedom Survive Same-Sex Marriage?* FIRST THINGS (Aug. 26, 2013), https://www.firstthings.com/blogs/firstthoughts/2013/08/can-religious-freedom-survive-same-sex-marriage.

29. *Masterpiece Cakeshop*, 138 S. Ct. at 1732.

30. Id. at 1729 (quoting the transcript).

31. Id. 1729–30.

32. For an instructive account of the Christian "theology of segregation" to justify slavery and segregation, see MCCLAIN, supra note 18, at 80–86.

33. *Masterpiece Cakeshop*, 138 S. Ct. at 1751–52 (Ginsburg, J., dissenting).

34. 388 U.S. 1, 3 (1967).

35. 390 U.S. 400, 402 n.5 (1968).

36. 517 U.S. at 632, 634.

37. Id. at 636, 646 (Scalia, J., dissenting).

38. 138 S. Ct. 2392, 2435–40 (2018) (Sotomayor, J., dissenting).

39. *Masterpiece Cakeshop*, 138 S. Ct. at 1733 (Kagan, J., concurring).

40. FLEMING & MCCLAIN, ORDERED LIBERTY, supra note 5, at 146–76.

41. 319 U.S. at 642.

42. *Masterpiece Cakeshop*, 138 S. Ct. at 1740–48 (Thomas, J., concurring, joined by Gorsuch, J.).

43. See JAMES E. FLEMING, SOTIRIOS A. BARBER, STEPHEN MACEDO & LINDA C. MCCLAIN, GAY RIGHTS AND THE CONSTITUTION 78–82, 419, 426 (2016); SOTIRIOS A. BARBER & JAMES E. FLEMING, CONSTITUTIONAL INTERPRETATION: THE BASIC QUESTIONS 41–45 (2007).

44. FLEMING & MCCLAIN, ORDERED LIBERTY, supra note 5, at 174–75.

CHAPTER TEN

1. THE BURGER COURT: THE COUNTER-REVOLUTION THAT WASN'T (Vincent Blasi ed., 1986).

2. Adam Liptak, *Former Justice O'Connor Sees Ill in Election Finance Ruling*, N.Y. TIMES, Jan. 26, 2010, https://www.nytimes.com/2010/01/27/us/politics/27judge.html.

3. 505 U.S. 833 (1992), *reaffirming* Roe v. Wade, 410 U.S. 113 (1973).

4. 539 U.S. 558 (2003), *overruling* Bowers v. Hardwick, 478 U.S. 186 (1986).

5. 576 U.S. 644 (2015).

6. *Casey*, 505 U.S. at 1000 (Scalia, J., concurring in the judgment in part and dissenting in part).

7. Id. at 849 (joint opinion of Justices O'Connor, Kennedy, and Souter).

8. Id. at 847–48.

9. On December 1, 2021, the Supreme Court heard arguments in a case—Dobbs v. Jackson Women's Health Organization, No. 19-1392—challenging a Mississippi law that banned abortions if "the probable gestational age of the unborn human" was determined to be more than fifteen weeks. The law included exceptions for medical emergencies or "a severe fetal abnormality." The lower federal courts ruled that the law was unconstitutional, with the United States Court of Appeals for the Fifth Circuit stating: "In an unbroken line dating to Roe v. Wade, the Supreme Court's abortion cases have established (and affirmed, and reaffirmed) a woman's right to choose an abortion

before viability." (The point of fetal viability is around twenty-three or twenty-four weeks.) The specific question the Supreme Court agreed to decide was "whether all pre-viability prohibitions on elective abortions are unconstitutional." Id. On November 1, 2021, the Court heard arguments in two cases—Whole Woman's Health v. Jackson, No. 21-463, and United States v. Texas, No. 21-588—in which abortion providers and the Biden administration challenged an even more radical state law. The Texas Heartbeat Act, S.8, bans abortions once cardiac activity of a fetus is detected, usually about six weeks after a person's last menstrual period (before many know they are pregnant). It puts enforcement of the law in the hands of private persons, rather than the state government, in an attempt to evade review by federal courts. Under the statute, any individual can sue anyone who aids or abets prohibited abortions, with an award of at least $10,000 and legal fees for any successful lawsuit. The federal district court suspended the law as an "offensive deprivation" of an important constitutional right, but the United States Court of Appeals for the Fifth Circuit reversed and reinstated it. The arguments in the two cases before the Supreme Court focused on procedural questions concerning whether abortion providers and the United States government could challenge the law by suing state officials in federal court instead of on the constitutionality of the underlying restriction of abortions. As this book goes to press, the Court has not yet issued its decisions in these cases.

10. At his confirmation hearings, then-Judge Kavanaugh said "I think all roads lead to the *Glucksberg* test." CNN, http://www.cnn.com/TRANSCRIPTS/1809/05/cnr.08.html.

11. *Obergefell*, 576 U.S. at 702 (Roberts, C. J., dissenting).

12. Douglas NeJaime, *The Constitution of Parenthood*, 72 STANFORD LAW REVIEW 261, 317 (2020) (discussing Pavan v. Smith, 137 S. Ct. 2075 [2017]).

13. *Pavan*, 137 S. Ct. at 2078 (citing *Obergefell*, 576 U.S. at 670 [majority opinion]).

14. Id. at 2079 (Gorsuch, J., dissenting, joined by Thomas, J., and Alito, J.).

15. NeJaime, supra note 12, at 317.

16. Despite his dissent in *Pavan*, adopting a narrow view of *Obergefell*, Justice Gorsuch took a broad view of Title VII's prohibition of discrimination on the basis of sex in his 6-3 majority opinion in Bostock v. Clayton County, 140 S. Ct. 1731 (2020), interpreting it to prohibit discrimination on the basis of sexual orientation or gender identity. Gorsuch wrote: "[A]pplying protective laws to groups that were politically unpopular at the time of the law's passage"—such as gay, lesbian, or transgender employees—"often may be seen as unexpected." However, he continued, to refuse enforcement for that reason would "tilt the scales of justice in favor of the strong or popular and neglect the promise that all persons are entitled to the benefit of the law's terms." This formulation seems to echo the opening words of Justice Kennedy's opinion in *Obergefell*: "The Constitution promises liberty to all within its reach," including same-sex couples seeking to marry. 576 U.S. at 651. I owe this observation to Linda C. McClain. I hasten to acknowledge that *Bostock* involved statutory interpretation, whereas *Obergefell* involved constitutional interpretation. Not surprisingly, Justices Thomas and Alito, who had joined Gorsuch's dissent in *Pavan*, dissented from his majority opinion in *Bostock*.

17. Adam Liptak, *How Brett Kavanaugh Would Transform the Supreme Court*, N.Y. TIMES, Sept. 3, 2018, at A1 (quoting Irv Gornstein), https://www.nytimes.com/2018/09/02/us/politics/judge-kavanaugh-supreme-court-justices.html.

18. Fulton v. City of Philadelphia, No. 19-123 (June 17, 2021). Roberts's narrow opinion prompted Alito to write a "caustic," "disappointed" concurrence, joined by Thomas and Gorsuch, criticizing the Court for passing up the opportunity to overturn *Smith*.

See Adam Liptak, *Supreme Court Backs Catholic Agency in Case on Gay Rights and Foster Care*, N.Y. TIMES, June 17, 2021, https://www.nytimes.com/2021/06/17/us/supreme -court-gay-rights-foster-care.html.

19. Adam Liptak, *The Supreme Court's Newest Justices Produce Some Unexpected Results*, N.Y. TIMES, June 18, 2021, https://www.nytimes.com/2021/06/18/us/politics/supreme -court-conservatives-liberals.html.

20. DANTE ALIGHIERI, THE INFERNO, canto III, verse 9 (Robert Hollander and Jean Hollander, trans., 2000) (1472).

21. See Bruce Ackerman, *The Court Packs Itself*, THE AMERICAN PROSPECT, Feb. 12, 2001, at 42 (discussing Bush v. Gore, 531 U.S. 98 [2000]), https://prospect.org/features /court-packs/.

22. Debra Cassens Weiss, *Scalia on Bush v. Gore: "Get Over It,"* ABA JOURNAL, Mar. 10, 2008, https://www.abajournal.com/news/article/scalia_on_bush_v_gore_get_over_it.

23. Carl Hulse and Jonathan Martin, *With a Transformed Judiciary in Sight, McConnell "Will Not Be Intimidated,"* N.Y. TIMES, Oct. 3, 2018 (quoting McConnell as saying "plow right through it"), https://www.nytimes.com/2018/10/03/us/politics /mcconnell-senate-judiciary-supreme-court.html.

24. See GERALD N. ROSENBERG, THE HOLLOW HOPE: CAN COURTS BRING ABOUT SOCIAL CHANGE? (2nd ed., 2008).

25. See RAN HIRSCHL, TOWARDS JURISTOCRACY: THE ORIGINS AND CONSEQUENCES OF THE NEW CONSTITUTIONALISM (2007).

26. https://ballotpedia.org/Nevada_Question_2,_Marriage_Regardless_of_Gender _Amendment_(2020).

27. Neil Vigdor, *Virginia's New Laws on LGBT Protections, Guns and Marijuana Reflect a Shift in Power*, N.Y. TIMES, Apr. 13, 2020, https://www.nytimes.com/2020/04/13/us /virginia-democrats-new-laws.html.

28. See Katie Lannan and Chris Lisinski, *Abortion Access Policies Become Law in Massachusetts Despite Governor Baker's Veto*, BOSTON GLOBE, Dec. 29, 2020, https://www.bostonglobe .com/2020/12/29/metro/abortion-access-policies-become-law-massachusetts-des pite-governor-bakers-veto/.

29. 554 U.S. 570 (2008).

30. See DAVID COLE, ENGINES OF LIBERTY: HOW CITIZEN MOVEMENTS SUCCEED (2016); ADAM WINKLER, GUNFIGHT: THE BATTLE OVER THE RIGHT TO BEAR ARMS IN AMERICA (2013).

31. See Charles M. Blow, *We Need a Second Great Migration*, N.Y. TIMES, Jan. 8, 2021, https://www.nytimes.com/2021/01/08/opinion/georgia-black-political-power.html.

32. Astead W. Herndon, *Georgia Was a Big Win for Democrats. Black Women Did the Groundwork*, N.Y. TIMES, Dec. 3, 2020, https://www.nytimes.com/2020/12/03/us/pol itics/georgia-democrats-black-women.html.

33. See, e.g., Jeffrey Rosen, Opinion, *States' Rights for the Left*, N.Y. TIMES, Dec. 4, 2016, at SR 4, https://www.nytimes.com/2016/12/03/opinion/sunday/states-rights-for-the -left.html.

34. See Goodridge v. Department of Public Health, 798 N.E.2d 941 (Mass. 2003); Baker v. State, 744 A.2d 864 (Vt. 1999).

35. See EMILY ZACKIN, LOOKING FOR RIGHTS IN ALL THE WRONG PLACES: WHY STATE CONSTITUTIONS CONTAIN AMERICA'S POSITIVE RIGHTS (2013).

36. 489 U.S. 189 (1989). For a forceful criticism of *DeShaney*'s vision and a cogent defense of a conception of the US Constitution as a charter of positive benefits, see SOTIRIOS A. BARBER, WELFARE AND THE CONSTITUTION (2003).

37. See, e.g., *Goodridge*, 798 N.E.2d at 959; *Baker*, 744 A.2d at 197.

38. E.g., Douglas Ginsburg, *Delegation Running Riot*, REGULATION, No. 1, 1995, at 83, 84 (coining the phrase "the Constitution in Exile"); RANDY E. BARNETT, RESTORING THE LOST CONSTITUTION: THE PRESUMPTION OF LIBERTY (2004).

39. See, e.g., United States v. Morrison, 529 U.S. 598, 628 (2000) (Souter, J., dissenting).

40. See, e.g., Citizens United v. Federal Election Commission, 558 U.S. 310, 393 (2010) (Stevens, J., concurring in part and dissenting in part).

41. National Institute of Family and Life Advocates v. Becerra, 138 S. Ct. 2361, 2369 (2018) (Breyer, J., dissenting).

42. See, e.g., Eric Posner, *The Far-Reaching Threats of a Conservative Court*, N.Y. TIMES, Oct. 23, 2018, https://www.nytimes.com/2018/10/23/opinion/supreme-court-brett -kavanaugh-trump-.html.

43. Many observers were relieved that the Supreme Court, as well as the lower courts, uniformly rejected Trump's and his supporters' lawsuits seeking to overturn the results of the 2020 presidential election. In doing so, they acted like courts rather than an arm of the Republican Party.

44. Barry Friedman, Opinion, *The Coming Storm over the Supreme Court*, N.Y. TIMES, Oct. 8, 2018, https://www.nytimes.com/2018/10/08/opinion/kavanaugh-supreme-court -conservative.html.

45. See, e.g., WILLIAM E. LEUCHTENBURG, THE SUPREME COURT REBORN: THE CONSTITUTIONAL REVOLUTION IN THE AGE OF ROOSEVELT (1996).

46. Friedman, supra note 44.

INDEX

abortion, right to. See *Planned Parenthood v. Casey* (1992); privacy, right of; *Roe v. Wade* (1973)

Abrams, Stacey, 225

Ackerman, Bruce, 26, 261n21

Adarand Constructors, Inc. v. Pena (1995), 116

Adkins v. Children's Hospital (1923), 22, 233n7, 233n8

Alito, Samuel (Justice), 69, 121, 195, 206, 221

Alvarez, United States v. (2012), 258n11

American Booksellers Ass'n v. Hudnut (1985), 83–84

Anderson, Ryan T., 206, 247n9

antidiscrimination laws: conflicts with religious liberty, 13, 201, 206; and formative project, 122, 211; and freedom from compelled expression, 205, 211, 213; and moralization of commerce, 211–13; and "the price of citizenship," 13, 204–5, 210, 212, 213; religious exemptions from, 13, 201, 207, 211–13; as securing status of equal citizenship, 206, 210–11

Arkes, Hadley, 140

aspirational principles: as a conception of tradition, 28; Constitution as a "basic charter" of, 32, 39; contrasted with historical practices, 28–30, 40, 43, 62, 66, 157; Due Process Clause as furthering, 28–32, 38, 50, 63; Equal Protection Clause as furthering, 40, 66

autonomy, right of. See deliberative autonomy; Due Process Clauses of Fifth and Fourteenth Amendments; privacy, right of

Baker v. Nelson (1972), 93, 198

Baker v. State (1999), 226

Balkin, Jack M., 155, 236n53, 255n1

Barber, Sotirios A., 254n45, 261n36

Barnett, Randy E.: as libertarian conservative, 138–39, 140, 143, 244n15; and presumption of liberty, 102; and restoration of the lost constitution, 262n38

Barrett, Amy Coney (Justice): confirmation to Supreme Court, 14, 186, 223, 228; and counterrevolutionary conservatism, 69; in *Fulton*, 221–22; and future of substantive due process, 218, 219, 224; and *Glucksberg*, 34, 220; as originalist, 2, 219

Bernstein, David, 138–39, 140

bigotry, 12, 174, 190–94, 209

Black, Charles L., Jr., 20

Black, Hugo (Justice), 26

Blackmun, Harry (Justice): and controversy over *Roe*, unanticipated, 255n23; dissent in *Bowers*, 35, 65, 107–8, 154, 164; gender equality justification not available at time of *Roe*, 181, 185; intertwining privacy and gender equality justifications in *Casey*, 36, 175–76, 177–79, 184; in majority in *Geduldig*, 181, 183; majority opinion in *Roe*, 11, 164, 178, 180, 182, 185

bodily integrity, right to, 5, 34, 36, 146, 175

Bolling v. Sharpe (1954), 29, 238n44

Bork, Robert H. (Judge): criticism of *Roe*, 164; on legal enforcement of traditional morals, 166; nomination to Supreme

Harlan, John Marshall, II (Justice) (*cont.*)
accepted by *Obergefell*, 39, 41, 49, 67,
174, 188; conception of Due Process
inquiry fits and justifies cases protecting
basic liberties, 50, 63; concurrence in
Griswold, 26, 39, 55, 188; and *Glucksberg*, 63; and *Lawrence*, 66–67; and
Moore, 58–60; and moral goods, 40–41,
188, 200; as preservative conservative,
11, 39, 69; and rational continuum of
ordered liberty, 5, 6, 30, 46, 48–50, 69;
on tradition as a "living thing," 28, 30,
40, 49. *See also* rational continuum of
ordered liberty; reasoned judgment
harm, rights as permitting infliction of, 155
harm principle. *See* Mill, John Stuart
Harper v. Poway Unified School District
(2006), 249n70
Harper v. Virginia State Board of Elections
(1966), 237n23
Hart, H. L. A., 154, 165–66
Hebert v. Louisiana (1926), 238n39
Hirschl, Ran, 224
Hirschman, Albert, 76
historical practices: conception of tradition
as, 28; contrasted with aspirational
principles, 28–30, 40, 43, 62, 66, 157.
See also Due Process Clauses of Fifth and
Fourteenth Amendments; *Washington v.
Glucksberg* (1997)
Holmes, Oliver W., Jr. (Justice): dissent in
Lochner, 3, 131–32, 135, 137, 139,
149–50, 161; dissent in *Meyer*, 51–52
Hunter, Nan, 253n38, 256n23

Jackson, Robert H. (Justice), 202
Jeffs, Warren, 167
judicial under-enforcement of constitutional norms, 10, 141–42. *See also*
Constitution outside the courts
June Medical Services, LLC v. Russo (2020),
61

Kagan, Elena (Justice), 210, 222
Karst, Kenneth, 182
Kavanaugh, Brett (Justice): and counterrevolutionary conservatism, 69; and future
of substantive due process, 2, 13, 186,
217, 218, 219; and *Glucksberg* framework, 34, 220; nomination to Supreme
Court, 223, 224, 228

Kelley v. Johnson (1976), 253n29
Kelo v. City of New London (2005), 144
Kennedy, Anthony (Justice): acceptance
of Harlan's conception of Due Process
inquiry, 39–41, 48–49, 188; and *Casey*
framework, 31, 41, 48–49, 85; legacy of,
219–20; majority opinion in *Masterpiece
Cakeshop*, 204, 205–8, 210, 212; majority
opinion in *Romer*, 100, 110, 189–93,
197; majority opinion in *Windsor*, 190,
197, 198; minimalism of opinions,
186–87; nomination to Supreme Court,
218; as preservative conservative, 11, 39,
69; rejection of *Glucksberg* framework,
31, 38–39; retirement of, 2, 13, 33,
186, 217–18. See also *Lawrence v. Texas*
(2003); *Obergefell v. Hodges* (2015);
Planned Parenthood v. Casey (1992)
Kitchen v. Hebert (2013), 245n34

large commercial republic, 211–12
Law, Sylvia, 182
Lawrence v. Texas (2003): analogy between
intimate association for straights and
for gays and lesbians, 77–78, 81, 163;
and *Casey* framework, 31–32, 36, 38, 63;
concern not to "demean the lives" of
gays and lesbians, 36, 77, 190, 193–94;
desuetude and, 81, 106; and Harlan's
conception of Due Process inquiry, 66–
67; intertwining of liberty and equality,
36, 190, 194; liberty as an abstract principle in, 32, 44; Mill's harm principle
and, 81–82, 154–55, 158; and myth of
two rigidly maintained tiers, 5–6, 45–48,
66, 68; overruling *Bowers*, 31, 33, 46, 65–
66, 218; and rational basis scrutiny with
"bite," 50, 104, 107, 111, 116; and "right
to be different," 157–58; and Scalia's
claims regarding moral disapproval, 8–9,
99–100, 105, 106, 107, 111–12, 116, 166;
and Scalia's slippery slope to "the end
of all morals legislation," 3, 7–8, 73–74,
76–84; securing status of equal citizenship, 36, 100, 190, 193–94; tradition as
evolving consensus in, 32, 67
LGBTQ+, 14–15
libertarianism. *See* Barnett, Randy E.; *Lochner v. New York* (1905); Smith, Tara
liberty. *See* Due Process Clauses of Fifth
and Fourteenth Amendments; ordered

liberty; presumption of liberty; privacy, right of; religious liberty
living constitutionalism, 235–36n31
Lochner v. New York (1905): anti-paternalism in, 129, 131; ghost of, 2–3, 9–10, 30, 43, 127–28, 134–38, 146–47, 176–77, 178; Harlan's dissent in, 130–31; Holmes's dissent in, 131–32; invocation of Holmes's dissent in, 10, 139, 149, 154, 156; majority opinion in, 128–30; rehabilitation of, 138–40; repudiation of, 2, 24, 127, 132, 142, 182; what was wrong in, competing conceptions of, 130–37, 141–42
Locke, John, 160
Loving v. Virginia (1967): anti-miscegenation law as violation of Due Process and Equal Protection Clauses, 26, 56; liberty as an abstract principle in, 56; protection of rights "essential to the orderly pursuit of happiness," 26, 56; right to marry in, 56; strict scrutiny in, 50, 55–56; support for *Casey* framework, 36
Lunder, Matthew W., 234n19

Macedo, Stephen, 96, 246n65, 247n15, 249n72, 251n38
MacKinnon, Catharine, 176–77, 179, 247n12
Madison, James, 142–43
marry, right to: and moral goods of marriage, 8, 40–41, 79–80, 113, 158, 160, 163, 188–89, 195, 196, 199; and proposals to abolish marriage, 103. See also *Goodridge v. Department of Public Health* (2003); *Loving v. Virginia* (1967); *Obergefell v. Hodges* (2015)
Marshall, John (Chief Justice), 235n20
Marshall, Thurgood (Justice), 156–57, 242n17, 248n54
Masterpiece Cakeshop, Ltd v. Colorado Civil Rights Commission (2018): broad lessons about antidiscrimination laws in, 206; hostility toward religion in, 204, 205, 207–8; as not accepting broad claims of religious liberty, 207; as not reaching compelled expression claim, 205, 211, 213; and "the price of citizenship," 13, 205, 210, 213. See also antidiscrimination laws; religious liberty

McClain, Linda C., 248n57, 249n68, 255n75, 258n18, 259n32
McConnell, Mitch, 222–23
McCulloch v. Maryland (1819), 235n20
Meyer v. Nebraska (1923): contrast with Plato's ideal commonwealth, 51; Holmes's dissent in, 51–52; liberty as an abstract principle in, 22–23, 51, 53; and *Loving*, 22–23, 26; right of parents to direct education of children in, 23, 51, 239n66; support for *Casey* framework, 36, 38, 46, 63
Michael H. v. Gerald D. (1989): Brennan's dissent in, 29–30; *Casey*'s rejection of Scalia's framework in, 30; and *Glucksberg* framework, 31, 62; *Lawrence*'s rejection of Scalia's framework in, 66–67; and myth of two rigidly maintained tiers, 6, 47, 64, 68; Scalia's framework in, 28–29. See also *Washington v. Glucksberg* (1997)
Michelman, Frank I., 142–43
Mill, John Stuart: and "experiments in living," 91; and *Griswold*, 166; harm principle of, 10–11, 82, 94–95, 102, 150, 152–55, 159; and *Lawrence*, 158; Millian principle of autonomy or individuality, 10–11, 151, 156; and polygamy, 165–69; and "right to be different," 152, 156–58; Roberts's dissent in *Obergefell* and, 9, 10–11, 149, 152–58, 160
Miller v. California (1973), 249n75
Mississippi University for Women v. Hogan (1982), 176
Moore v. City of East Cleveland (1977): applying a form of intermediate scrutiny, 50, 59; embracing Harlan's conception of Due Process inquiry, 58–60; family is not beyond regulation, 59; moral goods in, 59; protection of extended family, 58–59; protection of "private realm of family life," 58
moral reading of the Constitution: and *Casey* framework, 5, 220; common law constitutional interpretation as a form of, 122, 162–63, 165, 235n26, 235–36n31; defined, 3; distinguished from reading a moral theory into the Constitution, 150–51, 161–65; and *Obergefell*, 3–4, 10; and practice of substantive due process, 4, 34–35, 151. See also Dworkin, Ronald

reasoned judgment (*cont.*)
criticism of, 30, 76, 218. *See also* rational
continuum of ordered liberty
Reed v. Reed (1971), 181
Rehnquist, William H. (Chief Justice): as
counterrevolutionary conservative, 69;
as critic of substantive due process, 38,
45, 60; *Glucksberg* framework of, 28, 31,
38, 47, 61–64, 69, 164; and myth of two
rigidly maintained tiers, 47–49, 60, 68–
69. See also *Cruzan v. Director, Missouri
Department of Health* (1989); *Washington v.
Glucksberg* (1997)
religious liberty: conflicts between gay and
lesbian rights and, 12–13, 195–96, 201,
203–10; invoked to strike down COVID-
19 pandemic regulations, 146; and
religious exemptions, 13, 201, 207, 210,
211–13. See also *Masterpiece Cakeshop,
Ltd v. Colorado Civil Rights Commission*
(2018)
Reynolds v. Sims (1964), 237n23, 256n29
Reynolds v. United States (1878), 90
Roberts, John G. (Chief Justice): claim
regarding bigotry, 195; claim that
Obergefell enacts Mill's *On Liberty*, 9,
10–11, 149–50, 152–58, 160; claim that
Obergefell has no basis in the Constitution or precedent, 1, 4, 32–33; claim
that *Obergefell* repeats the "grave errors"
of *Lochner*, 9–10, 127, 140; claim that
same-sex marriage imperils religious
liberty, 12, 201; dissent in *Windsor*, 198;
majority opinion in *Fulton*, 221–22; and
"marriage problem," 114; on negative
liberty, 159–60; opposition to moral
reading, 161–65; on slippery slope to
plural marriage, 7, 73–74, 83, 84–87,
88–94, 96, 165; support for *Glucksberg*
framework, 38, 45, 164, 220
Robertson, Pat, 168
Roberts v. United States Jaycees (1984), 35–
36, 119
Rochin v. California (1952), 239n66
Roe v. Wade (1973): calls to overrule, 2,
219; calls to "rewrite," 11, 173, 174–75;
charges of "Lochnering" in, 2, 127,
128, 134–38, 147; concerns for family
stability and planning in, 11, 158; Ely's
criticism of, 134–35, 136, 178; gender
equality justification for, 178, 180–82;

Ginsburg's criticism of, 88; liberty as an
abstract principle in, 28–29; and Mill's
harm principle, 153–54; revival of substantive due process, 27; "rewriting" of
in *Casey*, 175–76, 178–79, 185; right of
privacy in, 2, 57–58, 239n66; strict scrutiny for fundamental rights in, 6, 46, 50,
57–58; support for *Casey* framework,
36, 58, 63. See also *Planned Parenthood v.
Casey* (1992)
Romer v. Evans (1996): on "animus," 110,
189–93; moral disapproval and, 110,
111–12; rational basis scrutiny with
"bite," 46, 111; Scalia's dissent in, 94,
107, 112, 166, 192–93; and status of
equal citizenship, 89, 100, 193
Roosevelt, Franklin D., 24, 132
Rosen, Jeffrey, 261n33
Rosenberg, Gerald N., 223, 261n24

Sager, Lawrence G., 141, 236n49
*San Antonio Independent School District v.
Rodriguez* (1973), 27, 183, 242n17
Scalia, Antonin (Justice): on *Bowers*, 6,
46, 64, 68; on *Bush v. Gore*, 222–23;
charting a middle course between Scylla
(Scalia) and Charybdis, 43–44; claim regarding bigotry, 190, 192, 194–95, 209;
claims regarding moral disapproval,
8–9, 99–100, 105, 106, 107, 111–12,
116, 166; claim that gay and lesbian
rights imperil religious liberty, 206; on
comparative constitutional inquiry,
83–84, 93–94; as counterrevolutionary
conservative, 11, 39, 69, 217; dissent
in *Romer*, 107, 112, 190, 209; dissent
in *Windsor*, 87, 197, 198; on *Dred Scott*
and substantive due process, 21; and
ghost of *Lochner*, 30, 147; and *Glucksberg*
framework, 38; *Michael H.* conception
of Due Process inquiry, 23, 29–30, 31,
62; myth of two rigidly maintained tiers,
5–6, 45–48, 49, 68–69; as originalist
conservative, 138–40, 217, 218; rejection of common law constitutional
interpretation, 75–76; rejection of
substantive due process, 5, 39, 146,
218–19; and slippery slope to "the end
of all morals legislation," 3, 7–8, 73–74,
76–84; on substantive due process as
"oxymoron," 1, 20, 137; tradition as